SALTWATER

Saltwater

GRIEF IN EARLY AMERICA

Mary Eyring

Published by the
OMOHUNDRO INSTITUTE OF
EARLY AMERICAN HISTORY AND CULTURE,
Williamsburg, Virginia,
and the
UNIVERSITY OF NORTH CAROLINA PRESS,
Chapel Hill

The Omohundro Institute of Early American History & Culture (OI)
is an independent research organization sponsored by
William & Mary and the Colonial Williamsburg Foundation.
On November 15, 1996, the OI adopted the present name in honor
of a bequest from Malvern H. Omohundro, Jr.,
and Elizabeth Omohundro.

Cover illustration: Watercolor (untitled). By Henry B. Eyring. 2023

Complete Cataloging-in-Publication Data for this title is available from
the Library of Congress at https://lccn.loc.gov/2024047388
ISBN 978-1-4696-8538-0 (cloth: alk. paper)
ISBN 978-1-4696-8539-7 (epub)
ISBN 978-1-4696-8757-5 (pdf)

For Kathleen Johnson Eyring

And for my father, who now has the watch

Preface

Almost twenty years ago, when she was about sixty-five, my mother's charming quirks took on a peculiar cast, which we gradually came to acknowledge as a symptom of early-onset dementia. The singularity of her character made it hard for us to see when her swerve from the fussy conventions of upper-middle-class life became inadvertent. She had always had a playful relationship with conformity. She was a mother of six and a preacher's wife, but she was also friends with Grace Slick when they were students at Castilleja High School in Palo Alto. She prepared and hosted elegant dinners, but once, after she had exhausted her patience for corporatized domesticity in the aisles of Albertsons, she came home and dumped everything, unpacked, in the chest freezer in our basement. I found the plastic bags encrusting their undifferentiated loads of laundry detergent, lunch meat, hairspray, Bisquick, and condensed tomato soup when they were dusted with ice crystals. What an elegant rebuke of grocery shopping's final tap into our emotional reserves, I remember thinking at the time.

I did not take particularly seriously the doctor who called during the first quarter of my graduate program to express concern that she had been found walking the halls of his medical center—the center to which she had taken all of us as children—with no clear idea which doctor she was to meet or why. Days later, unsettled by the conversation, I had to admit that her devil-may-care air always stopped short of intentionally discomfiting others or embarrassing herself. Although she had long rambled, she was now wandering against her will.

The advantage of our long goodbye was my keen appreciation of every moment we spent together, but I couldn't maintain the edge of it, and it became dulled by overuse. There were too many Last Things until, in effect, there were none. As I write this, she is still alive, but I can't remember the last words she said to me, or even which year she stopped speaking at all. I do remember the moment I realized she had already uttered those weighty last words, whatever they were, and that she wouldn't say anything else. One evening about ten years ago, I was washing my face in my Manhattan apartment when her loss struck me with the force of a telephone message conveying the news. Of course, there was no telephone call. She lingered on, in more or less the same condition she'd been in when I kissed her goodbye a few weeks before. But I suddenly stared down the truth that she hadn't said my name in years, hadn't registered any recognition of me that summer, would never know or talk to me again, was in every sense gone. She had died, and I had not realized it, and I had kissed a shade wearing her clothes. I cried on the floor of the bathroom that night and intermittently for a few days after. I had no one with whom to commiserate, since not even my siblings shared my impression of having lost someone who was still alive. There was only grief, and no event.

All this puts me in an uncomfortable position as a Christian and a scholar. I believe in an orderliness around birth and death. I believe in the eternal nature of the soul. If some academic fashion makes my life interesting to scholars four hundred years hence, they can responsibly interpret my relationship to my mother via the sacred texts from which I draw these articles of faith. If they are conscientious, their research will reveal that I regarded death not as an end, but simply as a transpositional event between one stage of existence and another. Yet they would be gravely mistaken to conclude that I found these beliefs comforting or even consistently relevant in the two decades preceding her death.

For, although I believe in eternal life, nothing in my theology can account for the location of my mother's soul now, in this heretical interregnum between her life and death. My theology simply does not accommodate the mess. Our doctrine of the soul assures me hers is still with her living body. But, if so, how dreadful. How could a loving God allow it? As recently as last winter, she would raise her head after days of drowsy silence, look at the screen broadcasting its unrelenting stream of iterations on the Hallmark Original Movie, and begin to cry. I imagined in those moments that her soul, which she refined at UC Berkeley and the Sorbonne and over a lifetime of studiously avoiding inane television programming, had suddenly accessed some remote unsnarled region of her brain and registered the horror of her straitened, speechless existence.

It was a comfort to me when those flashes of recognition ceased, but I have no theological basis for assuming her soul is now engaged more peacefully or productively elsewhere. One nurse told me my mother speaks with my deceased grandparents and aunt, but our church doctrine doesn't specify the mechanism by which such interactions could possibly be regulated, and I don't remember my mother enjoying unannounced visits from out-of-town family. Maybe she does now that she's no longer local herself. I can appreciate how the nurse's station along the border of an unfathomable abyss might have nudged her toward her side career in necromancy, and I hope she finds some comfort there. I think of myself as a strict textualist, and so I resist her speculation, but I find nothing in the text, strictly speaking, that gives me the doctrinal upper hand. Recently, I've been bothered to recognize some of my own grief in the writings of atheists. For years, I too have known how it feels to process the loss of someone dear without recourse to the prospect of something beyond. When my mother dies of Alzheimer's, I do believe she'll go to a better place. Until then, she can find no solace in the promise of heaven, but hell is real.

As a scholar, my association with grief has made me careful about assuming what even widely accepted religious doctrines can tell us about individual believers' experiences with the suffering the doctrines intended to organize. Perhaps, like me, devout early Americans had trouble stretching off-the-rack faith over the strange protrusions of their pain and privately devised some bespoke alternative. We know what ministers taught, and we know what people read in their Bibles, but over the question of what they drew from these doctrines to cushion their crushing personal losses hangs a curtain of uncertainty. Too few left extant records of their individual, no doubt highly idiosyncratic, recourse to theology in the midst of pain. Or perhaps they left records, in unfamiliar forms, in unexpected archives—archives that seem to have nothing at all to do with grief. Perhaps the atemporal, unwieldly dimensions of their grief infused every object they touched. Given the ways and degrees to which inhabitants of the Americas suffered in the age of colonialism, perhaps grief percolated through the whole of early New England history, collecting like groundwater, drifting like atmosphere.

This is a book about ragged, ongoing affliction in spaces constituting early America that takes the faith of people in pain seriously. But that cannot mean it gives more weight to formal sermons than to the myriad cultural and material histories so thoughtfully recovered by scholars of the last two generations. This Preface is in part my witness to future scholars that even devout American Christians of the twenty-first century had to retrofit doctrine to suit the impossible angles of their lived experience. It is also a warning to myself that most early Americans did not leave such a witness— and yet their faith was no less intricate and unlikely. In this book, I hold the material fragments surrounding a few suffering people against the religious expressions they were likely to have heard or read while in the throes of personal tragedy. My expectation is that the ways the materials and doctrines interact—complementing, contesting, or qualifying one another—will address some frustrating silences surrounding most early Americans' lives.

Puritans believed the mind created, as much as it manifested, the condition of the soul. "The mind is its own place, and in itself / Can make a Heaven of Hell, a Hell of Heaven," John Milton wrote.[1] If only this place were fixed rather than floating, we might finally determine the elusive quality of the New England mind. Instead, minds wander off, run riot, drift, degrade. What kinds of heavens and hells do these renegades discharge, and where do they deposit them? A great deal of Puritans' pain stemmed from the mind's inability to decipher the state and final destination of the soul. It caused them tremendous suffering, perhaps the kind of existential suffering against which other sorrows paled. Here, I can empathize. To watch my mother's tormented brain throwing up its wild projection of inner anguish is to encounter damnation in forms more lurid than the Puritan revivalist ever conjured. Yet the mind does not rest, and this damnation is only provisional. My mother's final words were almost certainly supplications to God, which gathered in fervor what they lost in coherence as the disease ravaged her brain but passed over the part of her that prayed.

If I cannot locate the souls of early moderns any more than I can hers, I can at least find in the archive curious souvenirs of their restless spiritual journeys through rough terrain that reflects but often distorts the cartographies ministers sketched on the page. And perhaps an excavation of the deep, messy archives of early American affliction will lead us to souls after all. Perhaps a desolated mind's determination to make holy places out of the rubble of catastrophe constitutes its own kind of afterlife.

Acknowledgments

With gratitude, I acknowledge those who supported the research and writing of this book. The Global Women's Studies program and the Humanities Center at Brigham Young University provided generous funding. A grant from the New England Regional Fellowship Consortium inspired archival research trips in Deerfield and New Bedford, Massachusetts. At the Memorial Libraries in Deerfield, I worked alongside David Bosse, who shaped my thinking about grief in early America and suggested materials that anchor several chapters. Penny Leveritt, Barbara Mathews, Annie Rubel, William Flynt, and William Sillin also went above and beyond in answering my questions about Historic Deerfield and sharing their deep knowledge of the people and places I contemplate in these chapters. At the New Bedford Whaling Museum, Mark Procknik pointed me toward materials in the logbook and journal collections that expanded my understanding of maritime disability and the emotions attending it.

Colleagues who read portions (or even the entirety) of the manuscript molded my arguments, acquainted me with scholarship I had missed in my solitary research, and helped me imagine how scholars in diverse fields would encounter my ideas. Other colleagues shared sources and ideas with me. For this aid, I thank Abram Van Engen, Sara Johnson, Mark Kelley, Zach Hutchins, Melissa Gniadek, Luke Hardy, and Seth Archer, as well as anonymous readers for the Omohundro Institute of Early American History and Culture and *American Literature*. Some of my colleagues at BYU also commented on sections of the book. I appreciate Matthew Wickman, Jenny Pulsipher, Chris Hodson, Brian Roberts, Brice Peterson, Sharon Harris, Jason Kerr, Jill Rudy, and Jamin Rowan, not just for their assistance with this project but also for making our college such a warm and vibrant place to work. Emron Esplin and Marlene Esplin, dear friends, deserve similar thanks. Students in graduate seminars on early American crisis, witchcraft, and disability have been vital interlocuters. Briley Wyckoff, Tricia Cope, Daniel Andersen, Kirsten Burningham, Annalisa Gulbrandsen, Lindsay Haddock, Brittany Maloy, Washington Pearce, Sam Jacob, Isaac Robertson, Abby Thatcher, and Sylvia Cutler have influenced my teaching and writing more than they know.

I hope my scholarship shows the influence of Nicole Tonkovich, my first friend and mentor in the profession. I am also indebted to (and wish I had thanked earlier and more often) LeAnn Drake and the late Cal Harris, who taught thousands of Bountiful High School students to write clearly and think critically about literature and American history.

At the Omohundro Institute, Catherine Kelly and Emily Suth saw promise in this study of early American grief. Their enthusiasm for the project and their astute, formative responses to the proposal and early drafts made the book much more than it would have been otherwise. Virginia Chew and her legendary team of editorial apprentices read the manuscript with remarkable care. Every page is better for their attention. Nick Popper expertly guided the book through the last stages of the publication process. Aaron Green provided invaluable assistance with the book's images, as did Jennifer Saldana.

Portions of this manuscript have appeared in "Choosing Death: The Making of Martyrs in Early American Criminal Narratives," *American Literature*, XCI (2019), 691–719, and "Archipelagic Deformations and Decontinental Disability Studies," in Michelle Stephens and Yolanda Martínez-San Miguel, eds., *Contemporary Archipelagic Thinking: Toward New Comparative Methodologies and Disciplinary Formations* (Lanham, Md., 2020), 177–189. I thank Duke University Press and Rowman & Littlefield for allowing me to reprint those portions in this book.

A beloved niece, Sarah Eyring, not only brings dinner to my home every Wednesday night but (imagine this) stays at my kitchen table after she clears the dishes to read what I've written during the week. Her visits make the griefs we share palatable, sometimes almost sweet.

I am grateful to all the friends and family members who care for me, most of whom have no reason to see this book. But some of them are so kind, so generous, that, despite having no particular interest in academia or early America, they will read this book simply because these things matter to me and are often on my mind. To you who are reading this page, your friendship is a blessing. If you have also been kind to my children, your friendship is our salvation. To my father, greatest among friends in this group, words fail. Anne Bradstreet's tribute to her father comes to mind: "Who heard or saw, observed or knew him better? / Or who alive than I a greater debtor?"

At this moment, my daughters are playing around me, dripping water from half-filled balloons across the floor as they dart between the bathroom and the front porch. I'm not sure where the balloons are going, but I'll wait a few minutes to investigate. Elle, Vivi, if you find your way to this book someday, I hope you will forgive your mother for the hours she spent at this kitchen table. I spent them in the company of other parents, all but forgotten, who also worked for and worried about their children's welfare. I suspect the children thrived in spite of their parents' anxiety, not because of it, but I empathize with the parents nonetheless. I hope your lives give you few occasions to think about grief. But if, after I am gone, you ever wonder how your forerunners lived with pain, I leave this little book for you. And in case you're ever moved to join our communion, I'll leave you the kitchen table, too.

Contents

Illustrations

SALTWATER

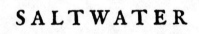

Grief in Early America

Around 1650, in Springfield, Massachusetts, something was working on Mary Parsons's nerves. She'd been divorced before, and now her second husband, Hugh, was acting strange. He had an off-putting demeanor anyway, and his behavior toward Mary, always odd, was verging on the cruel. But only verging. He picked up a brick and acted as though he would throw it at her head, then threw it on their hearth instead. He stayed out late at night, even when their children were sick and Mary was saddled with their care. Sometimes he didn't come home at all. He knew things about her she'd never told him. He was annoyed she was preoccupied with their ill baby and showed no sadness when the child died. He stopped short of violence, but she told neighbors she was afraid of him and shared what she was enduring in their home. They were appalled. They told the magistrates, who brought against Hugh the weightiest charge in the colonies' legal arsenal: witchcraft. One view of the New England witch hunts maintains that what officials saw and mirrored back to Mary was her fear. But some bereaved people are surprised to find that fear feels so much like grief.[1]

Grief is a volatile substance that mixes with other feelings in the air. It can become part of a decaying marriage, and certainly an abusive one, in ways that precede and exceed material loss and physical harm. Recalling an episode when Hugh harassed her to keep up with her chores while she pined for their dead child, Mary said, "When I saw my husband in this frame it added more grief to my sorrow." Sorrow is what she felt for her absent child. The grief her too-present husband added to it was something else—a feeling distinct from her sorrow before it infused and expanded it. This grief responded to losses that could not be seen and anticipated injury that had not occurred. It seeped into the cracks between the minor offenses that constantly replenished it and became an elemental building block of Mary's emotional life. It contributed to the mood that moved her to accuse her unkind, threatening husband of a capital crime.[2]

Since the American judiciary is well rid of the codes and procedures that allowed for the prosecution of witchcraft in the seventeenth century, some people may not realize how thoroughly modern systems have vacated not only the charge against Hugh but also the emotional grounds on which someone like Mary could bring such a nebulous claim of domestic anguish before a court. At the risk of taking readers out of the early American moment to which I will return momentarily and where the book will remain, I cite a recent example. In 2020, a fourteen-year-old girl in the tight-knit, highly religious city of Enoch, Utah, told the police she feared her father and was bothered by the way he "often [put] her mother down to her." When he put his hands around her throat, she was "very afraid," she said, "that he was going to keep her from breathing and kill her." The Division of Child and Family Services and the Enoch City Police Department investigated the incidents she described, and although the police saw evidence her father was "very close to assaultive," they were reassured by what they didn't see. "She stated that she did not suffer any injury," an officer reported. "She was mostly scared." No charges were brought, the county attorney's office explained, "likely based on an inability to prove each element of the offense(s) beyond reasonable doubt." Her mother didn't want charges filed anyway, hopeful the investigation would be a "wake-up call" for her husband. So the girl and her family were left alone, and for three years the police heard no more from them. And then she turned out to be right: her father killed her, her mother, her four younger siblings, and her grandmother inside their home two weeks after her mother filed for divorce. News reports regarded these deaths as a tragedy, rather than the end of a tragedy this girl endured but could not persuade outsiders to see. The tragedy might have materialized in a moment of violence, but it metastasized during the years the girl was mostly scared. Years during which she watched to see if she had keener intuition than the police officer who told her mother "there was no indication that there would be any violent behavior" from her father. Years during which she waited to find out whether her fear or her mother's desperate hope would prove prescient. I call this feeling grief, in defiance of the fact that only when there were seven bodies to mourn did the community she tried to alert acknowledge what she felt while she lived and what she knew when she died.[3]

While this girl was ignored, early New Englanders under the influence of grief compounded with other emotions are more often misunderstood within modern paradigms, and sometimes even pathologized. One book about the Parsons of Springfield grants Hugh's faults but downgrades them to the garden variety and blames the marriage's problems on Mary's disordered responses to his behavior. "He was moody, taciturn, avaricious; she depressive and delusional, perhaps suffering from paranoid schizophrenia or postpartum psychosis." The diagnosis of mental illness is not novel; this has been a standard view of Mary Parsons since the 1960s.[4]

As an alternative, if not precisely a corrective, to readings that rationalize away records of ambiguous grief in early America, my methodology in this book is to listen to expressions of emotional pain even when its sources are unclear, taking care not to minimize or invalidate the pain as I hold it in various theological, political, legal, or medical contexts. In the case of the Parsons, I don't see in extant records of their lives and legal woes evidence Hugh was physically violent. I can see ways Mary was not a perfect victim. But I believe she feared him, and I adopt the premise that her fear is understandable and the grief it spawned when it settled into her life should be granted the status of evidence, as religious experience and other affections have been, by those seeking to comprehend the stunning degree to which invisible forces shaped early American life.[5] As I apply this practice to other cases, I find the emotional notes of fear, anger, bewilderment, wariness, remorse, sympathy, conversion, and religious conviction we see or sense in early American sources are often constitutive elements of the chronic grief of people who said plainly, although with no dead body or visible wound to substantiate their claims, that they were in mourning—for safety, peace, wholeness, self-sufficiency, freedom, hope, surety, support, provision, beauty, faith, or something else. Because this grief was engrained in everyday experience and its antecedents were emotional rather than material, it has not always been acknowledged as grief and has sometimes been misread as the baser or baseless emotional reactions of primitive or hysterical people. My sympathetic interpretation of Mary's expression of grief is a throwback, not an innovation, since her devout Puritan community believed her, too. Springfield officials not only charged Hugh with witchcraft but, after a trial that elicited intimate details of their miserable domestic life, found him guilty. Like the girl in Utah, Mary came to local authorities with a strange story of staggering loss: an intimate protector had transformed into an enemy, leaving her bereaved of someone she loved and in danger of the shape-shifter in his place. She had a feeling this was her reality, not physical proof, but sometimes faith is more reasonable than doubt.[6]

My belief in the validity and evidentiary value of these expressions of grief fits within a field that follows the Puritans in treating emotional experience as something worthy of attention and analysis. Countering a nineteenth-century myth of stone-faced pilgrims beating thoroughfares of freedom across the wilderness, scholars of affect and historians of emotions have begun to sound the depth of Puritans' emotional lives and to acknowledge the common and public ways they shared a rich and complex array of feelings among one another and with other groups. "It no longer needs to be said that Puritans had emotions, nor indeed that their emotional range extended beyond lugubrious malice," Alec Ryrie and Tom Schwanda remark. Readers can see in Puritan writings people "intensely self-conscious of—and indeed, fascinated by—their own emotions." Fortunately for scholars in this vein, "the fiercely focused attention which many Puritans paid to their emotional lives generated rich bodies of source material." As they engage with this material, literary critics and historians have focused on emotion broadly construed as well as a range of specific emotions and affective states including happiness, devotion, desire, delight, anxiety, suffering, piety, sincerity, and sympathy.[7] My contribution to this scholarship is not to give grief its due as an emotion in its own right; it is to isolate the element of grief within these other emotions, to recognize and reckon with the degree to which the psychological force of grief integrated early New England experience and influenced belief, practice, and policy in the American Northeast.[8]

In the seventeenth century as now, theorists propose distinct definitions for words associated with feeling, and the terms help clarify this book's view of grief as an organic component of early New England life rather than as a periodic experience through which people and communities passed. Jonathan Edwards reasoned that "affections" are more "extensive" than passions; they are "actings of the will or inclination," whereas passions are more "sudden" and "violent." In A Treatise concerning Religious Affections, he used the word "affection" as a synonym for "emotion of the mind." Although this reasoning bears some relation to contemporary affect theory, affect theorists separate affect from emotions, treating affects as the irrational, preverbal, and preconscious forces that create the conditions under which emotions—which they assign to the realm of the cognitive—are experienced.[9] Most historians of emotions do not insist upon an elemental difference between affect and emotion because it was not recognized in or before the early modern era, when terms like *sentiment, affect, affections, passions,* and even *motion* described a range of what we would now call *emotion*.[10] When I use these words interchangeably, or when I draw on the thinking of affect theorists and historians of emotions in a single breath, it is because I wish to emphasize the degree to which chronic grief melded dispositions, feelings, and moods in early New England.[11]

Despite the pronounced influence of this renewed interest in affect and emotion on scholarship in the humanities and (to a lesser extent) the sciences, as Barbara H. Rosenwein and Riccardo Cristiani acknowledge, "outside of academic settings the impact of the history of emotions has been very slight." Fittingly for scholars of emotions, they add a lament: "This is a pity." In this book, I focus on grief associated with property loss, domestic tension, reproductive accidents and losses, and disability. I do so not just because these experiences were so commonplace in early New England but also because the feelings they invoke are still subjects of public controversy and consequence. The notion that some people do not suffer from homelessness or financial hardship but perversely prolong and profit from it inspired the fiction of Ronald Reagan's "Welfare Queen" and continues to justify austerity measures. Victims of domestic abuse must produce credible evidence of physical harm, not just psychological or emotional violence, to secure legal protection in American courts. People who do not grieve their pregnancy losses or whose pregnancies end in uncertain circumstances are subject to suspicion, and now (again) even criminal charges. And those whose disabilities are not visible or obviously painful are denied accommodations so frequently that the disability theorist Tobin Seibers, after an altercation with an airport gate agent who demanded he use a wheelchair if he wanted to claim early boarding privileges for a flight, wrote, "I have now adopted the habit of exaggerating my limp whenever I board planes. . . . despite the fact that it fills me with a sense of anxiety and bad faith, emotions that resonate with previous experiences in which doctors and nurses have accused me of false complaints, oversensitivity, and malingering." These unsympathetic responses to ambiguous or unseen losses sometimes draw on early modern precedent, as the public noticed with some alarm when Justice Samuel Alito's opinion to overturn *Roe v. Wade* repeatedly cited Matthew Hale, a Puritan English jurist who defended marital rape and presided over the execution of two widows for witchcraft in the seventeenth century.[12]

Yet the impulse to draw a line from Puritans' treatment of pregnant women to the John Roberts court's rulings on reproductive rights elides a circuitous emotional history. On the one hand, some historical cases seem to corroborate Nathaniel Hawthorne's caricature of the "grim rigidity" with which Puritans approached their "awful business" of policing women's bodies. In 1701, officials in Newbury, Massachusetts, charged a seventeen-year-old girl, Esther Rodgers, with infanticide in the wake of her traumatic pregnancy and delivery. Though she pleaded not guilty, they were unmoved, and she hanged for the crime. But as the case of Mary Parsons makes clear, Puritans could also be deeply sympathetic to the testimonies of vulnerable women. The mystifying logic by which New England Puritans denied Esther's claim to be a bereaved mother but credited Mary's claim to be an abused wife is no more uneven than the logic by which grief is validated in contemporary American society. In 2023, a national news outlet marveled at the credulity of the Enoch, Utah, community that published an obituary mourning the passing of a man who "made it a point to spend quality time with each and every one of his children" without mentioning that he shot each of his five children, mother-in-law, and wife before killing himself. But those community members were incredulous enough when his daughter came to them with warning signs of his escalating domestic violence. Grief responds to personal and local circumstances and in that sense has a historically specific quality to which this book is attuned, but many bereft people across the ages share this experience of having their grief doubted, ignored, misread, or dismissed outright. This book adopts some methods of contemporary historians of emotions to perceive anew the invisible grief in which some early moderns frankly believed. It opens the category of grief to anyone who claimed it in early New England, no matter the grounds, and in so doing proposes a study of grief that is smaller and yet more ranging than ones that have come before.[13]

Foundational scholarship on grief in early America has analyzed artifacts surrounding dead bodies, not disabled bodies, miscarried embryos, couples caught in unhappy marriages, or people mourning the loss of land or property, and for good reason. These things are hard enough to see as they happen. How is one to find them, or the grief they created, in the past? Death is easy to locate in the archive, and it has a geographically rooted quality—a deathbed or battlefield, a body, a gravestone, a funeral, a eulogist or an elegist, or a community of mourners located in a specific place—which makes its attendant signifiers easier to analyze according to familiar narratives foundational to the delineation of nations and the perpetuation of families. And the remains of dead bodies abound. There was no shortage of death during the seventeenth, eighteenth, and early nineteenth centuries—from the individual and expected to the collective and catastrophic—and no shortage of material illustrating the ways early Americans anticipated it, made sense of it, or instrumentalized the rituals surrounding it.[14] In a broader sense, attention to the most visible ruptures and catastrophes in early American life organizes historical periods and literary genres, which move through a series of controversies and calamities that call forth histories of settlement, captivity narratives, elegies, occasional poems, jeremiads, criminal narratives, and so on.[15] These units of history and literature take their cues from early moderns themselves, who structured their writings, rituals, and memorials around the spectacle or specter of tragedies on a grand scale. But nested within these forms, we find common, quiet pain no less powerful for its subtlety. Scholars have often read small-scale afflictions as tilting toward or accumulating into full-blown catastrophes—homelessness and burning homes initiate crises of settlement and captivity; uneasy marriages become legible in court records of physical abuse, homicide, or witchcraft; the suggestion of childbearing accidents loiters on the edges of infanticide cases; and bodies disabled by injury or disease presage death or depopulation crises. In chapters titled "Homeless," "Divorced," "Stillborn," and "Disabled," I cut off these familiar stories of early American tragedy before the climax, treating signs and shadows of pain as tragedies in themselves rather than portents.

These notices of minor affliction are obvious enough (the most famous early American captivity narratives open on the scene of burning homes, for example) that scholars' tendency to brush by them on the way to sites of death says as much about their interests as their methods. Early America was oversupplied with pain, which has worked against its value for those examining historical archives. Early Americanists initially tried to sharpen its stakes—to elevate private pain into matters of intergenerational (for Perry Miller) or national (for Sacvan Bercovitch) consequence—rather than contemplate it case by case where it seems idiosyncratic, unstable, inaccessible to expression or inference, insignificant, or simply unknowable.[16] The spiritual significance of affliction and the conditions and discourses of mourning, misery, and crisis have been granted the critical attention they richly deserve, but the perpetual discomfort of early Americans has become a first principle of early American scholarship rather than a subject of dedicated inquiry.[17]

There's an aphorism of uncertain origin but Churchillian timbre that chides those flagging in body, mind, or spirit: "Most of the world's work is done by people who don't feel very well." The sentiment turns on antipodean logic: low-grade, persistent suffering is so common it should not matter. A special issue of PMLA found the editors worrying about diluting the term *tragedy* ("If the word simply suggests something sad, banality is the consequence"), but the banality of early American sadness gave it incalculable psychic force. It is remarkable to consider that most of the world's work might be done, might have always been done, by people feeling unwell. Is it true? If so, is it possible that the influences of poor health, emotional distress, or mental discomposure do not impinge upon the work itself? The smallness of most pain in early New England allowed it to seep into the pores, to percolate the groundwater, to hang in the atmosphere. Pain was not all there was, but it was always there. Some observers take it for granted, but it is difficult to imagine that the pain of everyday affliction mattered less to early New Englanders, or left less of an impress upon early American culture, than the pain attending death. Untreated, unburied, and never memorialized, it endured. Early American grief has been considered as an event provoking certain rituals and forms. In the chapters of this book, I treat grief instead as a mood tingeing every kind of work early New Englanders performed and created.[18]

A MOOD OF GRIEF

The distinction between an event and a mood has to do with visibility as well as duration, intensity, and legibility.[19] Events happen, which is to say they begin and end, and they produce strong emotions that provoke material responses that leave imprints in the archive. In her study of New England misery, Kathleen Donegan invokes Hayden White and Alain Badiou to characterize events in terms of anomaly. She writes, "While the 'situation' is defined by an ordinary state of affairs in which all things can be accounted for, the 'event' forces a rupture, a break with previously known forms." As Badiou puts it, the event "is beyond what is." There can be no question that something has happened; the event is perceivable, even as the extreme feelings it produces—shock, confusion, horror, anger, terror, desolation, and so on—confound cognition and language. A long tradition of literature sought to manage these emotions by transmuting them (from despair into cries for vindication in the biblical psalms, for example) or subduing them (in Puritan sermons, by ordering and circumscribing them within God's providential design). When these literary forms failed, as they did when the crises of

English settlement in America overwhelmed the explanatory capacities of English writing, the disorganized emotions asserted themselves in a pageant of embodied horrors including "sieges, mutinies, desecrated corpses, slaughtered children, shipwrecks, [and] fire" that typified, Donegan argues, the "material condition" of misery during periods of English settlement in the new world.[20] Although it was not always part of such collective catastrophe in early America, death was always an event. On any scale, it terminated the routines of earthly experience. It called forth heightened emotions that ranged from devastation to resignation. And it left a body behind that had to be honored or interred or in any case handled by those most shaken and exhausted by the event. We have settled on the term *grief* to describe affective responses to death, though, as I've said, we're often startled to discover that what we took for sorrow is really fear, the anger of the betrayed, or love in search of a vanished referent. The expression of grief was an early American "project," to use Mitchell Robert Breitwieser's term, in which personal loss was reconciled to imperatives of communal survival. We can follow this arduous and imaginative labor through at least the nineteenth century in what Dana Luciano calls the "productions of mourners." Projects, productions, and even desecrated corpses present themselves for analysis in bounded forms that in some measure contain and preserve the anguish of desolated people. Just as Puritan ministers made meaning of the "tears trickling down the cheeks" of the sorrowful, field-defining scholarship on mourning in early America tracks the material traces that the work of grieving death left on the landscape.[21]

But death was only one of a host of losses early Americans grieved, many of which were neither events nor ongoing situations but things that didn't happen. Mary Rowlandson mourned the death of her daughter Sarah in her *Narrative of the Captivity and Restoration of Mrs. Mary Rowlandson*, but she also grieved the loss of her husband Joseph, who did not die. He is absent as the narrative opens on pandemonium in Lancaster, impotently petitioning leaders in Boston for protection against the Native attack on the town in 1676, and he never comes to redeem his wife in captivity. In moments of relative stillness, including when she reflected on her ordeal to compose her *Narrative*, Rowlandson troubled the murky pool of his whereabouts as she suffered alone. Had he tried to come for her? Had he forgotten her? The Pocasset Wampanoag saunksqua Weetamoo and her Narragansett husband Quinnapin, with whom Rowlandson lived during her captivity, suggested he was comfortably remarried in Boston, a possibility she did not dismiss out of hand. He was not dead, like Sarah, which would have been one thing.

He was "gone," which was something else. Countless early Americans wrestled such ambiguous losses. People who contracted diseases flowing among continents, islands, and oceans during the Age of Exploration, for example, attained statistical significance when they died, not when they became ill, so many historians who take depopulation seriously look past disability, the crisis that predicted and survived it.[22] In the literature of the depopulation crises colonists instigated and spread, the disabled are mostly invisible—the not-yet-dead, waiting in the wings for their moment to matter. The never-born and those who grieved them are another obscured group.[23] On a snowy day in Newbury, Esther Rodgers stole away from the baby she had delivered by herself in a field. She knew she could not possibly care for it, but she swore until the day she hanged for infanticide that she did not know whether the child was born alive or dead. Untold numbers of women did not see the deaths of their babies but clutched, or were shielded from, their miscarried or stillborn remains. They had to invent a happening where there was only silence. Had they murdered their children with their sundry sins? Esther was not alone in seizing upon and dramatizing this prospect just to give some semblance of a shape to an unbearable nonevent. There were no rituals, no genres, no familiar forms, not even language in which to mourn a child who was not born. That a few women crammed their immense sorrow into the ghastly conventions of the infanticide narrative is a testament to their resourcefulness, but the genre does not allow for the cipher at the heart of their tragedy and instead transforms the agonizing mystery of pregnancy loss into an event, a murder that summons legal procedures and the apocalyptic tones of ministerial writing. Infanticide convictions were mercifully rare in early America. Most bereaved mothers simply lived in the nimbus of their grief, where it assumed the properties of a mood surrounding something that did not happen rather than an emotion responding to something that did.[24]

Mood, like atmosphere, exists in excess of human thought and behavior. One can say of an empty room that it "has atmosphere," and people can be "in a mood" rather than a mood being in them. Mood and atmosphere can be charged, staged, and altered by human influence, but, just as frequently, they can bear down on humans and shift the quality of their thoughts, actions, even emotions. As Rita Felski and Susan Fraiman write: "Moods are usually described as ambient, vague, diffuse, hazy, and intangible, rather than intense, and they are often contrasted to emotions in having a longer duration. Instead of flowing, a mood lingers, tarries, settles in, accumulates, sticks around." The Patuxet Wampanoag *pniese* Tisquantum was kidnapped in 1614 by an English colonizer and did not return to Patuxet until the spring of 1619,

Introduction

when he found the Wampanoag stronghold devastated by an epidemic that killed most of its two thousand inhabitants and scattered the remnants, who were "not free of sicknesse" themselves. The once-teeming villages and fields were empty, the ground strewn with the unburied bones of his kin. When the *Mayflower* approached the coastline fringing Patuxet the next year, before the passengers saw any material vestiges of what the Wampanoag called "the Great Dying," they felt the icy chill of grief in the air and saw something dreadful in the way the pallid November light fell against the trees. "For summer being done, all things stand upon them with a wetherbeaten face; and the whole countrie, full of woods and thickets, represented a wild and savage heiw," William Bradford wrote.[25] The Separatists certainly did not grieve the deaths of the Patuxets, and only one of their own had died on the *Mayflower*, not under particularly tragic circumstances. They sailed into grief floating free of any event, grief that hung over Patuxet like weather. The environment itself seemed stricken. Within a year, an English Great Dying killed half the weary pilgrims, but it was only in a practical and political sense a second wave of death. A fog of grief penetrated the period historians including Bradford tried to put between the cataclysmic end of Patuxet and the harrowing beginnings of Plymouth, creating an affective continuity imbricating discrete historical events. Native space in America could be cleared and Native grounds claimed, desecrated, and transformed, but Native pain remained in forms the English felt but could not see, until they concluded and clung to the conviction these woods and thickets must be haunted.[26]

How does one recover a historical mood? Literary critics find it in the resonances of words and the structures of sentences, which, when writers are in command of their craft, create emotional properties in the writing that attach themselves to readers and begin to modulate their attitudes and thinking. Reading for mood came into fashion during a democratic era in literary studies, when the U.S. G.I. Bill (1944) made it reasonable for first-generation college students to study something as obviously pleasurable as English literature. For the sake of practicality as much as principle, professors assured these students that their modest acquaintance with the Western tradition posed no impediment to their future as English scholars. They taught short texts, mostly poems and stories, that were captivating and enlivening on their own merits, even if students knew nothing about the author's pedigree, oeuvre, anxieties, or inspirations. The theoretical apparatus supporting (or at any rate dignifying) this pedagogy, the New Criticism, revised the maxims of historically oriented criticism by promising that the essential meaning of a work was contained in the text itself. Variations on this promise still shape curriculum, particularly in high school English classrooms, for reasons substantially related to those influencing college professors in 1944 and exacerbated by economic policies that have stretched teachers' resources to the breaking point. The long association between mood and formalism means most studies of mood track it within a text or a literary movement. But Felski's work is revelatory for illuminating how wantonly mood defies boundaries, including those drawn by the New Critics. A multidisciplinary critical mood has spread its tendrils across vast swaths of the academy as we have been bent over our own fields.[27] Studying mood in a single text is like studying climate in a terrarium. To have any real sense of its origins and potential, we must follow it through the varied and unlikely spaces it draws into intimacy. Accordingly, I trace mood across a range of texts and artifacts— from naval logbooks to court records, primers, journals, newspaper articles, occasional poems, diplomatic correspondence, and sermons—to find an affective history of early America that wound a path through private and public life with no regard for the edges around historical epochs and literary forms. Felski's call for literary critics to moderate, or at least acknowledge, their own disposition toward the material they interpret has inspired my practice of "mid-level" reading, which aims for generosity in both scale and tone as it balances lateral readings across multiple sources with close readings of a few key texts. My objective is, to borrow Felksi's terms, "composing and cocreating," or "forging links between things that were previously unconnected," rather than traditional critique.[28]

This postcritical approach participates in the spirit and aims of the new Narrative History, which uses constellations of texts to tell dimensional, coherent stories about the past. Historical documents do not encode these stories; the most they supply, as Hayden White argues, are "story *elements*" from which historians assemble narratives. As we know, historians do not work from neutral ground. They approach their material and write with a certain attitude, so one can never be certain whether the mood captured in the narrative reflects the historical atmosphere, the mood enveloping the historian, or some interplay between the two. I offer no alternative to this phenomenon. My treatment of archival materials and scholarship is as moody as any other historian's, only more so, since in the chapters that follow I re-emplot familiar narratives of American settlement, colonial life, and exploration as stories driven by mood rather than action. Reading with an ear for tones rather than an eye for events, I find striking connections among texts that have been assigned to different historical narratives. My point is not to tell a more objective version of history but another subjective one, keyed into a different emotional pitch and sensitive to the thrum of mundane pain rather than the cacophony of catastrophe. That the moods of the present have attuned me to things historians might have missed about the moods of an early modern moment is impossible to deny, a circumstance I contemplate by way of concluding the book.[29]

THE NAME OF PAIN

The term I use for the source of grief in early American life is *pain*. I find the word useful for what it comprehends—beginning with the loss of what one had or for what one wished—as well as what it excludes. As Elaine Scarry and Cathy Caruth conceived of it, pain was punctual and extreme, the kind of consciousness-shattering and language-confounding occurrence associated with torture or the trauma of other limit events. Body and trauma theorists have since granted the power of less severe and more covert forms of pain and the potential for consciousness and language to adapt to the exigencies of trauma in ways that produce new forms of knowledge and discourse. I discuss pain that was traumatic in every sense—wounds sustained in war, limbs severed and bones crushed in maritime accidents, the bodily consumptions of leprosy and tertiary syphilis—as well as pain through which people routinely carried on with their daily lives, such as the weeping weight of post-partum recovery, the stiffness and twinge of old injuries, and the tightness of chest that accompanied respiratory infections. I discuss psychic as well as physical pain, which were closely related. The physiological encumbrances I just mentioned produced sensations of fear, frustration, thwarted hope, confusion, or despair. Captain Edmund Gardner was a hero at sea for surviving an encounter with a whale in 1816 that broke his shoulder, hand, teeth, and skull, but when he returned from the voyage to Nantucket, he began feeling "depressed." In Oceania, the fact that he did not die was a spiritual triumph, but on land, it became a psychological trauma commensurate with his physical disabilities.[30]

In naming pain and studying the names early moderns gave their pain, I am conscious, as Jill Lepore writes, that "words and wounds are not equivalent, but they are sometimes analogous." I use the words *sorrow, sadness, affliction, suffering, injury, illness,* and *discomfort* to suggest varieties and degrees of pain, not to delimit difference between wounds of the body and wounds of the mind or to suggest a threshold at which pain is too trivial to matter or too totalizing to represent. Yet I respect a distinction between *pain* and *trauma*. Many early Americans experienced, witnessed, or caused pain without

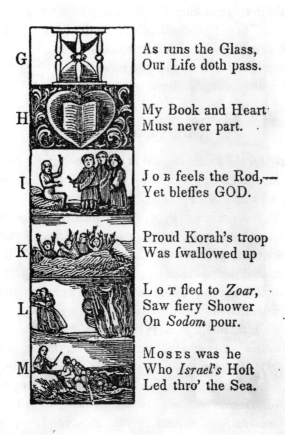

G
As runs the Glass,
Our Life doth pass.

H
My Book and Heart
Must never part.

I
J o b feels the Rod,—
Yet bleſſes GOD.

K
Proud Korah's troop
Was ſwallowed up

L
L o t fled to *Zoar*,
Saw fiery Shower
On *Sodom* pour.

M
M o s e s was he
Who *Israel's* Hoſt
Led thro' the Sea.

Figure 1. Drawing of the prophet Job. From *The New-England Primer Improved for the More Easy Attaining the True Reading of English; to Which Is Added the Assembly of Divines, and Mr. Cotton's Catechism* (Boston, 1777), n.p., image 20, Internet Archive

undergoing what we might consider trauma, and texts of the period show people absorbing or transforming pain in ways that produced something other than psychic wounds. They unsettled the dynamic between victims and perpetrators—not simply as the English assumed the posture of victims in the Native space they seized but also because some victims insisted on their status as agents of violence. Incarcerated and sentenced to die after delivering a baby without clear signs of life, Esther Rodgers used the conventions of the infanticide narrative to convert her victimhood into radical agency, wherein she became the author of her crime (not her injury), her reformation, and her potential salvation. I take seriously the testimonies of early Americans who couch their pain in terms that defy our understanding of trauma, and when I seek to contextualize their response to suffering, I do not presume to recharacterize their pain as more or less traumatic than it seemed to them. I am also careful to acknowledge a distinction between *pain* and *disability*, since some people with disabilities live lives free of pain, psychic or physical, and to assume otherwise is to create pain under the sham of ministering to it.[31]

I confess I use the terms *pain* and *suffering* somewhat interchangeably. Puritan ministers valued physical and emotional pain because they believed suffering inspired or deepened conversion, not because they were inured to pain's effects or took pleasure in its sanctifying potential. Puritans expected to experience pain as a condition of their fallen state, and the inevitable emotional and physical suffering it engendered made pain a potent didactic tool. John Cotton used the letter J in the *New-England Primer* to teach children, "Job feels the Rod yet blesses GOD." In William Perkins's view, "paine and pricking in the heart" should reorient the faithful back to God. And, as Charles Lloyd Cohen demonstrates, painful psychological transformations from states of "desperation" to "relief" initiated and regenerated the experience of Puritan conversion. Pain might be a punishment for sin, or a gentle chastisement from a loving God, or simply a trial that proved or further refined the saint. Perhaps inevitably, given this range of doctrinal interpretations, "men and women creatively negotiated their own relationship to this devotional tradition," as Adrian Chastain Weimer finds. Yet the writings of ministers and literate laypeople from which scholars deduce early modern theologies, and even try to account for discrepancies between the perspective from the pulpit and the view from the pews, preserve a relatively narrow record of pain in the early American Northeast. These writings do not reveal how people (even ministers) interpreted their pain when it was so consuming or distracting that it interfered with their ability to theorize it or when people, particularly Black and Indigenous Americans, had no means to write about their pain. These writings tell us that Puritans and those they sought to convert were admonished to find affliction meaningful, and that some did. But I study expressions of pain without assuming people always assigned it spiritual significance or experienced it according to the logic of ministerial directive. I exercise caution in making arguments by analogy that interpret one person's experience of pain by way of a contemporaneous theory of pain, since these theories might have caused pain as often as they explained it. I see evidence chronic pain could make doubters, and sometimes heretics, of the most-converted Christians. And I repeatedly encounter the possibility that a person's experience of pain overflowing the doctrinal forms meant to contain it was another source of suffering that added more grief to their sorrow.[32]

Pain turned the early modern world to water. In *Nine Books of Physick and Chirurgery* (1658), Daniel Sennert wrote, "If a soft part be dissolved by a thing that cutteth, it is simply called by the Greeks *Trauma*." In *A Compleat Discourse of Wounds* (1678), John Browne provided the definition, "Trauma, A Solution made by a Wound in the Fleshy parts."[33] This medical view of wounds as solutions and dissolutions owed a debt to Stoic cosmology, which held that all matter, including human and nonhuman bodies, existed on a continuum in a fluid universe. Early moderns understood their bodies as water that had temporarily taken human shape, and they watched anxiously for signs they were turning to water again. According to the Stoics, matter originates from a fiery liquid called *pneuma*, transmutes as pneuma acquires the properties of different elements and forms, and will finally return, by way of fire, to a liquid state. This philosophy was reflected in the third chapter of 2 Peter, which speaks of the antediluvian earth "standing out of the water and in the water" before the world was "overflowed with water" and prophesies an apotheosis of the cosmic life cycle in which "the heavens being on fire shall be dissolved, and the elements shall melt with fervent heat." The liquid universe was exceedingly precarious. As Kristen Poole observes: "This is not an environment of solidity and stability, but one that is labile. Like the Galenic body, with its four mutating humours, the cosmos is a shifting, living, liquid corpus." In a universe where trauma dissolved bodies and the heavens themselves were predestined to melt, the heart and soul were as soluble as anything else. The affective landscape flowed into the physical environment. In his occasional poem "Upon the Sweeping Flood," Edward Taylor illustrates the relationship among divine intervention, human emotion, and earthly ecologies, no less dreadful for being quite mundane.

> Oh! that Id had a tear to've quencht that flame
>   Which did dissolve the Heavens above
>   Into those liquid drops that Came
>   To drown our Carnall love.
> Our cheeks were dry and eyes refusde to weep.
> Tears bursting out ran down the skies darke Cheek.

Taylor's poem laments a catastrophic flood in August 1683—the cause of which, Taylor proposes, was a landscape too long parched by the spiritual indifference of its inhabitants, whose hearts would not melt and whose eyes would not cry until an enraged heaven addressed earth's water shortage. Although the tears of the sorrowful were a sign of pain in early America, they played a crucial role in maintaining cosmic equilibrium. The watery universe was a given, and better a landscape drenched with saltwater than one cleansed by liquid fire.[34]

I use the image of saltwater to evoke a sense of grief as elemental rather than episodic and pervasive rather than bounded, even within the forms and frames by which early New Englanders themselves sought to name and contain it. For better and worse, saltwater was a solvent that created coherence across a parceled early American world in the act of dissolving so many of its claims to autonomy and exceptionalism. Early New England grief had a globalizing thrust, by which I mean it resonated deeply and widely. Grief brought people into communion with one another and the world into communion with the cosmos, although communion is not always an unmitigated good. It is impossible to conceive of a mood so central to early New England experience without dramatically expanding our usual conceptual parameters around scale, space, and time.

I have a particular interest in grief that has been deemed small and insignificant, sometimes because it was invisible, or too widely shared, or too deeply personal to trigger conventions of mourning, but often because pain mourned by early Americans, especially English colonists, seems trivial to modern scholars relative to the pain they inflicted on others. For at least two generations it has been customary for early Americanists to come at the productions of English mourners from an angle, rather than meet white settlers' grief head-on. We take up these projects with a keen sense of our ethical obligation to read between the lines in order to see the stories of other people who suffered in early America, almost always to a much greater degree than the English staking their panicked claims to Native space. This scholarship has become increasingly generous over the past few years in the kinds of grief it is willing to see and sit with. Lisa Brooks, for example, reads the canonical documents surrounding King Philip's War to narrate the strategic vision by which Weetamoo guided her Wampanoag kin and their allies during an existential crisis. She does not dismiss Rowlandson's pain or her grief for her lost home and family, but she brings Weetamoo and her family into the foreground and asks Rowlandson to grieve alongside them, where the shared quality of their sorrow—as two mothers mourning dead babies in the crush of a brutal war—comes into relief. I follow on the heels of such inclusive scholarship. I consider pain, like anything else in the watery universe, to move somewhat promiscuously through Native space in early America. It was shared by people related through conflict and violence and felt by people who inflicted more than their share of suffering. People suffered whether they had any right to do so, and the practice of acknowledging slight and unworthy pain puts us in the habit of seeing suffering in unexpected places, where our attention might bring or at least precede some measure of relief.[35]

The promiscuity of mundane grief troubled the spatial boundaries of early America. It drew unlikely parties, such as Rowlandson and Weetamoo, into profound emotional entanglements. It sent sympathy sprawling across the landscape, unsettling national identities and making bedfellows of bereaved strangers and antagonists. Within families, affliction upset and realigned affinities we have taken for granted, such as the ideological consensus historians generally assume existed between husbands and wives.[36] It sent people in pain searching for forms in which to comprehend and express their suffering, producing artifacts of grief shaped by transcultural and transhemispheric influences. Although the first English settlers brought pain from England and Europe and called on long-established religious, legal, medical, and social traditions to address it, once they were in America their emotions mixed with the pain of Indigenous and Black Americans, producing new feelings and responses. In the writings I study, a diverse group of early Americans shared their pain with their children and grandchildren, who within a few generations began carrying their own pain around the world. I follow these travels because some dimensions of early Americans' grief are only apparent against the backdrop of unfamiliar environments, and because their grief absorbed qualities from their contact with other people. Although only the last chapter of this book is centered on spaces outside the American continent, each chapter takes up the rootless, slippery quality of grief to survey an affective landscape that dramatically exceeded the geographic footprint of early New England. Engaging the provocations of ecocriticism, Black and Indigenous American studies, and postcontinental American studies, the book tracks grief through the lands, waters, and shoals early Americans touched. By focusing on the oblique and invisible grief of individuals rather than the public expressions of mourners, the book finds a language of suffering understood and shared across diverse early American communities. And sensitizing ourselves to the pain of people divided between this world and another sends us to the underworld and the cosmos in pursuit of the pieces of their souls grief swept up and scattered.

As this turn toward the spiritual would suggest, grief has its own temporality. It gazes longingly behind at some vanished idyll, perhaps only ever a fantasy, that provided assurance or hope. It projects itself into the unfathomable reaches of a bleak future. It licks wounds in the present. In short, grief plays tricks with time. As Emily Dickinson put it:

> Pain—has an Element of Blank—
> It cannot recollect
> When it begun—Or if there were
> A time when it was not—
>
> It has no Future—but itself—
> It's Infinite contain
> It's Past—enlightened to perceive
> New Periods—Of Pain.

In the chapters that follow, I cast myself headlong into pain's element of blank. A mood of grief has a timeless quality that seemed stultifying to many early Americans, who desperately peered into the eternities for some sign of its origins and some promise of its end. I consider the faithful and imaginative ways grieving people nursed suffering that persisted but sometimes shifted under the influence of their emotional labor. They often tended to their pain alone, or within a very limited social sphere, since minor, invisible, and ongoing afflictions leave people grieving out of tempo with others, even those afflicted in the same ways. This kind of grieving rewards patient critical attention. From Tiffany Lethabo King, I adopt the practice of "shoaling," or slowing, over moments in texts that capture forms of quiet and subtle suffering before I pass to the larger crises that usually overshadow them. I find and give due consideration to moments when it seems the pain of the past intrudes on the present, which should not surprise us, given mood's propensity to linger.[37]

The chronology and methodology of this project betray my inclinations as an early Americanist planted in a department of English. I consider cases of grief ranging from the 1620s to the 1820s with close attention to tension and ambiguity in the language and form of historical sources and with no intention of covering the period or proposing a metahistorical narrative about American grief. Although the book's focus on minor griefs is microhistorical in the sense that "microhistory as a practice is essentially based on the reduction of the scale of observation, on a microscopic analysis and an intensive study of the documentary material," the chronological jumps within chapters and especially the leap from eighteenth-century New England to nineteenth-century Hawai'i in the last chapter will strike some readers as jarring departures from the other sections' granular, immersive pyschogeographies of early New England. But a project on early New England grief, especially on a microscopic level, that never leaves New England soil nor considers the inheritors of early New England pain misrepresents its force, which it gathered in persisting and in traveling. The chapter on disability focuses on the experience of physical suffering in Hawai'i because that is where a disabled descendant of Nantucket's first settlers voyaged and took the pain he incurred from working the nautical trade his ancestors bequeathed to him. Although disabled people in Hawai'i suffered within different ideological systems from those in New England, as oceanic industries brought these systems into relationship, new emotional communities emerged in response to the physical pain of colonial contact. These communities cut across social groups, geographic distance, and time in ways the last chapter contemplates at length.[38]

Barbara H. Rosenwein uses the term "generations of feeling" to underscore "the constant availability and potentiality of older and coexisting emotional traditions," which are so expansive, Elena Carrera argues, that the term "emotional communities" may be less apt than something like "transhistorical ideological groups." By the standards of historians of emotions, the temporal frame of this book is modest. Rosenwein's *Generations of Feeling* proposes a history of emotions from 600 to 1700; Carrera's edited collection *Emotions and Health* spans from 1200 to 1700; and Peter N. Stearns's *Shame: A Brief History* begins with premodern societies ("the term covers an immense amount of territory, and its generality can annoy many historical specialists who devote rich scholarly lives to exploring greater details in particular times and places," he admits) and ends in the contemporary United States. They use microhistorical techniques and yet treat only some representative groups and moments they consider significant—an approach Rosenwein, following archeologists, calls "judgmental sampling." Their point is that emotions resonate in specific contexts but also persist to some degree or in some sense across time. Within a much smaller historical framework, I make the same assumption in the last chapter of this book, when I trace the emotional imprints of early American disability as they traveled across geographic divides and passed through generational lines. If one of my methodological commitments is to listen to people in pain, another is to follow them. Some Americans wrote of grief for their children and anxiety about the pain in their children's future. They asked their readers to peer into these futures with them—to see whether the hearts of grieving children would turn to their fathers, and to wonder what they might offer them if they did.[39]

SATURATED

History is full of ponderous doors swinging on their slender hinges. Early Americans, and particularly the Puritans, seem to have reacted so operatically to provocations so slight that the stories of their struggles are often classified as hysterias of one kind or another. But between visible provocations and visible reactions runs a solution of invisible pain that conducts its own charge. The prophet Job, whose faithfulness under God's rod John Cotton taught New England children to emulate, met the serial losses of his sheep, camels, asses, oxen, servants, daughters, and sons with equanimity: "The Lord gave, and the Lord hath taken away; blessed be the name of the Lord," he said. But when he broke out in painful boils, his resolve gave way and he cursed the day of his birth. That a skin condition and not the deaths of his ten children finally punctured the surface tension of Job's emotional composure suggests what anyone who has lived in conditions of prolonged suffering knows, that the relationship between affliction and spiritual or psychic breakdown is neither linear nor additive. There is a continuity to Job's grief that gives the bundled mass of his losses soul-shattering heft. Yet each loss lends a distinctive note to the quality of his suffering. "Oh that my grief were throughly weighed!" he laments. Scholars of literature and history are adept at looking beyond the most proximate events when composing narratives of controversy and combustion. But scholars of affect and emotions are showing the value of looking beneath and above historical events to weigh hidden sorrows and moods of disquietude that were gnawing at people carrying out the work of the early American world. Like the Old Testament prophet, the weather-beaten inhabitants of New England were people sodden with the weight of accumulated griefs before the sudden eruptions by which we measure the march of early American life.[40]

Job's friends meant to comfort him when they promised, "Thou shalt forget thy misery, and remember it as waters that pass away," and they might have been right, for the story ends with a replacement set of animals, servants, daughters, and sons standing in place of the originals. But something about the way a vanished household miraculously reassembles itself points to the truth that waters don't pass away; they simply change shape and states. The determination of some sufferers to forget their misery accounts for a certain poverty in the archive, and we sift through the remains of what water left behind. But in fact water hangs in the air and collects in the ground beneath our field of study, invisible but not imperceptible. Most of us don't forget our grief, but we notice that it begins to slip from the forefront of consciousness to the atmosphere around us, no longer a deluge but a cloud. We remember it as water.[41]

CHAPTER I

Homeless

———

Nothing should be less surprising to students of Northeastern American settlement than the omnipresence of homelessness in the region and era. To be a settler, after all, was to be transformed by the crucible of dislocation. Settler colonialism depended on the forced homelessness and relocation of enslaved Africans. And temporary and prolonged relocations were central to Native subsistence activities. Given how unremarkable homelessness was, then, it is mildly surprising that the experience commands such emotional and aesthetic power in the literature of New England settlement and colonial life. "Farewell my Pelf, farewell my Store," Anne Bradstreet bids her family's belongings, destroyed along with their Andover home in 1666, in one of the most oft analyzed of early American texts. This was an unexpected moment of homelessness for Bradstreet, but as a Puritan exile in England, she had practice bidding "Adeiu, Adeiu" to her house. It was a recurring feature of the Puritan experience in North America, as well. Some of the most telling lines of Mary Rowlandson's captivity narrative appear as she regards the burning of her home, not with a sense of shock, but rather of resigned recognition:

"Now is that dreadfull hour come, that I have often heard of (in time of War, as it was in the case of others) but now mine eyes see it." In the wider context of American settlement, such a prosaic experience hardly seems worth dwelling upon, yet the loss of dwellings arrests the attention and inspires the pens of many early New England writers.[1]

Consider the number of canonical early American texts that open on or include the scene of flames consuming a home. A reader need take only a tentative step into the early American archives to catch the acrid whiff of something smoldering. This literature of sudden homelessness typically begins in medias res, which has the effect of impressing on readers the feelings of terror and dread the catastrophe ignites. Texts ranging from Bradstreet's poem "Here Followes Some Verses upon the Burning of Our House, July 10th, 1666" to captivity narratives written by Rowlandson, Cotton Mather, and John Williams cry "fire and fire" in their opening acts, if not in their first lines. But because they go on to describe or allude to tragedies that so totally eclipse the destruction of buildings (such as widespread death or spiritual apostasy), these texts are treated as stories of politics or faith—not as narratives about becoming suddenly homeless again. In fact, the burning home presents some impediment to our usual modes of interpreting these stories. The emphasis on houses in a litany of existential losses sits oddly against Native cosmologies and Puritan doctrine, which seem to privilege kinship networks or eternal verities over fixed domestic sites and worldly belongings. Given what we know, or think we know, about the values of English settlers and their first descendants, we might expect they absorbed this loss as the cost of doing colonial business. But the remains of thatch-roofed huts, wood-frame homes, wetus, lodges, forts, and even ships' berths, so conspicuously deposited in early American literature, call for excavation. In a space where homelessness was not a marginal identity but rather a life stage through which almost everyone passed—often more than once—what did homelessness mean, and why did it matter?[2]

The experience of homelessness was inflected, and these meanings and significances most apparent, when it occurred without warning or in conditions of coercion, as it did when violence or accident sent a family's dwelling up in flames. This chapter thus takes burning homes as its focal point, first as material objects embedded in Atlantic ecosystems and then as symbols deployed in literature to affectively collapse the globe and stretch time by uniting authors and readers in a circuit of shared vulnerability, grief, spirituality, and empathy. My interest in fire as a physical force and homelessness in early America as an affective experience brings to the fore what is more often implicit in a Reformed theological tradition that treats fire metaphorically and in historical scholarship that treats homelessness as a material condition. Within Puritan typology, a hermeneutical mode that translates secular history into sacred history by reading the Old Testament as prefiguring the life of Christ and postscriptural saints as imitating it, fire is a recurrent and central symbol. It represents phenomena ranging from God himself ("The Pillar of Cloud and Fire") to the depths of hell ("The Lake of Fire and Brimstone"), and even the apparent absence of the divine from some earthly events, as for the prophet Elijah, who found "the Lord was not in the fire." The figurative fires of Puritan sermons, perhaps most famously the one conjured in the jeremiad of Jonathan Edwards over which a sinful spider toasts, continue to shape the way Puritanism is introduced to students of early America. But for some Puritan writers, the astounding destructive and transformative potential of fire was literal, not (or not only, or not yet) a manifestation of God's anger or refining interference. I draw on foundational ecocritical approaches to early American literatures and history to contextualize Puritan writers' preoccupation with fire as a material element and not simply a conduit for spiritual meaning. But I also follow these Puritan writers in treating the homelessness created by fires and related disasters as a condition with metaphorical connections to the emotional experience of crossing cultures and leaving family behind and typological significance for strangers and pilgrims making their way from home to Home.[3]

In at least one sense, the burning home crossed these material and symbolic registers. The flames occasionally served as a signal between early American communities, alerting nearby friends of distress and summoning aid. When an alliance of French, Kahnawake Mohawk, and other Indigenous fighters took Reverend John Williams captive in Deerfield, Massachusetts, as part of a military campaign sometimes called "the conflagration of 1704," the burning of Deerfield's homes came to stand in for the greater catalog of violence (including the deaths of fifty-seven colonists and the captivity of at least ninety more) in written histories of the episode. But during the attack itself, the flames were the first sign of the catastrophe to neighboring allies. Isaac Addington wrote to Fitz-John Winthrop, "The fires being descried at Hatfield, Col. Partridge posted away a company of sixty souldiers, who came to the place about sunrise, beat the enemy out of the town, and thirty of them were left dead on the spot." While homes demarcated difference in early America—between families, communities, and the built and natural environment—*burning* homes connected communities across time and space, returned manufactured goods to their natural environments, and exposed the frequently fictive nature of geopolitical difference and even distance in the early modern world.[4]

I contemplate writings about North American fires and the homelessness attending them not to plot a chronology of grief related to this experience (readers will notice that texts do not appear in order of their composition) but to suggest that in a broadly—and sometimes imaginatively—construed early American world, the fires that appear at first blush to be devastating in their violence were in fact powerfully constructive forces of home making. Guided by foundational and recent work in ecocriticism, Black and Indigenous American studies, postsecular studies, book history, and postcontinental American studies, I follow fires through the terraqueous spaces they touched in search of the enduring homes early Americans forged out of the embers of collective catastrophe. In this world, homelessness as we typically conceive it was not an obstacle to finding a secure place within a protective kinship structure; it was a precondition for it.

HOME AND FIRE IN THE EARLY AMERICAN NORTHEAST

The prominence of burning homes in the canonical accounts of Northeastern American settlement and colonization alerts us to the ubiquity of fire in the region. In fact, setting fires was an act of settlement in North America long before it became part of a project of un- or countersettlement.[5] Native agricultural communities, including the Podunks, Nipmucs, Mahicans, and Tunxis, used fires to clear fields, to drive game, to create space and sunlight for corn crops, to reveal new soil mineral layers, and to produce dry logs to fuel fires for cooking and warmth. They deliberately burned "sprout hardwoods"—trees that regenerate from their roots—to stimulate germination, and because they set seasonal fires that routinely cleared underwood and fallen trees, their fires burned at low temperatures and quickly hit natural breaks in combustible material. These controlled burns had a salubrious effect on regional habitats, extending the benefits of what ecologists call the "edge effect," or the biodiversity that concentrates in areas where ecosystems overlap, as in the borders between forests and grasslands. Early English explorers like John Smith—who marveled that in New England "nature and liberty affords us that freely, which in *England* we want, or it costeth us dearly"—were in fact observing the effects of Native peoples' careful management of the space with fire. Timothy Dwight acknowledged as much when he wrote, "The object of these conflagrations was to produce fresh and sweet

Figure 2. *Pocumtuck, circa 1550.* By William Sillin. © 2004

pasture, for the purpose of alluring the deer, to the spots, on which they had been kindled." As William Cronon points out, "The effect was even subtler than Dwight realized: because the enlarged edge areas actually raised the total herbivorous food supply, they not merely attracted game but helped create much larger populations of it." Native hunters and farmers were not simply enjoying the natural bounty of the region; "in an important sense, they were harvesting a foodstuff which they had consciously been instrumental in creating." The Massachusetts General Court granted limited property rights to Native groups engaged in this kind of land management, conceding that the fires were part of a larger project of "subdueing" the land according to the directives of Genesis 1:28 and thus establishing a civil, not merely natural, claim to it.[6]

Although English settlers in some sense learned from the examples of Native hunters and farmers, they used fire in ways and to degrees unknown in the American Northeast. While Native planters set controlled burns to clear the undergrowth within a forest, English planters set fires to destroy the entire forest, clearing space for crops and agricultural practices imported from England. And while Native families collected fuel for household fires, the English settlers amassed firewood on an unprecedented scale. Some of this, Thomas Wickman argues, had to do with the colonists' difficulty tolerating frigid New England winters, especially relative to their Wabanaki neighbors, who adapted to the rhythms of winter as they did to other seasons. Some of this massive fuel consumption also had to do with Puritans' material aspirations. Prosperous settlers replaced roofs of thatch and slate with wooden shingles as a matter of course and, as soon as they were able, built larger half- or full-timbered structures and eventually brick homes. Fire was necessary to support these aspirations since settlers needed huge amounts of fuel to bake clay bricks and larger homes were harder to heat. And, in a broader sense, New England settlers' fuel consumption can be associated with a kind of resistance to environmental and seasonal changes (particularly the frigid winters) rather than a willingness to adapt their agricultural and economic activities to a space radically different from the temperate oceanic climate of their Atlantic isle. The "grossly inefficient design" of English fireplaces built in New England, which might be six feet long and five feet high and burned more or less continuously, drove firewood consumption to such an extent that it altered not only the regional woodlands but also the politics and even climate of the region. "Though well-adapted to traditional English culinary culture," Strother Roberts notes, "these fireplaces proved a poor fit for the harsher winters English settlers encountered in New England," prompting them to "compensate for the colder climate by consuming firewood on a level almost undreamed of back in England." The fuel demands of a single Connecticut Valley village required it to clear somewhere in the neighborhood of twenty-three hundred acres of woodland every fifty years. These unsustainable demands for firewood also put villages in competition with one another and with local Native communities for dwindling reserves and sent settlers north, west, and south in search of new supplies. The accompanying deforestation disrupted rainfall and wind patterns, which initiated devastating cycles of drought and floods. In making themselves at home in America, the English made it more likely they would be suddenly homeless in the future.[7]

As significant as these differences in English and Native uses of fire and their ecological effects are, the more pressing point—which can sometimes be obscured in comparative analyses of this kind—is that both Native peoples and English settlers used fire to become at home in the American Northeast. Without minimizing the competitive nature of firewood acquisition in New England, I wish to draw attention to the building of fires, which was part of the building of home, as a broadly shared enterprise in the region. Consider this exchange between Roger Williams and his Narragansett neighbors, as relayed by Williams: "This question they oft put to me: Why come the English-men hither? and measuring others by themselves; they say, It is because you want firing: for they, having burnt up the wood in one place, (wanting draughts to bring *wood* to them) they are faine to follow the *wood*; and so to remove to a fresh new place for the *woods* sake." The Narragansetts understand that English settlement is driven by proximity to essential resources, firewood foremost among them. For Williams, this understanding also reveals something about what the Narragansetts notice, or what they value. As they search for common ground from which to understand the other's rationale for moving through and within the space, firewood seems to be a point of tension and a source of suspicion on both sides. But wood *on fire* is a point of cultural commonality and connection. The Narragansets and the English set fires for a substantially similar purpose—to clear physical and affective space for a kind of communal survival. Not only is fire something both groups value; it is something both groups value for the same reason. We see that Williams and his Narragansett interlocuters appreciate acutely the ways fire shapes, subtly or dramatically, the natural landscape into something more capable of supporting not just the business but also the pleasures of domestic life.[8]

It is not only possible but also illuminating to see even fires of the kinds that open the captivity narratives of John Williams, Mary Rowlandson, and Cotton Mather as such tools of home building and preservation rather than agents of wanton destruction. The English settlers' incursions into woodlands further removed from their original sites of colonization threatened Native groups with the kind of homelessness the English feared from Native violence. The English ownership, bounding, and exploitation of forests, edge areas, and meadows made it harder if not impossible for Native agricultural communities to use the land, as they and their ancestors long had, for the subsistence activities that made meaningful kinship relations possible. In short, it left families dispossessed. Narratives that decontextualize the firing of English homes, as many do, elide the ways Native families used flames constructively. The first lines of Cotton Mather's account of Hannah Duston's captivity in Haverhill, Massachusetts, contain the iconography that already typified the popular genre: "On March 15. 1697. the *Salvages* made a Descent upon the Skirts of *Haverhil*, Murdering and Captiving about Thirty-nine Persons, and Burning about half a Dozen Houses. In this Broil, one *Hannah Dustan* having lain-in about a Week, attended with her Nurse, *Mary Neff*, a Widow, a Body of terrible *Indians* drew near unto the House where she lay, with Designs to carry on their Bloody Devastations." Mather was echoing the beats of Rowlandson's brisk-selling *Sovereignty and Goodness of God*, which opens: "On the tenth of February 1675. Came the *Indians* with great numbers upon *Lancaster*: Their first coming was about Sun-rising; hearing the noise of some Guns, we looked out; several Houses were burning, and the Smoke ascending to Heaven." In this genre, isolated maternal figures broiling in the fires of "Indian" violence against their homes stand in for the vulnerability of supposedly pacific colonists in a New World, but, of course, the trope sells short both the sophistication and aggression of colonial enterprise by the late seventeenth century and the Native economic and political strategies with which it interacted. As Abenaki scholar Lisa Brooks argues, "Raids, such as those on Lancaster . . . were not only reclamations of land but of sovereignty in that land." The fires warriors ignited were integral to their recuperation of Native space. "The burning of the hay, the barns, and the houses on these old planting fields represented a symbolic act of forceful recovery. As they had in the past, the Nipmuc men were firing the old meadows, with the idea of planting anew." Fire was not only a tool for home building; it was also a tool for home restoration. If fire appears in the literature of early American settlement as one of the most common instigators of homelessness, it must also be recognized as one of the most potent responses to and defenses against it.[9]

Fire thus etched the dynamic boundaries of home in Native space and determined where early Americans felt comfortable and safe. Regarded in this way, Native homes tended to be much more extensive than English homes. When she traveled with her Nipmuc captor Monoco, Rowlandson found herself a foreigner in a "vast and desolate wilderness" when she was "a mere 10 miles from her home." John Winthrop recorded a story of becoming so disoriented in the woods only "about half a mile" from his house in Mystic, Connecticut, that he could not find his way back until morning. Indeed, for English settlers having difficulty adjusting to colder New England winters, the limits of what fires made comfortable and safe could hardly be more constrained. Thomas Shepard wrote in a 1648 report of his missionary work, which all but ceased during the cold months, "I am not able to acquaint you very much from my owne eye and eare witnesse of things, for you know the neare relation between me and the fire side usually all winter time." Not only were some English settlers uncomfortable outside their homes, some were uncomfortable outside the largest room on the ground floor, the hall, where a fire burned night and day to warm a family as they prepared food, ate, conversed, and slept. But many Native groups practiced seasonal mobility and used fire to manage and thus make themselves comfortable in an expansive region of forests, meadows, and wetlands, creating "homeland spaces composed of intercropped fields, fishing falls, homes, and ceremonial grounds." The sense of homelessness that pervades the literature of early American settlement does not indicate the transience of the English, but

Figure 3. Woodcut of the raid on Lancaster. From *A Narrative of the Captivity Sufferings and Removes of Mrs. Mary Rowlandson, Who Was Taken Prisoner by the Indians . . . Written by Her Own Hand . . .* (Boston, 1771), 4. Courtesy of the Edward E. Ayer Digital Collection, The Newberry Library

rather the smallness of their homes relative to the wilderness—physical and metaphorical—surrounding them. Ironically, they felt vulnerable in New England in some measure because of the sturdy construction of their houses and the size of their roaring fires. The dimensions of their capacious fireplaces delimited the space in which they felt at home. But for Native Americans like Monoco, "the environment itself was his fortification." Especially in winter, when Native technologies and ecological knowledge gave them great advantage over their English neighbors, Native peoples commanded vast homelands. As Brooks tracks Rowlandson's growing disorientation against the Nipmucs' increasing comfort with each "remove" into the wilderness, she surmises, "The deeper [they] went, the more secure [they] felt."[10]

To return to the central question of this chapter, then, when did early Americans become homeless, and what did it mean for them? Although Anne Bradstreet, Mary Rowlandson, and Hannah Duston were made homeless when their houses went up in flames, the process of becoming homeless was more complicated and protracted for others, like people in and around Deerfield, the land of the Pocumtucs, in the early eighteenth century. When John Williams writes in *The Redeemed Captive* (1707) that, on the morning of February 29, 1704, he "saw many of the houses of my neighbours in flames, perceiving the whole fort, one house excepted, to be taken," he speaks of a long-standing conflict, not a single assault, that had unsettled Deerfield. Many of the homes the Mohawk and allied fighters burned were empty. News of conflicts among Indigenous communities and among Spanish, French, and English forces in Europe and America—which collectively constituted the Third Anglo-Wabanaki War—had reached the village and prompted many settlers to relocate to the central fort Williams mentions, a cluster of homes encircled by a wall (which the Native forces easily breached as they ascended, on snowshoes, the snowbanks outside it). That is, the people of Deerfield had made themselves homeless as a defense against death. This was true again on August 25, 1746, when Deerfield farmers and Abenaki warriors exchanged gunfire in a meadow south of the fort to which Deerfield families had relocated amid another period of heightened conflict among Wabanaki, Iroquois, English, and French forces, sometimes called King George's War. The families involved in the attack, Deerfield historian George Sheldon writes, "had deserted their homes to lodge in the forts, at Wapping, or at the Street." The story of early American settlement is replete with families who chose homelessness as the lesser of two evils. Of his Puritan companions in England, William Bradford writes, "hunted and persecuted on every side, . . . the most were faine to flie and leave their howses and habitations, and the

Figure 4. *Deerfield, circa 1700.* By William Sillin. © 2004

Figure 5. *Deerfield, 1704.* By William Sillin. © 2004

means of their livelehood." Against the looming specter of physical or spiritual devastation, exile took on a different aspect. A period of homelessness, wrenching as it was, set the stage for other kinds of survival.[11]

HOMES AMID THE SHOALS

The poet Lucy Terry, an enslaved resident of Deerfield during the 1746 skirmish, composed a ballad memorializing the incident called "Bars Fight." The poem's historical value has been granted since the nineteenth century, when Josiah Gilbert Holland printed it in his 1855 *History of Western Massachusetts*, and Sheldon, in his 1895–1896 *History of Deerfield*, called it "the fullest contemporary account of that bloody tragedy which has been preserved." In the late twentieth century, critics argued for the poem's broader cultural significance, considering Terry's status as the first African American poet. Frances Smith Foster reads "Bars Fight," for example, against the backdrop of the ten fires that engulfed homes and businesses in Manhattan in 1741 and led to the arrest, expulsion, or execution of more than 260 Black New Yorkers. No evidence directly links Terry to that crisis, but the stunning degree of racial prejudice it manifested discourages a reading of Terry's poem that laments, in Jean Wagner's words, it "has nothing specifically Negro about it." Positing that reverberations of the legal violence Manhattan's Black residents faced might have reached Deerfield, or simply that Deerfield's enslaved residents saw other expressions of it, Foster argues that, in this climate, Terry's poetic attention to an incident "not directly resulting from slavery or racial prejudice" and her command of the ballad's impersonal voice demonstrate "a sense of empowerment and social awareness" now recognized as a hallmark of eighteenth-century African American writing. Foster writes: "By assuming the role of historiographer without acknowledging this as an unusual position for one of her sex, race, and class, Terry is using silence to amplify her message. The absence of racially explicit references . . . indicates that on this occasion, in this speech act, Lucy Terry chose to speak as significantly as possible." Sharon M. Harris argues for the poem's aesthetic, not merely cultural, significance as a literary production that does not faithfully represent a historical event as much as it satirizes it by setting an American captivity narrative inside the folk ballad form, an imprecise fit whose voids reveal Terry's implied critique of transatlantic slavery. Harris makes a persuasive case for closely reading the poem—that is, engaging with it as a literary work as well as a historical artifact, an exercise popular eighteenth-century ballads rarely reward so richly.[12]

Influenced as I am by each of these critical approaches, I find the poem offers more than the fullest historical account of the 1746 skirmish, the earliest extant example of written African American poetry, and a coded condemnation of a slaveholding society and American racial prejudice. It also presents a layered and sensitive rendering of homelessness in and around Deerfield, likely informed by the poet's personal experience and attuned to the ways histories of homelessness connected members of her diverse audiences. The full extent of this connection is still becoming apparent. Terry was captured in West Africa as a child and forced across the Atlantic to North America, where she was purchased by Samuel Terry of Mendon, Massachusetts, around 1729, when she was probably between five and ten years old. When Samuel Terry faced legal and financial scandals in 1730, she was purchased by a childless couple, Ebenezer and Abigail Wells of Deerfield, in a sale possibly facilitated by Terry's Harvard classmate Stephen Williams, son of John Williams. In 1717, Ebenezer Wells had purchased a house from his brother Thomas, which later caught fire. Apparently, the destruction was total. In their 1996 history of the Wells homelot, part of an effort to "extend and correct" the lot histories George Sheldon published in his History of Deerfield, Susan McGowan and Amelia F. Miller note that both Sheldon and another nineteenth-century historian, Pliny Arms, record the burning of the Wells home, but neither identify the date of the fire. "The reason," they argue, "can probably be explained by the fact that the fire occurred at such an early date that no one in either Arms's or Sheldon's time could remember the year. Knowledge of the fire would then have been legendary." Based on aesthetic features of the existing structure on the lot, they suggest the home must have burned before 1730, observing that "the burned house was replaced by the present ell whose architectural style dates from 1720 to 1730."[13] Lucy Terry's biographers assume she lived in the newly constructed Wells home from her arrival in Deerfield around 1730 at least until her marriage in 1756. And because Ebenezer Wells's home burned and was rebuilt before Terry arrived in Deerfield and thus has little to do with her experience, they do not mention the fire.[14] But dendrochronological testing of the timbers in the Wells house performed after McGowan and Miller published their history reveals "that the ell was in fact framed after the 1746 growing season ended, most likely in 1747." It is possible Wells did not immediately rebuild his home after it burned, since a 1726 record shows he held a grant to another homelot in Deerfield on which he could have lived, but it is unlikely he would have left his property unimproved for many years after the fire. It is much more probable the house fire occurred after Terry arrived in Deerfield, and it is even

Figure 6. Wells-Thorn House. Courtesy of Historic Deerfield

possible the home burned in 1746, the year of the skirmish called the Bars Fight.[15]

Although it is reasonable to assume that Terry was living in the Wells home when it burned, it is unclear how the loss affected her. It was the only home she had known in Deerfield, but she was an enslaved laborer within it, far from her homeland. The fire might have been a tragedy for her. It might only have been part of the ongoing tragedy of her captivity. It might not have been a tragedy at all. There is no record of her commenting on the fire, but she did comment at length on a loss that occurred in Deerfield in 1746, and she paid particular attention to the fate of a captive child made homeless in the tragedy. Terry's poem, "Bars Fight," reads:

> August 'twas the twenty-fifth,
> Seventeen hundred forty-six;
> The Indians did in ambush lay,
> Some very valient men to slay,
> The names of whom I'll not leave out.
> Samuel Allen like a hero fout,
> And though he was so brave and bold,
> His face no more shall we behold.

Eleazer Hawks was killed outright,
Before he had time to fight,—
Before he did the Indians see,
Was shot and killed immediately.
Oliver Amsden he was slain,
Which caused his friends much grief and pain.
Simeon Amsden they found dead,
Not many rods distant from his head.
Adonijah Gillett we do hear
Did lose his life which was so dear.
John Sadler fled across the water,
And thus escaped the dreadful slaughter.
Eunice Allen see the Indians coming,
And hopes to save herself by running,
And had not her petticoats stopped her,
The awful creatures had not catched her,
Nor tommy hawked her on her head,
And left her on the ground for dead.
Young Samuel Allen, Oh lack-a-day!
Was taken and carried to Canada.[16]

In these verses, Terry mostly represents factual details of the event: Samuel Allen took his children (Eunice, Caleb, and Samuel, Jr.), two neighbors (Oliver and Simeon Amsden), two guards who were supposed to protect the party, and his brother-in-law, Eleazer Hawks, to gather hay on the meadow near the homes they had recently abandoned. When Hawks (who joined the party for sport rather than work) shot at partridges near the meadow, Native soldiers concealed in the brush, on high alert during this period of military conflict, returned fire.[17] One English guard fled; the other guard, along with Samuel Allen, Sr., the Amsden boys, and Hawks, were killed; and Eunice fell under a hatchet blow from which she famously—although never fully—recovered. But Terry ends the ballad with, and thus gives special emphasis to, the fate of the youngest member of the Allen family, who actually survived the skirmish without injury, in the couplet, "Young Samuel Allen, Oh lack-a-day! / Was taken and carried to Canada." For a time, the eight-year-old boy became one of Deerfield's unredeemed captives. One of the warriors took Samuel, unharmed, to Odanak, a village of Abenaki and Sokoki families on the bank of the Saint-François River. Like the Amsdens and Allens, the families of Odanak had to temporarily abandon their homes owing to threats of violence (from the English) in 1711, and they periodically relocated the village as climate, population size, and political expediency required. Samuel stayed there for a year and nine months before he was reclaimed by his uncle, John Hawks, the commander of the recently conquered Fort Massachusetts. According to Stephen West Williams, who interviewed Eunice Allen about the events surrounding the ordeal, Samuel "was extremely loth to see Col. Hawks, . . . and when he came into his presence he refused to speak the English language, pretending to have forgotten it."[18]

Hawks and the Deerfield community he represented in his diplomatic post would not have missed Samuel's resemblance to the Reverend John Williams's daughter Eunice, taken captive during the conflagration of 1704. Eunice was nearly Samuel's age when her home was burned and she was taken from Deerfield, and, like Samuel, she refused (or was no longer able) to speak to her English family when they tried to reclaim her from her adoptive Mohawk family. Although she converted to Catholicism, married a Mohawk man named Arsoen, and spent her life in Kahnawake, she remained close to members of her English family (particularly her brother Stephen Williams), whom she visited in and near Deerfield three times between 1740 and 1743. Her appearance during these visits—leggings, greased hair, a sleeveless tunic—confirmed her cultural transformation, and apparently her relatives pressed her "to put off her Indian blankets" in exchange for "English dress." Just three years later, Deerfield locals were alarmed again by the appearance of a recalcitrant captive. According to Eunice Allen, although Samuel "was dressed most shabbily, fared most miserably, and was covered with vermin, he was very much opposed to leaving the Indians." Finally, he consented to leave the Abenaki village with Hawks, but "he asserted to the day of his death that the Indian mode of life was the happiest." By ending her recital of the Bars Fight with Samuel's experience, Terry draws particular attention to the stories of early American survivors who were made homeless, adapted to altered conditions during periods of conflict, and finally made new homes among their captors in the aftermath of violence.[19]

Terry was one such survivor, making a home (and possibly more than one) with Ebenezer and Abigail Wells in Deerfield and another after she married Abijah Prince, a free, property-owning Black man from Wallingford, Connecticut. Abijah inherited one hundred acres of land in Guilford, Vermont, which the couple moved to claim in 1764. But their neighbors in Guilford, Ormas and John Noyce, repeatedly tried to contest the Princes' right to make a home by, among other things, burning their property. According to town records: "There was much trouble between 'Bijah and the Noyes families, for some reason which we are unable to discover, and 'Bijah was harassed and annoyed in many ways, his fences torn down, hay ricks burned and otherwise troubled and injured to such an extent that recourse was had to the highest tribunal within the state, the Governor's Council." It was Terry who in 1785 took the case before Governor Thomas Chittenden and his council on behalf of her then-elderly husband. The council ruled in her favor, finding "that the said Abijah, Lucy and Family are greatly oppressed and injured by John and Ormas Noyce" and fearing that, were the Noyces' harassment to continue, the Princes "must soon unavoidably fall upon the Charity of the Town." After Abijah's death, and when Terry was in her late seventies, she lost the farm she fought to protect—to the Noyces, who purchased it when she was unable to maintain the family property.[20]

Although the fires the Noyces set did not make the Princes homeless immediately, they were a reminder, and a warning, of possible homelessness always on the horizon. In fact, "warning out" was the formal system by which New England town authorities identified and removed people who had "no legal claim on the town treasury." Abijah Prince never fit this description during their marriage, but once he died Lucy became vulnerable to this attention. Rather than draw down funds to support elderly, ill, or impoverished people, town officials spent, as Ruth Wallis Herndon found in hundreds of eighteenth-century cases, "considerable time and money" sending undesirable people back to their "hometowns." According to elected town leaders, only those people who were "legally settled" (through birth, apprenticeship, marriage, or acquisition of property) in a place were entitled to that town's material aid; if they never settled or were unsettled through widowhood or financial hardship, they became the responsibility of the place where their parents or masters settled. This narrow definition of "hometown" does no justice to the complexity of conditions of early American home making. Those like Terry who made multiple homes and hometowns throughout their lives could be at a legal disadvantage in these cases, where their adaptability to crisis and change too often read as transience. These potentially dangerous circumstances demanded new modes of settlement and survival—affective strategies that rewrote white colonial scripts and allowed for more resilient forms of home.[21]

During all this time, Terry was reportedly fond of rehearsing "Bars Fight," which could be seen as one such strategy. The poem existed only in oral form during her life, but the version finally preserved in print in Holland's *History of Western Massachusetts* shows lines never amended to reflect Samuel Allen's return to Deerfield less than two years after the skirmish. To the degree that the published version represents Terry's artistic vision (a complicated question with respect to much eighteenth-century occasional poetry), it seems that, for more than seventy years, Terry held the boy suspended between his homes in Deerfield and Odanak, negotiating sympathetic affiliations with the Abenakis among whom he was making a happy life before he reunited with his English family.[22] Scholars have made much of the poem's canny appropriation of the captivity narrative genre and the possibility that its "damning" final couplet satirized a slaveholding society's sense of despair over Samuel's capture and the fate of his companions.[23] Certainly, Terry was capable of engineering such a critique. In the 1790s, when a neighbor tried to enclose land that belonged to the Princes, Lucy took the case to the United States Circuit Court for the District of Vermont, where she personally argued for her family's property rights before the Honorable Samuel Chase of Maryland and against the playwright Royall Tyler (who became Vermont's chief justice). Chase ruled in Terry's favor, remarking that she "made a better argument than he had heard from any lawyer at the Vermont bar." Terry could see the flaws in other people's views. But Chase's comment and other accounts of Terry suggest she could also use her uncommon rhetorical skill to draw people in, rather than keep them at arm's length, and that her poem about the Deerfield skirmish might have more sympathetic overtones.[24]

When Terry died in 1821 at age ninety-seven, her obituary in the *Franklin Herald* praised not only "the fluency of her speech" but also the degree to which she was "respected among her acquaintance, who treated her with a degree of deference." Late in her life, she had successfully made another home in Sunderland, Vermont, where she won a rare financial settlement from the town's selectmen that made her comfortable until she died. As David R. Proper remarks, that this relatively lengthy and detailed obituary notice exists at all is a testament to Terry's influence and renown in the several communities she called home. In "Bars Fight," she draws attention to the fortitude of her "brave and bold" Deerfield neighbors, particularly the heroism of Samuel Allen, Sr., who died trying to defend his children. These lines must have taken on special meaning as Terry performed them live for the survivors and mourners of the skirmish as well as friends and family in Vermont and Massachusetts who took in the conflict from a remove. Given her ability to generate currents of respectful understanding among disparate groups, it seems possible, even probable, that she highlighted young Samuel's story in "Bars Fight" not (or not merely) to covertly chastise the hypocrisy of her white audiences but because Samuel was the figure who best represented, for the widest variety of people, the fraught experience of making and remaking homes in early New England.[25]

The protracted process by which Samuel was made homeless and then made his successive homes among the Abenaki and English must have resonated with Terry as she composed "Bars Fight" and then must have connected with the people in and around Pocumtuc country whose faces she engaged as she projected her rhymed verses. Although few early Americans identified with the whole of Samuel's ordeal, almost all experienced some part of it, and many to a much greater extent than he. There was the home in Deerfield his family abandoned because it no longer protected them from existential threats. The lore of conflagrations in the recent past. The relocation to a fort enclosing its gaggle of frightened, displaced people, forced suddenly into the proximity of family. The horror of the meadow fight, where he saw his father and friends killed and, as tradition has it, made "a sharp resistance with [his] teeth, nails and feet" before he was "secured unhurt as a prisoner, and carried to St. Francis." The terror of captivity. The strangeness of a new place, populated by people weathering their own storms of threats, violence, dispossession, and homelessness. The emerging sense of kinship with erstwhile strangers and antagonists. The beginning of a "happy" new life. The inevitable pull of past homes and absent family, conjuring memories both Edenic and traumatic. More relocations, more adjustments, and, finally, a life lived between worlds.[26]

The word "Bars" in the title of Terry's poem refers to a location in Deerfield, the portion of the meadow on which the Amsdens and Allens made hay. But as Sharon Harris points out, the title also encompasses the image of sandbars, points of transition between land and water—and between stages of life, as in the nautical idiom "crossing the bar." Although it is possible Holland, not Terry, gave the poem its title (which both he and Sheldon use to introduce the text), it is also possible Terry referred to her work this way. Like other Deerfield residents, she would have recognized the site of the fight as the "bars"; it is not a stretch to imagine she called her artistic treatment of the event "Bars Fight." And reading this term figuratively, as the poetic form of her rhymed history encourages readers to do, illuminates the global sweep of the homelessness she lived and saw. A reading that assigns significance to particular words mediated by the local historians who brought Terry's work into print history admittedly imputes meanings to the poem that may outstrip the author's intentions. But literary critics have long embraced this as a feature rather than a flaw of close reading. Following Foster's call to read Terry's doggerel verse "as significantly as possible" as a necessary counter to the refusal of some critics to acknowledge the authenticity or literary quality of early African American poetry, I entertain the possibility that the ambiguity of a term that denotes two geological forms, and that Terry knew in both senses, allows the poem to comment on a history that exceeds the Deerfield skirmish and proposes a wider context in which readers might situate that local violence. The word "bars" had particular resonances for people who crossed water to arrive at or navigate through Native space in early America. In a reading that grants the status of the text as a literary production as well as a historical record, the poem's title, paired with its concluding couplet, opens up reflections on the series of transitions between settlement and unsettlement—sometimes peaceful, sometimes painful, and often at the crosscurrents of consent and coercion—that constituted early American home life.[27]

Sandbars were shifting sites of literal and metaphorical significance for those who shared in the experience of Terry's performing "Bars Fight." Tiffany Lethabo King notes in her study of shoals (a designation that includes sandbanks and bars) as guiding metaphors for reconsidering Black American and Indigenous relations: "As an ecological space, [the shoal] represents an errant and ecotonal location made of both water and not water. Ecotones are classified within environmental science as a combination or meeting of at least two distinct ecological zones." These bars were edge areas beyond the shore, as valuable to those who fished as the edge areas Native agriculturalists and hunters created with their controlled fires, because "a school, or gathering of fish, also sometimes described as a shoal, often gathers at the sandbar's edges to feed on vegetation." These areas also had meaning for Terry and other survivors of the Middle Passage, who possibly touched bars before they touched America. King notes that sandbars and limestone formations often prevented slave ships from approaching shorelines. Instead, vessels anchored near the shoals and relied on small boats to carry cargo and crew to shore. King writes: "Captive slaves from the hold could stand, sit, and wait on the sandbar for a boat or could wade to shore themselves. For the members of the community / shoal that emerge from the ship's hold, it is perhaps the last shallow place to rest your feet before the last canoe ride or swim to shore. It is another in-between space other than the hold to temporarily squat and reassemble the self on new terms." In this description of enslaved Africans like Terry finding their footing on the edge zones, sandbars were more than a landing place; they were the site of a first home in America, the watery ground upon which captives "temporarily squat" to regain their bearings and, more urgently, construct new terms on which to carry on in a radically altered environment.[28]

King insists we attend to the ways sandbars forced mariners to pause the expected course of their voyage or slow down—to "shoal"—lest the vessel run aground. It is intriguing to think of Terry's rendering of the skirmish between the Abenakis and the English on Pocumtuc land, not in the frenetic time span of military engagements, but as a moment of stillness in ecological time, a rupture in normal routines that forced the combatants and the families they interpolated into the event to pause and reassemble not just their conceptions of self but also the components of home. In this temporal frame, Samuel's two years of resourceful, conflicted home making in the context of captivity stretches to seventy years, and more.

The license that the title of Terry's poem grants readers to imaginatively restage the conflict on the "bars" offshore makes legible one more point about this squatting and reassembling of the self and the home: the environment itself is a dynamic participant in these entanglements. Not only are sandbars a mixture of the elements—accretions of rock, sand, coral, and animal matter deposited on the river, bay, or ocean floor—but they shift, grow, shrink, disappear, and reappear as the waves lap over and against them. Their exact size and location are not possible to predict or preserve. They are crucial sites of subsistence and survival, but they can be homes only to those willing to accept the inevitability of homelessness. As Michael LeVan puts it, "Rather than forming a boundary between land and water, shoals are spaces of contact, friction, and interaction among land and water." The stakes of the bars fight include but exceed land; what the combatants grapple with is not just property ownership but the right and ability to call a place home and to maintain or reassemble the comforts and security of home as the dirt, rock, water, and air collaborate to support or vanquish those claims. This was a contest among humans and the very elements out of which they must constantly, and often without warning, constitute new versions of themselves adapted to a suddenly changed environment. To become homeless in early America said next to nothing about a person's skill with lands, timber, money, or the legal tangles that came to ensnare Native space. Time and again, families watched the homes their ingenuity, material investments, and faith had built go up in flames. Canonical accounts of early American housefires such as John Williams's, Mary Rowlandson's, or Cotton Mather's often associate the burning of homes with human agents of destruction, but Terry's poem invites readers to consider the settings that witness homelessness as active participants in the loss and powerful sources of restoration.[29]

Those who read Terry's poem as satire see her as commenting on a relatively minor episode of violence on a piece of property in which she had no investment, and which must have appeared trifling relative to the centuries-long horrors perpetrated in the service of white settler colonialism. In such a reading, the lines about Eunice Allen snarling herself in her petticoats before being "tommy hawked" on the head are intentionally irreverent, and the bathos of the lines "Young Samuel Allen, Oh lack-a-day! / Was taken and carried to Canada" points out the vast disparity between the Native fighters' relatively humane treatment of war criminals and the brutal force with which white colonists held millions of Black and Indigenous people in lifelong slavery. But if readers construe the "bars" expansively, not just as the small plot of land the farmers worked but also as the many and mutable shoals within and around America, then Terry herself and her audiences appear as survivors of the conflict rather than critical bystanders.

In this environment, her sympathy for the Allens, her neighbors, seems genuine and pregnant with other kinds of pain. Eunice's injury and Samuel's captivity are dreadful—but these are not isolated incidents, nor isolated victims. These bars are a site of conflict many people know. They are a point of convergence upon which countless early Americans congregate, despite the immense differences between the sufferings of white children like Eunice and Samuel and the intergenerational trauma of Black and Indigenous Americans. "Bars Fight" contains sedimentary layers of meaning, some of which could only be fathomed by people who knew much more of captivity and physical violence than the white combatants in the Deerfield conflict. But the poem seemed "accurate" enough to two nineteenth-century historians, clearly sympathetic to the white settlers of Deerfield, that they printed it in their accounts of the town. Terry's "wit and shrewdness" have long been praised, but not as frequently her imagination or her generosity, which allowed many people to recognize themselves in her artful telling of this difficult story. Her poem grants emotional access to anyone familiar with some portion of the unfathomable pain of early American homelessness, and a literary interpretation of the title allows readers to acknowledge what diverse participants in the 1746 skirmish shared. The last eight lines of the poem focus on the survivors of the event (including Abenaki warriors), those who will continue to encounter the shoals. For them, as for Terry and her listeners, the bars fight—to make oneself at home in moments of unexpected violence and in conditions of perpetual flux—goes on.[30]

THE WORLDS FIRE MADE

These terraqueous connotations of home for Black, Indigenous, and English peoples living in early America help us understand why they more frequently depict themselves as moving between worlds than simply between homes. Terry's poem is a remarkably dimensional example of a meditation on homelessness nested within more familiar and legible themes (in this case, captivity and colonial warfare), but it is not an especially early example of this phenomenon. In seventeenth-century America, writers often dignified their grief over homelessness or transience within discourses of faith or transcultural navigations, where the most mundane aspects of this grief, thus disguised, were neglected by readers. Homelessness is almost always, in early American writings, part of some larger condition of rootlessness or liminality. To a degree, this obscuring of the materiality of homelessness seems part of the writers' deliberate strategy—to remind themselves, and their readers, not "to look on that was lent, / As if [one's] own, when thus impermanent," as Anne Bradstreet wrote. But this expansive conception of home also acknowledges forms of existential global and spiritual displacement of which physical homelessness was only a symptom. The notion of losing and rebuilding a singular "dwelling place" like the Bradstreet house is too narrow for peoples whose lived experiences integrated, in the words of Seneca scholar Mishuana Goeman, "indigenous conceptions" of "land and water as always connected" and constitutive of spiritual as well as material homelands. Our study of home making and homelessness must then account for the kinds of spaces—visible and invisible—early Americans inhabited and left behind. Tiya Miles and Sharon Holland find the images of "crossing waters" and "crossing worlds" appropriately evocative of this process of "buil[ding] metaphysical as well as physical homes on Native lands and within Native cultural landscapes." As early Americans moved among lands and waters, they stretched their homes across the oceans, rivers, islands, continents, and cosmos.[31]

Home making, as part of the larger project of world making, was a spatial, temporal, and spiritual process during the early modern period. The discourse of "worlds" emerged during this period to "synthesize new global experiences into a structure that would bind individual fragments into a collective unity" even as the emergence of the colonial term *worlds* itself indicated that colonial expansion had forever shattered the fiction of an "ideal integrity" that contained a singular globe. Early modern writers frequently engage the terms "old world" and "new world" to underscore their sense of rupture as they moved across a globe fragmented by colonial contact and settlement. But this fragmentation also had temporal dimensions, as the terms *old* and *new* can as frequently demarcate distance in time as distance in space. "Worlds are spaces, but they are also processes; or rather, what makes a world is its endurance of process, its persistence across time," as Samuel

Fallon argues. "If *new* and *old* suggest displacement of one world by another, they also insist on the durability of their connection." Finally, and surely in part because of this enduring connection between historical epochs, the term *world* has, for many early modern writers, aesthetic and spiritual resonances rooted in ancient texts. "Through faith," they read in Hebrews, "we understand that the worlds were framed by the word of God, so that things which are seen were not made of things which do appear." Early American world makers had faith in the permanence of worlds that were both invisible and literary (that is, framed by God and framed by words), toward which earthly homelessness guided them.[32]

When the Wampanoag scholar Caleb Cheeshateaumuck demonstrated his elite education in an eloquent letter to the financial benefactors of the Harvard Indian College, from which he graduated in 1665, he retold a story about crossing between worlds that might have reflected his spatial experience of moving from his island homeland of Noepe (Martha's Vineyard) to English continental homes in Roxbury and Cambridge as well as his spiritual conversion to Christianity. The affective influence of his writing stretches to the present moment. The letter seems to grow out of a hope the administrators of Harvard had that their emphasis on the college's Christianizing mission would generate financial support not only for the new Indian College but also for the maintenance of the already decaying structures surrounding it. Possibly, Caleb's letter to the benefactors also captured some dimensions of the world-crossing experiences of his Wampanoag classmate, Joel Iacoomes of Nunnepog (Edgartown). Their homelands ravaged by epidemics, they shared the circumstances of many early Americans who made new homes partly because their old homes could no longer offer the comfort or protection they once had. Their fathers were impressed by the reasoning of English missionaries who taught that God's power held the only cure for the contagion, and so they sent their sons to preparatory school in Roxbury and to Harvard so they could acquire religious training, skills, and possibly also political connections that could help their kin adapt to an environment altered by English settlement. We see in Caleb's sole piece of extant writing some evidence of the tension he felt as he left his home in the hope of returning to save it.[33]

Figure 7. Caleb Cheeshateaumuck's letter to his English benefactors. Caleb Cheeshahteaumauk (Caleb Cheeshay) to [Robert] Boyle, 1663, Boyle Correspondence (BL 2.12), Archive of the Royal Society, London. © The Royal Society

Honoratissimi benefactores.

Referunt Historici, de Orpheo musico, et insigni Poeta
quod ab Apolline Lyram acceperit, eaqꝫ tantum valuerit
ut illius Cantu sylvas, saxaꝙ moverit, et arbores ingentes
post se traxerit, ferasꝙ ferocissimas mitiores reddiderit, Imo
quod accepta Lyra ad inferos descenderit, et Plutonem et
Proserpinam suo Carmine demulserit, et Eurydicen uxorem
ab inferis ad superos evexerit: Hoc symbolum esse statuunt
Philosophi Antiquissimi, ut ostendant quod tanta et vis et virtus
doctrinæ et politioris literaturæ ad mutandum Barbarorum Ingenium:
qui sunt tanquam arbores, saxa, et bruta animantia: et eorum
quasi metamorphosin efficiendum eosꝙ tanquam tigres cicurandos
et post se trahendos.

Deus vos delegit isse Patronos nostros, et cum omni sapientiâ, in-
timâꝙ Commiseratione vos ornavit, ut nobis paganis salutiferæ
opem feratis, qui vitam, progeniemꝙ à Majoribus nostris ducebamus
tam animo, quam Corporeꝙ nudi fuimus, et ab omni humanitate
alieni fuimus, in Deserto huc et illuc variisꝙ erroribus ducti fuim̃?

Otergo, quatergꝫ ornatissimi, amantissimiqꝫ viri, quas quantasꝙ
quam maximas, immensasꝙ gratias vobis tribuamus: eo quod
omnium rerum Copiam nobis suppeditaveritis propter educationem nos-
tram: et ad sustentationem Corporum nostrorum: immensas, max imasꝙ
expensas attulistis.

Et præcipuè quas quantasꝙ Gratias Deo opt: Max: debimus, qui
sanctas scripturas nobis revelavit, Dominumꝙ Iesum Christum
nobis demonstravit, qui est via veritatis et vitæ, prætter
hæc omnia, per viscera misericordiæ Divinæ, aliqua spes relicta
est, ut instrumenta fiamus, ad declarandum, et propagandum e-
vangelium Cognatis nostris Conterraneisꝙ ut illi etiam Deum
Cognoscant et Christum.

Quamvis non possumus par pari reddere vobis, reliquisꝙ Benefactoribus nostris
Verumtamen speramus, nos non defuturos apud Deum suppli-
cationibus imposterius exorare pro illis piis misericordibus Viris, qui
supersunt in Vetere Angliâ, qui pro nobis tantam vim auri, ar-
gentiꝙ effuderunt ad salutem animarum nostrarum procurandam:
et pro vobis etiam, qui instrumenta, et quasi aquæ ductus fuistis
omnia ista beneficentia nobis conferendi.

Vestræ Dignitati devotissimus: Caleb Cheeshahteaumauk

In his epistle, written in Latin, Caleb demonstrates his proficiency in languages, his knowledge of classical literature, and his familiarity with Calvinist doctrines as he subtly draws attention to these environmental changes wrought by the English. He retells and comments on the myth of Orpheus, able to play music upon his lyre so powerful "that he made the great trees follow behind him" before he "descended into the underworld, softened even Pluto and Proserpina with his song, and led Eurydice, his wife, out of the underworld into the upper world." He then offers this elaboration: "The most ancient philosophers make this a symbol in order that they might show how strong the power and virtue of education and of refined literature are in the transformation of the barbarians' nature. They are like the trees, the rocks, and the unthinking animals, and a metamorphosis, as it were, of them must be brought about." In this artfully compressed reading, sensitively translated by Lisa Brooks, Caleb emphasizes worlds and trees, two images that appear repeatedly in the brief text. I follow Brooks in noticing that, in associating himself with trees, he acknowledges that Native homes encompass objects and humans as parts of and agents within the interconnected worlds of sky, lands, and water. Also, in associating himself with trees, which the English feed to their insatiable open hearths in order to make their homes and settlements into self-contained new worlds at odds with the natural environment, he invites sobering contemplations on what a domesticating "metamorphosis" might portend for himself and his kin.[34]

Did Caleb fear that he, his homeland, and his people would be used as expendable resources by the English and in some sense *become* the pervasive fires of North American settlement? Perhaps he could already sense the toll his move from the island world of Noepe to the drafty quarters of the Indian College, this journey from convert to missionary-in-training, had taken on his body. As Brooks points out, among other changes necessitated by this relocation, he exchanged his nutrient-rich island diet for a dreary regimen of bread and beer in Cambridge, and he died of consumption just after he graduated. Joel died in a "shipwreck upon the island of Nantucket" just before graduation in 1665 (where he would have taken "top honors" among his class of nine). Two of the other Native students who attended Harvard Indian College (and there were only five total) died of disease—or possibly "malnutrition." The costs of undergoing "transformation" under the power of Western education were staggering. And even Orpheus, for all his humanizing power, does not successfully cross between worlds. He tries, but ultimately fails, to save his beloved Eurydice from the clutches of the underworld, a detail Caleb does not include in his letter—and perhaps could not include, given what the benefactors might imagine it implied about the impotence of the ministers and instructors they were asked to support financially. To the extent that Caleb's Harvard training was supposed to equip him to carry the Christian gospel from the halls of Cambridge back to Noepe and elsewhere, he was also reflected in the figure of Orpheus—a gifted but ultimately stymied ambassador between this world and a lower one.[35]

The word *homeless* is a poor fit for this existential transience, too small and too specific to describe either the liminality of the classical hero or the experience of Native Americans, whose homes were designed for adaptability and mobility but whose entire homelands went up in flames, contracted, or otherwise metamorphized under English interventions. In this letter, Caleb gestures toward a more fitting concept, *worldless*, to fully capture his experience of shifting among religious paradigms, cultural traditions, and geographies—an experience that gave him sympathy not only for Orpheus but also for the hero's physical surroundings, which "follow" him on this audacious but ultimately futile pilgrimage. Yet, even in the face of this futility, and perhaps sensing what the crossing between English and Native worlds was costing him and would cost "the trees, the rocks, and the unthinking animals," Caleb manifests a remarkable faith that his and his Native colleagues' investment in this kind of travel would allow them to meaningfully connect the worlds of the English and Natives, the geographies of their island home and the mainland, and ultimately this life and the afterlife. Their intellectual and spiritual work, Caleb and Joel must have hoped, would have long-lasting cultural and religious significance not just for themselves but also for others this work would allow them to touch and bridge. As we will see, their influence persists into the contemporary moment in meaningful, concrete ways.

In this faith in multiple worlds and in their own power as intellectual and spiritual ambassadors between them, Caleb and Joel had much in common with another world-crossing scholar, Anne Bradstreet, their near contemporary in Massachusetts. From the deck of the *Arbella* off the coast of Salem, Bradstreet says she "found a new world and new manners, at which [her] heart rose." But the home in the old world she fled with her family to undertake the voyage to North America was only the first she would lose in her pilgrimage, in part because of the abandon with which the English felled and fired trees. In 1634, the Pennacook sachem Cutshamache sold a piece of land, called Cochichawick, for "six pounds and a coat" to John Winthrop, Jr., with the understanding that some Pennacook families would still use the land for planting and retain access to a stream running through the space. In 1645, Anne's husband Simon Bradstreet erected a sawmill on the Cochichewick

Brook. The Bradstreets, along with Anne's sister Mercy and her husband, John Woodbridge, made plans to relocate from the homes they had built in Ipswich to this new settlement, which the English renamed Andover. Simon built a fine house in the English fashion, which is to say, a large, somewhat drafty building centered around a voracious fire. When Bradstreet took on the voice of Fire in "The Four Elements," she described the role it played in her family's daily life:

> Ye Cooks, your Kitchen implements I frame
> Your Spits, Pots, Jacks, what else I need not name
> Your dayly food I wholsome make, I warm
> Your shrinking Limbs, which winter's cold doth harm.

But like Fire in Bradstreet's poem, which not only supports the economy and comforts of domestic life but also lays waste to civilizations, the fire in the family's enormous fireplace turned suddenly destructive. On the evening of July 10, 1666, after they had lived in their home for twenty years, the Bradstreets were jolted awake by cries of "fire and fire." Anne, together with Simon, their daughter-in-law Mercy, their granddaughter Anne, and their younger sons, rushed out of the house, stood back, and watched "the flame consume [their] dwelling place." The house burned to the ground. Furniture, paper, trunks and chests with their bolsters, bedding, and clothing—all reduced to ashes. Simon Bradstreet, Jr., who had just accepted a position as minister in New London after graduating from Harvard, lost "his books and many of his clothes" in the fire. Simon estimated the value of his lost goods at "50 or £60 at least," or nearly 70 percent of his annual salary, which was only ten pounds less than "some of the most noted ministers in New-England at that period." He petitioned the church at New London to compensate him for this loss, which they could not do for three years. One can only imagine the value of the books and working manuscripts that his mother, who kept all her earthly belongings in the home, watched go up in flames.[36]

The fire occurred during a five-year period of pronounced suffering in Bradstreet's life. In 1664, her oldest son, Samuel, then living in Boston, sent his wife, Mercy, to deliver their first baby under Bradstreet's practiced eye in the Andover home. Less than a year before the fire, the baby, then a year-and-a-half-old and still living with her grandparents, sickened and died. The grief-stricken mother named her next child Anne, a tribute to the mother-in-law who nursed her through these pregnancies and lavished such care on the babies. Three years later, in 1669, little Anne died, only to be followed by

Mercy's son, Simon, born in October and dead by November. In September 1670, Mercy had one more baby (another girl called Anne) before both she and the infant died. Samuel, bereft of children and wife, made a new life far from his parents in Jamaica. By 1671, Bradstreet was suffering from consumption, the illness from which she would die the next year. Yet, at some point during this period, in addition to elegizing these lost ones and preparing (perhaps longing) for her own death, Bradstreet penned the now-famous lines about her lost house. Seen in the context of this profound, existential suffering, the tragedy of the house fire pales considerably, and the notion of elegizing it as one would a toddler or daughter-in-law seems indulgent even by modern standards. The elegies on her grandchildren, written between 1665 and 1669, insist on the value of their short lives and the meaning to be found in grieving them, a rhetorical practice more often associated, as Abram Van Engen argues, with nineteenth-century sentimental writers than with Puritans supposed to have weaned their affections from their progeny. It is harder to see Bradstreet as ennobling grief over lost property in the poem about her house or to defend this kind of mourning. No life was lost in the blaze. The Bradstreets were wealthy, and they soon rebuilt an impressive home. The fire was accidental, not part of some larger military campaign in which it accrued geopolitical significance. The loss, though staggering, was entirely material. At this moment, why did the material matter?[37]

The poem's most obvious crossing of worlds occurs as Bradstreet elevates the event by contemplating its spiritual significance; clearly, an understanding of the shiftless material world as a shadow of a permanent heavenly world is central to Bradstreet's theology and many of her personal poems. In the midst of the horrors of that July night, Bradstreet suddenly collects herself and comes to a higher vision of the smoldering wreckage:

> And, when I could no longer look,
> I blest his Name that gave and took,
> That layd my goods now in the dust:
> Yea so it was, and so 'twas just.

But her grief turns out to be more complicated and rises again from the cooled ashes wherein Bradstreet often spies the unburied remains of the "pleasant things" she "counted best." Ultimately, Bradstreet quiets this grief as she addresses the larger problem of the homelessness she experienced first in England, as she and her fellow Puritans "from house and friends to exile went"; again after stepping off the cramped quarters of the *Arbella* onto bars off the coast of Salem; then shifting between provisional lodgings in Charlestown during a miserable first winter in North America; and finally as she and Simon built homes in Newtowne (Cambridge) and Ipswich. These periods, punctuated with other kinds of hardship, prompted her to question, "Was ever stable joy yet found below?" And the destruction of her home in Andover, the commanding structure supposed to put a definitive end to this rootlessness, seemed to supply the answer: certainly not. Even those who prospered in this space could not control the elements out of which they made their domestic lives. Yet, for Bradstreet, God provided the stability the environment could not. She testifies:

> Thou hast an house on high erect,
> Fram'd by that mighty Architect,
> With glory richly furnished,
> Stands permanent tho: this bee fled.
> 'Its purchased, and paid for too
> By him who hath enough to doe.

There would be one final move, which conversion prefigured and death effected, and then she would move no more. And, significantly, for a weary pilgrim whose arrival in North America had preceded the framing of her home there, God's house was ready for her and would require no season of homelessness.[38]

Yet, despite the conviction of Bradstreet's line, borrowed from Ecclesiastes, "Adeiu, Adeiu; All's vanity," it is not quite the case that she actually renounces the material world in favor of the spiritual in this poem. Instead, her text itself creates an intriguing bridge between the two worlds, allowing what she seemed to hope would be bidirectional traffic. Bradstreet's interest in opening this bridge grew keener in the last years of her life, when she invited her children to find her voice within an object, a brief spiritual autobiography, which she created to sustain their souls in or around 1664:

> This Book by Any yet unread,
> I leave for you when I am dead,
> That, being gone, here you may find
> What was your liveing mother's mind.
> Make use of what I leave in Love
> And God shall blesse you from above.

The papers containing Bradstreet's poems and other writings were meant to open up commerce between the earth and the afterlife, preserving expressions of faith and intellectual curiosity that would otherwise be lost and allowing for a continuance of dialogue between a mother and her offspring. In "Before the Birth of One of Her Children," a pregnant speaker fears she will die in labor but knows her poem will survive, and she asks her bereaved family to "kiss this paper for thy loves dear sake, / Who with salt tears this last Farewel did take." Writing allowed Bradstreet to excavate precious things from the "mouldring dust," even her own memory, and grant them a kind of immortality. And here lies an intriguing paradox: for Bradstreet, writing about the impermanence of material objects is, then, a costly investment that desperately seeks to make the promise of divine permanence into an earthly reality. Testifying in manuscripts to the insignificance of physical objects inverts the material and the immaterial. In the hours and with the resources she dedicated to writing, Bradstreet renounced the material and thus made it matter.[39]

The practical question of what exactly this New England woman must have had to sacrifice in order to produce the volume of poetry that became *The Tenth Muse* in 1650 was arresting enough that when John Woodbridge had these early poems printed in England, he addressed it head-on in a prefatory note. "It is the Work of a Woman, honoured, and esteemed where she lives, for her . . . exact diligence in her place, and discreet managing of her Family occasions," he wrote, "and more then so, these Poems are the fruit but of some few houres, curtailed from her sleep, and other refreshments." Vellum and paper were not readily available before 1690 in New England, nor (and more to the point) was time for writing. Bradstreet somehow accumulated and then traded the resources she possessed to purchase whatever permanence this world had on offer. Her elegies for people whom history was likely to forget—her pious but private mother Dorothy, for example, or her infant grandchildren—suggest she saw her writing as a defense against the obliteration she seems to accept in the verses about her home. In the physical existence of her elegies, we see strong evidence that she doubted whether even the spiritual reality of the human soul really mattered if it were not given some form of enduring earthly presence and that she considered pen and paper, and even the "Table" and "Candle" she lost in the house fire, as crucial resources in this quest to infuse this world with some degree of permanence, and the invisible world with some degree of tangibility.[40]

Rather than renouncing the material for the spiritual, Bradstreet, in writing "Some Verses upon the Burning of Our House," more accurately renounces wood and brick in favor of paper. Like Caleb Cheeshateaumuck, she recognizes that her homelessness places her at the margins between worlds and thus gives her both vulnerability and power as a kind of emissary. Unsettled (albeit temporarily) from Andover, she is suddenly free—even charged—to travel far beyond it, and the paper she transforms with her pen will be her conveyance. If ultimately, like Caleb, she hopes her spiritual work will convey her to heaven, she recognizes that her intellectual work can first carry her to specific places on earth. As she penned the lines about the fire, she might have looked up as well as out and deployed the image of her burning home to affectively collapse not only the distance between a divine home and an earthly one but also the distance between disparate points on the globe where people mourned the specific tragedy of watching a house go up in flames.

I proceed with caution here. We cannot know precisely the afterlives or reading audiences Bradstreet anticipated for the manuscripts—including the verses about the Andover house—she left unpublished at her death. It is intriguing, as Van Engen points out, to follow Bradstreet's career as she "*became* a public poet" and to notice that her "subject matter and her audience exist in inverse proportions: The more readers she gained, the more she turned to domestic concerns; the more public she became, the more she focused on private matters." But, as Margaret Olofson Thickstun reminds us, we have "no unmediated information about how Bradstreet organized her manuscript poetry or about how she prepared her texts for circulation." If the editors of *Several Poems* (1678) accurately represent her wishes, "she never meant" any of her personal occasional poems "should come to publick view." However, these editors and "some friends that knew her well" (who must have seen or possessed copies of these poems) saw fit to override her desires after her death. She knew this was a possibility. She claimed such friends, "less wise then true," were responsible for the publication of the poems in *The Tenth Muse*, which she possibly intended only for manuscript circulation in London when John Woodbridge took copies there in 1647. By the time of the Andover fire, Bradstreet's poetry had a transatlantic readership in manuscript as well as print, and among friends as well as critics, whose "carping tongue[s]" Bradstreet anticipates in her "Prologue." Still, we have no evidence she necessarily wanted the verses about her burning home, which were not printed until 1867, to be published to a wide audience.[41]

But we do have evidence she circulated the poem among her family, at least. Her son Simon had a copy of the poem, which he transcribed along with the spiritual autobiography Bradstreet specifically addressed to her "dear children"—an audience clearly on her mind in the 1660s. The copy of the poem in Simon's possession was written, not in "the booklet from which he transcribed the rest of his Andover manuscript," but rather upon "'a loose Paper'" (like the one the pregnant speaker in "Before the Birth" bids her survivors "kiss"), a form in which seventeenth-century writers commonly shared their work, and a form in which, as Meredith Neuman argues, Bradstreet "absolutely expect[ed] her poems to circulate." And when Simon titled the poem, he took unusual ownership of the topic: "Here Followes Some Verses upon the Burning of Our House, July 10th, 1666" (italics mine). (In titles he gives to other poems in the Andover manuscript, he indicates Bradstreet's perspective with the singular, not plural, first-person possessive.) The children who had not yet moved out of the house when it burned, or the beloved eldest son who sent his own family to live there, likely felt even stronger associations with the content of the poem. This is all to say that, despite the personal terms of the poem's grief, it invites, and found, a circle of fellow mourners to participate in its expression of suffering and faith. Even if Bradstreet shared it only with her children, the poem traveled beyond her settlement on the Cochichewick Brook. Copies of the poem or memories of its content went with her children around New England and as far as Jamaica, where it might have had special resonance for Samuel as he grieved the wife and child who had been forced to evacuate the home when it caught fire.[42]

Perhaps—and I tread with even more caution here—Bradstreet considered the possibility that these verses about her home would at some point be carried by family or close friends to England (the route her earlier poems took, with or without her express intention), where within nine weeks of the burning of her Andover home they would have particular poignance for the seventy thousand or so Londoners whose homes burned to the ground in September 1666. This fire was an epic event, on the scale of the civilization-wasting fires she personifies in "The Four Elements." It raged for five days through the city of London, destroying churches, businesses, and a multitude of homes in its path. Terrified residents attempted to "blow up" and pull down houses to create a break in the fire's path, "but all in vain, the Fire seising upon the Timber and Rubbish, and so continuing it self even through those spaces." It swept through Pope's Head Alley, where Woodbridge had taken Bradstreet's manuscript poetry to be printed, and where her work first appeared in the shop of Stephen Bowtell as The Tenth Muse, Lately Sprung up in America. The fire left the city devastated, and, although authorities considered various plots that might explain it, they were forced to "conclude the Whole was an effect of an unhappy Chance, or to speak better, the heavy hand of God upon us." We have no evidence that Bradstreet composed the verses about her house with the Great Fire of London in mind, and scholars have not presumed to bring the local Andover fire and the colossal London conflagration into a shared frame. But the possibility that Bradstreet was contemplating both by the late fall of 1666 is worth considering. My speculation would gather force if Bradstreet wrote her poem at least a few months after the Andover fire, and if she wrote with London on her mind, and neither is beyond the realm of plausibility.[43]

It would seem she was highly attuned to London in 1666. We know the Andover fire interrupted her revisions of her lengthy historical poem "The Four Monarchies." Serving as the centerpiece of *The Tenth Muse*, it recites a selective history of the Assyrian, Babylonian, Greek, and Roman empires in order to comment on the legitimacy and fortunes of the House of Stuart and the crisis of civil war.[44] Jane Eberwein argues that "Anne Bradstreet's profound concern about monarchy in a time of extreme political agitation motivated her to undertake this staggering historical project in a search for perspective on current events," including, when she attempted the revisions of the 1660s, the fate of the Commonwealth and the restoration of the monarchy. Eberwein even goes so far as to suggest that the modest scale of Bradstreet's adjustments to the original poem "had much less to do with changes in her personal life" than her waning enthusiasm, in the wake of the Interregnum, for a project initially inspired by "millennial hopes centered on dynamic English royal leadership." In or around 1666, Bradstreet admitted she was as entangled in this intellectual thicket as ever when she wrote in an addendum at the end of "Monarchies":

> To finish what's begun, was my intent,
> My thoughts and my endeavours thereto bent;
> Essays I many made but still gave out,
> The more I mus'd, the more I was in doubt.

Bradstreet's difficulty identifying specific solutions to the problems of monarchical excess she adumbrates in the long poem is likely a product of her acute understanding of the deepening complexities of English politics rather than a sudden lack of interest in them. I share with Wright the sense that Bradstreet's frustrated attempt to close the poem "testifies strongly to the conflicted loyalties which afflicted so many erstwhile critics of the English monarchy in the late 1640s and beyond." Only a writer less interested in ongoing political debate and less personally invested in English politics than Bradstreet could have offered a pat resolution to the sprawling history she unspools in "Monarchies." Instead, her close relationship to her father Thomas Dudley and to John Woodbridge, both directly involved in opposing the policies of Charles I, as well as her evident attention to the controversies underpinning civil war, nuanced her views. That she had returned to this unwieldy project during the summer her house caught fire suggests her continuing engagement with affairs unfolding in London.[45]

On the question of the timing of the composition of the verses on the house fire, it would be more surprising if Bradstreet wrote the poem immediately after her home (which is also to say her workspace and materials) burned to the ground and as she and Simon scrambled to secure provisional lodgings for their family. Bradstreet's poetic process was famously protracted; she alludes in "The Four Monarchies" to "dayes of rest," which then leave her "restless" to get on with her work. She also bemoans the "Shortness of time" in which she has to work each day, which forces her, she fears, "to a confus'd brevity." Even under the best of circumstances, as Woodbridge stressed (and his perspective as a family member and her neighbor in Andover put him in a position to know), her writing time was limited to what she could "[curtail] from her sleep, and other refreshments." The fire seriously disrupted her already labored writing process and threw the straitened conditions in which she wrote into disarray. Again, she herself remarks on the disruption in the apology appended to the version of "Monarchies" that she failed to revise to her satisfaction:

> But 'fore I could accomplish my desire,
> My papers fell a prey to th' raging fire.
> And thus my pains (with better things) I lost.

The fire must have made her a guest in someone's home, where she would have been expected to shoulder her share, at least, of the domestic tasks and pose minimal disruptions to the rhythms of the household. It seems likely she would wait until conditions were at all favorable for writing before she penned the verses about the house fire, which in any case document some period of time in which the narrator returned repeatedly to the site of the disaster and renegotiated her affective response to the loss. Certainly, the conversion process the poem describes could have taken place over the period of time it would have taken for the sensational news of the London fire to reach Andover.[46]

In positing that Bradstreet had time to learn of the fire in London as she organized her response to the fire in Andover, and that she seems particularly responsive to events in London in her writing during the period surrounding the disaster, I hope to return more fruitfully to the question of why a devout Puritan might have elegized something as ephemeral and worldly as a vanished house, and to what ends. I will try to distinguish carefully between fact and speculation in the argument that follows. Here is what we know. In the midst of revising her most ambitious poem, Bradstreet became suddenly homeless. She did not accomplish whatever she "desired" for "The Four Monarchies" either because she left it incomplete or was dissatisfied with what she fashioned. It is, in Paula Kopacz's words, "a concluded yet unfinished work." She cites the fire of July 10 as a significant reason she abandoned that project, and sometime after the domestic tragedy she wrote "Some Verses upon the Burning of Our House." In doing so, she turned from writing a politic history to writing an elegy—one that, unlike her earlier elegies, mourned an object rather than a person. The politic history is an expressly impersonal, objective genre, one whose narrator, as Wright points out, "is rarely a biographically individuated figure" but rather one whose "invisibility" foregrounds qualities of "discrimination, political judgment and apt expression." Bradstreet, knowing this, would have taken pains to obscure her own voice in "Monarchies," as generic conventions required. In contrast, the elegy is a fundamentally "sociable" form. "If seen from a critical perspective that incorporates rather than dismisses or apologizes for the 'social' functions of art," Jeffrey Hammond argues, elegies "emerge as models of cultural adaptation, as remarkably successful discursive performances." In the elegy, the narrator's willingness to offer up private pain for public contemplation allows her to support the psychic labor of mourning, as Max Cavitch proposes when he writes, "Elegies seek to apprehend the ultimate, most unknowable condition of privacy, while pointing, in their language of loss, toward the sheer commonality of human experience." In other words, the burning of her home might have prompted Bradstreet to shift from a deliberately impersonal genre to a specifically social one. But, possibly (and here I branch into what we can only imagine), Bradstreet was oriented toward states of crisis in London as she worked on both poems, one before and one after the fire that destroyed her house. And, possibly, for a poet whose authorial influence was blunted (and, after her death, complicated) by her position at the margins between worlds, Bradstreet's sudden homelessness in 1666 might have been less a problem than a solution to a problem that her sturdy English home in America created.[47]

In the politic history, Bradstreet's position between old and new worlds kept her at a literal remove from the conflicts scholars see her poem responding to, a separation mirrored in the poem's guarded emotional remove from its readers. In "Monarchies," she offers cautious critiques of the Stuarts, but she remains impartial on the contemporary political questions—particularly the conflict between parliamentary and monarchical power—her ancient history surfaces. For many critics, Bradstreet's stance mutes the artistic and affective impact of the poem. Elizabeth Wade White calls "The Four Monarchies" a "barren exercise in rhetorical ingenuity, unreadable by present-day standards." For Eberwein, "what 'Monarchies' has been universally condemned as lacking . . . is evidence of the author's presence." This lack of presence is a literary as well as historical quibble: scholars have suggested that, since Bradstreet was first published, the problem of her double homes in America and England played a critical part in the failure of supposedly "listless" poems such as "Monarchies" or elegies to Elizabeth I, Philip Sidney, and Guillaume de Salluste, seigneur du Bartas to resonate with readers. When it appeared in Bowtell's shop, *The Tenth Muse, Lately Sprung up in America* was, as Fallon argues, at once a sign of "the widened horizons of a transatlantic literary culture" and a "novelty" object that "raised the question of just how traversable the distance between imperial center and colonial periphery really was." The title page foregrounded the author's American home ("By a Gentlewoman in Those Parts") even as it advertised her contributions to English political debate ("Wherein Especially Is Contained . . . a Dialogue between Old England and New, concerning the Late Troubles"). English readers might have wondered whether their political institutions were being criticized by a member of the family or an in-law, so to speak, a question reproduced in a long-running scholarly debate about whether Bradstreet is rightfully the "first American poet" or "rather an Englishwoman abroad—a visitor residing in America only 'at present.'" As Fallon puts it, "Caught in the middle, Bradstreet fits comfortably into neither history; instead, she indexes the limits of the worlds that criticism guided by the nation can accommodate." This worldlessness caused Bradstreet herself enough consternation that she felt moved to assure her readers, or herself, in a line she added to her elegy for Sidney, that "English blood yet runs within my veins."[48]

But when her Andover house went up in flames, Bradstreet was momentarily set free from the landlocked paradigms that made her either an outsider looking in on English affairs or an insider who had wandered from home. Her physical location was suddenly immaterial. And in these conditions of immateriality, Bradstreet did not repress her "inappropriate grief" over a material loss (as we might imagine a Puritan doing in these circumstances) but instead chose to advertise it as a new condition for her solidarity with readers outside Andover, who clearly included her adult children and possibly included her English kinsfolk stretched across the Atlantic. While the house in Andover had hosted meals and pleasant talk among guests, by design it constrained the Bradstreets' sphere of sociality. That was the trade-off for the English home in American space, after all—it exchanged openness for protection, accessibility for security, adaptability for rootedness. Once it went up in flames, Bradstreet was able to dramatically enlarge her circle of relationality via the sheer power of elegiac sociality. If she had really taken the spiritual message of "Some Verses upon the Burning of Our House" to heart, Bradstreet would have recognized the relative insignificance of the loss, sublimated her grief about it along with her attachment to her treasured possessions, and resumed the work of discovering providential designs in monarchical history. That the elegy for the house exists at all, and that she did not complete "Monarchies" in the way she once envisioned, indicates that she instead redirected her authorial attentions to dwelling on, prolong-ing, and inevitably publicizing not just a material tragedy but her own sorrow about it.[49]

In the larger scale of her professional life and oeuvre, this may not be as surprising as it seems. Planted on American soil, Bradstreet's literal distance from crisis in England allowed her to take an academic interest in its woes. It was never clear when or whether the reverberations of English conflicts would reach New England's shores. Her attempts to grieve with people in England over the civil war, and even her belated elegies for public figures like Elizabeth I and Sidney, had always been marked by her particular subject position. She did not precisely share their sorrows, even if she worked to un-derstand them, and she grieved in both spatial and temporal registers that were out of tune with her English fellows. This changed by late 1666, when Bradstreet no longer had to exercise her powers of imagination to fathom what it would be like to synchronously share the precise grief of those per-sonally affected by the dominant tragedy in London. Temporarily unsettled, like them, by fire, Bradstreet emerges as a vulnerable, empathetic figure in a poem mourning a worldly loss. I find it more than coincidental that in or around 1666 she should work on both the historical poem in which critics most lament her absence and the personal poem—probably the most famous of her works—in which critics most relish finding her presence. It also seems more than possible that losing her structural connection to New England soil was the juncture between the revising of "Monarchies" and the composition of "Some Verses upon the Burning of Our House" that inspired Bradstreet to reconceive her connection to the English residents with whom she had always sympathized and to find in their shared tragedy new, more personal, possibilities for world making.

Although Bradstreet had long related to kinsfolk across the world under the banner of "transnational Protestantism," in the verses about her home her faith in a spiritual world that supersedes the boundaries of an earthly one rests on an ecological rather than a religiopolitical basis and is unusually generous (and specific) in its vision of succor for the suffering.[50] Protestants were united by persecution in wildly different contexts and locations, as John Foxe's *The Actes and Monuments*, so cherished by Puritans, graphically describes. But the terms of salvation this paradigm offered were rooted in Reformed theology, with the individual bringing herself into alignment with God's will and thus discovering her justification. Within this doctrine, the individual must take action to cross from the fallen world to the realm of a heavenly one. This journey is an arduous, painful one, as exemplified in the poem in which Bradstreet takes up the same themes of the verses on her house, but without yet having had the experience of watching a house burn down, "The Vanity of All Worldly Things." In it, she asks,

> Where shall I climb, sound, seek search or find
> That *Summum Bonum* which may stay my mind?
> There is a path, no vultures eye hath seen,
> Where Lion fierce, nor lions whelps have been,
> . . . Its hid from eyes of men, they count it strange.

But in "Some Verses upon the Burning of Our House," fire, not human exertion, is the agent that uncovers the path to God and to the "house on high" he has prepared. Fire is a remarkably democratic force—and a global one, as Bradstreet illustrates when she traces its path across the world in "The Four Elements." This form of spiritual epiphany is available outside her Puritan settlement and to those who may not share her relationship to God. The Bradstreet house fire is an affliction, handed out by a God who gives more than he takes, not a punishment for rebellion or corruption, as some London preachers interpreted the Great Fire and as Bradstreet sometimes read her misfortunes. She felt the displeasure of a God who "boyle[d]" her "burning flesh in sweat" during a fever she memorialized in another occasional meditation, but she did not find God's wrath in the image of her burning house, only his providence. And although other elegies show Bradstreet accessing this comfort in the first person, her poem on the house fire begins in the first person ("In silent night when rest I took, / For sorrow neer I did not look") but closes in the second person: "*Thou* hast a house on high erect, / Fram'd by that mighty Architect" (italics mine). To whom is she speaking? Although she clearly buoys herself with the couplet, the change in voice alerts us to subjects for her reassurance who exist outside herself, outside Andover, and possibly even outside the continent.[51]

Although by 1666 she shared neither the doctrinal nor the political views of a majority of Londoners, she shared with them the very specific circumstances of their suffering, and we might imagine these final couplets of her elegy to a vanished house positing a radically inclusive basis for fellow mourners to unite across geographic space. We might also imagine that when she penned these lines, she identified for the first time on utterly apolitical terms with people who were united, not in a partisan cause, but in an undiscriminating tragedy. Her promise of salvation applies to those who grieve and those who believe, which in one form or another must have applied to the vast majority of the newly homeless population of England. Even if Bradstreet did not think of her own loss in terms of the related tragedy in London as she wrote her elegy (although if she had to wait until the mid-fall or later to find the time, presence of mind, space, or resources to write, it is inconceivable she did not make the association), before the end of 1666 the connection would not be lost on her as a "reader" of her own experience, nor could it be lost on readers of her poem. In the wake of war and Restoration, when the Puritans' position in London had so dramatically shifted, Bradstreet's poem proposes a new basis of affiliation unattached to either old or new world paradigms but rather rooted in the homelessness that turns out to afflict both the pilgrim and those who stay planted. This world, the one populated by the unsettled, might have been the most expansive of the early modern period.

Little wonder that it is in the "global turn" of early American literature and early American studies that Bradstreet has found her most secure and comfortable place, no longer hampered by concerns about where she lived when she wrote. It certainly helps that in one of her latest and most popular poems, Bradstreet stressed the point that she lived nowhere. Setting herself free of spatial paradigms in this personal verse also allows Bradstreet a remarkable degree of timelessness, or an ability to cross between worlds of then and now. Her poem seems born of the sentimental nineteenth-century literary culture in which it was first published, increasingly resonated with readers and writers drawn to confessional writing in the twentieth century, and continues to captivate undergraduate students encountering American literature for the first time. Doubtless this has much to do with the degree to which the poem is not invested in the politics of a specific place, as so much of The Tenth Muse is, and instead deliberately announces the portability of the narrator and her craving to adapt in the face of changing environments. Allison Giffen has commented that Bradstreet uses the infinitival form of the verb consume in the line "The flame consume my dwelling place" to lend the scene a "sense of timeless horror." But the line also invites endless sympathy for a domestic tragedy that happened once in history but unfolds eternally in the elegy. Even as Bradstreet wrote the lines, "That fearfull sound of fire and fire / Let no man know is my Desire," she knew her hope was a futile one in a transatlantic world of English open hearths and insatiable appetites for the comforts fire fueled. There had been two "great fires," one in Salem and one in Boston, in a single week in April 1645, and fires in Boston in 1676 and 1679 would consume "some hundreds of houses and warehouses." Countless men and women knew, or would come to know, that fearful cry. The Bradstreets' fire turned out to be one more unexceptional feature of their colonial venture in North American Native space. But there's power in the typical, as Puritan writers well knew. Bradstreet's burning house forever throws up its signal of distress, and a call to commiserate, with those who literally or imaginatively came to share her sorrow.[52]

WAITING FOR ULYSSES

In an elegy for a mundane disaster, Bradstreet turned her house into paper and set it ablaze and then adrift on what has turned out to be—whatever her desires—a world-crossing and world-connecting voyage. In this way, her sheet of loose paper participates in a shared enterprise with the sheet of paper Caleb Cheeshateaumuck transformed into a letter to the benefactors of Harvard Indian College and a witness of his own and his colleagues' world-crossing journeys. He gave his life to leave this filament of himself in the archives of early American literature. And a piece of paper is not a trivial thing—in many ways it is more stable, and more substantial, than the homes of the seventeenth century. Caleb's letter preserves not just his own erudition and experience but also a vital piece of the history of the college and the journey he shared with his Native colleagues. In 2011, Tiffany Smalley became the first Wampanoag student to graduate from Harvard College since Caleb received his degree in 1665. She also accepted a printed diploma on behalf of Joel Iacoomes, 346 years after his untimely death. When she reflected on her experience as a student at Harvard, she paid tribute to Caleb's influence, which survives, against all odds, on the Cambridge campus. "I've felt really at home, knowing Caleb did this," she said. "It gives you perspective. He was just thrown into it, and for him, it was a whole different world." We moderns are connected to these other worlds by such thin slips of paper, yet the connection holds.[53]

The New England landscape bears irrefutable witness that English settlers in America used wood in shockingly unsustainable ways, devastating the ecosystems Natives had so carefully nurtured. Still, for all their differences, English writers and Native writers who used print in addition to the other materials of Native arts are similar in the ways they transformed paper into texts, which turned out to be one of the most sustainable of seventeenth-century American industries. When the English used wood to construct their houses, they eschewed the practices of the Natives, who moved to access the area's abundant resources, and instead demanded these resources be brought to their doorsteps. And the roaring fires the English burned to heat these houses rerouted the environmental history of New England in ways we still feel today. But when they wrote about the wood-fueled conflagrations that reclaimed their intransigent houses back into the rhythms of the land, English writers joined Native writers like Caleb and his colleagues in transforming the pain of homelessness into world-spanning signals that continue to summon kinsfolk to a sympathetic world that offers sustenance to the displaced.

I make this claim about the sustainability of the writing that mourns early American homelessness advisedly, in light of the ongoing debate about what sustainability involves or even what it signifies. Since the 1980s, the term *sustainability* has taken on meanings in the realms of economic development, education, and social equity that the verb *sustain* did not have in the seventeenth century. Still, the idea dates back that far. In 1664, the English agriculturalist and writer John Evelyn, in his treatise *Silva*, described a vision of agroforestry that aligns with a contemporary definition of "sustainable development" as "development that meets the needs of the present without compromising the ability of future generations to meet their own needs." In fact, Evelyn's 1664 treatise (revised in 1670 to include reference to "that Deplorable Calamity, the Conflagration of [the] Imperial City") makes the needs of future generations *the* consideration guiding the management of natural resources. In light of England's deforestation, a problem since the thirteenth century and one of the crises driving imperial expansion, Evelyn urged his landholding countrymen to think of their children as they came into their estates, "that such *Woods* as do yet remain intire, might be carefully *preserved*, and such as are *destroy'd*, sedulously *repaired*." They might take as their model, he suggested, the providence of an ancient parent:

Homeless

When *Ulysses*, after a ten-years Absence, was return'd from *Troy*, and coming home, found his aged *Father* in the Field planting of *Trees*, He asked him, why (being now so far advanc'd in Years) he would put himself to the Fatigue and Labour of Planting, *that* which he was never likely to enjoy the Fruits of? The good old Man (taking him for a Stranger) gently reply'd; I *plant* (says he) *against my Son Ulysses comes home.*[54]

While English settlers repeated the sins of their ancestors in the forests of North America, a few early Americans husbanded another precious resource, paper—still produced on a small scale in France, Holland, and England and imported to the colonies in the seventeenth century—and cultivated it for the benefit of those Bradstreet called the "After-comers." In the last years of their lives, when their work would not redound to their personal profit, Anne Bradstreet and Caleb Cheeshateaumuck bent their energies, training, and considerable skill to fashioning paper boats, which have carried them on a sea of shared sentiment to kinsfolk in distant times and places and have limned the footprint of a home readers are invited to share. They join Lucy Terry, John Williams, Cotton Mather, Mary Rowlandson, and others who sent their vanished houses up in literature in exchange for admission to this other place, where dislocated souls find the permanence the early modern world denied them. Paper production would become something else entirely by the nineteenth century, but in this preindustrial moment, writing about the grief of homelessness stands as one of the most forward-looking of American enterprises, one that made material loss into material objects that wait on the chance Ulysses comes home and, if he does, that beckon him to a world impervious to flame.[55]

CHAPTER 2

Divorced

———

For people in the American Northeast during the seventeenth century, the death of a husband or wife might have been heartbreaking, but it was at least straightforward: *Your husband is dead.* In the archives of the period, we see traces of people tormented by a more complicated and horrifying loss: *Your marriage is dead, but your wife is alive.* For most people, this did not mean the marriage had ended in legal divorce but rather that it persisted in a state of unease, outright misery, or chaos. A dead spouse could be eulogized, laid to rest, and mourned, and the surviving spouse could, and usually did, remarry. Unhappy marriages, those in which affection, trust, cooperation, or intimacy had died, produced another kind of grief—uneven, unpredictable, unending. If grief over the death of a spouse gradually calmed and resolved, the grief of those in unhappy marriages accreted over time, with fresh afflictions layered upon old to create sediments of suffering.[1]

How was one to endure, let alone talk about, this kind of pain? The very nature of it—a marriage fractured but the partners left standing— confounded the familial narratives and material rituals by which kin were typically mourned and memorialized. It was a tragedy both too small and too cataclysmic to discuss. And it rarely was. For example, in the vast body of writings about Puritan marriages and family life, we mostly see marriages clustered around the extremes ends of conjugal experience. On one end, we see Puritan marriages in all their idealized glory: Anne Bradstreet addressing erotic poems to her husband Simon in his sickness and absence; John and Margaret Winthrop exchanging tender letters during their courtship; Edward Taylor delighting in the union to and then lamenting the loss of his beloved Elizabeth. We find the minister Benjamin Wadsworth instructing spouses to "endeavour to have their affections really, cordially and closely knit, to each other"; John Cotton admonishing couples "transported with affection" to remember that God must be the ultimate object of desire; Puritan wedding sermons assuring the joyfully gathered that *"Matches are made in Heaven"*; and popular conduct books like William Gouge's *Of Domesticall Duties* assuming that husbands and wives replicated the relationship of Christ to his church. At the other extreme, we see marriages so catastrophic they launched themselves into public records of ecclesiastical discipline, criminal prosecution, or civil court proceedings. These are ghastly cases, too many to mention here, in which husbands and wives accuse one another of violence or stand trial for murdering their partners in cold blood. One longs for the mediocre middle. Where are the records of early Americans—surely, the majority of the population—whose marriages were neither reliable transports of pious delight nor homicidal nightmares? Where are the marriages that were difficult or disappointing in ordinary ways? Where are the marriages that were emotionally afflictive rather than physically abusive? Where are the stories of those whose marriages foundered outside enclaves of Puritan proscription or protection? And how did this pervasive, intimate suffering influence the quality of early American life in the Northeast?[2]

Although it is true we find few stand-alone contemplations of these experiences in the literature of American Puritans, it would be a mistake to say they ignored these stories. With incredible regularity, they incorporated them into their writings, but the larger crises or concepts these sources reflect have pulled critical attention away from the cryptic, mostly unexamined references to conjugal unease stitched through them. In many cases, the central crises of these writings have defined their genres—as religious histories, captivity narratives, witchcraft documents, jeremiads, and so on. That couples may be merely unhappy as antinomians foment, warriors menace, witches cavort, or God rages seems somewhat beside the point. Modern readers mostly move past the private pain to arrive at the catastrophe it portends. But Puritans themselves paid attention to the pain of people whose marital unions, supposed to designate saints' bond with God, faltered and failed. They paused on this pain and bore witness to it even when they did not elaborate and thus left future generations to make sense of it. We might imagine unhappy marriages as just one more piece of sediment irritating the glands and producing the pearl of Pilgrim fortitude, a grain hardly worth considering relative to the other traumas they endured. This would be understandable, since we would take our cue from the literature, which always encloses brief references to marital unhappiness within narratives of much more dramatic crises. But these enclosed references, however fragmentary, are not meaningless.[3]

Even the writings that testify to the blissful quality of the remarkable marriages mentioned earlier contain within them clear allusions to the proposition with which this chapter began: *My marriage is dead, but my spouse is alive.* Anne Bradstreet despaired at the prospect of distance from Simon, and never more so than before she gave birth, when the potential separation was permanent. In "Before the Birth of One of Her Children," Bradstreet speaks of their love and friendship and addresses herself to Simon as one "who long lay in [his] arms." Elsewhere, she wrote, "If ever two were one, then surely we, / If ever man were loved by wife, then thee," but her passionate affection for her husband makes her circumstance more dreadful. She may die giving birth to the product of their loving union and believes (as all Puritans) that her death will dissolve their marriage. But Simon will survive. She flirts with the idea he may remain faithful to her memory ("Love bids me / These farewell lines to recommend to thee, / That when that knot's untied that made us one / I may seem thine, who in effect am none") but then accepts as a given that her beloved will remarry (as he did when she died, in old age, in 1672). She then seriously considers the possibility the second bride he chooses may be so antithetical to herself and her values as to pose a threat to her "little babes." She begs him, "And if thou love thyself, or loved'st me, / These O protect from step-dame's injury." Bradstreet did not die in childbirth, but it is sobering to consider that someone who enjoyed one of the most famously sanguine relationships in Puritan America lived with the hunch her husband would outlive her marriage and the vivid fear he would betray her and imperil their children when he did.[4]

Embedded in John and Margaret Winthrop's amorous correspondence during their engagement is fear of spiritual rather than emotional betrayal, a fear that afflicted other devoted couples. "The great and sincere desire which I have that there might be no discouragement to daunt the edge of my affections, whyle they are truly labouringe to settle and repose themselves in thee, makes me thus watchfull and jealous of the least occasion that Sathan might stirre up to our discomfort," John writes to Margaret. The issue at hand is Margaret's fashion, which John senses might be designed to appeal to something other than God's pleasure. His fear is not that Satan will assail the union from without; it is that Margaret will kill trust in the marriage from within. And in expressing this fear, he alerts her to the contingency of his own affections (even in the halcyon days of their courtship), to the possibility they might be unsettled by her conduct in matters he acknowledges as mere "trifles." Edward Taylor sounds a similarly disquieting note in an otherwise stirring love letter to Elizabeth Fitch when he writes: "My Dove: I send you not my Heart: For that I hope is sent to h[ea]ven long since and (unless it hath utterly deceived me) it ha[th] not taken up its Lodgen in any ones Bosom on this Side the Royal City of the Greate King." The passion of the letter, directed toward an earthly object, raises a question pursuant to its opening lines: Has Taylor's heart deceived him? The question reflects his belief (again, shared by all Puritans) that the heart is capable of such deception, and even ardent attachments may be misdirected. Whatever else these celebrated romances reveal about Puritan affections, weaned or otherwise, they illuminate insecurities at the heart of New England's basic societal unit. *Can I trust him? Can I trust her? Can I trust myself?*[5]

When the answer was a demonstrable "no," Puritans, like modern readers, took notice. But their interest (unlike ours, I suspect) was not in what made these cases sensational but what made them common. In 1715, a Boston man named Jeremiah Mecham murdered his wife and sister-in-law with an axe and then cut his wife's throat with a penknife before setting fire to their house. A crowd detained him as he attempted to escape the conflagration, and he was hanged a few weeks later. The *Boston News-Letter* briefly reported the bare facts of the incident just after they occurred and then elaborated on their significance when it reported Mecham's death. At his execution, Mecham publicly embraced "his Sense of his Sinfulness and Repentance for Sin" and implored his audience "to take Warning by his Example of coming to an untimely End, and of Profaning the Lord's Day, and Sinning against the Light of their Conscience." Finally, he "Cautioned Married Persons to Guard against Strife and Contention in their Families, and acknowledged that he suffered justly for his Great and Capital Transgressions, and the Justice of the Sentence past upon him." In this longer report, the grisly details of the case are entirely absent, replaced by references to spiritual qualities—of sinfulness, repentance, and submission to God—and emotional experiences of interpersonal tension. The story of the miserable Mechams reaches its climax when Jeremiah warns married people to guard against domestic discord and acknowledges that he justly dies for failing so spectacularly to do so.[6]

This story, spread out over weeks, precisely inverts the arc we have come to expect of the early American criminal narrative. Instead of building from ordinary spiritual sins to extraordinary physical violence, the newspaper account begins with the homicide of two women and concludes its catalog of the traumas Jeremiah Mecham inflicted on his wife with the most prosaic, "Strife and Contention." These seem to be the "Great" (in excess of "Capital") transgressions for which Mecham feels he deserves to die. What makes this marriage newsworthy is the unusual abuse that kills it; but what makes this marriage tragic is the afflictive state in which it existed. Domestic tension is much less sensational than fatal domestic violence, but it was also far more common, even among ostensibly happy couples, and was thus a much more powerful force in the spiritual and emotional registers of early American life. Puritans took seriously both the prevalence of this suffering (Mecham urges spouses in the crowd "to Guard against Strife and Contention in their Families" [italics mine]) and its toll. "Contrary to mutuall peace are contentions betwixt man and wife: which are too frequent in most families, and by which the common good is much hindered," Gouge lamented. For those looking in on disastrous marriages like the Mechams', strife and contention—the psychological assaults we might term microaggressions—were not mere preamble to a story of crisis. They were the point.[7]

And what, precisely, was the toll such ordinary suffering took on those who experienced it? How did marital unhappiness influence the mood of early American life in the Northeast, and how was this mood manifest? In short, distrust within marriages generated widespread suspicion of faithlessness. It was such a powerful psychic force for so many people that economic, social, religious, political, and ecological harms were commonly understood and amplified in the terms of intimate partner betrayal (forsake, seduce, ravage, beguile, and so on). In stressing the marriage relationship as a central object of faith and betrayal for people living in the early American Northeast, I wish to make a case for the absolute reality of faithlessness during the period and for the emergence of an attitude of suspicion as a necessary, and sometimes salubrious, response to this crisis.[8]

The paradoxical impulses of this argument—faith in faithlessness, and trust in suspicion—align closely with a discernable mood in the historical record, but long-standing critical trends (which traffic in these same impulses) have made this mood difficult to take seriously or to perceive as a

Divorced

phenomenon separate from the twentieth-century critical climate. American Puritans were constantly suspicious that the faith of their partners, children, and contemporaries was on the ebb, as scores of jeremiads indicate. But Perry Miller, after reading exhaustively in the genre, suspected the authors themselves of faithlessness. "There is something of a ritualistic incantation about them," he suggested. "Whatever they may signify in the realm of theology, in that of psychology they are purgations of soul; they do not discourage but actually encourage the community to persist in its heinous conduct. The exhortation to a reformation which never materializes serves as a token payment upon the obligation, and so liberates the debtors." In the mid-twentieth century, other critics converted Miller's caution about his subject matter into a conviction that the only real referent of Puritan faith was suspicion itself, a position captured in H. L. Mencken's oft-reprinted quip, "Puritanism—The haunting fear that someone, somewhere, may be happy." But in the last generation or so, from fields of history, philosophy, and literary studies have come calls to modulate this suspicion run riot. Historians brought renewed attention to their own role in shaping narratives that foreground certain historical attitudes and sublimate others. As Hayden White proposed,

No given set of casually recorded historical events in themselves constitute a story; the most it might offer to the historian are story *elements*. The events are *made* into a story by the suppression or subordination of certain of them and the highlighting of others, by characterization, motific repetition, variation of tone and point of view, alternative descriptive strategies, and the like—in short, all of the techniques that we would normally expect to find in the emplotment of a novel or a play.

And, if so, the emergence of faithlessness and suspicion in the historical record suggests not so much a real state of affairs but moments of affinity between historians and Puritans—moments when the distrust of readers was drawn to expressions of distrust in the historical record. That affinity, more than any found evidence, provides the basis for stories about early American faith that highlight hypocrisy and deception and interpretations that seek to demystify the beliefs of Puritans. Paul Ricoeur called critical faith in faithlessness in the writings of Marx, Freud, and Nietzsche a "school of suspicion," which, as Rita Felski has pointed out, is such a charismatic mode of thought that the peculiar reading practices it inspires—to create distance, survey warily, unmask, decipher, and expose—have thoroughly permeated the academy as the essence of critique rather than one method of it. Certainly, these practices influenced early American studies over the past two generations.[9]

Despite the welcome provocations of these claims, suspicion is not an easy thing to shake. Ricoeur and Felski are suspicious of suspicion. John Winthrop and his contemporaries, beyond the reach of postcritical theorists' ministrations, can still be found persisting in their suspicion, even if they can also be found (under a sympathetic storyteller's eye) alight with other virtues. Furthermore, the historical record thoroughly validates the suspicion of the Native Americans, Africans, and African Americans who transacted business with European settlers. Even the alternative Ricoeur proposes, a "hermeneutics [of] restoration," is complicated: "The contrary of suspicion, I will say bluntly, is faith. What faith? No longer, to be sure, the first faith of the simple soul, but rather the second faith of one who has engaged in hermeneutics, faith that has undergone criticism, postcritical faith." At first blush this seems congruent with the notion, widespread though certainly not universal among critics during the twentieth century, that Puritans, possessed of suspicion in unholy amounts, were not actually faithful or that their faith was of the primitive sort. Surely this is an impoverished view of Puritan theology. We can come to a deeper appreciation of Puritan faith by putting a higher value on their suspicion, and on the suspicion of those who dealt with them. Beginning in the context of intimate partner relationships and emanating outward, faith was not always warranted, nor wise. Many people in the early American Northeast relied on suspicion as a defense strategy, which they deployed for their own protection and on behalf of other imperiled people. We rightfully suspect suspicion when it seems to be the aggressive, unfounded compulsion of people in positions of influence. But we should be reticent to criticize the suspicion of vulnerable people whose apparent lack of faith is a justified faith in faithlessness. What I call for and hope to practice in this chapter is not a return to suspicious reading; rather, it is an openness to the suspicion of Native Americans, Puritans, and English colonists of other faiths who found themselves in intimate relationships of startling instability and who oriented themselves to their environments accordingly. I consider marital suspicion as a mood that hung in the background of thought and subtly informed a variety of engagements across the American Northeast. This mood is traceable through historical records and literary productions, where we find evidence that suspicion of intimate partners led to safety, sympathy, and horror—but, above all, toward a clearer sense of reality. In reality, the crises of early American life did not destroy marriages. When they seemed to do so, they revealed marriages that were already dead and had long since leeched the dust of their discontent into the groundwater.[10]

MARRIAGE AND MOOD IN PATUXET

When a band of English Separatists caught a glimpse of the rocky coast edging the disease-ravaged Wampanoag town of Patuxet in 1620, they regarded this environment as wholly foreign. As William Bradford recalled in his history *Of Plymouth Plantation*, "What could they see but a hidious and desolate wildernes, full of wild beasts and willd men?" Notably, the space lacked any semblance of domestic life: "They had now no freinds [sic] to wellcome them, nor inns to entertaine or refresh their weatherbeaten bodys, no houses or much less townes to repaire too, to seeke for succoure." The settlers' view of their situation changed as the Wampanoag liaisons Hobbamock and Tisquantum introduced the English to the systems of hospitality, agriculture, diplomacy, and trade operating in the region and Bradford's language of stark difference gave way to the terms of intimate familiarity. For example, Hobbamock, a high-ranking Wampanoag Council member, was more than an ambassador between the paramount Wampanoag sachem Ousamequin (whom the English called by his title Massasoit) and leaders of the new settlement in Patuxet called Plymouth; he was a trusted confidant and strategist who "continued very faithfull and constant to the English till he dyed." This is not to say the English stance turned from one of suspicion to one of trust. More accurately, the English converted their suspicion of the unknown into suspicion of the familiar. Despite the complexity of their faith, their initial suspicion of North America was rather primitive and uninformed (a vague fear of desolate wilderness, wild beasts, and wild men). In the first few years of settlement, their suspicion became more sensitive, although not necessarily more sophisticated, since the complexity of Native confederations and cultural practices often escaped them. Their Wampanoag allies, whose position between the vast trading networks of the Atlantic and the continent gave them expertise in matters of kinship and betrayal, practiced a more attuned and nimble suspicion, capable of comprehending the turn of strangers into partners and partners into enemies.[11]

A famous example of the bounty of suspicion in a season of scarcity showcases a contest between faith and distrust that manifested as an intercultural conflict but mirrors in suggestive ways private tensions inherent in the marriages of the principal players. In March 1622, after a grueling winter that taxed the already meager resources of the Plymouth inhabitants who

Figure 8. Map of Port Saint Louis (Plymouth Colony, Massachusetts), including Native American settlements. From Samuel de Champlain, *Les voyages du sieur de Champlain Xaintongeois, capitaine ordinaire pour le Roy, en la marine* . . . (Paris, 1613), 80, Internet Archive

had managed to survive the first cataclysmic year of settlement, the English were planning a visit to trade with the Massachusett people. But Hobbamock heard a rumor that put him on edge and that he passed on to Bradford: the trading visit was a trap. The Massachusetts, according to his sources, had secretly formed an alliance with the Narragansetts, who saw the weakened condition of the English and plotted to attack Plymouth while the trading party was away. The English were desperate for supplies and, determined to proceed with the voyage anyway, on high alert. Their ship was still within shouting distance of the shore when a single man, whom the English traders recognized as a relative of Tisquantum, came tearing into view. An army of Narragansett warriors were descending on Plymouth, the panicked messenger warned, joined by the Pocasset sachem Corbitant and possibly—he couldn't be sure—Ousamequin himself. As he spoke, he threw terrified glances over his shoulder, as if the attackers "were at his heels." The English struggled to comprehend these alarming, bewildering pieces of intelligence. The Narragansetts they already feared. But had they been betrayed by their Wampanoag allies? As they turned to their Native liaisons to help them make sense of this terror, Hobbamock was surprisingly calm. He doubted very much he was looking at a man in distress, much less a man being pursued by his own Wampanoag kin. Instead, he trained his suspicious gaze on the passenger next to him in the boat, Tisquantum, whom he suspected of creating conditions of chaos in the Wampanoag-English alliance that would allow him to play the role of protector to both sides.[12]

In reality, suspicious familiarity was the basis of the bond between these Wampanoag ambassadors. They were both on the boat because the English declined to take one or the other on the trading voyage "in regarde of the jelocie betweene them." Ousamequin had recently installed Hobbamock and his family on the outskirts of Plymouth to create a line of communication between the Wampanoags and the English that bypassed Tisquantum, who was already living among the English as an interpreter and adviser, and whom he distrusted. Neither the Wampanoags nor the English could be certain of Tisquantum's loyalties, which he had learned to recalibrate in response to stunning betrayals. He was born around 1590 in Patuxet, then the center of northern Wampanoag trading and cultural activity. In 1614, a member of John Smith's New England exploring expedition, Thomas Hunt, kidnapped him and nineteen other Patuxet men and forcibly conveyed them across the "Red Atlantic" to a slave market in Málaga, Spain. Tisquantum left Málaga for London, without his Wampanoag compatriots, enslaved by the wealthy merchant John Slany. He resided in the merchant's grand residence in central London until the spring of 1617, when Slany sent him with an expedition to Newfoundland. There, he met the Englishman Thomas Dermer, who arranged to bring him back to the American Northeast in the spring of 1619. Tisquantum returned to Patuxet to find his home, two thousand strong when he was captured, devastated by disease and littered with the unburied and bleached bones of his kin. Dermer puts it in spare, bleak terms: "I arrived at my Savage's native Country (finding all dead)." The seat of Wampanoag power had moved west to Sowams, the central Pokanoket town. When they traveled to Noepe (Martha's Vineyard), they were attacked at the orders of the sachem Epenow, who had himself been briefly enslaved by the English. Tisquantum was captured, this time by fellow Wampanoags, and held at Noepe until Epenow turned him over to the Pokanokets, who eventually sent him to live in the fledgling settlement, Plymouth, the English were building on his Patuxet homeland.[13]

Little wonder neither the Wampanoags nor the English could gauge Tisquantum's loyalties, or that he sought protection by practicing what Anna Brickhouse calls "motivated mistranslation." The terms of a treaty Tisquantum had helped facilitate between the Wampanoags and the English in 1621 did not convince Bradford that the Wampanoags were not a credible threat in the spring of 1622, and the terror of the messenger on the shore as he shouted about advancing warriors seemed persuasive enough. Yet the warriors never materialized. Still leery, Bradford directed Hobbamock to send his wife to Pokanoket country to untangle the skein of these claims of imminent attack. She learned there was no truth to any of them. Tisquantum, with the help of a supporting actor, had concocted the fiction of a Wampanoag plot against Plymouth to destabilize their fragile peace with the English, cementing his status as a traitor. Ousamequin wanted him killed for this treachery, and he was never welcome among his kin thereafter. The English granted Tisquantum asylum in Plymouth, not because they trusted him, but because they were united with him in a suspicious attachment to the Wampanoags. And, for his part, Tisquantum's only available allies were two groups that had betrayed and enslaved him. Faith in fidelity was in short supply in this arena, but faith in faithlessness abounded.[14]

Behind this public pageant of American misgiving in Plymouth were private marital dramas whose essential contributions to this atmosphere of rampant distrust must be recognized. For, although historians have mostly ignored or touched lightly upon the marital relationships of these leaders, the marriages, or lack of marriages, among Tisquantum, Hobbamock, and Bradford reflect to an extraordinary degree the tensions, instability, and unknowability that came to typify Native-Anglo relationships in the region. For example, scholars have struggled to account for Tisquantum's marginal position in both Wampanoag and English cultures, given his remarkable language abilities and worldliness and the initial openness of both groups to cooperation. Some have suggested that his marital status made him suspect among Natives and English.[15] He was unmarried or possibly widowed in the Great Dying that desolated Patuxet during his enslavement by the English, and his identity as a single adult man made him anomalous in the region.

The Puritans' distrust of unattached men is famous and features prominently in Bradford's history of Plymouth, beginning with the wariness between saints and seamen on the *Mayflower*—the latter being, understandably, "loath to hazard their lives too desperatly" in service of the Separatist cause. This was the crux of the issue: Puritans saw single men as more likely to be motivated by self-interest than communal aims. (The 1630 showdown between the Pilgrims and the English colonial traders living in nearby Merrymount did nothing to rehabilitate the reputation of unattached men in the area.) When Hobbamock's wife returned from her mission to Pokanoket with evidence of Tisquantum's attempt to foment war between the English and the Wampanoags, Bradford condemned his individualism rather than his morality. "They begane to see that Squanto sought his owne ends," he recalled, "and plaid his owne game, by putting the Indians in fear, and drawing gifts from them to enrich him selfe; making them beleeve he could stir up warr against whom he would, and make peace for whom he would." In his history, Bradford dispatched Tisquantum in a few more sentences summing up the uneasy months before he died in late 1622, which indicate the English tolerated but never trusted him again.[16]

Among the Wampanoags, Tisquantum was suspect even before he bragged, or threatened, that he could command the English to unleash the "plague" of their gunpowder. For them, his individuality read as a kind of infidelity. He was captured with nineteen of his kinsmen but returned to Patuxet alone. The mother of three of these men confronted him and one of Bradford's key advisers, Edward Winslow, "weeping and crying excessively," insisting they recognize that "she was deprived of the comfort of her children in her old age." Her lament, which must have been directed at Tisquantum as he translated for Winslow, suggests the woman was not merely sharing her grief but also accusing Tisquantum of deserting his kin in Málaga. In addition to arousing suspicion of self-dealing, his singleness also hampered his access to legitimate routes of power, since Native leaders commonly gained, expanded, or protected their positions through strategic marriage alliances, which were not necessarily monogamous nor lifelong. Betty Booth Donohue argues that Tisquantum surely knew this, and that he remained unmarried should cause us to doubt Hobbamock's insinuation "that amassing power was Tisquantum's primary concern." It is not certain, however, that he chose to be single until his death in 1622. Neal Salisbury finds it probable that he was married when Hunt kidnapped him. If so, when he returned to find "a literal boneyard" on the site of his Patuxet home, he faced down the brutal fact that neither his marriage nor his extensive kinship network could withstand the ravages of English slavery and disease. He was alone, for reasons beyond his control. He lived for only three years after his return, perhaps unable to make another (or a first) marriage alliance among the "remnant[s]" of his kin stricken with the lingering effects of sickness and grief and forced to find new homes in other Wampanoag towns. English sources paint a portrait of Tisquantum as an opportunistic free agent rather than a man alienated, disempowered, and disoriented by profound tragedy. In the course of a short life, he lost his family, his freedom, and his homeland. We cannot know why Tisquantum was not married when he lived among the English, but we must consider the possibility that his single status was not just a source of intercultural bad faith but also a product of it.[17]

Hobbamock seems to provide the counter in this case, since his large family suggested sociable stability to the English and political power to the Wampanoags, both of which were manifested when his wife resolved a diplomatic crisis and protected the fragile peace recently brokered in the region. But his marriage is a perfect illustration of what is unreliable, slippery, and ultimately unknowable within an intimate alliance. Bradford reports that after Tisquantum's kinsman breathlessly gestured behind him at the phantom of Narragansett and Wampanoag warriors, Hobbamock expressed his confidence that Tisquantum, not Ousamequin, was the faithless actor. Yet "the Gov[erno]r caused him to send his wife privatly, to see what she could observe (preten[d]ing other occasions), but ther was nothing found, but all was quiet." One of Hobbamock's wives, then, was a trusted diplomat in her own right and had an area of expertise that recommended her, not Hobbamock (whose role, after all, was to facilitate communication between Ousamequin and the English), for the mission. Even if the English commanded Hobbamock to send her because they were naive enough to think a woman would be a less conspicuous presence in the sachem's residence, Hobbamock would have disabused them of this notion. Women could be powerful leaders among the Wampanoags, managing affairs that ranged from the ongoing business of planting and land management to wartime strategies. Ousamequin's own daughter-in-law, Weetamoo, would become an expert at the colonial "deed game" and a potent leader during the colonial conflict called King Philip's War. Hobbamock's wife seems to have established her own relationship with the sachem or his councillors, and there must have been something particular about the way she could probe for intelligence without inflaming a volatile situation. That the English took the step of bypassing their usual liaison and engaging his wife instead makes it clear that this was an unusually delicate affair. Furthermore, it makes it clear that in some crucial way, Hobbamock and his wife, while they were allied in a politically influential marriage, were not necessarily aligned.[18]

Far from being a flaw in the marriage, this misalignment might have been a survival tactic in which members of this union sought safety by intentionally creating distance between themselves and their ostensible allies. It was common for married Wampanoag men and women to protect themselves and advance their individual interests by conducting their own business and staking out their own positions relative to kinsmen and foreigners, but this practice was especially prudent given the vulnerable position Hobbamock and his wives inhabited. They occupied a diplomatic post that removed them from their Pokanoket kin and exposed them to every conflict, real and imagined, that arose between the Wampanoags and their jittery English allies. When they most needed the support of a kinship network, normally the greatest affordance of an Indigenous marriage, they were isolated and exposed. We can see even in an incomplete historical record how this arrangement stressed the relationship between Hobbamock and his wife as each grasped toward security in circumstances of utter novelty and unpredictability. In these circumstances, she—apparently more than he—developed the ability to protect herself via stratagem. Both Bradford and Winslow use a specific phrase to describe the essence of the mission: she will go to Ousamequin's residence "pretending other occasions." Simply put, this is an act of espionage, and Hobbamock's wife preserves peace at a decisive moment in Wampanoag-English relations because she successfully deceives. Although Donohue argues that Hobbamock's "several wives and extended family" constituted "a stable matriarchal power base" that gave him enduring credibility in the eyes of the English, it is telling that this household owed its stability not to a foundation of trust but to a protective net of shared suspicion.[19]

We get a sense of the ways Hobbamock's wife apprehended and managed risks as we consider the removes at which she kept potential threats to her own and her extended family's well-being. Each of these removes shows a careful balance between faith and suspicion, with her suspicion providing a critical tether for occasional flights of faith. To begin, we see the deliberate distance this diplomat established between herself and the English in Plymouth. The English engaged with Native women leaders and the wives of male leaders directly, as Winslow indicated when he described visiting the Pocasset town of Mattapoisett with Hobbamock in 1623 and, finding the sachem, Corbitant, away, enjoying "friendly entertainment" and even diplomatic aid from his wife, the saunkswka. Given that the English were willing to communicate with women diplomats, it is probable they "caused" Hobbamock to send his wife to visit Ousamequin because she refused to engage directly with them. The English did not have enough faith in her husband to trust his strong intuition that Ousamequin remained loyal to Plymouth unless she verified it, so perhaps she reciprocated their faithlessness. Yet she also kept Ousamequin and her kin in Pokanoket at a remove, pretending other reasons for her visit rather than revealing to them the reality of English misgivings. Had her geographic remove from her kin tilted her allegiance, ever so slightly, toward her Plymouth neighbors? Or did she doubt Wampanoag restraint, given the demonstrated faithlessness of the English? Was she seeking to protect the Wampanoags with this stratagem or the English—or both? Was it possible to remain faithful to her kin while advancing the interests of their unreliable allies? Implicitly, she asked those in Pokanoket to trust the loyalty that lay beneath her calculated lie to them. Future generations of Wampanoags, as they fended off full-blown assaults on Native lands and lives, had reason to wonder if these peacemaking diplomats had served Native interests or unwittingly betrayed them. Indeed, the rivalries between pro-English and anti-English Natives became as heated as hostilities between Native coalitions and English armies during King Philip's War, a fault line presaged in this moment of early Native-Anglo diplomacy and complicated because some Native people shifted their allegiances as geopolitical conditions deteriorated.[20]

These fluid loyalties were a wedge between tribes as well as individual warriors, but what about those bonded in marriage? Suspicion was the source of the 1622 diplomatic crisis in Plymouth as well as its solution and its legacy—and must have worked its influence on this Pokanoket diplomat's relationship to her husband, as well. Either Hobbamock's willingness to relay the English command to her signals his endorsement of this mission, in which case he and his wife were united in agreement that "pretending other occasions" was the best way to relate to their kin, or he relayed the command but doubted the strategy (which possibly explains why his wife, and not he, was the agent of this subterfuge among the Wampanoags). In either case, it is a fact that suspicion was a part of this partnership; what we must imagine is how their suspicion oriented them toward each other and toward their vexed environment. Hobbamock's wife engaged in duplicity, even if she did not embrace it, and her husband had strong faith in the faithlessness of Tisquantum and proof of the faithlessness of the English, who would not take his word that they should be more suspicious of a pretended friend at home than a potential threat abroad. He sought safety in caution and possibly even, like his wife, in pretense. He introduced himself to the English as Hobbamock—"the Indian 'bogeyman' and the equal of the European 'devil,'" as Nipmuc medicine man and author Kitt Little Turtle writes. "Sometimes called 'Cheepie,' this malevolent phantom is a source of pain, sickness, and emotional distress. He frequently materializes in various grotesque apparitions, including impersonations of departed loved ones—or enemies." A strange name for a high-ranking Wampanoag Council member. Unless, of course, he assumed it as an ambassador to make a point to his Wampanoag kin—the only ones who would appreciate the resonances of his name—that loved ones and enemies are equally likely to be devils in disguise.[21]

And what must the Wampanoag ambassadors have made of the vanished wife of the English governor? William Bradford, like Tisquantum, was a single man in 1622, and not even his friends in Plymouth could fathom the crisis that left him widowed. The historical record preserves only the bare facts of the tragedy: On December 17, 1620, Dorothy May Bradford drowned in the waters off the coast of Cape Cod, where the *Mayflower* was anchored. Her husband recorded a single phrase about the death within his own biographical entry in *Of Plymouth Plantation*, which he wrote thirty years after the incident: "William Bradford his wife dyed soone after their arivall; and he maried againe; and hath 4 children, 3 wherof are maried." Upon this slender nail generations of historians tried to hang an explanatory narrative, beginning in 1702 when Cotton Mather wrote in *Magnalia Christi Americana*, "At their first Landing, his dearest Consort accidentally falling Overboard, was drowned in the *Harbour*." Mather's assertion of new details—*dearest consort accidentally*—only pointed future storytellers toward the seamy allegations—*betrayed wife deliberately*—they imagined lurking behind them. Rumors of William's infidelity reached full bloom in *Mayflower* descendent Jane Goodwin Austin's short story "William Bradford's Love Life" (1869) in *Harper's New Monthly Magazine*, which supposes William's infatuation with Alice Carpenter Southworth (whom he married in 1623) before and during his marriage to Dorothy drove his neglected wife over the side of the ship. In case this was not propulsion enough, the story also imagines Dorothy sodden with grief and guilt over the toddler son, John, she left in Holland, and whom she loves better than her husband. Austin first claimed, and then denied, that she based her fiction on some "precious letters" between William and Alice and "a few leaves" of Dorothy's diary that had fallen into her possession. More restrained historians cleared their throats and redirected their suspicion from Dorothy's empty bed to her fragile head. Samuel Eliot Morison led in 1930 with officious concern for the abandoned William: "It may be that he suspected (as do we) that Dorothy Bradford took her own life, after gazing for six weeks at the barren sand dunes of Cape Cod." Morison had enough of a following that Francis

Murphy wrote in 1980: "Bradford's wife, Dorothy, 'fell overboard' from the *Mayflower* six weeks after they anchored, but most historians do not think it was an accident; she probably preferred to take her own life rather than face the certain rigors of the future." Even now, historians rarely mention Dorothy's death without at least glancing at the possibility she died by suicide. Intrigued readers, because they have nowhere else to go, seek Dorothy's inner life in the writings of her Puritan contemporaries, particularly her prolific husband. But they find much of others' psyches and none of hers, and only a fabulist would transform a man's journal into his dead wife's biography. As Stacey Dearing points out, even cautious efforts to recover the impetus of Dorothy's death reveal more about the minds and lives of readers than the unknowable circumstances that ended the Bradford marriage.[22]

But because we cannot responsibly infer why Dorothy died, it does not follow that we must draw a respectful curtain over the Bradford marriage. We know certain things of consequence. We know the marriage ended abruptly, while both partners were still relatively young. We know Dorothy and William had seen relatively young people die around them, including a seaman on the *Mayflower* stricken "with a greeveous disease, of which he dyed in a desperate maner." We know Dorothy was among the first Separatist settlers to die, but her death was immediately followed by a wave of others. In its first six months, Plymouth had a mortality rate of 50 percent, which reduced the number of intact married couples from eighteen to three. Although Dorothy's death has been an object of fascination in histories and fictions of colonial America, it did not necessarily have special status for the first inhabitants of Plymouth. We know that William Bradford left an atypical pause between his first and second marriages. He married Alice Southworth on August 14, 1623, nearly three years after Dorothy's death. (Bradford's counterpart in the Massachusetts Bay Colony, Governor John Winthrop, remarried sometimes months but never more than two years after the deaths of his first three wives.) These years between William's marriages, 1620–1623, represent a period of profound suffering for English setters in the Northeast. They also, as the story of the nearly aborted trading visit with the Massachusetts makes clear, represent a period of general suspicion and unease. And, finally, we know that when he looked back across three decades to write his history of the Plymouth settlement, William Bradford left his wife's death in the background, a fragment appended to the history proper.[23]

Readers and writers have tried to make Dorothy's death meaningful by shifting it from the background to the foreground of historical narrative, but if we hold Dorothy's death where William left it, we grant her suffering exactly the meaning it held for those in and around Patuxet—not as an isolated event, but as part of an omnipresent mood. Dorothy's tragedy manifests in her husband's history not as death but as dread, signaled by a constant sense of foreboding and hypervigilance that floats free of any single incident. In her study of the crises of New England settlement, Kathleen Donegan invokes the philosopher Alain Badiou to discuss and stress the significance of the event as a rupture in the normal state of affairs, "a break with previously known forms," that shocks existing systems of meaning-making and reveals their inadequacy.[24] Dorothy's death was in this sense an event because it suddenly revealed the precarity of the Separatists' claim on their promised land (if the faithful could hazard everything to reach it and still fail to set foot on it) and alerted historians to a prominent outlier that troubles the mythic narrative of Pilgrims' fortitude and perseverance. But the suffering that preceded, accompanied, and followed her death was not an event. It was not a rupture in the normal state of affairs; it was an elemental component of it. It cannot be brought to the forefront of thought and rationalized as an episode of betrayal trauma, mental illness, feminine weakness, or anything else without inventing events or interpolating emotions that do not exist in the historical record. If it seems Bradford omitted Dorothy's suffering in his history of Plymouth, it is only because readers search for it at the level of lexicon, when it actually manifests as ambiance. Here, Rita Felski's discussion of the way mood "bridges the gap between thought and feeling" and "accompanies and modulates thought" is particularly illuminating:

> Moods are often ambient, diffuse, and hazy, part of the background rather than the foreground of thought. In contrast to the suddenness and intensity of the passions, they are characterized by a degree of stability: a mood can be pervasive, lingering, slow to change. It "sets the tone" for our engagement with the world, causing it to appear before us in a given light. Mood, in this sense, is a prerequisite for any form of interaction or engagement; there is, Heidegger insists, no moodless or mood-free apprehension of phenomena. Mood . . . is what allows certain things to matter to us and to matter in specific ways.

As an event, Dorothy's death required little in the way of material or representational responses; the body buried itself, and a single phrase in *Of Plymouth Plantation* serves as cenotaph. But the mood enveloping her death slips into unexpected interstices of the narrative, tingeing other incidents, oddly, with not just the language but also the emotional notes of uneasy intimate alliances. Accommodation, suspicion, and sudden betrayals of greater and lesser degrees were fixtures in the backdrop of marriages forged in the crucible of early modern contact and settlement, and set the tone, as Felski puts it, for these engagements. Without knowing any more about the Bradford marriage than the facts I related above, we can see it involved two people steeped in suffering who did not need to doubt the fidelity of their spouses to have perfect faith in the unreliability of the marriage itself. It would fail before both of them were finished with it, a precondition they understood when they took their vows, and a proposition they accepted anyway. When William Bradford came back to the *Mayflower* to find his marriage abruptly ended, it was not the culmination but rather another manifestation of a tragedy that surrounded and survived those who sought safety in relationships but died alone in the lands and waters of Patuxet country.[25]

Reading Bradford's history at the level of tone allows us to keep intimate interpersonal experiences on the same plane as larger cultural engagements by dint of the mutually reinforcing moods of suspicion and suffering framing both. Days before Dorothy slipped beneath the icy water, William joined fifteen men to form a scouting party that would "discovere those nearest places" to the shore. The stance of these discoverers was not neutral. They expected to find conflict, and in arming themselves heavily they made conflict more likely. Yet, in the moment of contact, they were oddly conflicted within themselves, following five or six Natives "partly to see if they could speake with them, and partly to discover if ther might not be more of them lying in ambush." Thereafter, every interaction between the English and the Wampanoags modulated between these keys of desire and distrust. Early hostility gave way to strategic overtures. Both parties understood the necessity of a relationship, even if they feared the entanglements it invited. Expecting as much as fearing a cooling of affections, the parties sought to formalize their bond with a compact in March 1621—agreed upon, witnessed, and recorded. That fragile peace was renegotiated in September with a new treaty that preserved the alliance despite favoring the English and thus exaggerating a power imbalance between the yoked parties. Yet it was the English, more than the disfavored Wampanoags, who feared they were being betrayed in the diplomatic crisis of March 1622, even in the face of repeated evidence of Wampanoag fidelity. When Tisquantum's relative ran toward the coast carrying his tale of impending attack, the English feared the treaty had failed. But the truth of his tale was easy to test given that he represented violence as imminent. Hobbamock doubted; the rest waited; and no attackers appeared. Still, the English were not satisfied and dispatched Hobbamock's wife to discover whether the Wampanoags secretly schemed against them. Their question, it is clear, contained an implicit adverb: *Have you betrayed us—yet?* The faithlessness behind the question, as much as any Wampanoag aggression, eventually bankrupted the relationship. When their alliance with the Wampanoags finally dissolved, giving way to the enmity that preceded King Philip's War, the English must have felt confirmed, if not comforted, in the suspicions that prompted them to heavily arm themselves before they set out to discover the Wampanoag homeland. Corbitant pressed Plymouth's leaders to acknowledge that the treachery they saw in their relationships with the Natives was the uncanny reflection of their own faithlessness. "If your love be such, and it bring forth such fruits," he asked Winslow, "how cometh it to pass, that when we come to Patuxet, you stand upon your guard, with the mouths of your pieces presented towards us?" Bradford remarked on the "jealocie" between Hobbamock and Tisquantum and claimed the English finally learned to exploit the rivalry between the ambassadors, "by which they had better intelligence, and made them both more diligent." But he offers no examples of the intelligence or diligence thus obtained. Readers must accept Bradford's reasoning, which might have only been his hope, that a surfeit of distrust and competition should produce some tactical advantages, however difficult they may be to quantify, or even name.[26]

As the crisis of March 1622 unfolded, Hobbamock and Tisquantum knew Bradford's wife had died, and they might have been just as alert to the fact that he was waiting to remarry. Did the English governor have reason to question, after the first months of settlement culled half the Plymouth population, whether he wished to risk another attachment that might end just as abruptly as the first? Did he doubt, when unburied bodies littered the ground around the stricken settlers, the odds of his own survival? Did he wonder, as he returned to the anchored *Mayflower* and heard his wife was drowned, *What terrible thing has happened?* Future historians imagined he must have, and they find his disinclination to answer this question for his readers odd, possibly ominous. But if one attends to his history's tone of sustained, self-confirming dread, rather than to particular events, it becomes apparent Dorothy's death required no explanation. By the time Bradford was writing his story of Patuxet's resettlement, Dorothy's death had been utterly eclipsed by the cascade of death of which it was, at most, a portent. From its resting place as a biographical detail in an appendix to the history, it poses no challenge to the written narrative's persistent premonition that interpersonal relationships were always on the verge of giving out, for one reason or another. One suspects the news of Dorothy's tragedy struck William as a revelation more than a shock. *Finally, the Terrible Thing has happened.* It is difficult to resist the errant speculation that at some point, whether she died by accident or suicide, the same thought crossed Dorothy's mind.[27]

Hayden White argues that historians give events structure and significance by emplotting them, as one would a novel or a play, in a certain way. "Providing the 'meaning' of a story by identifying the *kind of story* that has been told is called explanation by emplotment," he says. "If, in the course of narrating his story, the historian provides it with the plot structure of a Tragedy, he has 'explained' it in one way; if he has structured it as a Comedy, he has 'explained' it in another way. Emplotment is the way by which a sequence of events fashioned into a story is gradually revealed to be a story of a particular kind." These marriages in Patuxet, which change emotional registers frequently and abruptly, present a challenge to historians seeking their meaning. Are they Romances? Tragedies? As White puts it, "The Romance is fundamentally a drama of self-identification symbolized by the hero's transcendence of the world of experience, his victory over it, and his final liberation from it. . . . It is a drama of the triumph of good over evil, of virtue over vice, of light over darkness, and of the ultimate transcendence of man over the world in which he was imprisoned by the Fall." Nineteenth-century historians tended to emplot the story of Plymouth in this mode, as a story in which the English settlers (and particularly their heroic male leaders) slowly but steadily triumphed over their environment, their political adversaries, and their personal afflictions to establish the footprint of an independent nation. As these historians interpreted *Of Plymouth Plantation*, Bradford himself emplotted the story this way, glossing periods of starving and sickness that threatened the settlement during the first winters, stressing gestures of good will on the part of the English as they negotiated with the Natives, and sublimating stories of abject loss like Dorothy's to stories of English protection, preservation, and dominance. But this emplotment is guided by a sequence of events, without accounting for a tone in the history that touches encounters of all kinds—for example, between passengers and a coastline, a scouting party and a half-dozen retreating Natives, or husbands and wives—with notes of suspicion and anxiety. If one emplots the story of Plymouth based on mood, it is unquestionably a tragedy. Unlike comedy, which "eventuates in a vision of the ultimate *reconciliation* of opposed forces," according to White, tragedy ends with "a *revelation* of the nature of the forces opposing man." Furthermore, he proposes, tragedy is a mode of emplotment "consonant with the interest of those historians who perceive behind or within the

welter of events contained in the chronicle an ongoing structure of relationships or an eternal return of the Same in the Different."

[We] arrived at my Savage's native Country (finding all dead).

William Bradford his wife dyed soone after their arivall; and he maried againe . . .

A most treacherous and hideous being, Hobbamock lurks in the night-time shadows. . . .
    Sometimes called "Cheepie," this malevolent phantom is a source of pain, sick-
ness, and emotional distress. He frequently materializes in various grotesque apparitions, including impersonations of departed loved ones—or enemies.

The tragedy of betrayal did not occur in the early American Northeast as much
as it hung in the air, occasionally materializing in various grotesque apparitions. When intimate partners faced distrust, disappointment, or devastation
in their relationships, they saw in fresh light something they already knew.[28]

"WITHOUT HER HUSBAND"

Although it is necessary to draw out and to some degree speculate about
implicit associations between the public dealings of prominent figures in
Patuxet and some ineffable but perceivable qualities in their marriages, in the
Massachusetts Bay Colony several years later such an association was made
explicit. There, controversies that ranged across matters of military, law, politics, church membership, and colonial governance could be traced, in some
leaders' eyes, to the unusual marriage between Anne Hutchinson and her
husband William. While this can only be characterized as an example of suspicion run amok, with mild alarm at Anne's propensity to conduct her affairs
beyond the oversight of her husband giving way to wild allegations of a monstrous bastard child she conceived with her chief political sympathizer, they
reveal that Puritans were immensely sensitive to the slightest suggestion of
marital discord or deviance. Later, when animosity between New Englanders
and the Native inhabitants they displaced erupted into war in the 1670s, some
Native couples entangled in domestic relationships with Puritans noticed
this sensitivity and added it to the arsenal of diplomatic and military weapons
they used to protect their own marriages and families from the twin threats of
English faith in their Christian God and faithlessness in those around them.

By 1636, almost every public issue in the Massachusetts Bay Colony revealed deep fault lines in popular opinion, trust, and cooperation. The English assault against the Pequot led by Captain John Endicott found mixed support, with some stout men openly denying their bodies to the cause. Three leaders—Thomas Dudley, John Haynes, and Henry Vane—had rapidly cycled through the governorship, and John Winthrop was eager to reclaim the office he lost in 1634 and that was now ill-filled, in his view, by Vane. Church membership had declined, for the first time since the colony's founding, as detractors of the Reverend John Wilson nominated another minister, John Wheelwright, to effectively replace him at the First Church of Boston. Historians have synthesized these branches of discontent as outgrowths of a single theological controversy between so-called legalists (represented most visibly by Wilson and Winthrop) and a group of "antinomians" or, more commonly in the words of their antagonists, "familists" (with whom Anne Hutchinson was associated), who disputed the significance of religious works given the all-encompassing affordances of grace.[29] However, most historians trace the schisms that surrounded Hutchinson only so far, assuming that a woman who broke ranks with erstwhile admirers, mentors, and allies in church and government moved in lockstep, to the end, with her devoted husband.[30]

The evidence in support of this view of the Hutchinsons as an irreducible fraction that resisted the multiple divisions of the Antinomian Controversy is spare but sturdy. Both natives of Alford, Lincolnshire, they married in London in 1612 and immigrated to the Massachusetts Bay Colony together in 1634. Within two months, they were both admitted to the Boston Church. They established a prominent household, and each rose to positions of influence in Boston—she as a midwife and spiritual adviser and he as a merchant and a deputy to the Massachusetts General Court, a position to which he was elected shortly after their arrival in 1634. By 1636, however, Anne's practice of hosting women and sometimes men to discuss sermons and church doctrine in their home drew interest and then alarm from political and religious leaders. The same year, William was dismissed as a deputy. He was not a controversial figure in his own right (John Winthrop, the most vocal of Anne's critics, called him "a very honest and peaceable man of good estate"), so historians assume it was his association with his wife that made him a political target as her conventicles and open scorn for the teachings of legalists attracted more attention. She famously faced both court and church officials in trials that resulted in her exile from the colony and excommunication. Although he did not face formal discipline, William left Boston with his wife and formed the settlement of Pocasset (later renamed Portsmouth) with others who sympathized with and supported her. In 1639, he told three messengers dispatched from the church in Boston to commune with the "wandringe sheepe" in Portsmouth that "he was more nearly tied to his wife than to the church, he thought her to be a dear saint and servant of god." He died two years later.[31]

Even in the face of this persuasive evidence of harmony and consensus that persisted throughout the Hutchinson marriage, their own close contemporaries suspected something was amiss in the relationship and that this blight had metastasized to infect the body politic. If William bore any responsibility for the problems in this marriage, it was that he was constitutionally, in Winthrop's view, "a man of very mild temper and weak parts, and wholly guided by his wife." Anne seemed to exploit this gentleness. Winthrop, who held the position of governor again by the time she was examined by the General Court in November 1637, noticed that Anne interrupted the apostle Paul when she invoked him to justify the gatherings in her home. Hutchinson reasoned that "there lyes a clear rule in Titus, that the elder women should instruct the younger." Winthrop was familiar with the passage of scripture and pointed out the prescribed object of the teaching, which Anne had elided: "But you must take it in this sense that elder women must instruct the younger about their business, and to love their husbands and not to make them to clash." In fact, Winthrop was hazarding an interpretation of his own. The verses in Titus read, "The elder women likewise, that they be in such behavior as becometh holiness, not false accusers, not subject to much wine, but teachers of honest things, that they may instruct the young women to be sober minded, that they love their husbands, that they love their children, That they be discreet, chaste, keeping at home, good and subject unto their husbands, that the word of God be not evil spoken of." Anne was leaving something out, but Winthrop was adding something to holy writ. The "clash" between spouses that women's sobriety and temperance may somehow forestall is his interpolation. It was a bold vision on the part of this embattled governor to imagine that clashes between armies, political parties, religious groups, and private citizens were rooted in squabbles between couples and that if only harmony could reign at home, peace could prevail in public. And this vision framed the examination, which was premised on the notion Anne was "the head of all this faction" precisely because she had become the head of her home. The Reverend Hugh Peters put it bluntly at her church trial in early 1638: "You have stept out of your place, you have rather bine a Husband than a Wife." Some entertained the possibility that Anne stepped out on William in other ways. Writing after Anne's banishment, Winthrop was appalled to recall how she and others of her ilk "laboured much to acquaint themselves with as many, as possibly they could" and then "would strangely labour to insinuate themselves into their affections, by loving salutes, humble carriage, kind invitements, friendly visits, and so they would winne upon men, and steale into their bosomes before they were aware." To her face, he accused her of trying "to seduce many honest persons" and "simple souls." Some went so far as to speculate that this seduction was physical as well as philosophical. After Anne delivered a mass of placental tissue and her supporter Mary Dyer had delivered a stillborn baby, a lurid report emerged and circulated to London, where one politician reported hearing it: "Sir Henry Vane in 1637 went over as Governor to N. England with 2 women, Mrs Dier and Mrs Hutchinson, . . . where he debauched both, and both were delivered of monsters."[32]

At the root of these bizarre allegations is a fact that merits our attention: unlike some readers of their history, people living in early New England did not assume married people were unified in feeling, thought, or conduct. They were disinclined to interpret the absence of controversy as proof positive of harmony. Historians generally take the opposite tack, assuming an unspoken alliance between married couples unless there is clear evidence to the contrary. The story of early American kinship is centered around dynasties—the Mathers, the Winthrops, the Dudleys, the Bradstreets, and so on—that are perceived to be riven lineally but rarely laterally. That is, historical analyses that follow Perry Miller's in finding divergences between parents and children that gradually tempered and transformed Puritan thought generally assume consensus between husbands and wives. Puritans themselves were much more open to the possibility that opinion, doctrine, and practice were being challenged within intimate relationships at least as much as they were challenged in the process of generational transmission. Historians sometimes use the term "Hutchinsonians" to describe those associated with an antinomian movement in seventeenth-century Boston, but Thomas Weld and John Winthrop preferred the terms "converts" or "followers." The designation "Hutchinson" was already too broad to encompass the diverse positions—physically, if not philosophically—of the single couple who shared that name. When Anne tried to compare herself to one half of the biblical couple Priscilla and Aquila, companions of the apostle Paul in his ministry to new converts, Winthrop balked. "See how your argument stands, *Priscilla* with her husband, tooke *Apollo* home to instruct him privately, therefore Mistris Hutchison without her husband may teach sixty or eighty." In 1962, Emery Battis proposed that Anne was one of those women in history "who have been tormented by fixed ideas and hysterical manifestations because their husbands have failed to guide their mental life." Battis speculated that "William Hutchinson seems to have lacked the power to provide adequate support and direction for his wife," forcing Anne to turn to John Cotton, Henry Vane, and God himself for this guiding authority. When this kind of speculative analysis fell out of fashion, scholars tempered their arguments about the marriage, inferring only that William's wealth influenced Anne's social status and likely explains what occupied his time while she was engaged in her own dealings. But economic and cultural historians are not necessarily closer than psychoanalytic critics to the concerns of early Bostonians, since for them William's absence from so much of his wife's business, whatever the reason, constituted a controversy in itself.[33]

Puritans were not alone in puzzling over the spectacle of women without their husbands or married men without their wives and wondering what it portended for the larger social structure. The Pocasset Wampanoag saunksqua Weetamoo and her Narragansett husband Quinnapin, who held Mary Rowlandson during her captivity in 1676, were not responsible for separating Rowlandson from her husband, Joseph, and they found the Rowlandsons' separation increasingly suggestive. Abram Van Engen argues that "the heart-tugging tragedy of familial separation" serves as "the central motif" of Rowlandson's bestselling captivity narrative and that her removals from her family—"and *especially* from her children"—structure the story. But Puritans, unlike the sentimental authors Van Engen sees Rowlandson anticipating, considered the relationship of parents to children secondary to the relationship between husband and wife (as William Gouge reasons, "*Adam* and *Eve* were joyned in mariage, and made man and wife before they had children"), and this foundational unit of the Rowlandson family is divided before they are attacked. Rowlandson's removals from her children may constitute, as Van Engen argues, the "motor of this text," but the removal that happens offstage, just before the drama begins, haunts the tragedy she rehearses.[34]

At the time of the Native raid on Lancaster in February 1676, Mary was with her family and neighbors in her home, which had been designated a "garrison house" in which people could gather in the likely event of escalating hostility between Nipmuc, Wampanoag, and Narragansett warriors and residents of exposed English towns. Joseph was away at Boston. There was nothing unusual in this; English men frequently left their wives in remote settlements as they traveled to centers of political and commercial activity. But Mary registered Joseph's absence from Lancaster on the morning she was taken as a source of particular affliction, and as her captivity stretched on and Joseph did not come to rescue her, Weetamoo and Quinnapin perceived that

A
NARRATIVE
OF THE
CAPTIVITY, SUFFERINGS and REMOVES
OF
Mrs. *Mary Rowlandſon,*

Who was taken Priſoner by the INDIANS with ſeveral others,
and treated in the moſt barbarous and cruel Manner by thoſe
vile Savages : With many other remarkable Events during her
TRAVELS.

Written by her own Hand, for her private Uſe, ar
public at the earneſt Deſire of ſome Friends, -
neſit of the afflicted.

BOSTO.

Printed and Sold at JOHN BOYLE's Print
to the *Three Doves* in Marlborough

Figure 9. Title page of A Narrative of the Captivity, Sufferings and Removes of Mrs. Mary
Rowlandson . . . (Boston, 1773). Courtesy of the John Carter Brown Library

she sensed his absence as a kind of abandonment, even betrayal, rather than an unfortunate necessity. Both the Native and the English couple were united in marriages that were supposed to provide forms of protection and prosperity. Because Indigenous marriages were adaptable alliances forged and restructured in times of crisis rather than monogamous lifelong commitments made in times of relative calm, Weetamoo and Quinnapin's relationship delivered on this promise at precisely the moment the Rowlandsons' failed them.[35]

Both marriages were made in conditions of flux and with an eye toward what the alliances could provide materially as well as socially. Weetamoo married "at least four men," and, according to Lisa Brooks, her "multiple marriages over the course of a lifetime would not have been seen as out of the ordinary." Indigenous marriages linked kin as well as individuals, and leaders like Weetamoo renegotiated these alliances in response to new threats. As tensions between Natives and English came to a head, she left her third husband and married Quinnapin, a powerful Narragansett sachem and military leader, who already had two wives. The marriage solidified an alliance between the Wampanoags and the Narragansetts and dramatically strengthened their resistance to the English. Early in the war, the warriors they commanded mounted a formidable, even devastating, challenge to English aggression in the region. Taking advantage of an extensive network of supporters who contributed provisions and fighters to the cause, the Wampanoag-Narragansett alliance, together with the Nipmucs who bordered English towns including Lancaster, crippled English power with a series of ambushes and surprise attacks from the fall of 1675 to the late winter of 1676. The twenty "removes" Rowlandson recounts in her captivity narrative were not random wanderings; they were strategic relocations to gatherings of kin located throughout the Connecticut River valley. Weetamoo and Quinnapin's marriage ensured they were never far from family willing—and, by the demands of their marriage bond, obligated—to provide vital aid.[36]

Although the Rowlandson alliance was inspired less by political than socioeconomic logic, it was strategic nonetheless. Before their marriage, Mary White and Joseph Rowlandson were recent arrivals in Lancaster. Mary's father had amassed substantial landholdings and investments in Wenham and came to Lancaster in pursuit of more land and property. Joseph Rowlandson was from an impoverished, scandal-ridden family based in Ipswich, headed by a father frequently summoned to court for various financial delinquencies. As Neal Salisbury puts it, "While the Whites were pillars of the community in Wenham, the Rowlandsons were near the bottom of Ipswich society in wealth, social status, and reputation." Determined to improve his status, Joseph graduated from Harvard College in 1652 and moved to Lancaster to become the town's first minister, bringing his indigent parents with him. Mary White's mother was active in church and likely favored a match between her daughter and the minister, which would make her daughter the only mistress (rather than goodwife) in town, and the Rowlandsons had even more to gain through the marriage of Joseph and Mary, which was solemnized around 1656. Once allied with the Whites in Lancaster, and availing himself of their financial resources, Joseph Rowlandson set about accruing his own sizable landholdings.[37]

At the time of the attack on Lancaster in February 1676, Joseph was trying to wield his influence in Boston, seeking troops to protect the town from Native assaults. Although troops arrived shortly after the raid, it was two Nipmuc spies, James Quanapohit and Job Kattananit, not Joseph, who had alerted English settlers nearby of the planned attack and persuaded them to send aid. Joseph remained in Boston where, after failing to protect his family, he turned to the intractable task of redeeming them. There, too, he would have failed if not for the interventions of two pro-English Nipmucs. His daughter died and his wife and children languished in captivity for three months before Nepanet (otherwise known as Tom Dublet) and Tatatiqunea (Peter Conway) opened successful negotiations for the English captives' release.[38]

Historians are uniformly satisfied with the sincerity, if not the efficacy, of Joseph Rowlandson's efforts to protect and reclaim his wife, which are various and well documented, including petitions to officials in Boston and pleas to Christian Natives. But Mary, even when she looked back on her experience to compose her narrative, had difficulty accounting for his absence throughout her ordeal. Instead, the facts of his failure—to procure the protection for Lancaster that prompted his trip to Boston, to shorten her time in captivity, or to personally effect her redemption—loom large. His absence might have been common and unavoidable, but it was remarkable for her. The first night of her captivity, as she took inventory of her griefs, the ambiguous absence of her husband ranked first among them. "All was gone, my Husband gone (at least separated from me, he being in the Bay [Boston]; and to add to my grief, the Indians told me they would kill him as he came homeward) my Children gone, my Relations and Friends gone, our House and home and all our comforts within door, and without, all was gone, (except my life) and I knew not but the next moment that might go too." In a moment of relative clarity, Rowlandson makes what Mitchell Robert Breitwieser calls the "first leap from astonishment to explicability." She attempts to make sense of a world-shattering crisis by naming what she has lost—children, relations, friends, house and home, comforts within doors and without—and to come to terms with the tragedy by emphatically pronouncing them *gone*. But she stumbles to come to terms with the loss she considers primary. Her husband is *gone*, she begins to explain, but then she catches and corrects herself; he is not gone, but only "separated" from her, "being in the Bay." The distinction is not meaningful. So, rather than holding her husband in a special category of things that are gone but still exist, she quickly folds her separated husband into the jumble of things she has permanently lost by anticipating his inevitable death. He might as well be gone. But this perfunctory treatment of his absence creates problems because his being and then *remaining* in the Bay complicates her ability to grieve him, or even make sense of his relationship to her. As Breitwieser argues, "The havoc does not conclude with things being laid to rest, instead they are prompted into grotesque and unprecedented motions, motions akin to the unrest that still uncoils itself within Rowlandson as she writes." Joseph is a recurring absence in the narrative, never dying en route to Lancaster but never appearing to rescue her either. When she has contact with people outside Weetamoo's family, she repeatedly asks after her husband. Nepanet and Tatatiqunea respond that he is *"well, but melancholy."* Shortly after, she says, "I durst not send to my Husband, though there were some thoughts of his coming to Redeem and fetch me," as if his absence could be explained by her failing to summon him, and as if the thought of his coming belongs to someone besides herself. As the *Narrative* unspools, it is evident that Joseph's "being in the Bay" is a loss more confounding to Mary, more utterly resistant to explanation, than his death.[39]

Weetamoo and Quinnapin must have sensed this because they and members of their family introduce strained explanations of their own that sought to convince Mary that, one way or another, she had survived to see the death of her marriage. "Some of them told me, he was dead, and they had killed him: some said he was Married again, and that the Governour wished him to marry; and told him he should have his choice, and that all perswaded I was dead." Their purpose, Breitwieser contends, might have been "to disconnect her from her past and reconcile her to the captivity, rather than, as she believes, to indulge cruel humor." But they might also have been probing for openings in their enemy's front line. They understood marriage bonds primarily as tactical relationships that protected families in conditions of crisis such as this and might have hoped Joseph's impotence in the matter of redeeming his wife signaled systemic disfunctions among the English that

Figure 10. Woodcut of the captive Mary Rowlandson with Tom and Peter. From *A Narrative of the Captivity Sufferings and Removes of Mrs. Mary Rowlandson, Who Was Taken Prisoner by the Indians . . . Written by Her Own Hand . . .* (Boston, 1771), 4. Courtesy of the Edward E. Ayer Digital Collection, The Newberry Library

would hamper their ability to sustain a united military effort. From the other side, the English had precisely the same question about what the Rowlandsons' division suggested about the potency of their enemy. The author of the first preface to Rowlandson's printed *Narrative* (probably Increase Mather) dismissed the "coy phantasies" readers might indulge about Rowlandson's time in captivity, which she addressed when she vouched, in a rare tribute to the character and restraint of her captors, that *"not one of them ever offered me the least abuse of unchastity to me, in word or action."* Although the war devastated Wampanoag sovereignty, it was deeply unsettling to the English, too, and we see in these insinuations evidence that some English wondered whether the vanquished Wampanoag, Narragansett, and Nipmuc warriors were powerful enough to have inflicted lasting violations on the English who tried but failed to eradicate Native presence in the North American space they seized.[40]

As negotiations for the captives' release progressed under the influence of Nepanet, the sachems who were communicating with the English instructed Rowlandson to set the price for her redemption. As she recalled, "The *Saggamores* met to consult about the Captives, and called me to them to enquire how much my husband would give to redeem me. . . . They bid me speak what I thought he would give." The question is pointed. They are not asking her to estimate her value; they are asking her to imagine how her husband estimates it. The question, she said, put her "in a great strait," and she frets over the calculus. After some internal deliberation, she arrives at a figure neither too low to hinder her redemption nor too high for her husband to meet—twenty pounds. Joseph Rowlandson indirectly (this time through the Concord lawyer John Hoar) offered the sum, and Mary was redeemed. In fact, Joseph thought his wife was worth much more than the price she named. He accepted an offer to become the minister at Wethersfield, Connecticut, in the spring of 1677. Of the career promotion, Salisbury writes, "Capitalizing on Mary's fame, he was able to command a starting annual salary of one hundred pounds with annual twenty-pound increments over the ensuing five years, making him one of the highest paid clergymen in New England." The sachems asked Rowlandson's companion in captivity, her Lancaster neighbor Elizabeth Kettle, the same question they put to Mary, but Elizabeth and John Kettle did not share the Rowlandsons' keen appraisal of the value they each brought to the marriage. The Harvard-educated Nipmuc scholar and community leader Wowaus (James Printer) wrote on behalf of the Nipmuc sachems to the "Governor and the Council at Boston": "Whereupon we ask Mrs. Rolanson how much your husband willing to give for you she gave an answer 20 pounds in goodes but John Kittels wife could not tell." Wowaus and the Native leaders for whom he wrote might have been trying to judge how English stores held up, given their own dangerously dwindling provisions, but they were clearly also trying to understand the relationship between these English women and their absent husbands. English husbands did not offer their wives reliable physical protection, so what, precisely, were they good for? It is difficult to say whether Mary Rowlandson, who could answer with an exact figure, or Elizabeth Kettle, who couldn't even guess, gave the Natives greater insight into the complicated private lives of early New Englanders.[41]

But one thing was clear: the reunions of Joseph and Mary Rowlandson and John and Elizabeth Kettle signaled the end of Weetamoo and Quinnapin's marriage, which was always bound up in the larger Wampanoag-Narragansett alliance. The Nipmuc sachems began to negotiate the release of the English captives because their resistance to the English was flagging by late spring of 1676. As Rowlandson indicates in her *Narrative*, Weetamoo's company was running out of food. Native marriages allowed couples to draw on the pooled resources of the kin implicated in their bond, but a severe shortage of provisions across the anti-English forces, because the war had disrupted normal planting and hunting activities, rendered that tactical advantage moot. Amid growing demoralization and significant military defeats, they decided to begin trading their captives with the English, which created the conditions under which Rowlandson was released on May 2, 1676. By this point, Salisbury writes, "many natives had begun to recognize that the colonists would prevent them from resuming their normal lives in their homelands." In fact, "the return of the English captives was part of a larger process whereby the Indian opponents of the English were scattering." As the forces arrayed against the English broke down under heavy losses, so, too, did the marriage between Weetamoo and Quinnapin, which existed as a constitutive part of that military resistance. Colonial forces apprehended Quinnapin in mid-August and executed him at Newport. Weetamoo died either during or just after her last heroic battle against the English near Taunton. The marriage was over—both in the sense of the partnership between the two leaders and the united Wampanoag-Narragansett challenge they mounted to English aggression. The English immediately seized the lands of Montaup, Pocasset, and Assonet this Native couple died defending. They crowed over the dismembered bodies of Metacom and Weetamoo. But the scattered remnants of this resistance retreated to sanctuaries where they bled and mourned, then regenerated, and rose time and again to fight for their homelands and culture. They persist in the struggle Weetamoo and Quinnapin's alliance advanced, and they model Weetamoo's dedication to protecting and leading her people.[42]

Joan Tavares Avant (Mashpee Wampanoag) bears witness to the enduring power of the Native women fighting to revive and protect Indigenous language, oral stories, ancestral teachings, dance, song, arts, and crafts. "Native Wampanoag women since Creation have been politically active by being linked to the preservation of the well-being and quality of life for their relatives and the extended family which equals community," she writes. "Today as I look at the Mashpee Wampanoag community and other Native societies the women continue to be politically involved. . . . Like the corn, beans, and squash, and the quahog, have been our main staple for sustenance, our women's collected wisdom is what makes our Indigenous community persevere." Weetamoo made marriages to create and nourish a tightly networked community. The intertribal and intergenerational implications of her alliance with Quinnapin gave it a power and longevity that English marriages lacked and transformed a familiar colonial tragedy into a promise of restoration and resilience: *Your marriage is dead, but your relations are alive.*[43]

In the cases discussed thus far, a stance of suspicion helped people on novel or uneven terrain to negotiate political and intercultural encounters, but suspicion played an equally essential role in helping people in situations of domestic unease or danger understand and gain some distance from threats at home. The examples of suspicion as a protective measure in private contexts we see in documents from early America surely represent only a fraction of the historical cases in which intimate partners sensed their own vulnerability and watched warily for signs of danger and ways to anticipate or respond to them. I wish to dwell on one case in particular, Mary and Hugh Parsons of Springfield, Massachusetts, the unhappy couple discussed in the book's Introduction.

Hugh and Mary Parsons were both charged with witchcraft in 1651, and, for that reason, their story is firmly ensconced in the annals of early American witch-hunting. Scholars have considered the Parsonses in terms of the gendered, regional, transatlantic, sociological, political, and theological dimensions of early American witchcraft, where the case affords insights into the endlessly engrossing portrait of a dark epoch in the nascent American judiciary. As compelling as these earlier analyses have been, rather than build upon them here, I propose to re-emplot Hugh and Mary's relationship as a story of faithlessness and suspicion, one in which a woman experiencing psychological violence within her marriage accessed the discourse of witchcraft in order to give her suffering meaning, visibility, and urgency. The problem of the pain in their relationship was that it defied comprehension as well as language, leaving Mary exposed to ongoing harm unless she could make sense of it and describe it in a way that attracted the attention of people who could intervene. That a woman in profound personal crisis happened to grasp at the grammar of witchcraft has disciplined readings of her story ever since, but if we attend to the threads of Mary's story as she unwinds it, without reading it backward through a history of which it is already an interwoven piece, we see an unwieldy and tragic story of a woman whose suspicions of her husband ultimately incriminated her, as so many women's claims of abuse have done and continue to do.[44]

Readers will notice a shift in my approach to this couple, which is dramatically less evenhanded than my treatment of other married couples in this chapter. Thus far, I have avoided imputing the challenges of particular marriages to the actions, character, mental health, or attitudes of one partner, since the evidence is inconclusive and the conditions of early modern life (with its cycles of cultural contact, diplomacy, settlement, betrayal, warfare, diaspora, and resettlement) taxed marriages in ways that often fell outside the control of either party. But it is irresponsible to imply that marital suffering in this region, and in this period, cannot be tied to individual human actors. Some early Americans suffered grievously at the hands of their intimate partners, and their stories are only half-told. We see these kinds of stories in the archives, certainly, but we see only a particular kind in any detail, when an abused person's complaints were validated by local authority or vindicated by the victim's death at the hands of the abuser. Thus, for example, we can read of Jeremiah Mecham's horrifying violence toward his wife and her sister, mentioned at the outset of this chapter, or William Waters of Suffolk County being "admonish't for his cruelty and unkindness" toward his wife, Elizabeth. Cases of men and women being admonished, fined, whipped, or jailed for afflicting their spouses abound, but in the majority of these cases colonial courts found in favor of the complaining party. Less frequently, the court found fault with the complainant, as in the case of George and Ruth Lock of Suffolk County, who appeared before the county court in November 1674 and were both admonished and fined for the abuse Ruth tried to bring to light. "George Lock and Ruth his wife appearing before this Court, the sd Lock being complained of by his wife for severall abuses offered to her: The Court upon hearing of the matter doe Sentence the sd George and Ruth Lock to bee admonished and to pay fees of Court and Order the sd Ruth to live with the sd George Lock as her husband." The last line of the sentence transforms a case of domestic violence into a living horror story, a horror I wish to surface and contemplate in the remaining pages of this chapter.[45]

Ruth Lock, failing to convince the Suffolk County Court that her husband George was, as she testified, abusing her in several ways, was sentenced to live with him. This is a devastating paradox of colonial law that demands our attention. Although Puritans condemned cruelty and considered it a compounding offense in divorce cases involving grosser crimes, cruelty by itself was not a reason for any divorce granted in a New England colony in the seventeenth century.[46] Colonies that granted divorces, and most did, granted them in cases of irreconcilable distance between the partners, primarily "adultery, desertion, and absence for a length of time to be determined by the civil government." Bigamy and failure to provide were also grounds for divorce. That is, the government would acknowledge when a marriage between estranged people had effectively ended and free the innocent partner to remarry. But when people could get no distance at all from their emotionally, verbally, or physically abusive partners, the government refused to recognize the marriage as dead and forced the survivors to carry on, confined within the rot. Consider the domestic situations that awaited the men and women who heard these judgments in court, which Edmund Morgan recounts in *The Puritan Family*:

> Henry Flood was required to give bond for good behavior because he had abused his wife by "ill words calling her whore and cursing of her." The wife of Christopher Collins was presented for railing at her husband and calling him "Gurley gutted divill." Apparently the court agreed with her, for although the fact was proved by two witnesses, she was discharged. On another occasion Jacob Pudeator, who had been fined for striking and kicking his wife, had the sentence moderated when the court was informed that she was a woman "of great provocation."

What, exactly, did these men and women gain through the ordeal of charging a spouse with cruelty, calling witnesses, appearing before the court, and recounting their trauma? Were abusers who were humiliated and punished in public more likely to reform in private or to punish the victims who had tried to expose them? Often, abusers tried to deflect from their offenses and defend themselves by reframing the reactions of their provoked spouses as acts of abuse or insanity in themselves, and so the record usually shows us a high-conflict couple rather than an obvious perpetrator and victim. (Joseph H. Smith wrote of Mary Parsons, when he edited the "Pynchon Court Record" in 1961, "Obviously a mental case, she now concentrated upon spreading reports that her husband was a witch.") This process must have had a chilling effect on men and women in abusive marriages who saw the futility of bringing their pain to court, only to have it invalidated or the charges bent back on them. Even if the abuses were confirmed, the court only compelled, to the best of its ability, repentance and reconciliation. The couples were condemned to live together, and so the victim succeeded only in ensuring he or she was barricaded with a freshly antagonized enemy. In all likelihood, most victims of domestic violence heeded these stiff penalties and never petitioned the courts, so their stories are forgotten. Others obeyed the counsel of Puritan ministers like John Allin not to "rip up private failings, and make them publique," their compliance and discretion a great comfort to their tormentors. But a few victims faced the long odds and, at profound personal risk, tried to alert their contemporaries that they were trapped inside horrific marriages that perpetuated abuse and protected abusers.[47]

Because of the risks involved in reporting this pain, I am inclined to take claims of domestic violence, including emotional violence, seriously. In the case of Mary and Hugh Parsons, there is a preponderance of evidence on her side, given that her allegations of her husband's abuse were corroborated with eyewitness testimony, while Hugh tried and failed to have his neighbors vouch for his version of events. But even if I err in my judgment and afford too much sympathy to a woman who only pretended to be a victim of her husband's abuse, treating Mary Parsons as a credible victim allows us an unusually intimate view into this kind of suffering in early New England. Because marital closeness in the form of violence was not taken as seriously as marital distance in the forms of neglect, abandonment, or adultery, it was sketched hastily in court records. Unless it assumed grotesque proportions, as in the case of the Mechams, the record preserves the judgment of the magistrate, not a full picture of the experiences—to say nothing of the emotions—of those directly involved. But Mary gave Hugh's abuse a name that ensured it would be scrutinized and that preserved a wealth of shockingly private information about the Parsonses' married life in the historical record. We can see from this unusually detailed account of the Parsonses' marriage that neither they nor their neighbors regarded diabolical activity as the most troublesome thing about this relationship, although it was the charge of witchcraft that finally compelled them to bear witness to the suffering they had seen. People convicted of witchcraft in early America have become famous for the benighted conditions under which they died. But if we take Mary and her sympathizers in Springfield at their word, the tragedy is not how she and Hugh died; it is how they lived.

Mary, like so many victims of domestic abuse, had a biography that diminished her credibility when she appeared in public to claim abuse at Hugh's hands. She was born in Wales, and Hugh in England, but both were living in Springfield by 1645. Mary's relationship with Hugh (what William Pynchon called "a league of amity") began while she was still married to her first husband, "one Lewis a papist." In order to marry Hugh, she had to testify that she had not cohabited with Lewis for "above 7 years," the amount of time Springfield and Boston officials considered irrefutable evidence of his abandonment of her. Lewis's religious views, whether simply off-center from the relatively tolerant Puritanism practiced under minister George Moxon's stewardship in Springfield or actually Catholic, might have influenced the way Mary Lewis was seen in the community and contributed to the isolation she experienced, albeit in different forms, in both her unhappy marriages. For although Hugh did not desert her, his manner was grating and aggressive in a way that alienated the couple from their neighbors. Their early spats in Springfield show them united in these social controversies, as when Mary accused the Widow Marshfield of witchcraft in 1649 and Hugh paid a fine to prevent her being whipped for slander. When their unity as a couple broke down, or was revealed to be a fiction, Hugh stopped coming home, even as Mary nursed sick and dying babies (they lost two in quick succession in 1650 and 1651) and fretted over sounds that seemed amplified in the darkness of her lonely home. For some reason, the Parsonses had invited a local man named Anthony Dorchester and his wife to live with them before 1650. It may be that the couple fell on hard times, perhaps because Hugh's proficiency as a brickmaker and wood sawyer could not compensate for his quarrelsome demeanor. But given Mary's anguish during nights when Hugh was out "till midnight," and she startled, she said, when "about half an hour before he comes home I shall hear some noise or other about the door or about the house," it is possible she found companions to dampen the sound of being left for the second time by a man who did not die but would not live with her.[48]

Mary's second abandonment had none of the finality of her first. Hugh kept her off-balance with attention that vacillated between estrangement and unbearable closeness. He seemed to be everywhere at once and possessed an unnerving ability to "come to know" everything she said to her friends, though "by what means," she said, she could not tell. She was terrified to be alone, but when Hugh came home, she realized the real danger was beside her in bed. She suspected her husband was a witch "because he useth to come home in a distempered frame so that I could not tell how to please him[;] sometimes he hath pulled off the bed clothes and left me naked a bed and hath quenched the fire[;] sometimes he hath thrown peas about the house and made me pick them up." Added to these strange behaviors were more common threats of violence, such as when, "after on a light occasion," Hugh "took up a block and made as if [he] would throw it at her head but yet in the end [he] did not but threw it down on the hearth of the chimney." Hugh said at first that he did not "remember that ever he took up a block to throw at her," but on further reflection and debate, he conceded "at last that he took up a block but remembered not the occasion" and then finally said "that he took up no block on that occasion." His qualified denial leaves open the possibility that he took up something else and threatened to throw it at her on another occasion, perhaps more than once.[49]

Hugh also had a habit of threatening residents of Springfield, as their depositions show, and people who watched his relationship with Mary were alarmed by his indifference to her and his children's suffering. He expressed "no kind of sorrow" for their youngest child's sickness or death, and in fact spent the night before the baby died, as was his wont, sleeping outside his house. He claimed he was "loath to express any sorrow before his wife," given "the weak condition that she was in at that time." But his defense did not stand up to Mary's complaint that he added to her sorrow by demanding she help him with his chores in the midst of their tragedy. Her housemate, from his perch within the house, witnessed Mary's pain and readily validated it, specifically countering Hugh's claims that he "often blamed her for doing work and bid her do less": "Anthony Dorchester who lived in their home stood forth to testify that he never knew him to blame her for doing too much work except (saith he) that she helped my wife at any time which work did not bring in any profit to him [and] saith I saw nothing he did to comfort his wife but he did often blame her that she did not throw in the corn from the door." The person who, in the grand vision of Puritan marriages, should have shared Mary's grief was at this wrenching moment only another source of it, a fact that unsettled those looking in on the marriage. For long stretches during the depositions, Springfield residents abandoned all questions of diabolism to press on this point. Again and again people volunteered or were asked to recount Hugh's strange behavior on this tragic night, when he slept outside as his baby died and stopped to smoke a pipe between hearing the news and returning home.[50]

After the loss of two children and the stress of two harrowing marriages, the only faith Mary had left, even when moments of wonder befell her, was faith in faithlessness. She experienced a miracle in the form of a vision of her dead child but was sure the vision came from the devil. John Hale recorded it this way: "She had lost a child and was exceedingly discontented at it, and longed; Oh that she might see her child again! And at last the devil in likeness of her child came to her bedside and talked with her, and asked to come into the bed to her, and she received it into the bed to her that night and several nights after, and so entered into covenant with Satan and became a witch." It is a sign of her resilience that her experiences with abandonment, divorce, and abuse had not turned her off the idea of commitment entirely, if only she could find the right man. Perhaps she took comfort in the fact that this devil was forthcoming about his identity before they solemnized their union. But although she might have imagined Satan himself was the only partner who could not manage to disappoint her, she found other, unexpected advocates closer to home. Her faith in faithlessness was supported and validated by her friends, neighbors, and even enemies in Springfield, who took up her suspicion of Hugh and magnified it in legal testimonies. She might have been Hugh's first and most strident accuser, as he claimed, but she was soon joined by a veritable chorus. Thirty-five people from Springfield's thirty-nine households made depositions before the magistrates, where they testified about Hugh's shiftiness, selfishness, verbal aggression, short temper, and vindictiveness. The general tenor, if not the details, of Mary's complaints were echoed by others who dealt with Hugh, such as John Lombard, who testified, "I have often heard [Parsons] say when he hath been displeased with anybody that he would be even with them for it." William Branch said that "he hath often heard Hugh Parsons say when he is displeased with any-body I do not question but I shall be even with him at one time or [an]other." Rice Bedortha confirmed, "I have often heard him use such threatening both against myself and others when he hath been displeased." Hugh's character was at least as much at issue as his theology or the strange phenomena with which he was associated by people who reported supernatural experiences. Although the trial jury at the Court of Assistants found Hugh guilty of witch-craft in May 1652, it was his aggression, more than anything, that aggravated or scared the scores of people who testified against him in Springfield—including his wife.[51]

This show of support for a victim of domestic affronts was not an iso-lated incident in Puritan New England. In 1650, in a province of Maine, Jane Bond's friends and neighbors gathered to testify against Robert Collins, who had sexually assaulted her. Collins was tried by jury, fined, and sentenced to "forty stripes but one," the harshest corporal punishment New England courts administered. In 1672, the residents of Salem, who would become infamous for their immoderate sympathy to the stories of afflicted young women, were horrified to hear that Elizabeth Goodell feared her brother-in-law John Smith would kill her, kill her children, or hurt her "creatures" if she admitted that he was stalking and harassing her. Her sympathizers, not Goodell herself, brought the issue to the attention of the magistrates, who thoroughly investigated her claims of Smith's unwelcome advances and threats (which stopped short of physical violence), believed them, and sen-tenced her abuser to be whipped.[52]

In the end, Mary's accusations against Hugh seem to have misfired since she was accused of witchcraft just days before him—caught up, as many vic-tims of domestic violence are, in the legal action her complaints generated—and, although Pynchon seems to have concurred with her claims of innocence to this charge, she confessed to murdering her baby during her examination (of which no record survives) and was indicted for infanticide. She was transferred to the Bay to be tried by the General Court, where in May 1651 the court found that the evidences against her "were not sufficient to proove hir a witch" but had no choice but to convict her of killing her child, given that she had confessed to the crime and pleaded guilty. She was sentenced to hang, although she might have died in prison. The tangle of guilt, grief, and spiritual agency that might have prompted her confession are closely studied in the next chapter. But Mary might have gotten something she needed from the witchcraft trials, as well. Hugh claimed Mary was in control of their abusive relationship and countered that he was afraid of her. "She is the worst enemy that I have considering the relation that is between us," he said. "If ever any trouble do come unto [me] it will be by her means and that she would be the means to hang [me]." His fear seems twofold: he worried she would expose his domestic cruelty, and he was especially concerned that she would aggrandize it as witchcraft, and thus bring about his death. He might not have been wrong. It is possible that, just as he feared, Mary named his violence witchcraft because her situation was galling enough that she had no interest in the symbolic victory of having her husband dressed down in court and then freed to return to her home, and she instead fitted her charges to one of the few legal discourses that could effect a permanent separation between a domestic abuser and a victim.[53]

During these legal proceedings, Mary might also have realized a psychological victory commensurate with the psychological abuse Hugh committed against her. She insisted on appearing in William Pynchon's court to testify against her husband. She was present for at least one of his two examinations and heard some of the statements that were made under oath to Pynchon on thirteen separate days from February 25 through April 7, 1651.[54] When she had appeared in court to accuse someone of witchcraft before, she had been charged with slander and sentenced to be whipped. She was not likely to command a position of respect as she stood before Pynchon again, nor is there anything in the historical record that suggests she expected to be regarded "but as a dreamer." Accusing one's husband of witchcraft was not something a dignified person did. It was something a desperate person did. So it must have been a surprise to her, and possibly a relief, when neighbors began to file into the room to corroborate her complaints about Hugh. He had not been physically violent toward her, but she felt threatened and unnerved by him, and it is precisely this threatening, unnerving demeanor that bothered her neighbors and to which they specifically spoke as they catalogued their experiences with him. They did not consider mere threats to be slight, or imaginary, or incapable of doing harm. In fact, they took Hugh's words and the psychological harm they inflicted more seriously than physical violence, since they followed Mary in couching them in the terms of witchcraft rather than assault, which amplified the case and made his actions into potentially capital offenses. And they were not just offended on their own behalf; they were aghast at his lack of consideration for his wife. George Colton recalled telling her, as she held her dying child and ignored Hugh's complaints about the chores she was shirking to do so, "Your husband had more need to get you some help than to keep ado at you to help him." Although Mary's case ended tragically in one sense, this is a form of validation many victims of domestic violence do not experience and dare not seek. To have a line of people bear witness to the devastation of emotional abuse in a court of law, and to have it recognized and condemned in the strongest possible terms by a magistrate, is an extraordinary thing, something most survivors of this kind of violence can only imagine.[55]

In 1898, the historian Samuel G. Drake wrote of Hugh Parsons's case in his *Annals of Witchcraft*, "The Testimonies amount to Nothing, being a collection of as childish Nonsense as ever was got together." In 1961, Joseph H. Smith conceded that "by present-day standards this condemnation is just," and he wondered how it could be that "William Pynchon, enlightened as he may have been in some respects, clearly accepted the existence of witchcraft as a supernatural phenomenon." Both historians are too fixated on the spectral dimensions of the case to see the undeniable suffering of the victim at the heart of it and are thus unable to appreciate that Pynchon and his contemporaries might have been moved by something more credible, and more humane, than religious hysteria. The Puritans' sensitivity to invisible harms cut both ways. Unenlightened as they were in ways we have recognized for centuries, their willingness to recognize verbal and psychological abuse as real and serious forms of violence puts even twenty-first-century American family law courts to shame, where someone in Mary's situation (with stories of domestic agony but without any signs or stories of physical harm) would almost certainly fail to get a protective order from her abuser.[56] After all, Hugh never threw anything at her, and it was (and is) against no law to make one's spouse pick up food off the floor or prevent them from sleeping. It was merely strange, aggressive, confusing, and wearying. It was just enough to make Mary hypervigilant in her own home, in her own bed. In Pynchon's court, someone suffering the insidious effects of emotional abuse inflicted by an intimate partner was not "obviously a mental case," although it takes a discerning observer to perceive the difference. Mary died as an indirect result of bringing this charge against Hugh. But before she died the people around her confirmed that her invisible wounds were not imaginary. She heard her neighbors say that she had suffered, and they had seen her suffering, and they would tell each other of it. She heard a magistrate say that she was not a witch, but in very fact lived with one—that during these dark years she had been afflicted by evil itself.[57]

Hugh claimed to be a victim in his own right, and he might have been. If he was, I hope the Massachusetts General Court's decision to overturn the trial jury's verdict and acquit him in 1652 granted him some measure of re- lief and that the life he carried on after this ordeal was kinder than the one he shared with Mary. But if Mary was, as she claimed, a victim of his do- mestic violence, there was something redemptive in the outpouring of sus- picion that flowed around her as she testified of her trauma. It is impossi- ble to imagine any other form of consolation for a woman in her agonizing situation. She had been granted a divorce before, and it only brought new periods of pain. She was familiar with her options at the moment a marriage becomes unbearable, and she weighed the fear of dying against the reality of living in unending emotional torment. She decided to bring a charge that would kill Hugh, even if it killed her too. We know witch hunts and trials could be used to harass and intimidate people. But if there is a single docu- mented moment of companionship and comfort in Mary Parsons's desolate life, it is when a group of people gathered to bear witness to her misery and tried, in their deeply flawed way, to help her. And for a bereaved mother ac- customed to being abandoned, abused, and admonished, this show of sym- pathetic suspicion—even if it could not forestall future suffering—must have been a grace.[58]

THE SENTIMENTAL PURITAN MARRIAGE

Most of the marriages discussed in this chapter featured in literary works of the nineteenth century. In *The Bay-Path; a Tale of New England Colonial Life* (1857), Josiah Gilbert Holland imagines the timid courtship between Mary and Hugh Parsons that preceded their ill-fated marriage. He depicts them both as social outcasts in Springfield but invents a backstory for Mary in which she is not an immigrant but rather the daughter of one of the first white settlers of the Connecticut River valley. In the scene in the novel in which she and her father are introduced, he threatens to beat her as he makes a "characteristic allusion to a rod that hung upon the wall," and she sits as he rages and laughs, "staring into the fire, with her thin lips pressed firmly together, and her eyes strong with anger." Ebenezer Weaver Peirce, a farmer, real estate investor, and a colonel in the Union Army who also wrote *Indian History, Biography, and Genealogy: Pertaining to the Good Sachem Massasoit of the Wampanoag Tribe, and His Descendants* (1878), was curious and contemplative about the breakdown of Weetamoo's second marriage. Her second husband, Petonowowett, "was predisposed in favor of the English," and Peirce speculated about the competing loyalties she must have considered as she chose her side on the eve of war. "She had been told that the English had poisoned her former husband, and the evidence was plain that they had seduced the present one, and her warriors would disobey her commands and desert her if she did not ally herself with the Indians in their cause against the English," he reasoned. "The course which a woman under such circumstances would be most likely to take, was that which Weetamoo did take, though it forever separated her from her husband, who still adhered to the English and assisted them in the war then about commencing." When they separated, Weetamoo married Quinnapin, and, in so doing, as Peirce puts it, "to [Metacom's] fate and that of her countrymen she united her own; and hence, in the language of an ancient publication now called the 'OLD INDIAN CHRONICLE,' she came in people's minds to have been justly chargeable 'next unto Philip in respect of the mischief that' was 'done.'"[59]

Nathaniel Hawthorne shared Peirce's interest in the psychological texture of early American domestic life—which requires some imagination to perceive—but did not share even the pretensions of a historian's fidelity to facts. He puzzled over the cipher of William Hutchinson in the written record when he wrote "Mrs. Hutchinson" (1830) and then proffered his own opinion: "In a little time [after proceeding to Rhode Island], also, she lost her husband, who is mentioned in history only as attending her footsteps, and whom we may conclude to have been (like most husbands of celebrated women) mere insignificant appendage of his mightier wife." He goes further when he theorizes about the marriage of Hannah Duston, a captive taken from Haverhill, Massachusetts, by Abenaki warriors, who was sometimes confused with Mary Rowlandson in literature published after the colonial period. Compelled to explain why Duston, like Rowlandson, was separated from her spouse when she most needed the putative benefits of an English husband, Hawthorne speculates that Thomas Duston "had such knowledge of the good lady's character, as afforded him a comfortable hope that she would hold her own, even in a contest with a whole tribe of Indians." Duston slew her captors and their families and returned to Haverhill with their

WILLIAM BRADFORD'S LOVE LIFE.

I.—ALICE CARPENTER.

"ALICE, will you give me your answer? I have traveled many leagues and run no little risk to ask this question."

"And after all may get no answer at all," interposed Alice Carpenter, pouting her pretty lips, and glancing mutinously into the grave face bent toward her.

"Nay, child, be not froward, nor trifle with what is or should be solemn earnest to both of us. I have already told you that this is the only hour I can call mine own while we remain in England. It is true, I accepted the mission with the full intention of seeing you while here; but, having accepted, I must fulfill it, and to-

he saw it not, heeded it not—thought only of the merry girl, who, suddenly deserting her playmate, stood beside him, and mockingly exclaimed: "What! not gone yet, Master Bradford! Truly the elders of your church did ill to intrust their mission to such a dreamer and laggard as yourself."

But her jesting drew no responsive smile to the face of the young man, as, laying a hand lightly upon her arm, he gravely answered:

"You have had your jest, fair Mistress Alice, and you have taken your time. Now I will pray you to give me a serious answer to my most serious petition. Will you be my wife, and fare with me to Holland, or it may be farther still—for our people are minded to remove to some country over seas where shall be room for all and opportunity for all to thrive by hon-

Figure 11. Title page of Jane G[oodwin] Austin, "William Bradford's Love Life," *Harper's New Monthly Magazine*, XXXIX (June 1869), 135–140. Courtesy of HathiTrust

scalps, an action Hawthorne muses might tell us something about the emotional temperature of their marriage.[60] Lydia Maria Child took even greater liberty with the record when she used the Plymouth settlement as a set piece for a novel about the marriage of an English girl named Mary Conant to a "young Indian" called Hobomok. Although *Hobomok* (1824) invokes the names of some historical figures, it wholly fictionalizes the life of the eponymous Wampanoag warrior, beginning by imagining that he is willing to sacrifice his connections to his kin and culture to pursue a monogamous relationship with Mary. At the end of the novel, Hobomok divorces her "by Indian laws" so she may marry an Englishman. Then, brokenhearted and grieving the child he shares with Mary and leaves in her care, he flees New England to live "far off among some of the red men in the west." This transformation of the historical diplomat into a fictional lover foreshadows Jane Goodwin Austin's focus on Dorothy and William Bradford's erotic, rather than spiritual or political, affairs when she published "William Bradford's Love Life" in 1869.[61]

Certainly, these speculative or lurid narratives reveal more about their authors and audiences than their source material, but something at the heart of them rings true to early American perspectives on the centrality of domestic life as the affective foundation of public thought and engagement. Nineteenth-century Americans sought a deeper understanding of their national progenitors by fully fleshing out the emotional dimensions of their lives, but their miscalculation was in assuming that these details had to be imaginatively constructed from scratch and then interpolated into the history proper. In fact, texts of early America contain a wealth of details about the personal lives, including marriages, of those who lived in the seventeenth and eighteenth centuries, but this material tends to be understated in the extreme and can be easy to miss. Recall, for example, George Colton's spare and sensitive estimation of Mary Parsons's survival of horrific domestic abuse: "Your husband had more need to get you some help than to keep ado at you to help him." The comment contains multitudes. This desperate woman needed some help, and almost everyone in the courtroom, by their presence as much as their testimonies, showed that they agreed with what Colton hinted at and left unsaid—her husband was the source of, not a potential solution to, her misery, and the machinery of justice must be called upon to do what it could to address her needs. If nineteenth-century Americans were looking for florid descriptions of intimate betrayal, violence, or suffering in early New England, they would have to invent them. But even in their inventions, the writers mentioned here seem attuned to the fact that actions that might not rise to the level of legal action on their own, such as threats and distasteful jokes, signaled something seriously amiss in interpersonal relationships and inevitably influenced public life. On this point, they were in perfect concurrence with their ancestors. It is easy to dismiss the overwrought fantasies of nineteenth-century writers intent on tarting up the colonial past, just as it has been possible to ignore troubling suggestions in the early American historical record that multitudes of people, most of them unable to leave an imprint of their experience, suffered constant, commonplace afflictions that must have worked on their nerves as much as the grand controversies and calamities that have riveted historians' interest and defined early American literary genres since the inception of the field of American studies. But early Americans themselves were on the watch for clues that people in emotional distress needed some help. We often fault them, particularly the Puritans, for reading too much into small signs, especially in cases of intercultural suspicion and bad faith and unmitigated disasters like the witch hunts. But their attention to things gone awry in slight or inconspicuous ways made them careful readers of human experience who perceived and responded to a metastatic mood of affliction before it progressed into the crises that are legible to historians.

The familiar plotlines of early American history generally take their cues from physical rather than emotional suffering, but early American writing springs from deep wells of invisible pain. By the time people were at war, or captured, or banished, or executed, or murdered, the real tragedy—of living in a state of hypervigilance, fear, isolation, alarm, chaos, or numbness—was over. And the corrosive effect on the minds and souls of people who experience these forms of affliction is so total that they are often unable to write of it, speak of it, or even make sense of it. We can hardly fault scholars of early American literature and history for failing to grasp that something as common and apparently trivial as marital unease could have influenced the course of settlement, diplomacy, warfare, jurisprudence, religion, or politics. This pain appears to us in forms that have been distorted by time but were also warped by historical actors' own minds, which had to sublimate and disguise it if they were to carry on with the business of daily life. Recovering the experience of living with this pain requires us to re-emplot not just events but also tones and moods in American documents. Hugh Parsons's distrustful neighbors and wife saw him menacing them in the form of a dog, a snake, and "a little boy, with a face as red as fire." Native Americans saw Hobbamock in the form of "various grotesque apparitions." These were people familiar with the shape-shifting of abusers, manipulators, and betrayers. Their suspicion was an expression of faith in unseen threats, invisible harms, and their own power to survive. And they knew emotional horror, like physical horror, could take various forms. When Weetamoo and Quinnapin saw Mary Rowlandson's loneliness and contempt, they spoke to her as if they were really seeing her fear. Those contemplating the carnage of Jeremiah Mecham's marriage knew they were seeing a particularly gruesome variety of ordinary strife. Histories of mourning in early America tend to handle the relationship between dead bodies and their kin. But when we sit long enough in the archive, we find loneliness and despair in the most unexpected places—more frequently among the living than the dying. And more than that, we discover that anger between people who once trusted, regarded, or even loved each other is often grief in another guise.[62]

CHAPTER 3

Stillborn

Fragments of the common story of stillbirth in early New England are buried within a number of archives like so many unmarked graves. Town and church records note the tragedy, although the count of stillborn babies in these vital records increases in the nineteenth century, while the demographic data suggests stillbirth and infant mortality declined as industrialization rose.[1] Some early records of stillbirth, then, must be missing or lost. We can complement the official record with information gleaned from sermons and diaries, which record women like Hannah Sewall delivering dead babies. We can find traces of the story in graveyards in eastern North America, in which a few stones list a single date—possibly, although not certainly, a stillbirth. One gravestone in Deerfield, Massachusetts, shows an image of a woman cradling a tiny bundle above the engraved lines:

In Memory of
Mary the Wife of
Simeon Harvey

Who Departed this
Life December 20th
1785 In 39th year of
Her age on her left
Arm lieth the Infant
Which was still
Born.

But even this complement of the usual and unusual sources elides the record of an entire group of women who delivered dead babies but were denied access to the registers of stillbirth: the *alone*. If a woman gave birth to a dead baby without a witness, she was not the mother of a stillborn; she was presumptively the murderer of a newborn. In Puritan towns, the group of women who gave birth alone was almost coterminous with another group who struggled to have their childbearing tragedies recognized as accidental: the *transient*. The more women moved, the more likely they seemed to find partners who also moved. And when they gave birth in places far removed from their homelands and family, often unaccompanied by partners who were, as was their wont, someplace else, their solitary tragedies could become spectacularly public ordeals. The stories of their stillbirths now rest in the archives of early American court cases and criminal narratives.[2]

Sarah Smith, for example, born in New Jersey, accompanied her much older husband, Martin (on his second marriage), to Deerfield in 1693. When he was captured by Mohawk warriors and taken to Canada for five years, Sarah fell under the protection of a cadre of permanent guards appointed to keep watch during an extended period of conflict along the northernmost zone of English settlement in North America. One of these watchmen, a married, longtime Deerfield resident named John Evans, came to her house on the evening of July 31, 1694, "discoursed a while with her," and then raped her. (Martin Smith had been credibly accused of sexual assault twenty years earlier, so Sarah was already vulnerable to this violence.) Two of Evans's fellow guards witnessed the crime from the door of her house, where they had been summoned by her cries, but, although Sarah brought a formal charge against Evans four days later in which she recounted the assault in excruciating detail, he was neither arrested nor excommunicated, and the young men who saw it did not come forward to corroborate her account. Three years later, she swore under oath the child she conceived with another soldier *"was Dead Born,"* but this time the court leaped into action, building a case against her with no eyewitness testimony. Her husband returned from Canada just in time to see her hang in 1698.[3]

Figure 12. Mary Harvey's grave marker. Photograph by Mary Eyring

Patience Boston, a Nauset woman born in Cape Cod in 1711, married a Black man and bound herself to his owner. After she became pregnant, her husband left on a whaling voyage, and Boston ran away from their site of indentured servitude. She became convinced that her newborn, born with "both its Arms . . . broken," must have been fatally injured in utero during her "Rambling." But although she begged a justice of the peace to arrest her for this death and the death of another baby born shortly after, the justice, "perceiving that [she] was in Drink, put [her] off." Ultimately, she did hang, but for the death of her master's grandson in 1734. And there was Esther Rodgers, who became involved with a Black man (probably from "Barbadoes or [another island] in the West Indies") in Newbury, Massachusetts, in the late 1690s, while she was living as a bound servant far from home. She moved from Newbury to get away from him, but then she moved back, and she became pregnant. The baby did not survive. Esther pleaded not guilty to infanticide and testified until the day she died that she could not tell whether her baby had been born alive or dead. She hanged for its murder in 1701, which brings us to the last essential thing these women shared: no one believed them.[4]

This is a notable departure from Puritans' willingness to believe women who were victims of emotional violence, including covert forms of domestic abuse. In the last chapter, I suggested that Puritans' credulity and sympathy

Upon the 4th day of Augu[st] 1694 ~~That~~ Sarah Smith
wife to Martin Smith Now in Captivitie this day appeared
in Hatfeild Before Joseph Hawley & Samll Partrigg Esqrs
Justices of ye Peace & Entred Complainte agst John Evans of Dereffeild [for]
that ye sd Evens On ye 31 day of July last past John Evans came to her
house in wch she Now lives in Dereffeild withoutdore but Neere ye fortificatio
she being alone discoursed a while with her then saying it was tyme to
Look after his watch & goeing to ye doce Lookt on ye starrs & sd it was
Not tyme yet & turneing toward me put his hand under my apron
at wch I startled to see him Soe Evilly mynded & drew back wth ye he tooke
hold of me & Moved me to ye house floore & there threw me down on my
back & got upon me holding me down pulling up my Coats wth I strove
to keepe down but he foce't than up & felt on my Naked body On my
prevy pts &c & after Opened his prevy pts So yt I Saw them & by foce
he brought his body Soe Neere as to touch me wth his prevy pts Next
& imeadiate to foreeing an Uncleane act upon me but with my Steire
ings I almost freed my self of him & a 2d tyme he got me under
him wch tyme he in my apprehention had done ye act but wch
my calling Out before Two of ye Souldrs as I am informed came to
the doce then & prvented him ye Souldrs can testifie wth they did see &c

Sarah Smith abovenamed hereby Entred into Bond hwin before Joseph
Hawley & Samll Partrigg Esqrs Justices of ye Peace to proseute her abovsd
Complt agst Jno Evans face to face before such Esqrs or Authoritie
as shall come before to wch she bindy her self in a Bond of fortie
Pounds to wch she Subscribeth this 4th day of August 1694

Sarah | Smith
her | Mark

Sarah Smith abovenamed acknowledged her abovesd
Bond & Subscribeing thereunto before Joseph
Hawley & Samll Partrigg Justices of ye Peace this 4th
day of August 1694 in Hatfeild &tt

Saml Partrigg Just
Joseph Hawley Just Peace

Eben(ez)r Stebbins aged 16 years and Henry White aged 16 years
both testifie

that on tusday y(e) 31 of July 1694 in y(e) Evening we being upon the
watch in doors: walking out att y(e) south gate: we heard a noyse
att y(t) hous whare y(e) wife of Martin Smith lived (so hous being
about 10 rods distant from so gate) we heard y(e) voyse of s(d) Goodwife
smith as though she ware in some distress: we hastned down to y(e) hous
whare we saw: (y(e) dore being open and y(e) moon giving light)
so goodwife smith lying upon the flore and Jn(o) Evans upon her or
indeavering to be upon her: but before we came to y(e) hous we heard
s(d) goodwife smith say let me alone or els I will call out: and
after we came to y(e) dore and saw as afore so: goodwife smith very
striving and strugling to get from s(d) Evans: and said once and
again let me alone or els I will call out: s(d) Evans replyd if
thou dost call nobody will hear you: she said yes y(e) watch will
here: so Evans replyd no: y(e) ar gon to y(e) other gate: she had once
almost got from him: but he tuck new hold of her and being
will doe it: but by her striving: she with(stood) his evill intent: he
he were greiting up: whereupon we ran away from y(e) dore: being
(as we might have said before) so surprized a little feare and trem=
ling att such actions y(t) we durst not goe in to y(e) house to y(e) woman's
assistene

Eben(ez)r Stebbins & Henry white abovenamed appeared this
4 th day of August 1694 & made oath to their abov(e)
testimonys before Joseph Hawly & Jn(o) Pertrig
Justis of y(e) Peace

Figure 13. "Complaint against John Evans by Sarah Smith," Aug. 4, 1694, [1], [2], L02.148, Memorial Hall Museum Online Collection. Courtesy of the Pocumtuck Valley Memorial Association's Memorial Hall Museum, Deerfield, Mass.

must have been a comfort for people who endured this kind of pain, even when it did not end or prevent their suffering. But Puritan sympathy ran in many directions, as Mary Parsons discovered when her neighbors found and favored a victim of unseen injury they deemed more helpless, and more worthy of defense, than her. Although they believed and even corroborated her allegations of her husband's emotional abuse, they also believed she committed infanticide, a crime for which she was convicted and likely hanged or died in prison. The ultimately disheartening arc of her Puritan community's response to her suffering has the virtue at least of being consistent: primed by their steadfast faith in faithlessness, Puritans did not require physical proof that a person had committed violence against someone else. But to endure a childbearing tragedy and then be blamed for it must have been another source of profound suffering that added, to adapt Mary's phrase, more grief to her sorrow. Many early modern women lost babies during pregnancy and childbirth or soon after delivery, and most were not charged with a crime. But the cases of those prosecuted for reproductive catastrophes center on a question relevant to every mother in early New England: To what extent is a woman responsible for the outcome of her pregnancy? Because the question could not be answered, it was an unending source of theological, medical, and legal debate. The theories, confessions, doctrines, and laws this controversy elicited sometimes conflicted with and even contradicted one another, but they shared a common motive, inspired by the grief of people determined to wring reason out of random tragedy.

Like Sarah Smith, Patience Boston, and Esther Rodgers, Mary Parsons was not born in the town in which she lost a baby and was charged with infanticide, and her abusive relationship with a man who constantly antagonized their neighbors isolated her within her community. But what do isolation and transience have to do with women's credibility on the subject of their own bodies? The writings about these women suggest that the more disconnected they were from the protective structures of extended family and community, and the more mobile, the easier it became to augment what was unknown about their reproductive experiences with what was invented. That is, in the absence of eyewitness testimony and character witnesses, and given all the intrigue that their foreign backgrounds and connections generated, those tasked with making meaning out of a cluster of mysteries at the heart of these mothers' tragedies turned to fiction. What they did not know, and what they could not know, they made up. The women's very isolation and mobility suggested they enjoyed an excess of liberty, and however much that supposition contradicts their sworn testimonies, their putative freedom became a central theme in the stories about their reproductive tragedies. And something about the range and apparent rootlessness of these women's lives pointed physicians, magistrates, and ministers in the direction of diverse sources as they searched for forms and themes by which to organize the chaos of maternal loss. As we see most clearly in the case of Esther Rodgers, these storytellers did not turn to the most proximate texts as models for their complex narratives. Instead, the early American narratives that rationalized the agonizing mystery of infant death often reached across centuries and oceans in search of the component pieces from which to fashion a new genre, the Puritan criminal-martyrology, in which writers theorized concepts as fundamental to American identity as liberty, justice, and consent. If we examine Esther's case and the diverse archive of religious, medical, and legal sources it integrates, we see how a record of stillborn babies and their martyred mothers deposited in early American criminal archives shows grieving women, not just their accusers, telling stories in order to process the tragedy. It is the utility of fiction, after all, that gives it such power.[5]

There are some things about Esther we do know. In 1693, at the age of thirteen, she left her home in Kittery, Maine, to live as a bound servant in the home of Joseph Woodbridge of Newbury, Massachusetts. The Woodbridges were a prominent Puritan family (Joseph was a nephew of Anne Bradstreet and the brother-in-law of her son Simon) and took an especially active role in establishing and managing Newbury's first grammar school. As a part of their household, Esther learned to read and memorized "Mr. *Cottons* Catechism." The *New-England Primer* in which Esther was most likely to have encountered Reverend John Cotton's catechism, *Spiritual Milk for Boston Babes*, also featured a woodcut illustration of the English Protestant hero John Rogers burning at the stake in central London in 1555 as his children watched. The facing page presents Rogers's apocryphal "Advice to His Children," spiritual warnings inflected with the terror and solemnity of his violent death. Esther read and memorized, but she was unmoved. She is quoted as saying, "[I] had frequent opportunities of going to Publick Meetings; but was a careless Observer of Sabbaths, and Hearer of Sermons; no Word that ever I heard or read making any Impression upon my Heart, (as I Remember)." She might have remembered, eight years later, when a crowd of thousands gathered to watch her own public execution, the face of the Marian martyr, smiling faintly as he burned within the pages of her primer.[6]

Esther's adolescence ended in a series of tragedies. She conceived a baby with the man living with or near the Woodbridges, perhaps not the first baby she had conceived with him. The pregnancy alarmed and unsettled her. "[I] was continually hurried in my thoughts," she said, until "I went forth to be delivered in the Field, and dropping my Child by the side of a little Pond,

Figure 14. Drawing of John Rogers burning at the stake. From *The New-England Primer Improved for the More Easy Attaining the True Reading of English; to Which Is Added the Assembly of Divines, and Mr. Cotton's Catechism* (Boston, 1777), n.p., image numbers 38 and 39, Internet Archive

(whether alive, or still Born I cannot tell) I covered it over with Dirt and Snow, and speedily returned home again." There she was "Suspected" of having delivered a child and subsequently "Examined." The next day, neighbors found fetal remains and presented them to Esther, to her considerable "Terror" and "Confusion." Her neighbors interpreted her distress as an indication of culpability. Her guilt then seemed to be assured at a trial at Ipswich, and critical notices of Esther have without exception followed the Ipswich court in considering her as the murderer of this child and another she purportedly delivered a few years earlier. Her presumed guilt is resonant enough—indexing as it does tensions related to American Puritans' sense of community, religious belief and order, law, political life, race, economic status, and gender—that the question of her potential innocence has been ignored, if not dismissed outright, in the scholarship surrounding her case. And this omission has a strong base upon which to rest. If she did not murder the child whose lifeless body occasioned her arrest, she was certainly guilty of delivering and disposing of it in an incriminating way.[7]

But here I consider Esther between her trial and her execution as a mother grieving a baby who might have died in utero. Is it such a stretch to imagine that a woman foreign to Newbury, who moved frequently, who attached herself to another person who traced his origins far outside the English town, and who gave birth alone excited extreme skepticism and then unfair judgment in the aftermath of a disastrous pregnancy? Viewing Esther as a bereaved mother *made into* a criminal stands to produce a rare and valuable insight into the emotional response to one of early New England's most common—and most silenced—forms of loss. To be clear, I am not insisting that Esther knew she did not cause the death of the infant found half-buried near the Newbury meetinghouse but rather pointing out that she could not know whether she was responsible for the death of that child, much as any mother, then as now, must wonder if any of her actions contributed to pre- or postnatal complications. She recognizes as much in that profoundly suggestive parenthetical aside: "(whether alive, or still Born I cannot tell)." What I am arguing, then, is that the initial uncertainty surrounding Esther's dead baby—originating with the mother's own ignorance about her possible role in her child's death—created a sense of grief strongly inclined toward guilt. This sense of guilt to which Esther might have already been disposed as a marginalized, mobile Puritan woman was helped along enormously by early modern medical, legal, and religious authorities, who sought to settle perplexing questions surrounding fetal death and infant mortality, and even human agency itself, by associating these outcomes with maternal wrongdoing. And, although Esther's circumstances are in some respects unusual, in this state of guilt-inclined maternal grief (supported by a transnational congress comprising the era's most respected authorities on childbearing), she is quite ordinary. Grief appears in coded rather than overt terms throughout much of this discussion, visible only if we consider the possibility that criminalized mothers' expressions of religious conversion and conviction are in fact manifestations of their grief in desperate search of meaning and resolution.

THE STORIES OF STILLBIRTH

How common were miscarriage and stillbirth in early America? The notation "stillborn" appears fourteen times next to entries for deceased babies in Newbury town records kept between 1660 and 1730, but this figure, gleaned from a sample too small to attain statistical significance, captures a very limited history of neonatal loss in early America.[8] Even if detailed records of stillbirth were routinely kept and preserved in early New England towns, this data would not reflect losses suffered by women disinclined to publicize their miscarriages (which in any case did not become a matter of official record) and the many women who lived or moved outside the boundaries of English towns in America. We might expect childbearing tragedies were more likely (owing to early modern prenatal care) and more numerous (because of the relatively high birth rate) than they are now in the United States, where more than 20 percent of all pregnancies end in miscarriage and 1 in 160 ends in fetal death after twenty weeks' gestation. The likelihood of complications increases now, as it presumably did in early modern America, if the mother is poor or lacks access to medical care. We know this for certain: childbearing catastrophes in early America were common enough that they organized Esther's response to her pregnancies and to her dead babies, although this arresting detail of her case has heretofore escaped the scrutiny it warrants.[9]

Most of what we know about Esther's case comes from a 167-page book titled *Death the Certain Wages of Sin*, printed by Bartholomew Green, Sr., in Boston in 1701. It opens with a preface by the Ipswich minister William Hubbard and a second preface, "To the Christian Reader," by ministers Nicholas Noyes and Joseph Gerrish of Salem—both active in the witch hunts a decade earlier. It then features three sermons that John Rogers, Hubbard's nephew and successor in the Ipswich ministry, taught on the occasions of Esther's trial, sentencing, and execution. The execution attracted so many spectators ("Four or Five Thousand People at least," according to the ministers) that Rogers and his ministerial colleagues saw a built-in audience for a book. To fill it out, Rogers added a 30-page criminal narrative, introduced by Samuel Belcher, after the third sermon. It begins with a first-person narration of Esther's biography and crime, details her conversations with various ministers and friends during her imprisonment, and ends with a third-person narration of her dying speech, prayer, and execution. If Rogers's first readers of the book were anything like modern scholars, they skimmed the first 130 pages of sermonizing before fixating on the riveting true-crime story at the end.[10]

Scholarship on this criminal narrative takes seriously—and for good reason—Esther's confession therein not only that she killed two of her infants but also that she premeditated the murders. She says of her first pregnancy, "After I perceived that I was with Child, I meditated how to prevent coming to Publick Shame; Satan presently setting in with his Temptation, I soon complyed and resolved to Murder the Child, if ever I should have one born alive: and continued in my wicked purpose all along, till I had the fatal Opportunity of putting it into Execution." The words seem to derail my supposition that Esther, like many early American women, had occasion to mourn a miscarried or stillborn baby. But consider the provocative conditional buried within the carefully qualified confession: *if ever I should have one born alive.* Her gentle emphasis on "ever" suggests, not that Esther premeditates the murder of her infant, but that she considers a live birth necessitating such a crime a remote possibility. Her confession does indicate the course of action she is prepared to take: she will deliver the baby, determine whether it was fortunate enough to survive the pregnancy and childbirth,

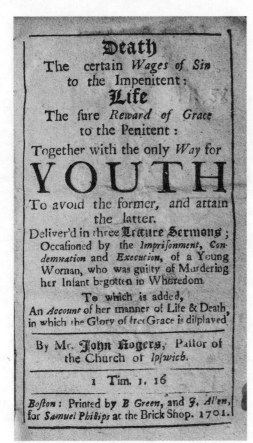

Figure 15. Title page of John Rogers, *Death the Certain Wages of Sin to the Impenitent: Life the Sure Reward of Grace to the Penitent: Together with the Only Way for Youth to Avoid the Former, and Attain the Latter* . . . (Boston, 1701). Courtesy, Special Collections, Thomas Prince Collection, H.15.58, Boston Public Library

and then succumb to Satan's temptation. But when Esther delivers her second baby, she *cannot tell* whether it was born alive. Her infant's form was indistinguishable to her from a stillborn baby's body (unusual in the extreme for a viable newborn). Rather than a deliberate murderer, we seem to have in Esther's case a woman familiar enough with reproductive traumas to know that the odds of her actually raising an illegitimate child are slim, and who is confirmed in this grim forecast when her own baby dies—as she more or less expected—without her ever raising a hand against it.[11]

But, at some point during her interactions with John Rogers as she awaits trial and then execution in Ipswich, Esther aligns herself with the judgment of the court and resolutely prepares for death. That she deliberately embeds the possibility of her technical innocence within a confession of her spiritual guilt manifests the remarkable ways Esther uses her religious beliefs to give meaning to the chaos of childbirth, without at all attempting to resolve its mysterious, excruciating messiness or to absolve herself of wrongdoing. What we finally discover in archives surrounding Esther's case—comprising court documents and sermons as well as, less obviously, a number of ancient and antique sources on sacrifice, maternity, and martyrdom—is a grieving woman who finds some degree of comfort, perhaps even cheer, in claiming responsibility for her infant's death and then radically projecting that agency forward to arrogate accountability for her public execution and ultimately for her own salvation.

As we examine the legal and theological complexities of a single mother giving birth to a mixed-race baby who did not survive, we see the ways early New England magistrates and ministers employed a transhemispheric archive of religious and gynecological sources to foreclose the possibility of maternal innocence in too-common cases of childbearing tragedy. In exchange, ministers like John Rogers offered women something more valuable: a kind of agency that, if it could harm a baby, could also offer a bereaved mother assurance of salvation, the pinnacle of knowledge most Puritans desperately sought and yet lacked. Some grieving mothers rejected this notion of accountability outright, like Sarah Smith, who Cotton Mather claims "*slept both at the Prayer and the Sermon*"—the Reverend John Williams's sixty-four-page jeremiad, preached just before Smith hanged, in which he railed against the rape survivor's "unbelief, hypocrisie, worldliness, hardness and carnality." One must appreciate this woman's exhaustion with a justice system that had so spectacularly failed her. But other mothers grieving dead babies, like Esther, were impressed by their own effect on the tragedy as well as their opportunity (granted rarely in Puritan theology) to turn that agency toward redemption. We can see these processes dramatized in Rogers's *Death the Certain Wages of Sin*, which presents Esther as a murderer and then, after her conversion, styles her in the mode of martyrs from North Africa, Europe, and England, like the saints Perpetua and Felicity and the English Protestant hero from Esther's primer, John Rogers.[12]

Esther's transformation from murderer to martyr replicates some elements of Puritan deathbed confessions preserved in printed texts and manuscripts of the late seventeenth and early eighteenth centuries. A decade before he added his preface to Esther's narrative, William Hubbard transcribed the dying words of Mary Dane and sent them to her father, who copied them into his journal along with his wife's deathbed testimony. In recording and circulating this record, Hubbard was enacting the counsel of his counterpart in the Cambridge ministry, Daniel Gookin, who in March 1681 urged his congregation: "How good a thing it will be to have the testimony of a good conscience in a dying hour." The quality of these consciences was sometimes hyperbolized, and the dying occasionally were likened to martyrs based on an understanding, as Adrian Chastain Weimer puts it, of "the Christian life as a kind of martyrdom" to the extent that Puritans "embrace[d] everyday hardships (such as avoiding the alehouse) with the same form and consistency as the martyrs had shown when they embraced the flames." As Weimer demonstrates, "the category of martyrdom . . . was tremendously elastic, encompassing many kinds of holy suffering"—elastic enough, even, to encompass the converted Esther. As they sought to stress the "good" in the horrors of suffering and death, both deathbed confessions and the stories of martyrs were less concerned with manipulating historical facts—such as the biographies of their subjects or the political contexts of their religious convictions—than with manipulating mood. No matter how gruesome the suffering, and no matter how misguided the sufferer (after all, Puritans venerated many martyrs whose particular causes they suspected or disputed), the stories of those who clung to faith in the face of death could be made into something inspiring.[13]

Deathbed sermons achieved this redemptive tone by presenting, as Sarah Rivett argues, "exaggerated evidence of grace" available to all believers but particularly emphasized in accounts of faithful women, whose "social role and covenantal responsibility" expanded as female church membership grew following the passing of the Halfway Covenant. Martyrology, on the other hand, achieves its triumphant tone by presenting exaggerated evidence of agency; its emotional hallmarks are zeal, willingness, and cheer. In this sense, the rhetoric of martyrdom offered even more comfort than ordinary deathbed confessions to Puritans seeking reassurance in the wake of childbearing loss. Martyrs do not simply suffer an inevitable death well; they rush toward the flames to advance the cause they love and are redeemed for the action that kills them. The analogy must have heartened some women who stared down death every time they conceived.[14]

Yet a third version of Esther lives within the pages of Rogers's tract, a figure we do not commonly associate with English communities in North America: a dutifully resigned sacrificial offering meant to appease the cosmic author of inexplicable tragedies. The shadowy depiction of Esther as a victim against the vivid portraits of her as cold-blooded murderer and celebrated martyr captures the full dimensionality of the tortured grief of faithful Puritan women, who saw at once the truth of their agency as mothers, and potentially martyrs for the cause of Puritan prosperity—but also the absolute limits of that agency, which ministers and magistrates (many of them bereaved parents themselves) could not bring themselves to acknowledge. Medical literature and ministers' sermons insisted that mothers held the fate of generations in their wombs—which is to say, according to early modern gynecology, in their minds. But in the terror of pregnancy, and in the trauma of childbirth, and in the desolation over stilled heartbeats, grieving Puritan women recognized something else. Their agency was the source of New England's posterity, but it was also its price.

ANCIENT AND ANTIQUE ORIGINS OF EARLY MODERN AGENCY

The Puritans reached to the distant past and across space to find models according to which they could make sense of human agency in tragedies like Esther's. In the book of Judges, for example, the Israelite judge Jephthah sacrifices his only daughter to fulfill a vow to God, although God did not initiate or require the covenant. The episode clearly discomfited Puritan ministers, who regarded human sacrifice as the devil's "fearful Imitations" of "the Prophecies concerning the *Sacrifice* of the *Messiah*," in the words of Cotton Mather, and found in the practice a major and recurring point of difference between God's faithful and the ancient Egyptians, Greeks, Romans, and Gauls, to say nothing of Indigenous Americans, whose ritual sacrifices were sensationalized or alluded to in narratives of European invasion and captivity. Human sacrifices in Mesoamerica invoked or imagined in the literature of colonialism leant a sense of urgency to the invaders' Christianizing mission. Yet Mather takes pains to justify Jephthah's "Real and Bloody *Sacrifice* of his Daughter" in his *Biblia Americana*, which suggests the "obscure" passage had surprising urgency for Puritan leaders judging the parents of dead children. Human sacrifice was not a controversial issue in Puritan New England, but Mather's commentary on the passage reveals tensions between guilt and innocence in relation to consent and constraint, which were at the heart of Puritan law and the literature supporting it. The episode in Judges, Mather's commentary, and infanticide narratives each reveal a deep engagement with the issue of human will—not just its ability to produce guilt if left unbridled but also its potential to produce innocence via conversion and consent. Read comparatively, as they were in Puritan New England, the texts illuminate the complicated function of agency in Puritan theology and the foundation of the Puritan criminal-martyrology, a hybrid genre that negotiated the competing claims of judicial power and personal liberty through antique and ancient religious forms.[15]

Christ's antitypical sacrifice rendered human sacrifice theologically irrelevant and thus morally indefensible, but the concept of personal sacrifice was embedded in Puritan belief and practice, particularly for women who prepared to sacrifice their lives to deliver children. The thin literary record of their personal responses to childbirth suggests women resigned themselves to maternal outcomes beyond their control. In "Before the Birth of One of Her Children," Anne Bradstreet bids her husband farewell as a hedge in case she falls victim to "death's parting blow." When her daughter-in-law died after childbirth, Bradstreet advised her son to find solace in God—"Him alone that caused all this smart." Ministerial literature advances a different understanding of cause, one that located control over childbearing accidents primarily in mothers themselves. Puritan physicians in England and America maintained that "betweene the Brayne and the wombe there is very great consent," and they monitored the effects of a mother's thoughts on her developing fetus. When Anne Hutchinson delivered a mass of placental tissue after her excommunication and banishment from the Bay Colony, Thomas Weld attributed these "deformed monsters" to her "mishapen opinions." Ministers offered biblical support for these gynecological views by citing the doctrine that women are punished (because of Eve's transgression) to bring forth children in "sorrow" of their own making. Even as women like Bradstreet saw childbirth as a sacrifice—a personal offering with an eye toward posterity—Puritan ministers, following ancient authorities, refigured labor and childbearing tragedies as earned consequences of maternal action.[16]

Scholars have considered these cases of personal sacrifice—from Bradstreet's childbearing to what Hutchinson described as the "free will offering" of her time to host conventicles—in terms of Puritan ministers' inclination to neglect (in Bradstreet's case) or reject (in Hutchinson's case) the offerings and instead treat their reproductive traumas as "visitations of divine justice" for ordinary feminine weakness or extraordinary wickedness. The Puritan criminal-martyrology, which engages the conventions of antique martyr literature to stress the agency of allegedly criminal women and their complicity in their public executions, should be seen as another example of this insistence on women's choice and accountability. But criminal-martyrology negotiates an even more complicated relationship among procreation, consent, and speech. Because it dramatizes conversion, its ideal subject committed the most heinous of all crimes—murder of her own offspring—before embracing God. Her agency is both the means and the end of this ordeal. In the text, a converted "Saint" retrospectively orders and justifies highly ambiguous plot points (complicated sexual relationships, unexplained infant deaths, her macabre postconversion execution) as products, all, of her consistently free will. But because the genre requires the criminal-martyr's death as denouement, it replaces the maternal speech that guides our understanding of Bradstreet's and Hutchinson's sacrifices with ministerial overwriting that elides the possibility that women could be subject to coercion or random tragedy and argues for maternal responsibility for childbearing accidents. Further, ministers' manipulation of maternal speech to produce the performance of martyrdom in their literary accounts of infanticide brought them full circle—back to the conventions of sacrifice, the very offerings they engaged martyrology in order to avoid.[17]

Martyrology exaggerates the agency of martyrs and deemphasizes the role of executioners, features that must have appealed to Puritan leaders seeking theological explanations for and legal responses to omnipresent reproductive catastrophes. Crucially, as a genre, martyrology also aligns the American colonists with Christian European rather than Indigenous American religious traditions. But the distinctions between the role of sacrifice in New England colonies and Indigenous American communities were not so clear-cut. As a public ritual and a doctrine, sacrifice does not deny the agency of its adherents as much as it acknowledges that personal offerings—public or private, Christian or pantheistic, ancient or early modern—are always enacted in contexts of theological, political, and biological constraint. In its inadvertent conceptual recourse to ritual sacrifice, the Puritan criminal-martyrology grafts early American grief into transhistorical, global genealogies. And, as it ranges across time and space in search of answers to the unanswerable, it illuminates the real and fictive constraints under which mothers, ministers, and magistrates exercised agency in cases of catastrophic maternity. The Puritan criminal-martyrology also reveals the slippery, sometimes competing articulations of consent that finally produce an early American figure who is at once bereaved mother, captive criminal, willing martyr, and sacrificial victim.

Esther's criminal narrative is a particularly compelling example of this hybrid genre. Even though she was technically guilty of crimes associated with her baby's conception, delivery, and partial burial, she swore her baby was born without clear signs of life. However, only a trace of the terrified, confused mother who faced the trauma of stillbirth alone in Newbury survives in John Rogers's narrative of Esther's crime. Instead, we see in *Death the Certain Wages of Sin* a character who bears an uncanny resemblance to the English martyr John Rogers in the well-worn *New-England Primer*, "not in the least daunted, but with wonderful patience [dying] courageously for the gospel of Jesus Christ."

> When she walked the dolorous way to the place of her Execution, and approaching near to it, after a little Reluctancy of the Flesh, as soon as she ascended to behold the fatal Tree, her Faith, and courage revived, and she lift up her Feet, and Marched on with an Erected, and Radiant Countenance, as unconcerned with the business of Death, at once out doing all the old *Roman Masculine* bravery, and shewing what Grace can do, in, and for the Weaker Sex.

These lines appear in Samuel Belcher's introduction to Esther's criminal narrative, and they comport with Rogers's description of Esther's execution in the last pages of the text. In one of the two prefaces, William Hubbard compares Esther to Pomponius Algerius of Campania, "that holy Martyr, who suffered Martyrdom in *Lyons* in *France*," and Rogers describes Esther's "undaunted Courage and unshaken Confidence" on the gallows in a way that echoes the ferocious composure of other martyrs in the Puritans' beloved *Book of Martyrs,* as John Foxe's *Actes and Monuments* was commonly called.[18]

The ministers' repetition suggests the metaphor of martyrdom did not easily bear the weight of interpretive pressure. While classical martyrs are free to convert (the choice for which they die) and then appropriate execution as a radical demonstration of faith, most Puritans understood criminals like Esther within a discourse of constraint. Because criminals would not sublimate their will to God's, they were *"Led Captive by Satan at his will,"* according to Cotton Mather. The very nature of their captivity, Daniel E. Williams argues, suited them for service in Puritan ministers' elaborate allegories, where "an individual's capital crime . . . represented the collective crimes of everyone who defied the sacred order (as it was interpreted by New England's ministers and magistrates), and his or her desperate struggle to escape damnation through redemption reflected the larger drama of New England itself."[19] Women criminals like Esther were especially "encumbered," as Wendy Brown engages the term, because of their nonautonomous position within the network of "dependencies and connections that sustain and nourish human life." This biological encumbrance—combined with her marginal status as a bound servant, an outsider to Newbury, and the partner of a Black man probably born in the Caribbean—made Esther especially vulnerable to criminal conviction, imprisonment, and execution for infanticide.[20]

Yet Esther gained liberty of choice and speech as a Puritan martyr because of, not in spite of, the gendered nature of her alleged crime. Even before late-eighteenth-century political theorists were pressed to find in biological difference an apparently natural check on the putative liberty of all individuals, Esther's body presented a threat to Puritan order not just in its capacity to reproduce but also in its incapacity to reproduce—to malfunction, spontaneously abort, or deliver a baby without signs of life. As Puritan ministers and magistrates managed this threat by insisting on the ability of women to consent to matters of maternal function, they located in the very biological difference that would eventually exclude women from the liberal political arena a site of particular agency. At stake in recruiting an antique Christian genre to make martyred subjects of marginalized Puritan women, then, was the larger project of organizing the chaos of maternal bodies through narratives of choice.

In the pages of Rogers's tract, the historical trace of a possibly nonconsenting woman (visited by the tragedy of stillbirth and then victimized by a judicial system that criminalized certain pre- and postpartum behaviors) is replaced by the literary figure of a consenting one. Casting Esther and other isolated, transient mothers in the mold of willing martyrs seemed to resolve urgent questions about the women's guilt, the hidden order in apparently random reproductive catastrophes, and the moral respectability of the Puritan justice system in America. But ministers' interventions called attention to literary form itself and highlighted both a script and an editorial process very much at odds with classical martyrs' spontaneous, sometimes self-authored, declarations of personal will. In their insistence on Esther's freedom, first to cause the death of her child and then to consent to the religious and legal response, Rogers and his coauthors constrained Esther's agency, even if they did not ultimately preclude her from turning the conventions of martyrdom into a restorative conclusion of an agonizing period of mourning. Like other marginalized women represented in the genre of the American criminal-martyrology, Esther shares less with martyrs in Carthage, Rome, France, or England than with Jephthah's daughter in Gilead—asked to publicly articulate her consent to laws she cannot shape. Within communities on the cusp of religious and political transformation, New England Puritans made sense of individual choice, the main spring of liberalism, not by anticipating a political future, but by referring to an antique and ancient past and finding in religious texts complicated models for consenting—if not precisely free—subjects in America.

Of course, Esther's reasons for lending her voice and body to the Puritan criminal-martyrology were personal, not political, and deserve thoughtful attention against the backdrop of what we now perceive as unfolding historical developments. What value might Esther, as an isolated outsider in Newbury, have found in complying with a literary and rhetorical production that culminated in her death? Scholars have offered compelling insights into the way her criminal status operated in the public sphere generally or print culture specifically, but the literary construction of that criminal status shows Esther alternately using and sacrificing her speech and consent in order to construct a spiritually meaningful postlude to a horrific tragedy. To appreciate how Puritan authors transformed some women into Christian martyrs, we must first examine how Esther cooperated with her ministers to transform herself from a bereaved mother into a murderer. Rogers and his contemporaries engaged the conventions of transatlantic criminal narratives to organize the chaos of reproductive tragedy according to fictions of choice and the conventions of classical martyr literature to recast execution as a prelude to salvation. But in the spaces of misfit between the criminal's speech and the forms to which these authors suited it, readers could see a character who was something more—or less—than murderer or martyr: a mourning mother who found a counterweight to the constraints of maternity and early modern law in her ability to claim culpability and then transform it into religious conversion. And all this is to say that perhaps Esther discovered, in the nadir of her postnatal grief, new power to create life.[21]

MAKING MURDERERS OF MOTHERS IN THE EARLY AMERICAN CRIMINAL NARRATIVE

Let us take up this matter of the murderer that John Rogers and his colleagues shaped from the ashes of Esther's adolescence.[22] In his narrative of a repentant criminal, Rogers simplifies a complex case, making it appear as though Esther's guilty verdict and death by hanging were inevitable. But even the crimes to which Esther frankly confesses—interracial sexual relations, fornication, giving birth without a legal witness, and concealing fetal remains—were not ipso facto capital offenses in New England, or at least not always. Before 1635, Edgar McManus finds, magistrates were given wide latitude to mete out justice in individual cases. Their judgments could rely on transatlantic legal precedent or scriptural command, but they were not legally constrained; ideally, they would form decisions based on their "special wisdom, learning, courage, zeal or faithfulness." In 1635, when a Bay Colony faction called for a formal legal code "in resemblance to a Magna Charta" to prevent magistrates from abusing this power, John Winthrop argued that codifying laws was likely to have the opposite effect, preventing magistrates from considering extenuating circumstances and exercising mercy according to a higher moral standard regulated by conscience rather than code. In the absence of a written body of laws, most magistrates charged suspected women with fornication (a noncapital offense) rather than infanticide, possibly because they sympathized with mothers or perhaps because without a written code infanticide was "almost impossible to prove." Of course, proponents of a formal legal code won out over Winthrop's objections, and, for better or worse, magistrates' judgments became responsible to written statutes. But Winthrop's fears of public officials' constraint were never fully realized: officials could and did revise the code, and even codified laws did not always check the merciful inclinations of legal authorities. By the eighteenth century, infanticide was illegal, but courts were increasingly willing to overlook evidence of guilt in order to find women innocent of the crime. The greatest legal challenge to Esther's innocence, the English law that required an eyewitness to verify a live birth and made "concealment of the death presumptive evidence of murder," was not even enforced in New England until the 1690s—just a few years before her trial.[23]

In other words, the jurists who determined Esther's guilt understood that some of her actions were not violations of a universal moral code but were rather capital crimes produced by recent political processes in America. It is true that by 1701 "the burden of proof rested upon the woman" in infanticide cases, but juries were hardly accustomed to this shift in the balance of power; before the 1690s, McManus finds, "no woman who did not admit her guilt was executed for infanticide." If courts refused to convict a woman who did not plead guilty to infanticide before 1690 and declined to convict even women who did by the late eighteenth century, it stands to reason the jurists who found Esther guilty responded to particularly compelling forms of persuasion that put her culpability as a murderer—not just a fornicator or negligent mother—beyond doubt. That is, even before Rogers recorded a narrative of Esther's crime, his counterparts in the law had already arranged the complicated details of her case into a form that assured her guilt by insisting on her freedom to exercise choice in the conception, delivery, and death of her baby.[24]

These biographical details, which anchor Rogers's narrative, were almost certainly presented in court. Her freedom might have been indicated even by details of her birth in Kittery and then an adolescence spent in Newbury among other servants and the enslaved. Although they were bonded, Esther and her companions were not local, and that might have suggested to ministers concerned with stability a troubling freedom of movement. "About the Age of Seventeen," Rogers records Esther as saying, "I was left to fall into that foul Sin of Uncleanness, suffering my self to be defiled by a *Negro* Lad living in the same House." The relationship was consensual, then—more proof of the lovers' ostensible freedom. Esther's partner might have been one of the three Black men whose births were recorded in Newbury between 1662 and 1682. Much more likely, he was one of the "negro servants" whom "inhabitants of the town, engaged in agricultural, industrial, or mercantile pursuits . . . frequently imported . . . from the Barbadoes or other islands in the West Indies." If so, their relationship was a product of Newbury's reliance on commerce between the American continent and the islands that facilitated its rapid economic and political growth.[25]

Samuel Sewall, who traveled to Ipswich to judge Esther's case, believed a tragedy like hers was the direct result of global commerce in general and the slave trade in particular. His denunciation of slavery in *The Selling of Joseph: A Memorial* (1700) was only partly rooted in doctrinal concerns; at a practical level, he also worried that enslaved Africans could "never embody with us, and grow up into orderly Families, to the Peopling of the Land: but still remain in our Body Politick as a kind of extravasat Blood." Esther's mixed-race baby was a product, for Sewall, of a "sort of Servitude" that allowed, if it did not actually promote, "lawless" sexual behavior. In a relationship marked by this kind of suspicion, Esther conceives and supposedly murders a baby, but not the one whose lifeless body occasioned her arrest; that baby is born roughly two years later, after Esther leaves Newbury for a time and then returns to the Woodbridge house. We do not know where she went; the important detail to John Rogers seems to be simply that she did not remain rooted. Upon returning to Newbury, the first-person narrator of Esther's ordeal says, "And there I fell into the like horrible Pit (as before) *viz.* of Carnal Pollution with the *Negro* man belonging to that House."[26]

This background seems unnecessarily complicated. Two babies and two Black men—or perhaps just one man, if "that House" refers to the Woodbridges' and they have only one Black servant or enslaved man. And there are more complications. Esther does confess to murdering the first baby, using "means" to "stop the breath of it," but somehow manages to hide the body in an "upper Room" of the house and finally bury it in the garden under cover of night. It is possible, but not likely, that a young woman who gives birth in a crowded home, murders the baby, and hides the remains inside the house arouses no suspicion—but then is suspected after delivering a baby all alone in a snowy field. At least as possible is the literary creation of the first murder, which allowed those involved with Esther's case to relocate her from the margins of her own reproductive history to the commanding center.[27]

These Puritans' transformation of Esther from a lonely outsider facing childbearing tragedy into a calculating criminal is a testament not just to their imaginations but to their audacity, to their refusal to see themselves sidelined in the cosmic contests overhanging their lives. It is possible the ministers helping Esther make sense of her tragedy (and doubtless seeking some sense for themselves) reviewed her history for telltale signs of the tragedy to come, a progression of events that would transform the dead baby in Newbury from a random and unaccountable object into something logical— actually *earned*. Here, the genre of criminal narratives provided American magistrates and ministers with a form in which the possibility that Esther was the victim of a horrific but common maternal outcome to which she responded imprudently gives way to the certainty that she deliberately killed her baby. The long tradition of criminal narratives, adapted and popularized in America by Increase and Cotton Mather, imagines prisoners slipping from minor sin to major sin until they finally tumble headlong into the capital offense beckoning from the bottom of the slippery slope. This trajectory indicates their guilt by establishing their agency.

Although these narratives did not necessarily involve maternity, they established the logic by which mothers like Esther became criminals, fully responsible for childbearing tragedies. Cotton Mather's *Pillars of Salt*, for example, features James Morgan, led to murder after choosing habits of "Sabbath-breaking," "Lying," "Cursing and Swearing," and, finally, "Drunkenness," the condition in which he stabbed a male visitor (unexpected, apparently quite unwelcome) in his home. Hugh Stone, executed for murdering his wife, would not acknowledge a causal relationship among his early minor sins and his execution, so Mather solved this by presenting the criminal and minister in a dialogue that endowed Stone with agency in order to incriminate him.

> Min. But are you sensible, That you have broken *all* the *Laws* of
> God? You know the *Commandments*. Are you sensible, That
> you have broken every one of Them.
> H.S. *I cannot well answer to that. My Answer may be liable to some*
> *Exceptions.—This I own, I have broken every Commandment on the*

> Account mentioned by the Apostle James; that he who breaks one
> is Guilty of all. But not otherwise.
>
> Min. Alas, That you know your self no better than so! I do
> affirm to you, that you have particularly broken every one of
> the Commandments; and you must be sensible of it.
>
> H.S. I cann't see it.

In this dialogue, Mather assigns to Stone sins (the result of unbridled human will) the criminal refuses to own (another example of free will run amok). Two years later, in *Death the Certain Wages of Sin*, Rogers provided not just the familiar catalog of sins (Esther's casual Sabbath observance, a neglect of "Secret Prayer, or any other Duty that concerned the Salvation of [her] Soul") but also other incriminating patterns. Two lovers. Both of them Black men, probably from outside Newbury. A series of moves among New England towns. And two dead babies. How could a jurist or reader doubt the guilt of the protagonist? Esther was the murderer of the baby found in the field, probably, but if not, no matter—she was a murderer already. Esther's criminal case and the first part of her criminal narrative establish her excessive freedom, her inability to check human will, and the immoral choices that result. Presented with evidence of a dead body and not even a mother who knew for certain whether the baby was born alive, the magistrates and ministers amplified and extended Esther's presumptive agency in order to resolve fundamentally unanswerable questions about the tragic pregnancy. Rogers and his colleagues could persuasively transform a bereaved mother into a murderer because they so emphatically established Esther's freedom to exercise her will.[28]

MAKING MARTYRS OF MURDERERS IN THE EARLY
AMERICAN CRIMINAL-MARTYROLOGY

With the question of culpability settled, to the extent it could be, via this theological discourse of choice, the authors of Esther's narrative had prepared the foundation necessary to execute the business of beatification. The process of making Esther into a martyr further defended the court's judgment by stretching her theoretical excess of agency to an extreme, if logical, conclusion. If a mother chose to kill her own offspring, could she not also—under the ministrations of religious leaders—choose to convert, and then choose to die for her grievous sin? Like many elite New England ministers, John Rogers, educated at Harvard while his father served as president, studied a rich variety of print genres, including English, European, and Middle Eastern sources concerned with early Christian martyrology. That William Hubbard compares Esther to a venerated martyr before readers know anything about her eventual conversion suggests that ministers—perhaps Puritans generally—were generous in drawing such a comparison, strained though it may be. Hubbard, Belcher, and Rogers, in their various contributions to Esther's narrative, each insist upon her radiant courage, complacence, and even "Cheerfulness of Countenance." It is possible, of course, that a deeply devout woman could be reconciled to her fate, but it strains credulity to imagine even the most resigned victim of reproductive tragedy approaching the gallows cheerfully. The first readers of Death the Certain Wages of Sin, however, encountered Esther within a literary culture that immediately suggested the symbolic significance of that cheer. It is a crucial element of Christian martyrologies, a saint's response to death that compensates the martyr and her community with the promise of salvation. A martyr's cheer also hyperbolizes her choice in the matter of her public execution: she is consensual in the extreme.[29]

Esther's "Cheerfulness of Countenance" specifically echoes, for example, the account of Perpetua's and Felicity's remarkable composure in the face of imminent death in Carthage around 203 CE. Perpetua, a married noblewoman and young mother, and Felicity, her enslaved, pregnant companion, captivated the Christianizing world, appeared in the first (1563) edition of John Foxe's Actes and Monuments, and worked to establish key characteristics of a nascent genre. Perpetua penned much of the account of her martyrdom in Carthage before she died. Her account, surrounded by complementary narrative, constitutes the early-third-century text The Passion of Saints Perpetua and Felicity, which appeared shortly after their deaths and served as a source text for subsequent retellings, including John Foxe's. Foxe, an English Protestant persecuted during the reign of Mary I, wrote his stories of martyrs as a refugee traveling between Antwerp, Rotterdam, Frankfurt, and Strasbourg. He published his compiled stories of martyrs to an expansive audience, writing, "By this printing, as by the gift of tongues . . . the doctrine of the gospel soundeth to all nations and countries under heaven; and what God revealeth to one man, is dispersed to many, and what is known in one nation, is opened to all." He also drew inspiration from geographically diverse sources, as when he told the story of two mothers facing death in North Africa. These lines, from The Passion of Saints Perpetua and Felicity, may be among the first written by a Christian woman: "Now dawned the day of their victory, and they went forth from the prison into the amphitheatre as it were into heaven,

Perpetua and Felicitas

Figure 16. Martyrdom of Saints Perpetua and Felicity at Carthage, circa 203 CE. © The Granger Collection Ltd d/b/a Granger Historical Picture Archive

cheerful and bright of countenance; if they trembled at all, it was for joy, not for fear." The sixteenth-century English editions of *Actes and Monuments* refer frequently to the "cheere" of both martyrs and their communities. And the American Reverend Charles A. Goodrich's 1830 edition of the *Book of Martyrs* ("improved" with Goodrich's graphic examples of popish persecutions) represents the extent to which early American religious writers absorbed and reproduced these earlier texts' veneration for the affect. The word *cheer* and its variants appear in that revised American edition some twenty times.[30]

Beyond specifically noting her "Cheerfulness of Countenance," Rogers's narrative of Esther's death mimics even the formal characteristics of Perpetua's third-century account. Both center on the deaths of young mothers recently converted or reconverted to the Christian faith. Both begin with a first-person recital of autobiographical fact interspersed with professions of faith before a third-person narrator assumes the pen to record an eyewitness account of the public death. Both end with a short paean to the deceased female victim, and they connect the events of the narrative to either "the irresistible Grace and Mercy of God in Christ" (Esther's story) or "God the Father Almighty, and His Son Jesus Christ Our Lord, to Whom is glory and power unending for ever and ever" (the third-century text). The similarities seem remarkable, particularly considering the events leading up to the deaths: Why should infanticide, on one hand, and extreme Christian piety, on the other, both speak to the grace of God?[31]

The comparison alludes to the choices each class of individuals makes and owns: the capital criminal, we have established, needed to be understood as someone who chose to transgress a law, just as the martyr was someone who chose religious conversion and then maintained that choice in the face of death. By routing the biographies of early American criminals through imported religious forms, including the martyrology, Puritan writers sanctified their protagonists via a discourse of choice whether they were exonerated or executed. Even James Morgan and Hugh Stone appear as pilgrims in *Pillars of Salt*, guided by spiritual advisers toward repentance and at least the possibility of salvation. In another example, under the authorial influence of Cotton Mather, Hannah Duston's murder of Abenaki families (including six children) during King William's War becomes a demonstration of human will channeled in a godly, if unlikely, direction. A mother of seven surviving children, Duston was recovering in 1697 from childbirth in her home in Haverhill, Massachusetts, when a small group of Abenaki warriors raided the Dustons' community, burned their house, scattered Duston's husband and children, and forced Duston and the midwife attending her recovery, Mary Neff, to march toward Canada. (The warriors were already accompanied by a captive English boy, Samuel Lennardson.) Before they left Haverhill, one of the Abenakis swept up Duston's weeks-old infant and dashed her head against a tree. Days later, the bereaved mother enacted her revenge and secured her liberty. As her Abenaki captors slept, Duston stole their hatchets and slew them. The trio—Duston, Lennardson, and Neff—made a hasty escape, but Duston turned back to extract the scalps of all ten Abenakis.[32]

Cotton Mather helped Duston address her public relations challenge after she reentered her English settlement with bloody scalps in hand—potentially a signal that her journey into Native space had worked its influence on her, rather than the other way around. As he did with capital criminals, he took a narrative from her mouth, but, in Duston's case, he excused the capital offense according to a biblical precedent involving a woman's violent, strategic choice. In his *Magnalia Christi Americana*, published one year after *Death the Certain Wages of Sin*, Mather conceives of the Haverhill incident in terms of global, not local, geopolitics. He writes: "One of these Women [taken captive] took up a Resolution to intimate the Action of *Jael* upon *Sisera*; and being where she had not her own *Life* secured by any *Law* unto her, she thought she was not forbidden by any *Law* to take away the *Life* of the *Murderers*, by whom her

Child had been Butchered." Mather's allusion to a wartime episode in the book of Judges elides the military context of the Haverhill attack in order to situate the violence in a transhistorical, transcontinental struggle between figurative, not political, forces of good (or insiders) and evil (or outsiders). Duston, finding herself in a space outside the purview of English law, chooses to secure her liberty on her own terms. Notably, though, Mather exactly reverses what is native and foreign to the American continent, recasting the English colonists as within the "law" (itself an imported construct adapted to the space) and Native American communities as outside it. Like Esther Rodgers, Duston did not write her own story, allowing Mather and subsequent historians to form it for public consumption. When he dramatized her experience, Mather did not cast Duston as a criminal because he did not need to. Her choice to perpetrate violence directed outside the reach of Puritan law posed no threat to internal order. As a warrior woman in the style of Jael or Judith, Duston consolidated Christian values in a way that directed violence against children away from English settlements in America. But Esther's supposed infanticide, carrying its associations of interracial sexual congress, was a case of violence whose seeds were planted on the islands and in the waterways outside America and then directed inward, toward English communities on the North American continent.[33]

Puritan women learned to live with the disorder of reproduction: menstruation, infertility, miscarriage, birth defects, menopause, maternal mortality, infant illness and death, and on and on. Puritan ministers were less accepting, and they searched for schematic explanations. In this sense, one can understand their interest in the criminal narrative, martyr literature, and even the captivity narrative as an attempt to organize maternal chaos according to fictions of choice—good and ill. Duston did not remain long in captivity (as Mary Rowlandson had in 1676 or Eunice Williams did in 1704) because she preferred not to, choosing instead to avenge her murdered child and return home to care for the survivors. Esther's dead baby must also be her choice, the criminal-martyrology insists, followed by her choice to repent, and then her choice to die.

Esther Rodgers's "sort of Complaisantness in Carriage" as she approaches the gallows thus signifies as an indication of her agency in life and ultimate responsibility for her death—the hallmarks of early Christian martyrologies. Agency defines martyrs and distinguishes them from victims. As he compiled Esther's story, John Rogers reached far beyond America for templates to establish this agency. In Actes and Monuments, the English martyr John Rogers is given the chance to recant his Protestant testimony and save his life. "Maister Rogers aunswered and sayd: that whych I have preached, I wyll seale with my bloud." So great, apparently, was the desire of Saint Germanicus of Smyrna to prove his affinity with the crucified Lord that "when the Pro-Consul wished to persuade him and bade him have pity on his youth, he violently dragged the beast towards himself, wishing to be released more quickly from their unrighteous and lawless life." Prospective Christian martyrs in the Roman Empire became so eager to demonstrate their faith in this dramatic mode that Polycarp felt prompted to remind his disciples that Jesus waited to be apprehended: "For this reason, therefore, brethren, we do not commend those who give themselves up, since the Gospel does not give this teaching." In other ways, Jesus modeled the central role that agency was to play in the idealized Christian death. Although the earliest gospel, Mark, says only, "Jesus cried with a loud voice, and gave up the ghost," Luke-Acts elaborates on the speech act: "And when Jesus had cried with a loud voice, he said, Father, into thy hands I commend my spirit: and having said thus, he gave up the ghost." John, more overtly theological than the synoptic gospels, associates the power of this speech act with Jesus's ultimate control over his destiny and suggests not only that Jesus determined the moment he would die but also that the choice to do so was made in a moment of supreme agency. "When Jesus therefore had received the vinegar, he said, It is finished: and he bowed his head, and gave up the ghost." Following this example, the speech act itself becomes a demonstration of agency, an act of control in the face of otherwise overwhelming violence.[34]

In the biblical account of the figure later recognized as the first Christian martyr, Stephen, his unbroken stream of speech testifies to his command of mind and body in the midst of martyrdom. It also casts him in a position of authority over his murderers. Like Jesus, he not only controls the immediate outcome of the situation; he influences the spiritual repercussions as well. "Lord Jesus, receive my spirit," he says, adding, "Lord, lay not this sin to their charge." In the second century, Polycarp, led into the city of his execution on an ass on the high Sabbath, emulates both in his pious subversion of Roman authority. "I bless thee, that Thou has granted me this day and hour, that I may share, among the number of the martyrs, in the cup of thy Christ," he prays. He goes on, "And may I, to-day, be received among them before Thee." Lest the audience still wonders who controlled the fate of his soul and body, his martyrology affirms, "For every word which he uttered from his mouth both was fulfilled and will be fulfilled." In the speech acts that demonstrate their command of the situation, Christian martyrs assert control over their own executions, rewriting the events as dramatic exhibitions of personal agency.[35]

Although Puritan ministers present long, uninterrupted speeches of criminal mothers in their narratives of capital crime, unruly subtexts trouble this attempt to mimic the martyrology's form.[36] Consider Patience Boston, convicted in 1734 of the murder of her master's grandson. Exactly like Esther, Patience lost two of her infants (products of a complicated, mixed-race sexual relationship) under suspicious circumstances, and, although a jury declined to convict her even when she confessed to killing one of them, the infants' deaths eventually established the narrative arc that led to her conviction for the murder of a child with whom she shared a quasi-maternal relationship. Except for the third-person account of execution typical of martyrologies, "A Faithful Narrative of the Wicked Life and Remarkable Conversion of Patience Boston" presents itself in first-person narration. "Here is nothing false or feigned," the introduction promises, and yet it adds, "It must be confessed, that it could not be exactly taken in her own Way of expressing her self." Patience, like many servants in Puritan households, received a rudimentary education, so it was not illiteracy that disqualified her from contributing her own speech to her narrative. Rather, it was something about the way she had of expressing herself—or what she had to say—that did not comport with the conventions of an elite literary form. Father-and-son ministers Joseph and Samuel Moody, the authors of the preface (at least), disclose also the following: "The Account was not drawn up in haste, but Things were written down at twenty several Times—One Day Week and Month after another." So, although in the text Patience claims she was as comfortable during her several months in prison in "my Chains of Iron" as she could have been "with a Chain of Gold," and an eyewitness to her execution several months later noted the glimmer of "a Smile, which several others besides myself took notice of," adorning her face before the rope adorned her neck, the authors invite readers to consider the postmortem revision process that produced these testimonies.[37]

The Moodys' many revisions may be manifested in Patience's spastic vacillations between peace at the prospect of death and hysterical fear regarding her demise. Cotton Mather presents sinners like James Morgan treading a straightforward path, from small to serious wickedness and then to remorse and resignation upon the scaffold. Patience, in contrast, frequently regrets and repents of sins (particularly the murder of her baby) only to fall again into chasms of deep despair. Like Esther, she is imagined as wielding an excess of agency that can produce radical, sometimes deliberately silent, demonstrations of dissent. Only under close ministerial influence was Patience's disruptive will to withhold speech converted into the martyr's stabilizing articulations of consent. "[I] did not at first desire Visits from Ministers," she admits, "till I found how desirous they were to help me, and that I might speak freely to them, and that I needed their Direction." Finally, the taciturn sinner becomes the loquacious convert of conventional martyr literature.[38]

The freedom of speech both Patience and Esther find in captivity defines the early American criminal-martyrology as it marks this transformation of a criminal into a martyr. The agency that presumably led to crime now leads, after a religious conversion also predicated on free will, to the martyr's public consent to die. Of Esther, John Rogers writes:

> During her Imprisonment (which was more than eight months) she was frequently visited by Ministers, and other Christians of the Town and Neighborhood, to whom she gave little Encouragement for a considerable time, being very much reserved, partly thro' natural temper, partly by power of Temptation as was judged; that she could not open her mind or condition at all; nor make any other answer to Questions propounded, than yea or no: till after a while she obtained more freedom of spirit, and liberty of speech.

When he traveled to Ipswich to judge her case, Samuel Sewall found it harder to take words from Esther's mouth than to put them in. "She hardly said a word," he recorded. "I told her . . . Esther was a great saviour; she, a great destroyer. Said did not do this to insult over her, but to make her sensible." John Rogers likely found her choice to remain silent a threat not just to the success of his narrative but to Puritan order itself. We can appreciate his need, given the way his coauthors framed Esther's story, to insist upon her will to speak. The criminal's written speeches assure readers that the martyrdom is unfolding according to form. Silence suggests uncomfortable alternatives, such as the potential that the unbroken will that presumably produced sin is now engaged in disputing the judgments of magistrates, ministers, and God.[39]

How did the quiet girl in the Ipswich courtroom, the bored teenager in the Newbury church, the terrified outsider delivering a baby alone in a snowy field—how did she become the garrulous saint at the center of *Death the Certain Wages of Sin*? One imagines Esther's thoughts providing essential connective tissue among these developments, and Patience's narrative suggests how dramatically they might cut against the traditional martyrology's emotional crescendo. "I had *Blasphemous Thoughts* cast into me, such as are not fit to be mentioned," Patience told the Moodys. "My Terror increased, and I feared God might by a Thunder Bolt or some other Way, strike me dead; but

I strove against such abominable Thoughts. I think I can say, my Soul did, and does hate them. I cried to the Lord, and Help was unexpectedly sent in, after it was Night." By the end of her narrative, Patience's thoughts have given way entirely to her considerably more composed speech, which betrays none of the trauma of imprisonment or impending execution that doubtless occupied Esther's thoughts as well. The biographical information we have about Esther both in and outside Rogers's account suggests she was naturally reserved. But a reserved capital criminal is not reassuring, and in their desire to offer readers the drama of salvation in miniature, Puritan authors sensationalized their martyrs' freedom of incriminating and then exculpatory speech—and discouraged their freedom of silence.[40]

Of course, it can be true that ministers exerted real pressure on bereaved mothers to admit complicity in their infants' deaths, which then enabled them to present confessing murderers in their written accounts of the grieving mothers, published after the women's executions and thus obviously without their consent to or endorsement of the final published work. But it can at the same time be possible that Esther actually was impressed by her ministers' exhortations and by her spiritual sense of her role in, and perhaps sole responsibility for, her babies' deaths. This sense of guilt would not necessarily render her a victim of her ministers' overweening control; she might have arrived at—indeed preferred—a final stage in her grieving process that positioned her as a figure of remarkable power, somehow able to effect the death of her baby but also able, by the same token, to secure her own salvation. Consider her alternatives. If she maintained her innocence, her eternal life (looming ever larger on the horizon) was in jeopardy, since she could not possibly, by her own doctrinal understanding, consider herself innocent of the minor sins that might have incurred God's judgment and brought about the reproductive tragedies in her life. And such a protestation of innocence would endanger rather than protect her reputation even in the short run, since the ministers, magistrates, and other concerned persons around her esteemed her more highly the more fully she confessed to and owned her guilt. Finally, she had access to some of the social connections that might have protected her if she had delivered a stillborn in her own home, with her own family. Thus, it may be that Esther's own desire for salvation and the anxious interventions of her counselors and friends in fact aligned and in aggregate produced a sense of guilt that could be effectively addressed—even miraculously erased—through the religious diligence it excited in Esther.

Alone among the crowd gathered to watch the public execution, Esther had been assured by her spiritual advisers (and, it seems, by her own conscience) that God forgave her sins and stood ready to redeem her. Her ministers came as close as Puritans could, without flirting with outright heresy, to affirming that Esther had *earned* her salvation. Death is inevitable, but few will stand at its threshold and hear a minister promise, as Esther did after she prayed for spiritual deliverance upon the scaffold, "*The Lord is the Hearer of Prayers, and will hear thee.*" And for either Samuel or Joseph Moody to proclaim in 1738 of Patience Boston, "The dear Saint I doubt not quietly slept in Jesus," was nothing short of extraordinary. One blanches to think of women possibly grieving miscarriages or stillbirths in such a visible, ritualized way. But mourning such losses privately incurs its own pain, with no surer guarantee of restoration or relief. If few Puritans mourned postpartum tragedies more publicly than these women, surely none were compensated more dramatically.[41]

These grieving American mothers, guided by their ministers, reimagined themselves as murderers so they could become martyrs in the mode of Christians in Carthage. The metaphor did not precisely suit local circumstances, of course, and the gaps left room for wildly divergent interpretations of the ritual's stakes. (In an American geopolitical context, what was the cause for which they were martyred, and who were their tormentors?) But the strange formation that resulted from an attempt to convert their possible innocence into guilt and then guilt back into innocence works to explain the Puritan criminal-martyrology's formal complexity and complications. On one hand, ministers, in an attempt to assure audiences of the guilt of maternal figures and the innocence of public leaders, produced literary capital offenders who demonstrated the dramatic agency of early Christian martyrs. On the other hand, only a coerced and limited version of the agency of antique and early modern martyrs survives in the figures of American Puritan capital offenders, and none of their unmediated speech. Another literary model provides a better fit for the ragged edges of these criminal narratives, one based like the story of Jael in the Deuteronomist's writings. And in the adaptation we see how not merely mothers but all grieving Puritans struggled to see the meaning of their actions in a world beyond their control.

UNEARTHING NARRATIVES OF SACRIFICE WITHIN THE EARLY AMERICAN CRIMINAL-MARTYROLOGY

In the story of Jephthah and his daughter, the tensions of Puritan scaffold performances align in unexpected ways with biblical sacrifice. The laws with particular bearing on Esther's case—regulations around sexual relations, pregnancy and delivery, and disposal of fetal remains—proved as politically contingent as the covenant to which the judge Jephthah finds himself bound in ancient Gilead. Overwhelmed by opposing Ammonite forces, Jephthah approaches God with a proposition: "If thou shalt without fail deliver the children of Ammon into mine hands, [t]hen it shall be, that whatsoever cometh forth of the doors of my house to meet me, when I return in peace from the children of Ammon, shall surely be the LORD'S, and I will offer it up for a burnt offering." There is no biblical precedent for such a vow, and the outcome is disastrous. The first one to greet Jephthah on his victorious return is his only child, a beloved daughter. He deeply regrets the religious office his fidelity to a contract of dubious human origin now requires him to perform. "Alas, my daughter!" he cries, "thou hast brought me very low, and thou art one of them that trouble me." Despite his misgivings, Jephthah recognizes that the military victory he decided (inexplicably) to attach to human sacrifice comes at a dear price, and he apparently has no choice but to pay. Remarkably composed, Jephthah's daughter chooses to accept the consequences of a vow not sanctioned by God and that she had no influence in making. Although she does not cheerfully embrace the prospect of death—in fact, she strategically delays it—she ultimately articulates her consent. "My father," she says, "if thou hast opened thy mouth unto the LORD, do to me according to that which hath proceeded out of thy mouth." She only asks, "Let this thing be done for me: let me alone two months, that I may go up and down upon the mountains, and bewail my virginity, I and my fellows." Jephthah, whose ill-conceived vow initiated the devastating transaction, becomes uncharacteristically silent.[42]

Esther Rodgers, separated by millennia of political and legal history, and in a region that has long been understood primarily in terms of its close associations to England and Europe, nevertheless shares the instrumentalized agency of this ancient Middle Eastern victim. Both are subject by virtue of their participation in religious communities to the consequences attached to recent, spiritually inflected (but not necessarily divinely mandated) laws. They are finally granted the ability to consent to these laws, but not the ability to shape them initially. Esther's criminal narrative presents her as ultimately resigned to her fate, but what choice does she have? Unlike the condemned John Rogers in Queen Mary's England, she is given no avenue to escape martyrdom. Understandably, the narratives of Esther and Patience Boston record their equivocations during the months between their arraignments and deaths. Patience seriously considered pleading not guilty (as Esther did when she was indicted and again at her trial) and fretted over the welfare of her living child, at points becoming so agitated that the jailer and his wife feared she would die by suicide. Ultimately, according to the ministers' accounts, both Esther and Patience come to terms with their fate and, like Jephthah's daughter, use the occasion to publicly articulate their courage, faith, and resignation to God's will. The influence that Jephthah and New England's ministers and magistrates have in codifying, interpreting, or enforcing the laws to which these women find themselves bound abruptly ends; when they might presumably intervene to mitigate the effects of the covenants they created, they fade into the background. Hemmed in by religious and legal procedures supported by a sudden sense of their own constraint, all share Jephthah's lament: "For I have opened my mouth unto the LORD, and I cannot go back."[43]

The story of Jephthah's daughter presented serious problems to Puritan leaders, as it had to earlier Christian and Jewish commentators, but Cotton Mather resolved its conflict between judicial power and personal liberty the same way Puritan authors negotiated an individual's capacity to consent through the genres of criminal and martyr literature.[44] This negotiation reveals the central paradox of the Puritan criminal-martyrology and the tension at the root of early New England law: criminals are endowed with the capacity to consent (both to criminal activity and to the demands of justice), but in this literary form Puritan officials are *not* free to consent or dissent. The form recalls the fear of John Winthrop that a formal body of laws in New England would constrain magistrates' liberty, to the detriment of the marginalized people they could otherwise protect. Yet it implicitly exonerates the faction that won out over Winthrop's objection and that established the foundation of American jurisprudence (which did indeed expose people like Esther to disproportionate harm) by imagining that legal officials' agency was *already* constrained; it was God's will, not human initiative, that shaped New England's laws. In the Puritan criminal-martyrology, magistrates and ministers are the early modern counterparts of the biblical judge, activated by God and encumbered by cosmic constraints on their agency. In his commentary on the episode in Judges, Mather follows French Protestant scholar Louis Cappel in offering a typological reading of Jephthah's vow, one that renders Jephthah a captive to God and his daughter the consenting subject.

> And the Lord might particularly leave *Jephtah* unto the Action of bringing his Daughter to be a *Sacrifice*, that so an Illustrious Type, of our Glorious Christ, becoming a *Sacrifice* for us, might be produced among the People of God. *Jephtah* after some sort bought a Deliverance for his

People; and the lovely Creature that became the *Sacrifice* for it, enter-
tains with Joy, with a Joyful Triumph, the Honour of purchasing this
Deliverance, tho' it were by being made a *Sacrifice*. Behold, an admi-
rable Picture, of our Lord obtaining a Victory over the Enemies of His
People!

Jephthah's daughter is the more powerful consumer in this moral economy
(she makes good on Jephthah's attempt to purchase deliverance on credit),
and she is the one with real agency in the fatal moment of reckoning; she
joyfully acts, while her father is led into action by the Lord. Furthermore,
Mather's reading equates the impotence of Jephthah with the *"Power of the
Parents and Masters"* in New England society—not to be used "without the
Intervention of the *Magistrates*," who were themselves subject to God. This
power legally granted to some Puritans is thus always certified and circum-
scribed by God, who requires "direful Imprecations," once codified, to be
"terribly accomplished." In the fictive limits of their own authority, Puritan
leaders created a space where marginalized individuals were compelled to
demonstrate their consent to the outcomes of laws whose recent, local political origins—and spiritual legitimacy—become invisible.[45]

When John Rogers writes that Esther had demonstrated such sincere repentance, Christian charity, and faith by the day of her execution that "they
might in a humble confidence and hope, pronounce an Absolution, though
not from the Temporal Punishment, yet from the Condemning Guilt of all her
great Abomination," he relies on ancient Hebrew tradition rather than early
modern English political logic to satisfy those who might wonder—because
God has forgiven the repentant sinner's crime—whether execution represents the New England legal system's secularization, an inclination toward
rational rather than spiritual forms of justice. Rogers's recourse to the biblical presumption of official constraint, dramatically set against the cheerful
consent of sacrificial victims, assures audiences of Puritan leaders' innocence
(because of their impotence) and the victim's complicity in her death, if not
exactly her moral guilt. Furthermore, in emphasizing the victim's composure rather than the conditions of punishment, Rogers's authorial collective
places such conundrums beyond the field of New England political debate.
In the way he drew from ancient and antique sources to find analogies and
explanations for Esther's maternal ordeal and ultimate fate, Rogers deliberately dissociated the tragedy from American soil and restaged it on a theater that floated between, and above, particular legal jurisdictions. The move
seems calculated to downplay the material realities of Esther's trauma and

emphasize instead its emotional, otherworldly dimensions. "If the Prison of Martyrs be lookt upon as a Paradise," writes William Hubbard, who begs the question in his preface to Death the Certain Wages of Sin, "What will be the place of their Eternal Mansions in the Higher Heavens!" The purpose of the Puritan criminal-martyrology was to redirect potential critics' gaze heavenward. But the genre also redirected their gaze outward and backward, beyond the American continent and through a series of antique and ancient genres that show unexpected patterns of consent and coercion in capital cases. In asking sentenced criminals to articulate the expressions of faith and optimism of the early Christian martyrs, Puritan leaders complicated the central element of these martyrologies: the volition of the drama's protagonist. Instead, as they manipulated literary representations of convicts to assume the moods of willing martyrs, Puritan ministers inadvertently replicated conventions of ancient biblical sacrifice, a deeply conflicted form that argued against the freedom of elite officials and compelled the consent of victims. The tortured form underscored a truth Puritans must have felt about personal sacrifice: it might come from a devout soul, but the conditions of the offering were never prepolitical, and too rarely brought to heel the renegade forces of life and death.[46]

THE PROMISE AND THE PAIN OF
GRIEF-INDUCED GUILT

The magistrates and ministers involved with Esther Rodgers's infanticide case relied on patterns of declension in Puritan criminal narratives to substitute for the fatal question at the heart of her case—whether her baby was born dead or alive—a portrait of murder so persuasive that Esther has never been considered since except in relation to this crime. The payoff was not one individual's conviction for infanticide but rather the foundation of a genre that borrowed the structure of martyr literature to isolate sinners from political systems and engage them as their own prosecutors and executioners, no longer powerless victims but rather figures of fantastic maternal agency. Esther's choice to abandon God exactly mirrored the martyr's choice to embrace him, a dialectic easily resolved in a moment of personal conversion that provided the climax of the criminal-martyrology and prepared for a spiritual denouement that now replicated the martyr's fate.

Puritan authors' recourse to the drama of biblical sacrifice in their attempt to create martyrologies out of infanticide cases was inadvertent, and not simply because early New Englanders associated human sacrifice with communities imagined as utterly foreign to the Christian Eden they sought to establish.[47] More problematically, this textual route potentially revived the early-seventeenth-century debate about the moral legitimacy and implications of New England law itself by attributing the innocence of public officials to their fundamental constraint and the guilt of those executed to their freedom to consent to a range of actions and consequences. Most significantly, it potentially revealed the agency at the center of the Puritan criminal-martyrology (indeed, at the heart of Calvinists' ideas about law) as a fiction. Jephthah's daughter articulates her consent to her ritualized death but cannot be understood by any Christian commentator to be an author of the original vow, a subject whose initial choice or consent created the contract. Like Esther's, her agency is only called upon (perhaps only allowed) in order to assure audiences of the innocence of the true authors, now represented as bound servants to the contract's *cosmic* creator. If Esther's agency is granted only in the buildup to a final, fatal reckoning, perhaps she and other marginalized criminals were not free earlier. They certainly were not free to shape the shifting legal codes that required their deaths, and quite possibly did not even freely produce the outcomes—like neonatal death—for which they died. The truth of Esther's guilt or innocence eludes us. But the power of the fiction that established her guilt by insisting on her ability to exercise maternal agency persists, legislated through three centuries' worth of writings affirming or denying women's access to reproductive choice.[48]

By associating certain mothers with criminals via a complicated discourse of consent, Puritan ministers and magistrates laid the conceptual tracks and established the moral stakes for these old and ongoing debates about reproductive rights. Their embrace of maternal impression theories imported from Europe explained fetal abnormalities—and even normal genetic variation—as divine justice for mothers' choices. Building on this logic, a hybrid literary formation replaced some grieving mothers (whose children died in utero or shortly after birth) with murderers. The implications could be comforting—to many Puritan ministers and magistrates, and even to some Puritan women, who could seek salve for their aching hearts in rituals of repentance and find in their own agency their best chance of averting future reproductive tragedies. Indeed, the sense we have of Esther in *Death the Certain Wages of Sin* is of a mother whose grief, now transmuted into guilt, gives her short life a pressing and monumentally significant purpose. If grief dampens the energy of bereaved mothers in some eighteenth- and nineteenth-century American literature, Esther's guilt calls her into action.

But this putative power over the reproductive process is also a brutal liability. It fell like a weight on Puritan mothers like Esther, or Anne Hutchinson and Anne Bradstreet before her, vulnerable because of their marginal social status, unorthodox views, or presumed spiritual weakness, and resigned to labor under a provisional death sentence every time they conceived. The early American criminal-martyrology reveals women executed for infanticide as what they often were: sacrificial victims engaged to address the grief so frequently occasioned by premodern maternity. Some unfathomable concatenation of biochemistry, human interference, divine will, and bad luck robbed many Puritan parents of children they expected. But through the sheer force of their own faithful minds, mothers could reconceive, if not the lost child in this life, then the promise of immortality in another world.

CHAPTER 4

Disabled

Four years after Anne Bradstreet sickened for the last time and died in 1672, her husband married thirty-eight-year-old Anne Downing Gardner, the widow of Captain Joseph Gardner, who died leading an English company against the Narragansetts during King Philip's War. Records of the Gardner family suggest some of them knew as much physical suffering as Bradstreet, whose personal poetry chronicles a life suffused with sickness and punctuated by bouts of pain so extreme they conjured the specter of death and the stepdame who would replace her. Joseph Gardner's mother, Margaret, was pregnant when she sailed from England with Joseph, his older brothers, and their father, Thomas, on the *Zouch Phenix* in late 1623 with a company of Dorchester fishermen and farmers planning to establish a commercial fishing enterprise in New England. The voyage was arduous, and Margaret gave birth to another son, John, just after the company landed in the winter of 1624. She and John survived, against all odds, but their English settlement at Cape Ann did not; after two years of "trials, temptations, and hardships," the weary company admitted "that there was not enough good ground on Cape

Ann to raise fresh vegetables for the fleet, and that the fishermen there had to go out twenty miles to make their catch." In the autumn of 1626, the Gardners moved a few miles south to the homeland of the Naumkeags, where they and a few other Cape Ann planters began the settlement of Salem. Margaret died there in childbirth in the early 1640s. Thomas remarried Damaris Shattuck, a widow called before the magistrates at least once to answer the charge of being "'present at a Quaker meeting,' and for absence from her own church." According to family historian Will Gardner, her oldest son, Samuel Shattuck, was whipped and jailed for encouraging Quaker missionaries to address meetings in the homes of Salem settlers. Her religious influence on her step-children appears to have been profound, since in 1670 two of Thomas Gardner's adult children, Richard and John, left Salem to practice their Quaker faith and ply their nautical trades in Nantucket. Joseph and Anne Gardner remained in Salem. The Gardner family history hints at physical discomfort they must have shared with the Bradstreets—hunger, cold, sickness, strain, injuries, and deprivations associated with planting settlements in New England and waging war to maintain them, to say nothing of conceiving and delivering children in these conditions. But it also suggests afflictions Simon

Figure 17. Richard Gardner House. (left) P7501 South Elevation of the Richard Gardner III House, PH165 Photographic Print Collection, 1960s. (right) P22423 Richard Gardner House, Ph165 Photographic Print Collection, 1970s, Gift of Mr. and Mrs. Charles J. Gardner, RL2011.12. Courtesy, Nantucket Historical Association

and Anne Bradstreet did not know, pain associated with variance from Puritan orthodoxy and especially the physical toll of working the New England fisheries.[1]

The Gardners did not wax poetic about their pain. Several histories of Thomas Gardner repeat his contemporaries' estimation of him as "an able and expert man in divers faccultyes," and one surmises that "like their father, the six sons of Thomas Gardner evidently were 'able and expert' and all appear to have possessed 'diverse facultys.'" Of the Gardners' experiences with disability—with aging, or the effects of injury and exposure to the elements as they captained ships and hauled their catches back to shore, or fits of illness and "lingering sicknes" like those Bradstreet knew and described for her children—no seventeenth-century record remains. In this sense, the Gardners were as typical of Puritans in Salem as they were of Quakers seeking refuge in Nantucket. Relatively few personal papers of these settlers survive, and fewer still speak as openly as Bradstreet's to the emotional pain associated with acute physical suffering and chronic disability. If one assumes the jolting or haunting presence of this pain worked itself into early American life and should be reckoned with as a historical force, the problem of evidence immediately asserts itself. The story of the Gardners—like most early New England families—is preserved in records of land grants, legal and political appointments, petitions, probate inventories, transfers and sales of personal property, civil litigation, births, deaths, marriages, and wills that do not mention sickness, injury, or differences present at birth. At most they imply and could possibly be arranged to elaborate a history of family members' changing circumstances, including those associated with physical incapacity. In other chapters of this book, I have read into legal and political documents to discover or imagine the suffering the records encode, seeking comprehension of collective emotional experience by contemplating intensely local cases. But the closeness and intentional narrowness of this methodology poses an ethical challenge to the study of early American disability. Bearing down on the particular to get at the obscured and often untold history of disability risks perpetuating and exacerbating one of the most afflicting by-products of physical pain: the way it isolates sufferers from others and even from corners of their own consciousness.[2]

The contemporary poet and scholar Christian Wiman says of pain, simply, "It islands you." Like Bradstreet, who laments that severe illness frustrates her habit of seeing "evidence" of God's presence in her life, Wiman registers the isolating sensations of physical pain as a spiritual crisis. Of the cancer consuming his body, he writes:

It is a dull devouring pain, as if the earth were already—but slowly—eating me. And then, with a wrong move or simply a shift in breath, it is a lightning strike of absolute feeling and absolute oblivion fused in one flash. Mornings I make my way out of bed very early and, after taking all of the pain medicine I can take without dying, sit on the couch and try to make myself small by bending over and holding my ankles. And I pray. Not to God, who also seems to have abandoned this island, but to the pain. That it ease up ever so little, that it let me breathe. That it not—though I know it will—get worse.

It is challenging, but not impossible, to find textual traces of early New Englanders like the Gardners wrestling with pain of this magnitude, and Bradstreet's extant poetry testifies to the fact that some devout early moderns also found it severed or shrouded them from the divine. But locating and empha-sizing their individual pain obscures the degree to which the disabilities of Nantucket's English settlers, however isolating they seemed in the moment, bound them to the first inhabitants and the inheritors of the island and con-nected them to islanders around the world whose physical and emotional health came to be shaped by contact with English mariners, especially as the New England codfishery transformed into a center of the global whaling in-dustry in the early nineteenth century. Because islands, archipelagos, and ships stressed bodies in ways that continental environments did not, oce-anic disability was common throughout disparate regions of the globe. To consider the pain of Nantucket sailors without considering the other living beings their industry afflicted perpetuates in historical scholarship the very isolation the field of disability studies points out and pushes beyond. A study of disabled early New Englanders grounded in the American Northeast im-plies difference and exceptionalism when it could illuminate the ways the vulnerability of human and animal bodies created spheres of affective iden-tification that encompassed—even if momentarily—diverse groupings of people across the space America came to contain.[3]

Considering the individuating tendencies of pain, a relatively late record of disability in the Gardner family—the vivid, at points almost poetic, journal of Captain Edmund Gardner, the great-great-grandson of John Gardner—could (and perhaps should) be read for what it tells of pain transmitted through the Gardner line and shared with other islanded people. Although the journal entries, which begin in the early nineteenth century, seem too far removed from the early days of Nantucket settlement to reveal much about the period in which John Gardner, Joseph Gardner, and Anne Down-ing Gardner lived, Edmund Gardner reaches across the generations to stress his affiliation with these progenitors in the first lines of his history. "I was born and brought up on the Island of Nantucket. Born the 8th of 11th Mo 1784," he begins. "My Parents were Thomas and Anna Gardner, my ancestors were some of the first settlers of the Island. My Great Grandfather was the first Male white born on the Island, his name was John Swain, he married the daughter of Peter Folger, her name was Experience Folger. Thus 'twill be shown that my connections were with the first settlers of the Island." Al-though the journal often finds Gardner, who like many mariners suffered illness and serious injury, preoccupied with his own pain, it also shows him straining to make connections like these—both to his seafaring ancestors and also, throughout the journal, to other islanders he encounters during his voyages. His claims on these affiliates are sometimes tenuous; even his descendants doubt John Swain was the first white male born on Nantucket and wonder in any case about the births Gardner must ignore to assert his ancestor's primacy, and Gardner acknowledges the distrust with which many of his oceanic hosts regarded his ships and crew. Ultimately, however, it is less biological or political ties than these very emotions—doubt and distrust giving way to desperate faith in the ability of speech and writing to bring siloed sufferers into sympathetic communion—that connect Gardner to other people in pain. This mood flows through other chapters of this book (and a considerable swath of early American history), but its familiarity is especially striking when one encounters it in an unfamiliar place. So, to illuminate an affective continuity—the persistence across time and space of an emotional climate we have perceived before—the theater shifts from early New England to a locale drawn into American experience by Nantucket voyagers trailing pain as they traveled, charging global encounters with the atmosphere of early American disability.[4]

LIES, PAIN, BELIEF

On a clear morning in early 1822, Kahekili Ke'eaumoku, royal governor of Maui, Moloka'i, Lāna'i, and Kaho'olawe, sat on ground above Kealakekua Bay on the Big Island of Hawai'i, watching Edmund Gardner walk a few yards of the coastline. In 1819, Gardner had been one of the first two whaling captains to reach the Hawaiian archipelago, and he and Ke'eaumoku were on friendly terms.[5] Today, though, on his second voyage to Hawai'i, the Nantucket captain was making a pilgrimage to a site with a vexed diplomatic history. Ke'eaumoku could see that Gardner had brought one of his boats ashore to survey the stretch of beach where in 1779 Captain James Cook had attempted to seize Kalani'ōpu'u-a-Kaiamamao, the mō'ī (king) of the Big Island, and hold him hostage against the return of a cutter the English presumed stolen. In the struggle that ensued, thirty or more Hawaiians, Cook, and four English marines were killed. Gardner stood for a moment near the spot where they died, tamped the sand with his boot, then made his way toward the place where Ke'eaumoku sat with his family and advisers, sharing a morning meal of freshly caught fish. He invited Gardner to dine with them, but the American captain demurred—he had just eaten on his ship, he said. Ke'eaumoku stared at Gardner for a moment and then said two words in response: *You lie.*[6]

Gardner claimed "you lie" were the only English words Ke'eaumoku knew. He wrote: "I could but smile for this was the extent of his English. He had learned this much from sailors and nothing more." This was not true. Samuel

Mānaiakalani Kamakau, one of the most prolific Hawaiian historians and scholars of the nineteenth century, identifies Keʻeaumoku as one of four Hawaiian chiefs who entered an English-speaking school and were "able to understand and read the English language" in the early 1820s. Gilbert Farquhar Mathison, an Englishman who visited Hawaiʻi in 1821, wrote of Keʻeaumoku, "He speaks English better than any other native I had yet conversed with, and welcomed me in the kindest manner." The British missionary William Ellis recorded lengthy conversations with Keʻeaumoku, including some from his deathbed. "The illness that immediately preceded his dissolution, was painful, and somewhat protracted; at first some of the chiefs imagined he was suffering from sorcery, but afterwards imbibed more rational ideas," Ellis recalled. "I visited him daily during his illness, and hope and fear alternately occupied my mind respecting him. I sometimes found him engaged in ejaculatory prayer: 'Lord, thou knowest my deeds from my youth up: thou knowest my sins; Lord, forgive them: save me by Jesus Christ the only Saviour!'" Ellis spoke "excellent" Tahitian and "'plain and intelligible'" Hawaiian, so he and Keʻeaumoku might not have conversed in English, but they could have. Gardner says that Keʻeaumoku came "often" aboard his ship to dine with him, so he knew his host spoke English. He crafted a fiction in his journal to make some comment about the slippery nature of relations between foreign sailors and their Hawaiian hosts. Or, to put it another way, he lied.[7]

Although diplomatic relations between Keʻeaumoku and the visitors his family of Maui chiefs hosted could hardly be reduced to a single phrase, the issue of lying had a storied history on Kealakekua Beach. On the morning of February 12, 1779, Kalaniʻōpuʻu stormed aboard the ship Cook commanded, HMS *Resolution*, and demanded to know why Cook had returned after leaving the island eight days earlier. Before the English sailed, their formerly amicable relations with the Hawaiians soured when they interred one of their men inside a sacred Hawaiian burial site and accused the Hawaiians of stealing a jolly boat their carpenter's mate had simply misplaced. Cook returned to the island of Hawaiʻi because the foremast on the *Resolution* was sprung and had to be repaired, but Kalaniʻōpuʻu despaired at the sight of the two hundred rough, rapacious sailors he had just sent off reappearing on the horizon. "The King told the Capn that he had amused them with Lies that [when] he went away he took his farewell of him and said he did not know he should ever come again," wrote one of Cook's men in a letter. Whatever deceptions in the history of Hawaiian foreign relations since Cook's visits Keʻeaumoku was referencing when he addressed Gardner, he did not light upon the phrase "you lie" by accident, or because he knew no other English words suited to the moment.[8]

This chapter's interest, as I have suggested, is in what connected Keʻeaumoku to Cook and Gardner beyond their layered encounters with the coastline fringing Kealakekua Bay, which will bring us to the emotional properties of these lies. For, despite the fraught conditions of Hawaiian-haole relationships during the late eighteenth and early nineteenth centuries, these three men had meaningful things in common. Cook's voyages initiated a new era of global trade in which Keʻeaumoku (who served as admiral of the king's fleet) and whalers like Gardner played a central part. This commerce also connected them epidemiologically as it introduced novel pathogens to the Hawaiian archipelago that transformed the history of the Pacific. When Kalanimoku, the chief minister of Hawaiʻi, wrote to his cousins King Liholiho (Kamehameha II) and Queen Kamāmalu of the death of Keʻeaumoku in 1824, he gave this grim survey of conditions: "We here have been swept off by death from illness. . . . Keeaumoku . . . died, and was taken back to Kailua. Pihookaneakarora has died. Kiriwehe is dead. Eeka is dead. Taumuarii has died, the death occurring nine days ago. . . . Later, those of us here may all be dead from sickness; you should come back." The king and queen, who sailed to England in 1823, never read Kalanimoku's letter—they had died of measles in London. In 1817, just after Gardner returned to Massachusetts from a voyage to Peru, all three of his children died of fever in less than three months. The era of exploration inaugurated by the contact between Keʻeaumoku's kinsfolk and Cook fueled pandemics with resonances both wide and personal.[9]

To these connections among Keʻeaumoku, Cook, and Gardner that scholars have already considered can be added the significant fact that all three men had physical disabilities. This is not a particularly daring claim; the same thing could be said of many people mentioned in this book.[10] Their physical vulnerability owes much to their proximity to shorelines, since islanders, coastal inhabitants, and voyagers involved in oceanic exploration, warfare, hunting, and trade were particularly susceptible to injury and illness, and their watery environments shaped personal experiences with and communal responses to disability. Keʻeaumoku's and Cook's naval service and Gardner's whaling were especially dangerous. English naval and whaling ships routinely had surgeons on board, and although frugal American regulators did not place this burden on American whaleships, the grisly illustrations in maritime manuals that guided whaling captains through surgery make a compelling case for this financial commitment. The business of making war—no less than the business of harpooning, hauling in, cutting up, and boiling the remains of a forty-ton animal on a rolling deck slick with blood and oil—yielded disability as a constant by-product of the dead bodies warships and whalers intended to produce. Disability on ships was so common that it carried little of the stigma it attracted on land, and in some cases it was even a basis for solidarity, a sign of social status, or an indication of divine providence. Warfare was a fixture of Native Hawaiian life through the early nineteenth century, so disability resulting from injury was common on the islands, as well, as were other disabilities associated with labor, genetics, or environment. And the Hawaiian archipelago was (and is) particularly vulnerable to the ravages of epidemics, so the protracted sicknesses and disease-induced disabilities of Hawaiians like Keʻeaumoku were not anomalous events and are open to cultural and political analysis as much as medical diagnosis and study.[11]

Within this oceanic framework, I chart the social, material, and affective registers of early American disability by contemplating, in turn, the concepts of lies, pain, and belief as they relate to Cook, Keʻeaumoku, Gardner, and their kinsfolk.[12] It is impossible to locate disability in historical narratives without acknowledging how lying unsettles the search from the outset. Much of what we know of disability in and around Hawaiʻi comes from writings of those who did not understand Hawaiian life, such as the "Cook books" made by members of Cook's third expedition to the Pacific or Protestant missionaries who began arriving in 1820. I see the inconsistencies and obvious biases of English and American writings about Hawaiʻi and take care to read them as perspectives on experiences rather than facts about historical events. Whenever possible I use Native Hawaiian accounts of these encounters or foreground Indigenous perspectives. But I make no effort to push the lies aside because they are revelations in themselves. The lies people tell about their own minds and bodies, and the lies they tell about the minds and bodies of others, do not cover deeper truths about physical ability and disability; they are part of the web of attitudes, expectations, treatments, and outcomes that constitute health in any environment. Keʻeaumoku, Cook, and Gardner heard and told lies of various kinds, but those that involved their bodies were political gestures with a profoundly personal root. People who were injured or who experienced pronounced or prolonged pain in terraqueous spaces understood their disabilities in terms afforded by their environment and represented their disabilities strategically, which sometimes meant dishonestly. In disability studies, the illusions prostheses create (a form of "passing") or the exaggeration of a disability ("masquerading") are in some sense lies that respond to the social conditions in which people live and labor. But they are also a subset of the much more pervasive lie that there are such fixed categories as "able" and "disabled"—a lie that gives comfort to many able-bodied people who misrepresent, pity, or oppress disabled people until, inevitably, the reality of shared vulnerability asserts itself, shatters illusory self-images, and demands the construction of new narratives that more adequately explain what it means to be human.[13]

These narratives must contend with the most basic fact of humanity—that what it means to be human is to be susceptible to pain. As the disability theorist Tobin Siebers notes, most people avoid this knowledge. "Pain represents for most people a source of terror and an affront to human dignity," he writes. "A painful life is simply considered a life not worth living." Perhaps without realizing it, some scholars have looked away from the disabilities of early Americans and especially from the disabilities of Indigenous peoples. My insistence that disability bore heavily on the experiences and perceptions of people who lived in and visited Hawai'i in the eighteenth and early nineteenth centuries is not meant to reduce these individuals with disabilities to an undifferentiated category of "the disabled." That designation, comprising all of humanity at some point or in some sense, is meaningless. Instead, I wonder how diverse experiences of illness and injury in Oceania tinged the emotional palette of global early American life. Although disability is not often foregrounded in the literature or historical records of early America, it works itself into the archive in unexpected ways that require, and reward, careful attention. To perceive it, readers must look beyond assumptions about what disability looks like, how people with disabilities feel, or how disability was regarded in the waters and lands that sustained early American life.[14]

I follow Siebers's call to see disability, pain, and suffering as discrete experiences that do not always coexist. He argues: "In a world where pain represents the ultimate measure of quality of life, all disabled people risk having their experiences described as wrongful because disability and suffering are thought synonymous. Disabled lives are routinely described as lives not worth living, lives undeserving of human dignity, lives judged inferior to death." This is especially true of Indigenous people with disabilities, and it is not a recent phenomenon. Many foreign visitors to Hawai'i judged disabled lives as undeserving of serious contemplation, or—given how infrequently they appear in writings documenting their visits—even notice. "Many people sick" was a common refrain in the journal of one European living in Hawai'i in the early nineteenth century. Surely there is more, much more, to be seen and said about these lives. I search for the voices and impressions of people with disabilities in and around Hawai'i, but I proceed carefully. As I look at historical sources, I resist imputing pain to disabled people who tell us that they were not in pain, that they were not particularly traumatized by their injury or illness, or that they did not consider themselves in need of healing or correction. But, at the same time, I focus on and take seriously the expressions of other historical figures who report that they suffered profoundly because of illness and injury or who record impressions about their disabilities that changed over time. With extreme caution, I engage their expressions to consider how they might introduce us to the subjectivities of other people with disabilities, like Edmund Gardner's ancestors, who left no conventionally legible accounts of their lives. I also consider those whose faith in salvation of one kind or another alleviated their suffering even when it did not diminish their pain. In other words, I make a conscious decision to believe my sources as the experts on their own experiences of embodiment and to trust they had legitimate reasons for representing disability as they did in the public sphere and for responding to it as they did in their private, including spiritual, lives.[15]

The stories of a few people who stood on the same stretch of sand in Kealakekua Bay during the late eighteenth and early nineteenth centuries capture only a sliver of the larger portrait of those who experienced prolonged illness or serious injury during this period. But their pain was also common ground, and the lies and beliefs by which they managed it connect them to countless others whose lives were punctuated by pain but were nevertheless worthwhile and worthy of our contemplation. If pain is profoundly isolating, to believe in the pain of others and the validity of their responses to it is to turn outward, even if momentarily, and these periodic expressions of belief stand out as redemptive moments in a history of transoceanic contact and conquest laden with too much violence and cruelty to comprehend. Suffering was not distributed equally across the world Keʻeaumoku, Cook, and Gardner explored. Some Hawaiians thought Keʻeaumoku might have inflicted as much pain as he endured, and Cook and Gardner inflicted much more. But in spite of this, pain was in some measure shared, and sometimes offered the only terms on which people could relate across seas of mutual incomprehension. Perhaps in another world salvation means freedom from pain. But if any kind of redemption, however provisional, is possible in this world, it can only be redemption in the midst of pain, or redemption because of it.

THREE STORIES OF OCEANIC DISABILITY IN THE AGE OF SAIL

Because it is part of every human life, disability is as much a physical and historical fact as it is, to use the words of Rosemarie Garland-Thomson, "a story we tell about bodies." We begin, then, with the stories of three bodies, told in chronological order.[16]

James Cook was born in Marton-in-Cleveland, Yorkshire, in 1728. According to his biographer J. C. Beaglehole, Cook was "an infant strong, tough, and . . . large-boned, with a clutch on survival." This last characteristic apparently distinguished him from his siblings Mary, Jane, another Mary, and William, who all died in early childhood or infancy. By the age of eighteen, this hardy youth was apprenticed to and living with John Walker, a Quaker shipmaster, shipowner, and coal shipper. When the apprenticeship ended in 1750, Cook signed on as a seaman in the British merchant navy, and in 1755 he joined the Royal Navy and ascended its ranks by distinguishing himself as a surveyor and cartographer. He was commanding the schooner *Grenville* in 1764, at the age of thirty-six, when he suffered an accident while surveying the coast of Cape Norman in Newfoundland. The *Grenville* logbook entry for August 6 reads:

> 2 pm Came on board the Cutter with the Master who unfortunately had a Large Powder Horn blown up and Burst in his hand which shatter'd it in a Terrible manner and one of the people that stood hard by suffered greatly by the same accident and having no Surgeon on board Bore away for Noddy Harbour where a French fishing ship Lay, at 8 sent the Boat in for the French surgeon at 10 the Boat returned with the Surgeon, at 11 Anchord in Noddy Harbour in 6 fathom water.

Of the incident, Beaglehole writes: "This untoward affair seems to have disabled Cook as an active surveyor for the rest of the month, though not as a commander. It was his right hand; it healed, but it bore a gash between the thumb and forefinger, and a large scar as far as the wrist, that had an identifying function fifteen years later." Beaglehole refers to the days following Cook's death in 1779, which occurred during his third voyage to the Pacific. On this final voyage, those who had sailed with Cook before noted, in the words of his biographer Frank McLynn, a "personality change" marked by episodes of "mania" and "depressive interludes." According to midshipman James Trevenen: "He would sometimes relax from his almost constant severity of disposition and now and then to converse familiarly with us. But it was only for a time; as soon as on board the ship he became again the despot." Gone was the "surveying genius" of earlier decades; Cook was confused about the islands he encountered in the Bering Sea and uninterested in exploring the Samoan and Fijian Islands only a few days' sail from Tonga, where he spent an unaccountably long time. McLynn finds it "probable" he had become addicted to opiates used to treat his sciatica and speculates he was exhausted (at forty-eight, he was unusually old for a sea captain, and years of chronic pain must have exacerbated the ordinary stress of command-ing voyages). What we find in the historical record is evidence that Cook's crew found him given to what Trevenen called "paroxysms of passion" and prone as he never had been to take dangerous risks, including the gambit that culminated in his death.[17]

Cook and Captain Charles Clerke, who commanded the expedition's con-sort ship, HMS *Discovery*, reached Kauai in January 1778—the first, or among the first, Europeans to visit the Hawaiian archipelago.[18] They stayed for two weeks before sailing on to explore the west coast of North America. When they cruised around Maui and the island of Hawai'i in November and Decem-ber 1778, they were greeted, as on Kauai, by Hawaiian explorers in canoes who paddled out to meet the ships and initiated a lively trading relationship. Cook's decision to circle the islands for seven weeks rather than drop anchor and make landfall to provision maddened his half-starved crew and suggests to McLynn that Cook had "cracked and scarcely knew what he was doing or why." All the trade that occurred between the Hawaiians and the English was facilitated by Hawaiians who came to the ships. When Cook finally anchored on January 17, 1779, in Kealakekua Bay, some ten thousand people in fifteen hundred canoes came out to welcome his men, flanked by swimmers in the water and crowds standing on shore. Some Hawaiians might have regarded him, as they did other high chiefs, as an *attua*, or an avatar of a god—in this case Lono, the god of peace, light, and fertility. Others simply saw the advan-tage in dealing generously with this powerful stranger. But by the time the English were preparing to leave on February 4, the Hawaiian laborers had grown tired of the English seamen, who treated them with contempt, and Kalani'ōpu'u was eager to send off Cook and Clerke. When the *Resolution*'s damaged foremast prompted Cook to bring the ships back to Kealakekua Bay on February 10, the empty shore signaled that the Hawaiians were utterly disenchanted with their visitors. "'The Natives did not appear to receive us this time with that Friendship that they had done before," one midshipman commented. "Our quick return seemed to create a kind of Jealousy amongst them with respect to our intentions; as fearing we should attempt to settle there, and deprive them of part if not the whole of their Country." The Hawai-ians were not simply standoffish; after the first uneasy night forced to play hosts again on this interminable visit of the English, they embarked on vari-ous campaigns (although how officially coordinated is unclear) to drive them out. Price gouging, petty theft, and aggression preceded a more complicated and damaging plot to unfasten and abscond with the *Discovery*'s big cutter. When they succeeded, Cook's expedition was paralyzed, since without both the *Discovery*'s large and small cutters his quest for the Northwest Passage—the ostensible purpose of the voyage—was impossible, "for in polar regions it was dangerous folly to venture into the ice without the cutters as guides." Cook responded by ordering his men to blockade the bay and kill any canoe-ists trying to run it, but then he hatched a bizarre plot, without consulting his officers, to go to shore and arrest Kalaniʻōpuʻu. He lacked the manpower to carry out an arrest on land and a blockade at sea, and when he tried to force Kalaniʻōpuʻu to his ship, a crowd intervened to protect the mōʻī. Cook shot and killed at least one Hawaiian man before he was struck in the back with a club and then stabbed by two warriors.[19]

In the aftermath of the fray, Cook's wounded hand might have served the identifying function to which Beaglehole alludes. Cook and the four marines who died with him were ritually dismembered, and for several days Clerke tried and failed to persuade the Hawaiians to return their remains. Those of the marines were never procured. But six days after they and Cook died, a personal envoy of the high chief met Clerke on the beach and handed him a bundle wrapped in a feathered cloak. In the cabin of the *Resolution*, the officers opened the bundle. According to second lieutenant James King:

> We found in it both the hands of Captain Cook entire, which were well known from a remarkable scar on one of them, that divided the thumb from the fore-finger, the whole length of the metacarpal bone; the skull, but with the scalp separated from it, and the bones that form the face wanting; the scalp, with the hair upon it cut short, and the ears adhering to it; the bones of both arms, with the skin of the fore-arms hanging to them; the thigh and leg-bones joined together, but without the feet. The ligaments of the joints were entire; and the whole bore evident marks of having been in the fire, except the hands, which had the flesh left upon them, and were cut in several places, and crammed with salt, apparently with an intention of preserving them.

Cook's disability was thus made a centerpiece in one English story of his death, although the question of how it featured in his life and various posthumous representations remains for us to discover.[20]

The second case considered is that of Edmund Gardner, who provided a wealth of personal information in the journal he began sometime after 1826 and worked on until 1874, a year before his death. Gardner followed in the steps of his seafaring family in 1800 when he joined the crew of the sloop *Dove*. The trading voyage was "unsuccessful," and Gardner "returned without any remuneration for services." Still, he was enchanted with nautical life. Within three years he was an officer on the whaleship *Union*, and by 1807, when he was just twenty-two years old, he was tendered command of it. When the *Union* collided with a whale and sank, his clear thinking about the futility of trying to save the ship allowed him to bring the crew—although dehydrated and badly rattled—to safety in the Azores. His career was interrupted by the War of 1812, but in 1815 he commanded the ship *Winslow* on a whaling voyage that led him around South America and through the Pacific.[21]

During a hunt on February 21, 1816, Gardner grew frustrated with his boatsteerers, whose harpoons kept missing the whales the *Winslow* was pursuing. Like Captain Cook late in life, Gardner had a penchant for commandeering the tasks for which his more specialized subordinates were better qualified—with mixed, occasionally calamitous, results. He rushed to the head of his boat, deposing the boatsteerer and seizing his weapon. In his journal, he writes of the incident this action precipitated.

> Took harpoon in hand threw into the whale, took my other harpoon in hand, but have no recollection of what I did with it. I recollect of seeing the Whale's teeth but further I know nothing, 'till getting up from the bottom of the boat. Found I was much hurt and wounded, when I came to my senses after being stunned, called one of the boat's company to cut off the line and take me to the ship. I was bleeding copiously when taken on board, my shoes were quite full of blood. When on board, found one tooth had entered my head breaking in my skull, another had pierced my hand, another had entered the upper part of my right arm, the fourth had entered my right shoulder, from the shoulder to the elbow of the right arm was badly fractured[.] My shoulder was broken down an inch or more (where it now is), my jaw and five teeth were broken, tongue cut through, my left hand was pierced with a tooth and much broken and very painful. 'Twas favorable I retained my senses, my hand was very painful, many of the bones were broken in the hand.

Because Gardner, who served as the ship's surgeon, could not operate on himself, the ship was brought to the port of Paita, Peru. The detour to Paita took six days, during which he suffered grievously from blood loss, and for the last forty-eight hours members of the crew had to fan him "continually."

now on far famed Pacific. Had taken more than
two hundred barils of sperm oil in about two months after leeving St Catherines, was doing finely. On
21 st of 2o Mo 1816. was a beutifull day, with smoothe
sea when we saw many whales, went in pursuit
of them, my boatsteres had missed throwing their
harpoons five times, when they ought not to have
missed. I went into the head of my boat rowed
to my Mate teling him to go into the head of his
then went after others that hadnot been disturbed,
twas still weather were paddling after them, when
I got near to one lay down my paddle took harpoon in hand threw into the whale, took my other
harpoon in hand, but have no recollection of what
I did with it. I recollect of seeing the Whales teeth,
but further I know nothing, till geting up
from the bottom of the boat. Found I was much hurt and wounded, when I came to my
senses from the stund, called one of the boats
company to cut off the line, and take me to
to the ship. I was bleeding coppiously when
taken on board, my shoes were quite full of
blood. When on board, found one tooth had
entered my head breaking in my scull, another
had pierced my hand, another had entered the
upper part of my right arm, the fourth had entered
my right sholder, from the sholder to the elbow
of the right arm was badly fractured. My sholder
was broken down an inch or more (where it now is)
five and five teeth were broken, tonge cut through
my left hand was pierced with a tooth and much
broken and very painfull. Twas favourable I
retained my senses, my hand was very painfull
many of the bones were broken in the hand. —
          The ships course was directed for Payta whe-
re the land was sighted, twas thought to be
Payta head, but the anxiety of my officers
prevented their geting the Latitude, had they done

Figure 18. Page from Edmund Gardner's journal describing his February 21, 1816,
encounter with the whale on the *Winslow*. MSS 64, series G, sub-series 2. Courtesy of
the New Bedford Whaling Museum

"Soon after anchoring," he wrote, "had the Doctor from a Spanish King's Ship. He examined my wounds as I lay on my cabin floor. I talked with him through a linguist. He pronounced my wounds bad, my left hand must be cut off, my head was bad, (did not propose cutting that off) but recommended my having the Chaplain to come and confess me." Gardner's dry wit regarding his serious injury is a rhetorical move that appears in other accounts of whaling captains' disabilities, and which we will consider under the rubric of "lies" in the section that follows. Gardner's medical condition, however, was dire. The Spanish doctor saw "little chance" of his recovery. But Gardner knew another whaling captain who had his leg broken by a whale and had been miraculously revived by "an old Doctor" residing nearby in Piura. He directed his mate to go ashore and send for him. When the sixty-nine-year-old doctor came aboard the ship and examined Gardner, he was confident he could treat his patient and even save his badly wounded hand. But he recommended Gardner be conveyed to Piura, a little more than thirty miles inland, where he could reside near his own lodgings. To make the journey, Gardner was carried on a cot suspended between two mules, with an awning hung to protect him from the blazing sun. For six weeks Gardner lived in an apartment in front of the doctor's office. The doctor applied splints to both arms—one to set the right shoulder and one to set the left arm and hand—which left Gardner "entirely helpless" and in need of someone to feed, bathe, and dress him. The wound in the left hand had to be reopened so the doctor could remove bone, although Gardner would not allow him to break and reset the right shoulder so it would have more mobility. As the doctor predicted, it caused Gardner "much pain" to lift his arms, so he had to have shirts and jackets fitted with strings sewn inside them that enabled him to dress himself. After two months, he was well enough to meet the *Winslow*, which had returned to Paita, and resume command.[22]

If Gardner's disability impeded his ability to carry out his duties as captain, he mentions nothing about it in his journal, but when the ship returned to Massachusetts in 1817, he began to suffer from depression. "Having returned in an invalid state," he wrote, "few days passed without ill feelings caused by my weak state. It seemed doubtful to me if I should ever be able to do much more." Tragically, the cause for which he determined to work despite his suffering—to "do something for the support of my little family"—betrayed him in the months after his return as each of his children, in quick succession, succumbed to whooping cough. The trauma deepened his depression. "We buried all three of them in less than three months, leaving our house desolate," he wrote. "'Twas a severe dispensation but could do nothing ourselves but put our trust in divine Providence, where our whole support and strength lay." He started a school and for one fall and winter taught mathematics and navigation to aspiring seamen, but in the spring, when the owners of the *Winslow* offered him the command of another whale-ship being built in New Bedford, he accepted and revived his career as a captain. The price of whale oil fell to an all-time low in 1822, so in 1824, finding the business no longer remunerating, he gave up whaling and began commanding trading voyages.[23]

In 1826, at the age of forty-two, Gardner quit the sea, but his disability had not truncated his career. Most sea captains retired by the age of forty, and those who worked longer considered themselves "hard done by." This was certainly the case for Gardner, and for reasons that applied to many mariners: "I was ready to listen to anything that would divert me from the life of a sailor, having spent much of my time on the ocean for more than twenty years," he wrote. "Much of the time in rugged weather, I had little rest or comfort until fair weather, having had so many broken bones, I had little refreshing sleep." He reduced his exposure to the currents of the global shipping industry to the purely financial, investing in ships and moving his family from Nantucket to New Bedford, where he ran a gauging and coopering business and became a prominent figure in the community. But even on shore, old age brought new injuries that echoed those of his youth. Just before his eightieth birthday, when he was invited to tour the latest phase of construction on Fort Taber, Gardner fell through two wooden planks and broke his leg. He used crutches, and then a cane, until his death at the age of ninety.[24]

Kahekili Keʻeaumoku, unlike Cook and Gardner, did not experience serious disability until he suffered, as missionary William Ellis put it, "frequent attacks of disease . . . during the last years of his life." In this sense, his story represents one of the most common forms of disability in Oceania during the Age of Sail, as contact with Europeans exposed Indigenous people to novel and devastating pathogens. These *maʻi malihini*, as the Hawaiians called them, were particularly virulent in Hawaiʻi in the nineteenth century because trade winds had long carried large ships far to the north or to the south of the archipelago, leading to its relatively late encounters with English, European, and American mariners and contributing to the epidemiological insularity that made Hawaiians particularly vulnerable to the respiratory infections and sexually transmitted diseases foreigners carried. Keʻeaumoku was born in the wake of European contact, around 1784, to a powerful ruling family. His father, chief Keʻeaumoku Pāpaʻiahiahi, was one of five crucial supporters of Kamehameha I, who conquered competing polities to become the first ruler of the unified islands. In 1782, Keʻeaumoku Pāpaʻiahiahi led Kamehameha's forces to victory over Kīwalaʻō, the ruler of the island of Hawaiʻi, during the Battle of Mokuʻōhai. He was seriously wounded in the campaign. According to the American Protestant missionary Hiram Bingham, he executed the decisive action of the battle when he rushed upon the warriors of Kīwalaʻō, who then fell upon him, threw him down, and stabbed him first with a *pololu* (spear) and then a *pahoa* (dagger). At the same time, Kīwalaʻō "was struck by a stone and felled," diverting the attention of the warriors attacking Keʻeaumoku Pāpaʻiahiahi. "Though in the hands of his enemies, overpowered, and weak with fatigue and wounds," he used the distraction to rush to the fallen Kīwalaʻō. He "seized him by the throat" and killed him. "Thus, in the utmost straits," Bingham wrote, "he turned the scale of battle in favor of Kamehameha, who then rushed on, overpowered and routed his opponents." He was rewarded for his military victories with posts as governor of large areas of the island of Hawaiʻi and senior counselor to Kamehameha. He and his wife, Nāmāhānaʻi Kaleleokalani, had five children. Their eldest, Kaʻahumanu, became Kamehameha's most powerful wife and a prominent figure in his government and the governments of his two immediate successors. Kahekili Keʻeaumoku was their third child, just older than another son, Kuakini. The couple died of disease, possibly cholera, during an epidemic that ravaged Hawaiʻi in 1804 and that infected Kamehameha and many of his warriors.[25]

Like their father, Keʻeaumoku's brother Kuakini was seriously injured, although in an amorous escapade rather than a military campaign. Samuel Kamakau writes, "When his parents died of the cholera he was a grown man with a fine bearing, soft eyes like a dove's, and a feminine face very attractive to women." One evening, he arranged an assignation with the wife of the governor of Oahu. In the midst of it, "he was discovered by the guards and set upon by the husband. He fled and jumped over a stone wall, and the rocks fell on his foot and broke it so that he was thenceforth lame. . . . Kua-kini almost died of his broken foot, and his uncles Ka-uhi-wawae-ono and Kekua-manohaʻ came and took him to Puʻuloa and treated him until he recovered." The disability did not impede his political career; he and his brother were both governors and central figures in Hawaiian public life by the 1820s, a transformative decade in Hawaiian history during which the islands' economy and culture registered the influence of visiting whalemen, merchants, and foreign missionaries. For a time, Kahekili Keʻeaumoku served as commander of Kamehameha's navy while Kuakini served as commander of the army. But foreign visitors struggled to interpret Kuakini's disability, since he

Figure 19. *Kuakini, Governor of Hawaii* ("John Adams" Kuakini). Engraved by S. S. Jocelyn, from a sketch by William Ellis, circa 1823. Frontispiece from [William Ellis], *A Journal of a Tour around Hawaii, the Largest of the Sandwich Islands* (Boston, 1825). Library of Congress, https://www.loc.gov/resource/gdcmassbookdig.journaloftouraroooelli/?sp=6&r=-1.14,-0 .282,3.28,2.079,0

navigated his environment easily and only occasionally struggled to stand or walk. He boarded the Dutch merchant Jacobus Boelen's vessel with the aid of a chair designed for women disinclined or unable to "climb up the side of the ship," and when he stood up on the deck, "he fell over backward with such force that in truth the whole ship shook from the impact." But Boelen recalled: "He seemed to bother less about his fall than I should have expected. It is probable that unfamiliarity with the practice of wearing shoes, or possibly a dizziness from his being hoisted on the chair were the causes of his crash. As soon as the man had recovered from his accident, he shook my hand warmly and bade me welcome in the bay, in very intelligible English." Captain Louis-Claude de Saulces de Freycinet, an officer in the French navy, misattributed Kuakini's limp to obesity. He wrote, "I wished to see the shipyards and principal workshops of [Kamehameha]; Kouakini hastened to lead me to them, and I appreciated his actions the more, since he walks with some effort on account of his extreme weight." That Kuakini played host so enthusiastically even on uneven and unfamiliar terrain demonstrates his commitment to foreign trade and relations, which his brother shared. Both gave themselves names that referenced American and English industry or politics. Kuakini styled himself "John Adams Kuakini," and Keʻeaumoku used the name "George Cox" after King George and an Englishman named Harold Cox who married into his family of Maui chiefs.[26]

Keʻeaumoku was at least as interested in economic development as diplomacy after Kamehameha appointed him governor of Maui, Molokaʻi, Lānaʻi, and Kahoʻolawe around 1812. Gilbert Farquhar Mathison, traveling with a sea captain who purchased sandalwood from him, reported a conversation in which Keʻeaumoku "adduced the magnitude of his own wealth and possessions, which were the result of trade with the Americans." Mathison went on: "He is said to be worth twenty or thirty thousand dollars, and derives an increasing yearly income from the sale of sandal-wood, which grows upon his land. He is very covetous and fond of money withal, and knows how to drive a hard bargain. The mention of his wealth and power as very great, gives him infinite satisfaction." Although a few European and American visitors to Hawaiʻi found Keʻeaumoku indolent or distracted (possibly because his interest in the sandalwood trade preoccupied him) and many sources comment on his propensity to drink (which was not anomalous among rulers at the time), none offers evidence to refute Mathison's estimation of him as an uncommonly successful player in Hawaiʻi's expanding commercial markets.[27]

Figure 20. *Governor Cox of Maui* (George Cox Keʻeaumoku). By Adrien Taunay the Younger. 1819. Ink and watercolor over graphite. Collection of the Honolulu Museum of Art. Purchase, 1992 (21490)

Whatever else American and European visitors said about Keʻeaumoku's net worth or temperament and whatever they implied about his personal habits or character, almost all commented on his athletic build. If there was anything deviant about his embodiment, to these observers' eyes, it was that he was remarkably attractive and regal in bearing. Mathison, for example, introduced him this way: "He is a large, athletic, handsome

Disabled

man, of an ingenuous and good-humoured countenance." Ellis elsewhere quotes Mathison as fawning, as he watched Ke'eaumoku receive lessons in Christianity: "His tall athletic form and bust seen bending over the other's shoulders, and dignified demeanor, marked at one glance his rank and superiority over all around." Freycinet described him as "quite muscular, of a grave but agreeable appearance." Presbyterian, Congregationalist, and Dutch Reformist missionaries sponsored by the American Board of Commissioners for Foreign Missions were grateful for Ke'eaumoku's sanction of their presence on the islands beginning in 1820, even if it stopped short of conversion to their god. Their gratitude might have been manifest in their constant praise of his physical grace and prowess. When Bingham, who arrived with the first group of missionaries to Hawai'i, hosted a ceremony to open a printing press intended to distribute proselytizing material in Hawaiian, he wrote, "A considerable number was present, and among those particularly interested was Keeaumoku, who, after a little instruction from Mr. [Elisha] Loomis, applied the strength of his athletic arm to the lever of a Ramage press, pleased thus to assist in working off a few impressions of the first lessons."[28]

It was a dramatic shift, then, when the same missionaries began describing Ke'eaumoku as frail and sickly. The Reverend Charles Samuel Stewart, who arrived in Hawai'i to reinforce the mission in 1823, quoted Ellis's description of the "painful" and "protracted" illness that preceded Ke'eaumoku's death in Oahu in March 1824. Kamakau writes that Ke'eaumoku's sister Ka'ahumanu was "called home in February" by the illness of her brother. He goes on: "He was treated by foreign physicians but died March 23 [1824] at Pakaka in Honolulu. On the night that he died Kua-kini arrived from Hawaii, lay off shore with his ship, and secretly took away the body to Hawaii leaving Mr. Bingham to conduct the funeral services over an empty coffin." According to Kamakau, "The chiefs did not at this time take the missionaries seriously and some of them said, 'Let us see whether the foreign god has power to tell them that the coffin is empty.'" On the coffin that did contain the remains of his brother, Kuakini had engraved, in large letters, the name COX.[29]

LIES AND THE IDEOLOGY OF OCEANIC ABILITY

On these stories hangs a skin of representation, and the purpose in this section is to momentarily subordinate the interiority of subjects with disabilities to the issue of the public-facing presentations of their bodies they constructed or that were constructed for them during and after their lives.[30] I undertake a class-conscious reading of disability here, but with a caveat: in Oceania, disability signified differently than it did on the American continent. Although the term *disability* is unmanageably broad (a hand blasted by gunpowder or mauled by a whale differs fundamentally from sciatica or mental illness), and even the constrained category of oceanic disability during the late eighteenth and early nineteenth centuries risks erasing important differences (people injured in Tonga did not necessarily feel about it as people injured in Hawai'i or on an English ship measuring the distance between the two), the commonness of oceanic disability during this period created a natural basis for social connection and solidarity. The focus here is on disabilities associated with injury, and the next section considers the crisis of illness-induced disability in Oceania, although the two are in important ways related. While the statistical concept of the norm was not invented until the 1840s, the sense that illness and injury were unremarkable facts of life in these spaces during the latter half of the Age of Sail was not lost on their inhabitants. Disability was neither a recognized identity nor a subject of political awareness and activism because it did not need to be; it coexisted fluidly with oceanic experience. So those who experienced and represented oceanic disability were not saddled with the task of reconciling deviant bodies with unattainable, or at least unsustainable, standards of health, beauty, youth, or fitness fixed in the continental public imaginary. If, as Lennard Davis argues, "normalcy and disability are part of the same system," with the one concept invoking and constituting the other, we must recognize that poles of disability and ability, like so many continental paradigms, were unmoored in Oceania. Oceanic values inverted the ideology of ability that prevailed on land. To be disabled on early American land was to be pathetic, threatening, inconvenient, or invisible. Later, with some advances in the awareness and treatment of people with disabilities, it was to be hyperindividual, or, euphemistically, "special." But to have physical signs of past injuries on islands, archipelagos, and ships was to be normal—and because it is difficult and sometimes dangerous to be abnormal, it was even something to be desired.[31]

To get a sense of the particular strain oceanic environments put on human and nonhuman bodies, we need look no further than the journal of Reverend Charles Samuel Stewart, who sailed to join his companions in the Hawaiian mission on the whale ship *Thames*, which briefly fell into company with the *Winslow*, the ship on which Gardner had been wounded. Stewart found the voyage endlessly diverting, and his vivid descriptions of a whale hunt capture

Disabled

the danger of the enterprise in a way that logbooks kept by those immersed in the day-to-day business of whaling and inured to its occasional thrills (and bound by the constraints of the economical genre) seldom do. On December 23, 1822, he wrote:

> The boats [lowered to chase whales] are of the most light, and apparently fragile construction, formed to move with the utmost rapidity, and to ride even on the crest of a wave. The harpooner stands erect on the bow, with a firmness and gracefulness which practice only could secure, while the boat bounds from height to depth and from depth to height of the swelling sea. At a proper distance, his eye fixed on his victim, he darts the instrument with a force, which would seem, inevitably, to throw him from his narrow foot-hold into the water, while the floundering animal, writhing in the desperation of death, puts the boat in constant jeopardy.
>
> The danger is by no means imaginary; many boats are destroyed, and many lives are lost, in whaling voyages. The line, hundreds of yards in length, to which the harpoon is attached, is coiled in a tub in the fore part of the boat, and permitted to run off according to the power and speed of the whale to which it has been fastened; while one of the boatmen stands with a hatchet to cut it off, at a single blow, in case it should become entangled, as the delay of an instant, might prove fatal, and the boat be irresistibly taken down by the animal. It not infrequently happens, that an arm or leg of some of the men is caught in the line, as it glides with the quickness of lightning from the tub, and, should not the limb be at once severed from the body by it, the wretch is, in a moment, hurried to an irrecoverable depth.

As Stewart's rapt attention to the spectacle of torturing a whale to death attests, the industry's hazards were a feature, not a bug. Those who could stomach the financial risk an investment in whaling required could grow rich beyond all reason. Sailors on canoes, boats, and whaleships, which included islanders and Indigenous people from all over the world, endured long hours of tedium in exchange for adventures including the frenzy of the hunt, whose stakes were life and death. The risks whale hunters incurred are too many to catalog; any whaling logbook will mention injuries, whether minor (burns from sun, rope, and oil, for example) or critical (severed limbs or crushed bodies). The survivors of these injuries experienced disability temporarily, at least, and most bore lifelong scars or other physical manifestations of the incidents.[32]

Logbooks suggest most maritime injuries were not accidental. Naval and whaling captains aimed to disable at least as often as they aimed to kill. The powder horn that exploded in Captain Cook's hand is one injury stacked against a grim tally, which mounted steeply in the last years of his life, of injuries doled out at his command. On Cook's first voyage to the Pacific, twenty-one men guilty of crimes ranging from disobedience to assault received a total of 354 lashes. On his second voyage to the Pacific, twenty men received a total of 288 lashes. On his third voyage, from 1776–1779, forty-four men aboard the *Resolution* received a total of 684 lashes, some as many as 24 at a time, twice the legal maximum allowed by Navy regulations. This count does not include the Indigenous people Cook deliberately wounded during the third voyage, including a Tongan man flogged 72 times with the cat-o'-nine-tails, other Tongans whose ears he cut off, and still others he maimed with oars and boat hooks. English naval ships were notorious for their violence against friend and foe alike—inspiring, as Peter Linebaugh and Marcus Rediker have argued, uprisings among crew that reverberated across the waters during the Age of Revolutions—but they were not anomalous. Even Edmund Gardner, "born and educated a friend or Quaker, [and] consequently opposed to war" (he thought the terrapins in Australia, who stretch their necks until one's head outreaches the other's, had mastered "the only good way of fighting"), intentionally injured a member of his whaling crew during the same voyage on the *Winslow* when he was critically wounded. "On the early part of the voyage, for some misdemeanor, had to punish one of my men, from which time he behaved himself like a man," Gardner recorded. Far from bristling at the injury, the crew member considered the punishment routine and told Gardner, "You served me just right." Perhaps he counted himself fortunate to have been afforded the American maritime industry's version of due process, as Gardner assembled the crew to witness the flogging and "addressed him by telling him the laws of his Country were open for him if [he] had not done him justice." Many injuries were extralegal, even according to the loosely regulated judicial procedures of the sea. Joan Druett, in her history of the surgeons who joined nineteenth-century whaling voyages, tells of one watchman shocked from a deep sleep when a mate hammered a spike into his head. The bodies of tortured whales and the compliance of tortured men were not negative externalities of maritime enterprise during the eighteenth and nineteenth centuries; they were its most valuable products.[33]

And, in these conditions, the experience of disability formed an essential basis for class solidarity. Some sailors came to prefer visible signs of inflicted or accidental injury to able-bodiedness. Herman Melville, who was at sea from 1839 to 1844, suggests in his novella Billy Budd, Sailor, published posthumously in 1924, that a sailor's body unmarked by scars or other legible signs of maritime injury connoted immaturity at best and at worst an alarming degree of self-interest. Billy Budd is disabled in a conventional sense—he has a speech impediment, a stutter that prevents him from defending himself against a false charge of conspiring to mutiny on an English man-of-war in 1797 and thus propels the tragic arc of the narrative, which ends with his hanging. But, except for the moment when Billy, unable to muster a verbal response, lashes out and kills the officer accusing him, his speech impediment poses no challenge to his ability to fraternize or labor at sea. Unlike those who labored in landlocked environments, mariners had little difficulty bridging linguistic difference. After convalescing in Piura a month, Gardner itched for news of his ship. One day, a man watering a horse called to him, "Capitan tu Fragata es en Paita." Gardner wrote:

> I then called him to me, asking him how he knew my ship was at Paita. (Had of necessity to speak Spanish, no other language being spoken.) The muleteer informed me my ship was in Paita, had taken five whales, had lost one big one. I then asked him how he knew all this. He informed me 'Mudo oblace tutear.' My mate had enjoined it on all the ship's company not to inform me what they had done. I had one man who was a mute, the mate never thought to caution him. 'Twas from him the Spaniard was informed. I was fifty miles in the Country, learned through a deaf and dumb man my ship was in Port, had been successful.

Possibly Gardner thought his readers would be surprised at the thought of an informant who did not speak, but he couldn't have been; in Namibia, he communicated with the Khoekhoen "by signs," and in Kealakekua Bay a Hawaiian hunter alerted him to the presence of a large sperm whale and then later "shut his eyes and laid his head on one side in his hand" to inform Gardner that one of his boatsteerers had killed it. Almost every account of an oceanic voyage during the late eighteenth and early nineteenth centuries mentions Indigenous sailors who joined the crew. On his third voyage to the Pacific, Cook took two Maori boys when he left New Zealand; two Maui voyagers sailed with Gardner from Hawai'i to New Bedford in 1819; and a young Hawaiian man (who "had been on several of these cruises") left with Jacobus Boelen on his ship Wilhelmina & Maria in 1828 and sailed to Holland—just several of countless cases that illustrate the racial, ethnic, and linguistic diversity of the oceanic workforce. Although Billy Budd's stutter figures prominently in the climax of the novella, it is immaterial in the rest of the narrative, as such a disability would have been on a typical eighteenth-century ship.[34]

Instead, it is a counterintuitive disability, Billy's aberrantly able body, that distinguishes him from the ship's crew and sets the persecution plot in motion. Melville endows his protagonist with mythic beauty. "He showed in face that humane look of reposeful good nature which the Greek sculptor in some instances gave to his heroic strong man, Hercules," he rhapsodizes. "But this again was subtly modified by another and pervasive quality. The ear, small and shapely, the arch of the foot, the curve in mouth and nostril, . . . but above all, something in the mobile expression, and every chance attitude and movement, [was] suggestive of a mother eminently favored by Love and the Graces." The description goes on, but what becomes clear is that Billy is repeatedly isolated and disadvantaged by precisely these physical characteristics. For example, he is the only crew member on board the English merchant ship *Rights-of-Man* to be pressed into the king's service on HMS *Bellipotent*, the ship on which he eventually hangs.

> Plump upon Billy at first sight in the gangway the boarding officer, Lieutenant Ratcliffe, pounced, even before the merchantman's crew was formally mustered on the quarter-deck for his deliberate inspection. And him only he elected. For whether it was because the other men when ranged before him showed to ill advantage after Billy, or whether he had some scruples in view of the merchantman's being rather short-handed, however it might be, the officer contented himself with his first spontaneous choice.

His appearance then arouses the envy and ultimately the ire of John Claggart, the officer who accuses Billy and dies by his hand. Their relationship is defined by physical difference: "In view of the marked contrast between the persons of the twain, it is more than probable that when the master-at-arms . . . applied to the sailor the proverb 'Handsome is as handsome does,' he there let escape an ironic inkling, not caught by the young sailors who heard it, as to what it was that had first moved him against Billy, namely, his significant personal beauty." Billy's body is not just aesthetically appealing but also unmarked by scars, which was a social advantage on land but at sea in the eighteenth century suggested a lack of experience with the hazards of maritime life that bound sailors together in a sense of shared sacrifice.[35]

The novel introduces him in ways that underscore this professional inexperience: he is "Billy Budd—or Baby Budd, as more familiarly, under circumstances hereafter to be given, he at last came to be called." Billy is twenty-one when he is impressed (older than most sailors on their first voyage), and yet he seems to grow younger as the novella wears on—he *at last* came to be called Baby Budd. That is, his beauty increasingly seems to indicate immaturity, or perhaps even an aversion to the inevitable risks of maritime labor. In contrast, the oldest crewman on the *Bellipotent* wears his experience on his face, "a long pale scar like a streak of dawn's light falling athwart the dark visage." Scars in Oceania were documents of experience as well as expertise. One whaling captain sewed up at least one of his patients with a sail needle and waxed twine. Because he knew only one stitch—the one he used to mend sails—the man was left "with a distinctive scar in a neat herringbone pattern." As Billy's compatriots acquire such visible marks of their oceanic labor and knowledge, Billy's beauty becomes a pretext for his exclusion from the crew and perhaps even an indication of his narrow self-interest. In the context of a naval ship, his persistently able body is even more alienating than it was on the merchant ship. After armed combat, disability manifested commitment not just to a crew but also to a cause. But when Billy fights, as when he strikes Claggart, it is to defend himself rather than to advance a communal objective. It is portentous we first meet the "Handsome Sailor" on board the *Rights-of-Man*: as his unblemished body comes increasingly to signify, Billy is concerned with these rights in the singular rather than the plural.[36]

Scars served a similar signifying function on the Hawaiian Islands through the early nineteenth century, where Native warfare was a regular political force. As Cook arrived at the islands, Kalani'ōpu'u was attempting to conquer eastern Maui. Chiefs had attempted such conquests before, and they would do so again, and so battle scars were deeply etched into Hawaiian memory and bodies. Two days before Hawaiian warriors responded to Captain Cook's plot to seize Kalani'ōpu'u, they demanded to know whether Cook possessed a body marked by experience in combat or one (like Billy Budd's) that was tellingly unblemished. On February 12, 1779, amid the breakdown of relations that precipitated the deadly encounter at Kealakekua Bay, a Hawaiian chief boarded the *Resolution* and sat down at Cook's table. David Samwell, the surgeon's first mate on the *Resolution*, gives his version of the exchange that followed. The chief asked Cook

if he was a *Tata Toa* [*Hakaka Koa*]; which means a fighting man, or soldier. Being answered in the affirmative, he desired to see his wounds: Captain Cook held out his right-hand, which had a scar upon it, dividing the thumb from the finger, the whole length of the metacarpal bones. The Indian, being thus convinced of his being a Toa [Koa], put the same question to another gentleman present, but he happened to have none of those distinguishing marks: the chief then said, that he himself was a Toa [Koa], and showed the scars of some wounds he had received in battle.

Cook's answer was a lie by omission. The scar on his hand was not evidence of battle action; it was a souvenir of an accident during a surveying mission. But Cook understood enough about his environment to exaggerate his disability since it put him in company with the chief and suggested a basis for his superior rank over the other English man rooted in something like character rather than politics. Since the Hawaiians no longer trusted Cook's words, they might have turned to deciphering his intentions in Hawai'i based on the history of violent conflict inscribed on his body.[37]

Cook's right hand and the experience it archived was a site of controversy in representations made of him during and after his life as Native Hawaiians, his crew, and a wider public used the scar to establish his reputation and contest his legacy. John Webber, the official artist appointed to Cook's third Pacific expedition, was a great admirer of the captain, with whom he spent two years in close quarters on the *Resolution*. Webber adapted to the rhythms of naval life and doubtless absorbed some of its values. Shortly after Cook died, Webber made two portraits that idealized the wound of which Cook seems so proud in Samwell's account of the days before his death. Although he stopped short of showing the scar, in each portrait Webber depicted Cook's left hand bare but the right hand gloved, an asymmetry that points viewers to his disability. Webber shared with Samwell a sense, born of oceanic reasoning, of the scar as a sign of experience rather than a deformity. When Nathaniel Dance-Holland, an English artist who traveled to study in Italy but spent no substantial amount of time at sea, painted Cook's hands in 1775 ungloved and without the mark of the powder horn blast, he superimposed a terrestrial vision of the ideal human form onto Webber's terraqueous one. But when Samuel Kamakau created his own representation of Cook's right hand, he erased the scar as a political rather than an aesthetic gesture, one that refuted Cook's claim that his hand bore evidence of his experience as a koa. Although James King described the state in which Cook's hands— including the distinctively scarred right hand—were preserved and returned to the English, Kamakau flatly rejected the claim they ever left Hawai'i. He writes:

Figure 21. *Portrait of Captain James Cook*. By John Webber. Circa 1780. Oil on canvas. Gift of the New Zealand Government, 1960. Te Papa (1960-0013-1)

Figure 22. *Portrait of Captain James Cook* RN. By John Webber. 1782. Oil on canvas. National Portrait Gallery of Australia. Purchased by the Commonwealth Government with the generous assistance of Robert Oatley AO and John Schaeffer AO 2000

Captain Cook was a [man of] Britain famous for his explorations in the Indian, Atlantic, and the Pacific oceans. He discovered lands in the ocean which were [previously] unknown. He had been but a short time in Hawai'i when God punished him for his sin. It was not the fault of the Hawaiian people that they held him sacred and paid him honor as a god worshipped by the Hawaiian people. But because he killed the

Disabled

people he was killed by them without mercy, and his entrails were used to rope off the arena, and the palms of his hands used for fly swatters at a cock fight. Such is the end of a transgressor.

In this representation, Cook's hands are again unblemished (neither scarred by injury nor by postmortem gashing to preserve them as relics, as in King's account), but here Kamakau denies Cook the distinction of having a scar as a way of negating the equivalence between a colonial officer who fired on enemies from his ship and a Hawaiian koa engaged in hand-to-hand combat during the interisland conflicts of the eighteenth century. They both saw battle, but they were physically exposed to and marked by mortal danger in utterly dissimilar ways, and Kamakau does not impute to Cook's hand a scar that would elide the difference.[38]

These histories suggest that the Hawaiians' nickname for Edmund Gardner, "the crooked handed man," was closer to an honorific than an insult, as it might have been on the American continent. In New Bedford, a man who dined with Gardner gawked at his disabled body and then later wrote about it in the daily Morning Mercury. He foregrounded Gardner's disability in describing him, but with nothing of the spare candor of the Hawaiians. "It was the chewed-up right hand of the captain as he sat by me at table which had first excited my curiosity—(stimulating the inquiries which drew from him, at last, this thrilling story)—the stump, or what was visible below the coat-sleeve, looking like a twisted rope's end, but still retaining clutch enough to carry the chowder-spoon to his mouth," the author begins. After staring at Gardner eating with his "stump" and then prevailing upon him "at last" to tell the story of his disabilities, the author proceeds to prod (literally) his uncomfortable dinner companion. "The healing of the wound in the head left a cavity like the inside of an egg-shell; and . . . it tells, after forty years, the size of the tooth that did it. I laid the ends of my three fingers very comfortably in the hallow." The Hawaiian designation "crooked handed man" does not obviously convey either the flippant voyeurism or the entitled ableism of the New Bedford article. It is not clear the reference was meant to be pejorative, and when read alongside Samwell's account of the encounter on the Resolution, it seems unlikely it would have been. There was nothing unusual about a voyager and a hunter having a disability, as Hawaiians well knew. If the sobriquet was not intentionally laudatory, it was probably neutral; their reference to Gardner by way of his most distinguishing physical feature has a frank economy typical of cross-cultural and especially cross-linguistic encounters, when the objective is clear communication rather than subtlety or politesse. But "crooked handed man" might have had a note of admiration to it, since an oceanic people understood that a man who commanded a whale ship would have obvious signs of his tenure in a dangerous line of work.[39]

Part of the value associated with disability in these contexts had its root in the practical fact that in oceanic environments in the eighteenth and early nineteenth centuries, surviving a serious injury was a privilege reserved for the powerful and the fortunate. Gardner's journal describes the extraordinary measures his crew took to arrest their voyage the moment the whale crushed his body, to reroute the ship to the nearest port in Paita, to use his global connections to other captains and influential political figures to find an expert medical professional who dedicated weeks to his treatment, and to allow him the time on land he needed to recover from his injuries. In Piura, Gardner was a celebrity. A "dense column" of people assembled along the road to witness his arrival, and "many of them," he said, "tendered to me all the assistance 'twas in their power. Many of the females picked and prepared lint for dressing my wounds. Many little delicacies of fruit and flowers were sent me." He interpreted his miraculous recovery as a dispensation from God, but he was the beneficiary of human favor and favoritism, as well. Cook enjoyed similar preference when his crew dedicated themselves to responding to the blast that should have taken his hand and similar luck, or providence, when he found a nearby vessel with a French doctor qualified and inclined to care for his wound. Common sailors on American whalers were treated by the captain, who, armed with a few directions in a manual, a medicine cabinet stocked to his own specifications, and whatever grim experience he had accumulated in surgery, did his best to manage the injury quickly and cheaply enough not to hit the nerves of the ship's investors. The stakes were not terribly high; if a sailor did not survive, any port could supply his replacement.[40]

The reason we see more iconic ship captains—Ahab, Hook, Long John Silver—than ordinary sailors with the prostheses that indicate the successful amputation of a limb is probably less a matter of artistic fancy than a reflection of historical fact. As captains with disabilities, Cook and Gardner were not outliers. Magellan sustained a wound during an expedition to Morocco that left him with a permanent limp, and Horatio Nelson lost sight in one eye and most of one arm in combat. Before a 1670 voyage, Henry Morgan's pirates agreed to a schedule of "Recompenses and Rewards" to which they were entitled for lost limbs, and, like so much of piratical culture, the agreement manifests democratic aspirations—in this case, that the ordinary pirate could acquire the death-defying disabilities of ship captains. "For the loss of both Legs, they assigned 1500 pieces of Eight, or 15 Slaves, the Choice being left to the election of the Party. For the loss of both Hands, 1800 pieces of Eight, or 18 Slaves," Alexandre Olivier Exquemelin writes in *Americaensche Zee-Roovers* (published in English as *Bucaniers of America* in 1684). In dramatizing the riot of calamities that might have activated this contract, *Americaensche Zee-Roovers* makes it apparent that, for all their revolutionary ideals, pirate captains were not at great risk of having to pay out survivors of double amputations. Sailors almost invariably bore the scars of minor injuries, but to possess a prosthetic leg or arm in the medical conditions that prevailed at sea signaled either extreme good fortune or, more likely, that the man had a body whose value held its own against the potential returns of a voyage.[41]

A determinative feature that whaling, merchant, and naval ships shared with the Hawaiian Islands they visited was these striations in social structure that perpetuated disparities in health and encouraged class-based conceptions of disability. Although herbal remedies were familiar across the islands, a small class of elites including warriors, priests, chiefs, advisers, and healers enjoyed a higher standard of living than commoners, which predisposed them to better outcomes following injury. Beginning in the late sixteenth century, the maka'āinana (commoners) were required to give a portion of their crops to the ali'i (the ruling class) as a tribute. The maka'āinana called the ali'i "shark[s] that [travel] on land."[42] Diet alone was enough to increase their odds of surviving serious injuries, but ali'i also enjoyed labor routines and lifestyles that supported their health and recovery. In the early nineteenth century, when chiefs including Kamehameha and Ke'eaumoku became active in the sandalwood trade, they forced the maka'āinana to harvest the wood in the mountains, haul it to the shores, and load it on ships, arduous labor that kept workers from tending and harvesting their own crops. For this labor they were ill-fed and compensated poorly, or not at all. One popular nickname for Ke'eaumoku, "Pu'u-nui" ("Great Heap"), was a jab aimed squarely at the joint between social class and physical embodiment on the islands. Although he was likely larger than the average Hawaiian, and members of his family were according to many accounts obese, the name did not mock his body as much as it critiqued what it reflected: the political system that allowed Ke'eaumoku to garnish the hard-earned agricultural products of the maka'āinana even as he forced them to labor for his financial gain in the sandalwood system. He and his associates feasted on this taxed produce "until they could eat no more," according to Kamakau, but amounts exceeding what they needed or wanted to consume—great heaps—were left to rot. It's not that "Puʻu-nui" or anyone else was heavy that was risible to the 99 percent of Hawaiians outside the ruling class; the metaphor pointed out that chiefs and those in their elite circles grew fat off land they did not tend.[43]

Amid these pronounced divisions on ships and on the islands, we see a socially inverted form of disability oppression in which members of disadvantaged classes make satire from the embodiments, including disabilities, that signified rulers' privilege. I use the word "ruler" deliberately, for the notion of sea captains as sovereigns akin to the Hawaiian aliʻi is not so far off, even given the obvious differences in the origins and implications of their authority. Just as the American whaling captain served as surgeon on a voyage, the Hawaiian kahuna (advisers, priests, and healers) were considered part of the family of the aliʻi. Louis Freycinet remarked, "The chiefs and their wives are the ones who know best of all the art of curing wounds." On both ships and on the Hawaiian Islands, then, rulers dispensed medical care or had better access to it than commoners. They also wielded disproportionate power over political conflicts and judicial processes that inevitably produced wounds. Kamakau's history is peppered with descriptions of the injuries warriors inflicted in the course of advancing a chief's interests and the tortures chiefs devised for their enemies. Edmund Gardner was an example of temperance when he advised the crewman he flogged that he was welcome to seek justice on land, but he only underscored the bleak reality: for a common sailor unfairly used, there was no justice at sea. Until a ship reached shore, a captain's rule was absolute. Rulers' status-signifying disabilities thus became targets of comedy that offered catharsis for groups who mocked the figures they feared.[44]

For example, a Nantucket captain named Seth Coffin lost his leg in pursuit of a sperm whale in 1800 on the whaleship Minerva. He became legendary among officers for using his "mechanical genius" to direct his own amputation as he stretched across his berth and to fashion his own prosthesis while the ship was still at sea. His descendants say he pointed a pistol at his mate and said: "My leg has got to come off, or I shall die. I know how it should be done, and will show you how to do it. If you flinch one whit I'll send this instrument through you. I am ready. Begin!" But the popular lore among the seafaring underclass talked back to the myth of hypercompetence and absolute power Coffin's fellow officers and family circulated: "One of the men left onboard to take care of the ship [as the rest of the crew chased after a whale] didn't do promptly what [Coffin] had ordered him to do, so the Captain, not having anything convenient to punish him for his neglect, took off his wooden leg and threw it at him. The sailor threw it overboard and with one leg he could not pursue him." Although stories that make comedy or horror out of disabled bodies are distressingly common in the nineteenth century, some set in Oceania (including Herman Melville's most famous work, *Moby-Dick*) rest on the underclasses' presumption that, unlike the beggar, the washwoman, or the urchin, the monomaniacal sea captain could stand to be taken down a peg. The punch line of Coffin's tale maps precisely onto one told of Ke'eaumoku's brother Kuakini about the fall that injured his foot: "Thereafter, when he fought with his wife and she ran away from him he could not pursue her because of his lameness." There might have been something satisfying in the symbolic act of temporarily grounding this quasi-divine chief—known for being a "patron of thieves," a cavorter among women in a society of segregated and sometimes imbalanced gender roles, and an imposing ruler who enjoyed a position of power propped up by the labor of a buffeted underclass. The tales are political acts of literary rebellion, a mild counterpart to the armed conflicts these top-heavy regimes periodically ignited. The captain who beats people or the roving chief who eats the land are rendered motionless, and the women and men they pursue are granted a moment of respite. Gardner's own pass at comedy in his journal—after the whale's mouth engulfed his body, he wrote, the doctor "pronounced my wounds bad, my left hand must be cut off, my head was bad, (did not propose cutting that off)"—indicates that some oceanic elites were in on the joke. From the perspective of their social inferiors, they could afford to be. Their disfigured bodies were triumphs, not tragedies—disability snatched from the jaws of death.[45]

PAIN AND THE CRISIS OF INDIGENOUS DISABILITY

In pointing out that oceanic rulers were the objects of humor and myth rooted in their privileged conditions of injury and recovery, I have sidestepped the pain that produced the scars islanders and mariners read and valued according to oceanic reason. But I turn now from scars to wounds—that is, the personal experience of disability rather than its public representations—to focus specifically on moments when disability is attended by pain, rather than indicated by signs of past or presumed pain. Although I identified moments when such symbols afforded social opportunities, I do not suggest that the lived experience of pain in Oceania was beneficial or productive, a blessing in disguise. That has been a position advanced by body theorists, some of whom see "suffering and disability either as a way of reconfiguring the physical resources of the body or opening up new possibilities of pleasure."

This, Tobin Siebers argues, is simply another manifestation of the ideology of ability, which "requires that any sign of disability be viewed exclusively as awakening new and magical opportunities for ability." Sometimes pain was just pain, as difficult as that is to sit with and as much as it confounds the impulse of academic argument to search out resolutions and implications. The objective in this section is to bring to the fore the pain of people disabled by the diseases English and European ships introduced to the Hawaiian Islands. But because so much of this pain is left out of the archive, it is reached by way of the pain historical records include in extended discussions of prominent figures in Oceania and scattered references to legions of unnamed commoners. Although I recognize that the pain of rulers like Keʻeaumoku, James Cook, and Edmund Gardner presents ethical and practical impediments to our understanding of common pain in Hawaiʻi, it is a starting place with the potential to connect us to sites of private and less-frequently-contemplated suffering. Such contemplations stand to counter the long-standing assumption in early American studies that Indigenous death is a phenomenon more deserving of our attention than Indigenous disability, the crisis that always preceded depopulation, and in some ways exceeded and survives it.[46]

Dwelling on the personal pain of figures like Cook and Gardner is so difficult and unappealing it is little wonder only family historians and hagiographic biographers do it with any gusto. In the first place, theorists have long associated pain with what Judith Butler calls "abject beings," or those who are pathologized, victimized, and vulnerable. These captains were none of those things. Cook's blasted hand produced a disability, but it did not locate him in an abject position. Even though one of his biographers speculates about his episodes of "mania," "depressive interludes," and his occasional presentation of "the mentality of a gambler," that does not mean posthumous interest in symptoms associated today with bipolar disorder has any relationship to the way he saw himself or was seen by others during his life. On the *Resolution*, Cook was not a disabled person, even if we recognize him now as a person with at least one disability. And neither the scar on his hand nor the erratic behavior Cook's contemporaries documented proves he experienced lifelong or recurring pain associated with physical or mental disability (manic episodes, on the contrary, often produce welcome feelings of euphoria, grandiosity, and disinhibition).[47]

This points out another challenge to making meaning of his, other captains', or early New Englanders' pain: pain is notoriously subjective and changes over time. As Elaine Scarry argues, it overwhelms language and other forms of expression. Even in his journal, Edmund Gardner's pain is difficult to track. Just after the whale struck him, he says, "I had them put clothes around me and get me on deck." But when he had directed his ship to Paita, an old friend from Massachusetts, Captain Micajah Swain, came aboard, and his stoicism gave way. "It was the first time I had any weakness relative to my situation, seeing him in health and me lying on the cabin floor prostrated," he writes. "It made me feel my weakness. I said to Capt. Swain I was quite unmanned as I could not refrain from tears, so weak was I and un-able to help myself." Only a few days later, he had recovered his indifference to pain, or his ability to lie: "I told [the doctor] if he thought it best to take my hand off, 'to off with it.'" No more mention is made of his pain and little of his disabilities until the end of his journal, when back on land and con-fronted again with a continental ideology of ability and his own aging body, he writes, "I have been a cripple since 1816 having many things to contend with, and many poor feelings, was unable to do much." That Gardner felt psychic and physical pain and that the two are closely related is undeniable, and yet it is challenging to honor this pain in the face of the pain he inflicted on so many bodies during his career. In his journal, he mentions that his unlucky crew failed to haul in fourteen whales they successfully killed off the coast of Brazil and records his mounting irritation at seeing each gigantic animal, "as soon as life was extinct, sunk down like a stone." If it is difficult to contemplate the carnage—sometimes so pointless that it did not even produce perfume, candles, buggy whips, or corsets—that drove a species of whale to the brink of extinction, it is impossible to fathom the suffering Cook and his men inflicted on people in the Pacific. It is hard to hold the captains' personal pain against the pain they caused and not to see a kind of inevitability, if not justice, in a whale occasionally striking back. Cook's pow-der horn might be the narrative historian's version of Chekhov's gun: if one of the most powerful English naval officers in history went barging around the world carrying a cartridge of gunpowder, the powder owed it to those following the plot to go off, and his did so under circumstances less objec-tionable than most.[48]

So I mention Cook's torn hand, and Gardner's mauled body, with reser-vations. Their pain did not approach the pain to which they contributed, but the tendency has been to admit the limits of humans' ability to express or comprehend pain rather than to do our imperfect best, working in imper-fect archives, to confront and contemplate pain case by case as it appears before us. When we deem some people's pain unworthy of or inaccessible to consideration, whatever the grounds, we participate in a system of disability oppression that has hurt the truly abject far more often than it has censured the powerful. Cook and Gardner's pain coexisted with the pain they caused, but it is difficult to deny the one without downplaying the other. I simply acknowledge that physical pain was real, that even people whose privileged social conditions cushioned the blows of injury and illnesses felt pain and grief associated with their disabilities, and that pain and grief are capable of being shared and understood by others.[49]

This acknowledgement puts us in a position to give Keʻeaumoku's pain the attention and significance it deserves. He was a powerful person and by birth the beneficiary of an imbalanced political system. Forced labor in the sandalwood trade that made him wealthy contributed to poor health and population decline among the makaʻāinana, the effects of which are still felt in Hawaiʻi today. But his pain—and I stress pain, not just his illness—was a democratizing force. It is almost irresistible to think of illness in impersonal terms, particularly when it metastasizes into epidemic proportions, or to measure its impact in terms of numbers dead. We read, for example, of the Hawaiian "depopulation crisis" perpetrated by Cook's men and the English and Europeans who followed him. We recognize the diseases including gonorrhea, syphilis, tuberculosis, influenza, whooping cough, leprosy, mumps, measles, smallpox, and cholera that foreigners introduced to the islands. Scholars have debated how many Native Hawaiians lived on the islands during the eighteenth century—possibly, David Stannard argues, as many as eight hundred thousand. This number helps establish the precise severity of depopulation owing to death and deeply diminished fertility rates after contact, although no scholars debate the fact of dramatic decline. By the middle of the nineteenth century, as many as 90 percent of Native Hawaiians had died from the effects of introduced diseases, overwork, poor nutrition, and agricultural disruptions. Yet it is almost impossible to think of pain except in personal terms, so it is telling that we do not read of a contemporaneous Hawaiian "disability crisis" that affected Keʻeaumoku and thousands of others. This is not to say that the issue of health in Hawaiʻi in the decades immediately following Cook's voyages has not been the subject of academic inquiry. There have been studies of individual diseases, mostly leprosy, and their appalling influence on Hawaiian history. More recently, Seth Archer has argued that "disease, poor health, and population loss were not bit players in a cast of colonial disruption that tore at the heart of Hawaiian life. Instead they were colonial disruptions of the first order." Few people, aliʻi or makaʻāinana, escaped the pain associated with the forces of disease or poor health, but its presence is generally implied rather than examined. I pause on it here. There are additional insights into colonial disruptions available if we slow our analytic progression from individual case studies to wider implications by inserting the phenomenon of pain between keywords in these studies: "Indigenous health" and "culture," and "disease" and "depopulation." That is, I wish to briefly consider poor health as a personal issue before it becomes a cultural crisis and to give the painful periods of disability that precede disease-induced death their due as moments of vulnerability and transformation.[50]

We know two things about the disease from which Keʻeaumoku died: it was "painful" and "protracted." And, although his social situation differed from the majority of Hawaiians during his life, these two characteristics of his experience with disability were common. He might have noticed just before he became ill that, as Don Francisco de Paula Marín, a Spaniard living in Hawaiʻi, put it, there was "much sickness," but once he became "very sick" himself, the social dimension of his suffering faded in the face of his pain. We must speculate about the nature of this pain since Keʻeaumoku left no record of it, but it is possible to do so, because observers like Louis Freycinet documented the symptoms of diseases introduced to Hawaiʻi, and others like William Ellis visited his deathbed and wrote of what he witnessed. It requires some effort, however, to get beyond the mediation of these observers. In the first place, they have the habit of substituting their discomfort for the pain of others. Adam Smith argues such substitutions enable sympathy ("As we have no immediate experience of what other men feel, we can form no idea of the manner in which they are affected, but by conceiving what we ourselves should feel in the like situation"), but they put the pain of people with disabilities in the realm of inaccessibility, where it is easy to ignore. The French surgeon-naturalist Jean René Constant Quoy provides a typical example in an account of "Catarrhs," or tubercular symptoms, in Hawaiʻi. He writes, "I personally saw a young girl, stretched on some mats under a shed, dying from this terrible disease." He elevates his experience of seeing pain over the girl's experience of living it. He does not report intervening to alleviate her suffering; perhaps it did not occur to him to do so, perhaps he did not know how. Colonial visitors frequently found their Hawaiian hosts mystifying, but they found Hawaiians with disabilities confounding and often grotesque. The legacy of that impression endures: disabled people within Indigenous societies are the "other other," at least twice removed from the subject position of putatively "normal" (white, temporarily able-bodied) people and vulnerable to even greater oppression.[51]

Another habit of temporarily able-bodied observers is to ignore pain associated with disabilities that are not visible and impute pain to anomalous embodiments that are not necessarily painful. So, although he appears in the surgeon Joseph Paul Gaimard's list of suffering people, an "eight-year-old child with an atrophied right arm and a very thin left arm" in the neighborhood of Kailua Bay gave no indication of experiencing pain and differs categorically from the people who appear with him under the general heading of "Diseases" in Hawai'i, such as those "in a complete state of emaciation resulting from dysentery" or a woman with leprosy or tertiary syphilis "whose nose bones no longer existed and who was making a kind of whistling noise." One of the most remarked-upon features of the Hawaiian elite, their "really monstrous weight," sometimes caused no pain at all or contributed, as in Kuakini's case, to observers' inability to perceive physical conditions that did. Even people who share the same diseases or genetic conditions (such as the children born with birth defects a few years after Cook's men left their sexually transmitted diseases on the islands) do not necessarily share the same symptoms or experience them in the same way. Before I make any leap from Ke'eaumoku's pain to the groups with which it connected him epidemiologically or culturally, then, I assert only one thing he certainly shared with other Hawaiians of all embodiments: his pain was at various points and by various observers—even those trying to help him—misunderstood and misinterpreted, which does not change its essential character but must have added to his distress.[52]

The significance of this insight deepens when we consider that the experience of living with misunderstood pain is for many people a continuing situation rather than an isolated event. The impulse to look away from pain manifests in the historical record as brief mentions of illness-induced pain that belie that it is for many people, as it was for Ke'eaumoku, quite "protracted." "Many people sick" is all Marín had to say about an epidemic that was ongoing when Ke'eaumoku died, and Gaimard summarized "madness" in Hawai'i in two sentences: "There are no mad dogs in the islands, but insanity does exist. The maniacs are tied up and sometimes are left to die of hunger." The glosses cover unimaginable periods of pain. Death is the climax in the story of Indigenous health. It is staggering to read of the number of Native Hawaiians who died in the decades after Cook's arrival (and of Native Americans who died in the Northeast during the seventeenth century), and some of these people died of injury or illness almost immediately after contact with Europeans or others infected. But most died over a stretch of time, and many people with disabilities spend long lives in constant or recurring pain. Even when colonial agents did not wield pain as a weapon, it was itself an agent working on the psyches of individuals who were facing new and varied threats to their way of life. From contemporary disability studies comes a meditation on the significance of this phenomenon with transhistorical relevance:

> Many people with disabilities understand that physical pain is an enemy. It hovers over innumerable daily actions, whether the disability is painful in itself or only the occasion for pain because of the difficulty of navigating one's environment. The great challenge every day is to manage the body's pain, to get out of bed in the morning, to overcome the well of pain that rises in the evening, to meet the hundred daily obstacles that are not merely inconveniences but occasions for physical suffering.

Keʻeaumoku experienced "frequent attacks of disease . . . during the last years of his life," but even people who died of sickness more quickly had a window of time ranging from days to months in which pain of varying intensity worked its pernicious influence on their minds and bodies. Yet these were not fallow seasons for infected people, as the raw data on epidemics might suggest; most people worked through illness on issues of far-reaching economic, political, or spiritual import.[53]

Keʻeaumoku was weighing at least one issue of existential significance in the period between these entries in Marín's journal: "14 March. Governor Coks is very sick," "17 March. He is better," and "22 March. This day Governor Coks died." As Ellis wrote, "I visited him daily during his illness, and hope and fear alternately occupied my mind respecting him. I sometimes found him engaged in ejaculatory prayer: 'Lord, thou knowest my deeds from my youth up: thou knowest my sins; Lord, forgive them: save me by Jesus Christ the only Saviour!" Although Ellis might have embellished this account, it is certainly possible Keʻeaumoku had the Christian God on his mind as he died. By 1824, many Native Hawaiians, especially aliʻi, did. Keʻeaumoku grew up under the ancient kapu system of religion, which regulated what was divine (sacred and thus forbidden) and governed interactions among people, gods, and nature. But in 1819, six months after Kamehameha died, Keʻeumoku's sister Kaʻahumanu and her adopted son Liholiho joined other ruling chiefs to nullify it. This inaugurated a "cultural revolution" during which Hawaiians no longer strictly observed traditional planting and harvesting seasons and thus lost access to foods that had been staples of their ancestors' diets, gradually replaced their subsistence economy with a cash economy, and became increasingly (although not uniformly) receptive to Western merchants and missionaries.[54]

But before and after the chiefs took official action against the state religion, individual Hawaiians worked out their own relationships to the ancient gods. Keʻeaumoku's brother and sister regarded their personal health as a referendum on the gods' power. As Kaʻahumanu moved to abolish the kapu system, she was "complaining of feeling generally unwell." Two years later, she began entertaining the Christian missionaries' teachings after a bout of illness from which Hiram Bingham expected her to die. She asked Bingham to pray for her. "She was soon restored," he wrote, "and with her friends set a higher value on the religion which we were endeavoring to inculcate." Bingham thought Kuakini made the same calculation about the "defect, or disease in his limbs, which made it difficult for him to walk or stand." He reported, "Their *kahunas* took occasion to obtain from him many offerings, promising a cure. He at length discredited them, withheld his offerings, grew better, rather than worse, and was on that account more ready to turn away from the whole system." The missionaries did not report that the pendulum swung both ways. The sandalwood trader Peter Corney reported a conversation with Keʻeaumoku in 1818 in which the chief said he "sets the wooden gods and priests at defiance" and "that they are all liars, and that the white men's God is the true and only God." But, in 1822, Keʻeaumoku ordered the performance of traditional rituals for discovering the sorcerer who caused his wife's death, and sacrifices to ward off sorcery attended his own final illness. In the face of this ambivalence, Ellis was bearish about Keʻeaumoku's odds of redemption. "Keeaumoku died at Oahu with some faint hopes of his acceptance through the Redeemer" was his deflated summation of the effects of his daily deathbed ministry.[55]

Political and economic considerations weighed on the aliʻi and the makaʻāinana as they persisted in their allegiance to ancient gods or replaced them with new ones, but there might have been personal reasons for Keʻeaumoku's religious vacillations during a period of disability, as well. Ellis refers to the "frequent attacks of disease" . . . "during the last years of his life" before describing "the illness that immediately preceded his dissolution," which "was painful, and somewhat protracted." So during the period when Keʻeaumoku "uniformly befriended" the missionaries and yet persisted in some of his familiar religious rituals and activities, he did not feel well, at least, and was increasingly in pain. If he died of one of the respiratory illnesses sweeping the islands in the early 1820s, he probably experienced high fevers, coughing fits so severe he could not sleep, tightening of his chest, and sharp discomfort with every breath. Ellis's description of Keʻeaumoku's pain is only a representation of it, and one must look beneath his account to see the possibility that when he writes that "hope and fear alternately occupied my mind respecting him," he was claiming Keʻeaumoku's sensations as his own. For the missionary, these waves had religious undertones—he thought the chief despaired at his sins ("Lord, forgive them") and grasped at salvation ("Save me"). But for Keʻeaumoku, the pain in his body might have moved in waves of calm and anguish, which are a different source of hope and fear and pleas to be saved. The documents we have about his final years do not give us insight into the state or inclination of his soul as he lived with disease; they only offer others' observations, interpretations, and representations of his spiritual life—or, as he might put it, their lies. Arguments by analogy—what his sister or brother said about their religious activities or beliefs, how other chiefs responded to the influence of Catholicism and Protestantism in Hawaiʻi, or what a missionary thought as he attended his bedside, only get us so far. And if his faith is private and to a great degree unknowable, so, too, is the pain with which it was entwined.[56]

This is a modest and familiar claim, and yet it's also a dangerous one. Pain is always personal and often isolating. One view of painful disability is that it "makes narcissists of all of us." Toward the end of his life, lonely and bored in New Bedford, Edmund Gardner figured, "Few or none have suffered from personal injury more than myself." Just watching Keʻeaumoku suffer turned Ellis in upon himself: Were these the cries of a soul he had saved? There is no question some people used the idiosyncratic nature of pain to further isolate people already driven inward—by pathologizing, institutionalizing, and otherwise sequestering people with disabilities in the name of treatment or public safety. Others regarded the pain of Indigenous people as one more mystifying aspect of foreign and incomprehensible cultures and simply left it alone. And others have declined to dwell on the pain of others out of caution or respect—because it is too personal, inexpressible, or mundane to know, let alone study. In aggregate, these choices to deny or neglect or politely pass over pain have mounted into a wall of untreated pain behind which bodies continue to live, unseen and anguished. In the twenty-first century, Native Hawaiians have the shortest life expectancy of any ethnic group in Hawaiʻi, as well as the highest rates of infant mortality and death from heart disease, cancer, stroke, accidents, and diabetes. They share with Keʻeaumoku imperiling circumstances in which their pain is misunderstood or misinterpreted as they suffer.[57]

I have presented two polarized views of oceanic disability—one interior and embodied and the other public and symbolic. It takes a leap of faith to bridge the two, to believe that private suffering is a communal concern that is both expressible and intelligible. It takes a further leap to imagine the disabilities of Hawaiians, Indigenous Americans, and New Englanders from the seventeenth through the nineteenth centuries as sharing essential emotional properties despite their material and ideological distance. Those living with blindness, deafness, heart disease, mental illness, chronic pain, and other disabilities through the ages are not organically linked and did not necessarily perceive themselves in relation to one another. Disability theorists created this bridge across space by asking people with a variety of disabilities to accept, in the face of fundamental physiological difference, as Lennard Davis puts it, "that the subject position one occupies is to some extent capable of being shared by others in parallel circumstances." Their objective was to make disability studies as inclusive as possible and to demonstrate that people across a spectrum of complex embodiments share enough to sustain a community rooted in disability. From its outset, the field pulsed with the urgency of activism. Early disability theorists declared to the academy, "If ability is socially and symbolically produced in the manner of race, ethnicity, gender, and sexuality, then we can no longer conceive of disability as individual physical or mental defect. The defect is located in the environments, institutions, languages, and paradigms of knowledge made inaccessible to people with disabilities, and we have a responsibility to remove it." Given that living people were suffering oppression because of their disabilities, early Americanists were hard-pressed to justify pulling attention toward the physical pain of those long dead, and the two fields ran on separate tracks until relatively recently. But within Indigenous studies, writers and scholars have long been espousing and advocating the belief that one suffering body relates to many suffering bodies not just in the present moment but also across history.[58]

"Why are Native Hawaiians, the once healthy indigenous people of Hawai'i, suffering disproportionately?" 'Iwalani R. N. Else asks. One answer must come from the past, from the period when Ke'eaumoku and his family of Maui chiefs lived with their various disabilities. "The breakdown of the kapu system and the traditional subsistence economy, and the ensuing dependence on a capitalistic cash economy brought by Western influence have led, in combination with other factors, to the current decline in health and well-being among Hawaiians." Else argues that many Indigenous people are in pain now because they still exist in relation to people who lived in or visited Hawai'i in the nineteenth century.[59] At least one influential Hawaiian living in the nineteenth century shared this belief in the communal and transtemporal dimensions of personal pain. In his 1824 letter to King

Liholiho and Queen Kamāmalu, their chief minister Kalanimoku begins by acknowledging individuals who have suffered disease-induced death by name: "We here have been swept off by death from illness. . . . Keeaumoku . . . died, and was taken back to Kailua. Pihookaneakarora has died. Kiri-wehe is dead. Eeka is dead. Taumuarii has died, the death occurring nine days ago." He gives each person's encounter with protracted illness due consideration. But then he makes a synthetic leap: "Later, those of us here may all be dead from sickness; you should come back." Kalanimoku's ability to see beyond the divergent diseases, symptoms, and treatments that complicate the picture of Native Hawaiian health was a crucial step toward uniting a group of people subject to or suffering from physical disability and advocating for their interests. But the reality of disease-induced disability thwarted the attempt: the political rulers to whom he appealed could not "come back" because they were dead of disease, as many of the disabled, suffering, and exposed around Kalanimoku soon would be. Indigenous disability is sometimes undertheorized from Indigenous perspectives partly because it is such a consuming, ongoing crisis: the phenomenon of pain and poor health itself interrupts efforts to respond to it or to research and analyze it. So the study of Indigenous health calls on the belief that communities of disabled people can be imagined across time: "Later, those of us here may all be dead from sickness." Ma muli. Literally, "At later."[60]

By and by, we will all be sick.[61]

BELIEF AND THE TELESCOPE OF OCEANIC TEMPORALITY

Disability oppression is a problem of asynchronicity. Every baby is born into total dependence on others for physical survival, and every life ends in the breakdown of the body's ability to function. How is it that the essential characteristic of being human has ever been a category of exclusion? One answer is that people experience disability at different times, and most people lack or disdain Kalanimoku's ability to project themselves into disabled futures or disabled pasts. There is for most people only the insistence on the able-bodied present and fear or denial of the crises that transform our bodies and minds. But oceanic disability flowed through fluid temporalities. It was so omnipresent on ships, islands, and archipelagoes that Kalanimoku scarcely needed to project himself into another temporality at all—he could look to the right and to the left and surmise that he would be disabled again and dead in no time. He had been sick, off and on, since 1811 and was so afflicted by dropsy in 1825 that surgeons "tapped," or surgically drained, gallons of excess fluid from his body during five operations before he died in 1827. His condition was debilitating but common enough that it entered maritime vernacular as metaphor: Edmund Gardner complained about the "dropsical" condition of a ship he commanded from 1823–1824, which had to be "pumped morning and evening" and yet "continued to increase the leak." Oceania was filled with leaky bodies ever in the process of contracting, recovering, relapsing, and dying. There was no time apart from disability.[62]

As they languished in the tedium between hunts, whalemen scanned the horizon for the sight of another ship. When they fell into company with one, a pocket of fraternity gave some structure to the otherwise diaphanous folds of oceanic time. They shared news, sent messages home, were even willing to chase whales together and split the spoils. For a period, there was someone beyond themselves. The literature of Oceania suspends people like voyagers on ships. Those who venture into oceanic archives come across a text like a vessel, full of bodies with their news and messages from other times and places. And every so often we come across something that has been unsighted and floating alone so long there is something revelatory in whatever pent-up stories it carries.[63]

Keʻeaumoku is well known, and Cook outrageously so, but Kalanimoku's undelivered letter was swept up in William Ellis's papers and unpublished until 2010, and Edmund Gardner has received little attention since the early twentieth century. So this book is invested in an enterprise called "recovery work," although I trip now over the ableist connotations of the term. The aim of recovery was never simply to bring to light forgotten texts; it was also to bring to light the conditions that concealed them for so long. In literary studies, for example, the assumption was not that Susanna Rowson's *Charlotte Temple* or Nathaniel Hawthorne's brighter fiction was drifting alone, untouched since the days of its initial popularity, because of the happenstance by which ships pass in the night. These texts had been welcomed, and then scorned, and then pushed off the map of American literary history. For historians, it was not difficult to perceive the colonial currents that deposited a letter written by one of the most influential Hawaiians of his time, about a health crisis that rerouted political history, in an uncatalogued file within the Special Collections library of the School of Oriental and African Studies at the University of London.[64]

We reach toward stranded vessels to help us diagnose disabling features in our critical environments. And we hope they can recover us. But can we recover them? When I began to examine the less familiar writings to which

I was responsible as an early Americanist in my first year of graduate study, I was undone by the physical suffering I encountered. It seemed to me that no matter what we wrote, no matter what we taught, no matter how we held these texts up to the view of a largely indifferent public, nothing could ever touch the pain these people bore. We have undeniable obligations to the inheritors of their trauma. But their disabled bodies are outside recovery. To reach for them seems as futile as writing to a dead king and queen, "You should come back." And yet some of them wrote, and we write, and we teach of people who can't come back on the hope that we can still fall into company somehow and things will be better for the contact.

Those we recover will not be healed by our efforts, and we may not be saved. But they do not necessarily ask to be healed. Edmund Gardner was a religious man, and in a coda to his journal, he expressed his hope for salvation.

> In the early part of 1872 I lay down my pen thinking I might never resume it again, and have not until arriving to my 89 year, several times I have depressed feeling my time would not be long, but my guide and direction has been meted out to me by the aid of a blessed Redeemer whose hand has been stretch[e]d forth to guide and guard me from all dangers I have had many things, known to none but myself, but trust they have been all for the best. . . .
> . . . Eight y[ea]rs. have passed since I've lived a lonely life and declining health surrounded by many things for comfort and Consolation but a blank remains that nothing can fill but dependence on a blessed Saviour who died for me and all mankind that we might live.

Gardner believes in redemption but says nothing about expecting his wounded body to be transformed. He imagines a scarred hand stretching to meet his scarred hand, and his wish is simply to live. The Redeemer he needs in the midst of depression and poor health is one who waits, always in disability, not to prevent pain or erase it, but to understand it. "The fear of pain is often the beginning of oppression. But pain can also be the beginning of compassion," Seibers writes. "Compassion feels with the other person, granting this person's life value equal to all other lives. It places itself in service to another life on the other person's terms, assuming the commitment to help this person find a life worthy of a human being, that is, a life at the heart of and embraced by other human beings." Gardner reaches ahead toward a figure whose infinite experience with pain grants him all-encompassing capacities for compassion, but his journal reaches behind, offering to feel with others who know the loneliness of declining health.[65]

Gardner's prediction in the preamble of his journal—"Thus 'twill be shown that my connections were with the first settlers of the Island"—suggests ties beyond the biological, since he already established those in the genealogy he recites in the preceding line. But he does not return to his ancestors at the end of the journal, closing instead with this meditation on his own pain and loneliness. One of his indirect ancestors did something similar. Two years before she died at the age of eighty, Anne Downing Gardner, left in Salem by the family members who settled Nantucket and twice widowed with no children of her own, wrote: "Sept. 29th Anno Domini, 1711—I Anne Bradstreet of Salem in New-England Widow Being Weak of Body but Sound in Mind and Memory Do Make This my Last Will and Testament, hereby Revoking and disanulling all former Wills by me at any Time made." She goes on at length and in unsparing detail (down to the last bedpan) to bequeath her inventory to sundry friends and members of the Downing, Gardner, and Bradstreet families. In using a common legal phrase to foreground her weak body as she edges toward death, she connects herself not only to her great-great grandnephew but also to a deceased woman who considered their familial connection a threat rather than a comfort. Anticipating the pain of labor and the possibility of imminent death, the speaker of Anne Dudley Bradstreet's poem "Before the Birth of One of Her Children" begs her husband, if he loves her, to protect her children from "step-dames injury." But in her last testament, Simon Bradstreet's second wife is not the potent maternal rival of Anne Bradstreet's catastrophic imagination, only another weakened woman who feels her mortality, twenty years older than Bradstreet was when she died. During the eighteenth century, many widows used will making to proclaim "economic and social power" married women did not have, so Anne Gardner's inclination to disclose her weak body before demonstrating her sound mind should be recognized as a choice she made from a variety of conventional options, and one that echoes the openness of Anne Bradstreet's most personal poetry. Although none of them had to admit their frailty and isolation in writing, and it might have cost them some pride to do it, three people divided from one another by sentiment, time, and place immortalized themselves at their most physically vulnerable. Their honesty and manifest sympathy for those who will survive them make it possible for historians of disability and emotion to fulfill Gardner's promise—to show close connections among people who seem distantly or uneasily related, to draw islands of pain into archipelagic relation.[66]

Figure 23. *Captain Edmund Gardner*. By William Allen Wall (1801–1885). Circa 1840. Oil on canvas, 30.25 x 25.25 in. (76.8 x 64.1 cm.). New Bedford Whaling Museum, Gift of Mr. Henry Forster, 1992.10.2. Courtesy of the New Bedford Whaling Museum

Photograph of Edmund Gardner towards the end of
his life, showing the crippled hand.

Figure 24. Photograph of Edmund Gardner. From John M. Bullard, ed.,
Captain Edmund Gardner of Nantucket and New Bedford: His Journal and Family
(New Bedford, Mass., 1958), between 84 and 85

Like Anne Bradstreet, Edmund Gardner leaves a weather-beaten version of himself suspended in the archives of coastal New England writing. The original copy of his journal sits in the New Bedford Whaling Museum near a portrait of him, in company with other captains' portraits, his broken hand cropped out of frame. The portrait courts Keʻeaumoku's accusation: *You lie.* But the copy of his journal his descendants published in 1958 includes a picture that foregrounds it, with a caption that reads, "Photograph of Edmund Gardner towards the end of his life, showing the crippled hand." The power of historical writings and images is not that they heal people. It's that they don't. By preserving people in pain and holding them in conditions of disability or affliction, they solve the problem of asynchronicity that strands people in their private worlds of grief. The novelist Aleksandar Hemon calls these worlds aquariums. Of his own experience in one, he writes, "I could see out, the people outside could see me (if they chose to pay attention), but we were living and breathing in entirely different environments." That we are inexpressibly, impenetrably alone when we suffer is the most believable of lies. And we need it, for it covers a truth that is somehow darker. We are not alone in our saltwater worlds, and we are not contained. We are in the open sea with others who feel pain and who have caused pain, including ours, and forces we cannot fathom control the cycles of calm and storm and the currents to which we surrender or die fighting. People who know these waters offer strategies for survival. "When we were kids, our grandparents (*tūtū wahine* and *tūtū kāne*) would sit us on the shoreline and teach us how to watch (*nānā*) and listen (*hoʻolohe*) to the ocean. We studied its patterns and movements, its currents and weather conditions," writes the Hawaiian musician and author Brother Noland. "People drown because they are exhausted, panicked and unable to stay afloat. Don't swim alone, especially if you don't know the area well." Every so often, those of us at sea glimpse or search out a body that art or writing has held in pain and set adrift. And if these people can't come back and won't convey us home, they still bring news and offer company and show us something beyond ourselves. And we stay afloat a little longer.[67]

CONCLUSION

Where Does the Grief Go?

A book about early New England grief that ends on the shores of Hawai'i in the eternal present must make some account of itself. I arrived here by a series of turns that have, over the past generation or two, shaped the study of early American life—turns toward the global, the postsecular, the affective and emotional, the ecocritical, and the ontological. But even an attentive student of early America sealed off from academic trends might have traveled as far afield simply by following sufferers of ordinary pains as they went about their business. They might have arrived, that is to say, at the point of this book, which is that mourning death in early New England was local, punctual, visible, and bounded in ways that mourning other kinds of losses was not.

The business of early American life was markedly global by the mid-nineteenth century (if one allows the temporal boundaries of early America to stretch that far), but the global dimensions of early America were felt and seen much earlier. The "global turn" in early American studies, closely related to the earlier "Atlantic turn," illuminates a vast and intricate cultural circuitry that pulled early modern actors and objects into relationship.

While there is much interest and even some delight to be found in tracing world-spanning routes of travel and trade and discovering the connections forged therein, scholars have warned against "adopting the laudatory positions of those who tried to turn those connections to their own ends." As histories of slavery, colonialism, and empire have long demonstrated and in myriad ways, the substance of global connection in the early modern world was more often painful than not. Early New England grief was part of these histories. It had a transatlantic quality owing to the suffering of enslaved Africans and Indigenous people displaced by seventeenth-century English settlers. These settlers carried with them their own pain and their habitual responses to it, which included emotional reactions conditioned by communities, remedies prescribed in books of medicine, and relief supplied by legal code. And New England grief had a global quality in part because the text to which early Americans frequently turned for succor was the Bible, which bore the emotional residue of the scattered peoples who wrote, translated, heard, and read it and which then acquired fresh emotional imprints as it was read in the crucible of North American settlement and retranslated and deployed in the context of American imperialism. By the early nineteenth century, Americans were exporting grief to a greater degree than they were importing it, sharing with vast regions of the world the sense of sickness, privation, and alarm the early New England settlers felt so acutely. Whalers like Edmund Gardner contributed to economic, political, and cultural transformations on the Hawaiian archipelago that brought riches to a few and the pain of poverty and poor health to many more. Other Americans effected such transformations more deliberately, such as the Protestant missionaries who arrived in Hawai'i in 1820, the year after Gardner first visited the islands. Their journals, like Gardner's, record injuries and illnesses they endured as well as physical pain they noticed around them and to which they might have been more attuned because they felt their own vulnerability. New Englanders found an expanding sphere of fellow sufferers with whom to commiserate as the centuries wore on, a development that influenced both the experience and the expression of early American grief. They deserve credit for their role in creating this communion, since their own attitudes and actions in pursuit of imperial expansion enlarged the global community of mourners and perpetually refreshed the grounds on which they could sympathize.[1]

The religious dogma by which colonialism's purveyors of pain justified their incursions deserves the critiques heaped upon it since the early twentieth century. But the faith to which distressed early Americans of diverse religious traditions—many of them far from seats of imperial power—turned for comfort and direction merits the attentive curiosity that characterizes the work of postsecular critics. As these critics challenge the "secularization thesis"—in Bryce Traister's useful gloss, "a set of arguments which has, until quite recently, maintained the view that sometime around or about the early eighteenth century, and for a lot of reasons, religion just gave out"—they not only acknowledge the persistence of religious thought and affection beyond the eighteenth century but also the complexity and polyvocality of religion in a putatively unenlightened past. Grief was like religious devotion in early America in the sense that it was an affective disposition as much as, and perhaps even more than, a set of rituals and doctrines. When people grieved losses that were complicated and chronic and did not fit rhetorical forms or social conventions in which they could be organized, expressed, or laid to rest, grief was not a state through which they moved but a way of being in the world. Grief became part of a worldview, part of an identity. It was not simply like faith in this regard; it was the reason there was such a thing as faith. Grief measured the distance between heaven and earth, between trial and deliverance, between damnation and salvation. "In the world ye shall have tribulation," Jesus promised his disciples, "but be of good cheer; I have overcome the world." Without grief, why a savior? The religious doctrines of punishment and affliction to which Americans like Caleb Cheeshateaumuck, Anne Bradstreet, Lucy Terry, Mary Parsons, and Esther Rodgers might have subscribed can be found in the literature of their ministers and missionaries. I have quoted cautiously from these sources in this book, and less extensively than some readers may have hoped, because my interest is less in Puritans' cataphatic religion than in their apophatic faith, which can only be found in their own expressions—even manhandled as they were by those who disseminated their words—and these speak, not of doctrine, but of pain and the idiosyncratic beliefs they grasp in hope of surviving it. An intellectual history of the writings of Puritan leaders may reveal the New England mind, but this study of the writings of bewildered, bereaved people who looked for an absent God and listened to divine silence has tried to reveal the New England heart.[2]

The relationship between minds and hearts has been variously conceived through the millennia by those who have debated the origins and properties of emotions within the body, the relationship of thought and language to the experience and expression of emotion, and the degree to which individual minds and hearts merge with others to form communities or even meld with objects and environments outside the body. In some of the cases of grief I contemplated in this book, I have considered responses to loss within what historians of emotions call "bounded bodies." Esther Rodgers, for example, turned the language and intellectual frameworks of the magistrates and ministers who condemned her toward therapeutic ends, embracing rather than denying the title of "murderer" to contain the otherwise overwhelming maternal tragedy (or tragedies) she had endured and to find a path to relief through confession, death, and potential redemption. But at some point, the porousness of her body reveals itself and demands our attention. Was Esther's emotional reaction to her grief influenced by a pathetic woodcut in a copy of The New-England Primer she held as a child? And what of the uncanny way her countenance on the scaffold recalled the cheer with which the martyrs Perpetua and Felicity faced the crowd assembled to watch them die in the third century? Or was that cheer simply a projection onto her frame of the anxiety her minister John Rogers felt, which drove him to wrestle the omnipresent catastrophe of neonatal loss into a coherent narrative? Questions like these open onto broad vistas. "Emotions are contagious," Barbara H. Rosenwein and Riccardo Cristiani write. "They pour into the world—into things and the interstices between things." Inevitably, this close study of emotions has led us from individual minds and hearts to the spaces where New Englanders carried grief and within which they experienced additional losses.[3]

As affect theorists maintain, these spaces are not neutral. Even from a distance, the disease-ravaged Patuxet coastline signaled something ominous to the approaching English settlers—not because of what they saw, but because of what they didn't see. Accustomed to what Henri Lefebvre calls the language "common to country people and townspeople" of an "architectural, urbanistic and political . . . code which allowed space not only to be 'read' but also to be constructed," the Mayflower passengers found the desolated landscape illegible and thus foreboding. Recall William Bradford's summary as he surveyed it: No "inns," "no houses or much less townes," he laments. The materially stripped but grief-laden space into which the English settlers stepped to assert their colonial prerogative might explain, though it does not excuse, their stance of unwarranted suspicion and sometimes violent overreactions to slight stimuli. John Demos notices New England diarists' dutiful records of celestial phenomena ("comets, eclipses, meteors, aurora, even rainbows") and their obsession with floods, storms, crop disease, and insect infestations, and he correlates these astronomical, atmospheric, and environmental aberrations with bursts of interest in witch-hunting activity. The space in which disoriented early New Englanders stewed charged their emotional states and predisposed them to behaviors that appear irrational to modern eyes. If Mary Parsons had been left alone at night and woken suddenly by some strange sound in central London rather than in Springfield, Massachusetts, she might have registered the emotional force of her husband's cycles of abandonment and harassment to a different degree and in different terms. But, as it was, she reached for a legal charge that seemed consonant with the emotional pitch of her distress.[4]

As New Englanders sallied into new regions of the globe, this issue of spatial freight and the pressure it put on people in pain replayed on different stages. Kahekili Ke'eaumoku saw the familiar coast of Kealakekua Bay made strange as a foreign visitor sought out the portion of it on which, forty-three years earlier, Captain James Cook died in a violent conflict with his Hawaiian hosts. There was no obvious connection between the colonial past and present on this beach except the emotion that drew Edmund Gardner to the spot. But what that emotion was, Ke'eaumoku could not decipher, nor could he guess what it portended for his relationship with the English, Europeans, and Americans crossing into his space. Did he anticipate how totally they would penetrate it? He suffered his final illness in the company of one of them, the missionary William Ellis, so even his deathbed was a site of emotional contagion that makes it difficult, if not impossible, to read Ke'eaumoku's pain through the haze of the missionary's impression of it. The actions of English settlers of North America and, later, Americans abroad dramatically altered the spaces they explored or settled. When they depleted marine life, disrupted traditional agriculture, rerouted Native foodways, cleared forests and burned trees, made claims to land, and developed private property, they changed landscapes and climates in ways that contributed to poor health, economic hardship, political unrest, and warfare. These disasters changed the way people felt, and, acting out of these emotions, people behaved in ways that further modified their environments. In 1978, when William Rueckert coined the term "ecocriticism," he worried his readers might find his argument that literature relates to the biosphere "absurd"; now, activists hope the more emotional language of *crisis* and *emergency* can do something to turn complacency into urgency and mitigate the inevitable damage of what scientists once called climate change. But the new language only highlights the degree to which ecologies have long possessed and transmitted an emotional tenor to which humans in turn contribute. As the cases in this book have shown, Native inhabitants of what became America felt human-induced environmental change as crisis without anyone instructing them to do so, and English settlers and American voyagers who came to grieve in their space suffered in atmospheres they helped create.[5]

Emotions pour into things as well as spaces, and what finally carried me from New England to Kealakekua Bay was a book I held in the New Bedford Whaling Museum, where I had traveled to learn more about the pain of early American mariners in the Age of Sail. Although some familiar methodologies—for example, strict observance of historical periodization, a continental paradigm, or attention to specific literary genres—would have excluded Edmund Gardner's journal from a project on early New England grief, my focus on emotion drew it into relation with other objects I considered in this book. Like William Bradford and Mary Rowlandson, Gardner speaks at length about sensations of physical pain, confusion, alarm, and despair made more poignant because he experiences them in unfamiliar spaces. He feels his victimhood in these spaces much more deeply than his agency. The whales that stove in his ship and crushed his body feature as anthropomorphic antagonists in his personal narrative, whereas those he made a career of hunting feature hardly at all, and certainly not as sentient beings. And although Gardner lived mostly in the nineteenth century, his heart was often someplace else. He writes himself into history by way of his "connections . . . with the first settlers" of Nantucket, and he writes himself out of it by way of his connection to God: "I've lived a lonely life and declining health surrounded by many things for comfort and Consolation but a blank remains that nothing can fill but dependence on a blessed Saviour." Put another way, he begins his story of grief in the seventeenth century and ends it in pain's element of blank, which he hopes can be filled by some force outside himself, outside the world, and outside time. This is the way most of the grieving people in this book begin and end their stories of suffering, when they were able to tell them at all.[6]

Along with the range of its temporal span, Gardner's journal has a raggedness to its form—sometimes adventure tale, sometimes history, sometimes schoolbook, sometimes lament—that makes it difficult to categorize generically, but not more than any other object I contemplated in this book. The writings of Caleb Cheeshateaumuck, Lucy Terry, and Mary Rowlandson straddle literature and history and are pulled to different ends by people who have an interest in grounding them in one field or another. Anne Bradstreet's work, recognized as poetry even in her own day, seems to belong squarely on one side, except that when she bid her family to "kiss this paper for thy loves dear sake," she asked them to give due regard to the material object she managed out of her economy and industry to leave for them, not just the poetic lines. And Edmund Gardner's journal, at no apparent danger of being dragged into this debate, was treated by his children as a purely literary bequest. Lydia Hussey Gardner Spooner made a fair copy of the journal, correcting her father's spelling and adding detail where she felt he had been parsimonious. According to her great-grandson John M. Bullard, she "wanted the original destroyed" because she felt "the spelling reflected on her father." The actual object her father created in conditions of physical pain and disability and gifted to his children was embarrassing to her, an impediment to memorializing him the way she wanted and the way the content of his journal, if she prettied it a bit, could allow. Gardner's great-granddaughter Ruth Allen disagreed and settled the matter when she loaned the original to the Whaling Museum at the Old Dartmouth Historical Society in New Bedford, which is how it found its way into my hands. And now I throw it back into play. What makes an object literary as opposed to historical has a great deal to do with the way its inheritors, not just its creators, feel about it. "Some texts are born literary, some achieve literariness, and some have literariness thrust upon them," as Terry Eagleton quips. I have thrust literariness on some early American writings because I believe they yield insights about grief if we entertain the possibility they might have been written out of a suffering person's imagination rather than memory or understanding. The designations "early" and "American" may be no less emotional, bestowed out of the aspirations (for coherence, at the very least), affinities, or anxieties of readers and historians and certainly with inconsistent regard for the feelings of people living during the seventeenth, eighteenth, and nineteenth centuries who saw themselves as neither early nor American.[7]

While granting that "theories of affect might feel like a momentary (sometimes more permanent) methodological and conceptual free fall" for scholars accustomed to other ways of approaching historical material, I count myself among the scholars who find the discomfort a fair price for the view. For historians of emotions, the questions a project like this raises about the limits of traditional fields in the face of something as totalizing as personal grief are gateways to more expansive thinking. "Periods, like emotions, are not preordained," Rosenwein and Cristiani write. "We think that the history of emotions may—indeed must—help to tear down walls." Rosenwein uses the term "generations of feeling" to this end as she narrates emotional histories that run across ancient, medieval, and early modern worlds. The overlapping generations of feeling that shaped early modern experience even implicate people in the present who inhabit early American spaces or handle early American objects and find their moods strummed by the contact.

Scholars have debated the merits of this fact and the methodological conundrum it poses. In Stephanie Trigg's words, "How much of our selves do we, or should we, bring to the study of the habitus?"[8]

The emotional charge of historical material takes many researchers and teachers, at some point in their careers, to the verge of an "autobiographical turn," which some take for the avenues of recognition and identification it opens and others avoid as a primrose path into "overstatement and tabloidization" and other forms of "creeping anti-intellectualism." Of one case in point, the archeologist Sarah Tarlow writes:

> There is a terrible poignancy in the lists of names of children and babies following their siblings to the grave. The empathetic instinct has brought most graveyard recorders with whom I have spoken to the point of tears at least once; this profound sense of engagement with the past people is both a good and a bad thing: good because an emotional interest can be channelled into research or conversation, bad because it persuades us that we understand gravestones, that their meanings are transparent to us, and perhaps does not force us to probe as deeply as we otherwise might.

Medievalists such as Carolyn Dinshaw who foreground their personal connection to their material have made eloquent cases for "not only doing history ... but also ... constructing a community across time" by reading the past affectively and metonymically. D. Vance Smith calls this approach "redemptive partiality—focusing on what moves and compels, and on what resists the whole, the forms of totality." Yet Smith worries about what he sees as the narcissistic and ethnocentric foundations of affective and autobiographical approaches that attend more closely to individual responses than communal relations. "The authenticity of affect derives from its purported innocence of institutional forms of thought and control, an immediacy that allows us not only to reroute lost circuits to the past, but to clear them of the interference of the work of intellectual institutions in the past," he argues. Many scholars resist this emotional entanglement on principle. As Trigg writes: "Last year I attended a talk by an expert historian charting a history of loss and the destruction of her subject matter in the English reformation. In question time she was asked how she felt about that loss. 'I'm a historian,' she replied, 'it's not my job to feel.'" I'm a literary historian, so I may be allowed to feel, but there has long been, even among literary critics, as Rita Felski notes, "an understandable wariness of being tarred with the brush of subjective or emotional response." This spirit extends to the classroom, where it becomes part of the training given to students in the humanities. One of my college professors, on the edge of retirement, told our class he despaired to teach Anne Bradstreet because students who had no business becoming poets sometimes fell under her influence and made fools of themselves. He would have little to fear if he were still teaching, because students are enrolling in the course he taught in dwindling numbers. They seek salve for their well-founded worries in colleges of business, science, and engineering, where they pose no risk of desacralizing the distance between their increasingly distressed present and an increasingly distant past by identifying too emotionally with early American subjects. Some of us register this turn of events as a crisis.[9]

My own affective attachment to the stories of grief in this book has not been part of my methodology in an overt or critically contextualized way. But this work betrays my attachments nonetheless, and I conclude by way of frankly acknowledging them. The question "How much of our selves do we, or should we, bring to the study of the habitus?" implies a degree of agency scholars may not possess. We are emotional beings implicated in affective atmospheres we can ignore but cannot escape. The comment "it's not my job to feel" is a moody statement. Given this shared condition, autobiographical turns in historiography or literary criticism are not necessarily personal turns or turns devoid of institutional context or awareness. They make overt what is implicit or sublimated in other kinds of work, and these disclosures change the tone of academic writing in ways some readers, understandably, find objectionable. But they also reveal experiences and especially attitudes to which other readers relate and out of which new communities (or, in our profession, fields) may arise. They show what this book about unremarkable and often unremarked New England grief has tried to illustrate: to say that an emotional experience is common is not to say that it is trivial. Just the opposite is more often true. The commonness of most early New England pain is what made it matter.

Following historical and academic writers whose honesty I appreciate and with an eye toward students desperately seeking something the humanities are uniquely capable of providing, I veer into the autobiographical, and say, conscious of the risks, that the commonness of most early New England pain is what makes it matter still. As I write this, I am sitting on the edge of my mother's bed. Her glassy eyes are half open beneath waxy lids. Each time she inhales, her ribs retract and the fluid in her throat comes to a rolling boil. Two nurses are of two minds about whether she is in the "active" or "preactive" stage of dying. It's a question of whether her brain will wage its heroic, futile fight for hours or a day more. They speak of her oxygen saturation and blood pressure to my father, who sits in a suit at the other side of her bed, holding her blue fingers. He feigns interest in their debate, though we both know it does not matter. She has been actively dying—or is it passively dying?—for as long as we can remember. I feel guilty about working as she dies, but I couldn't work otherwise.

Throughout this book, my assumption has been that private suffering bled into everyday New England life in ways we might acknowledge more fully. In the pages that follow this Conclusion, I think out loud about the ways I see the persistence of this phenomenon through the lens of my own experience, which often intrudes on my intellectual work. My point is not that chronic grief is a through line that connects the past to the present. It's that acknowledging invisible pain allows us to see the emotional labor taking place in the wings as constitutive of the production on stage and that the history of emotional labor is as palimpsestic as the history of emotion more broadly. I wrote about people who fought for their homelands, learned new languages, conducted diplomacy, planted settlements, maintained households, voyaged, and traded as they endured homelessness, domestic tension and abuse, reproductive tragedies, injury, and poor health. And, as I wrote, I found their experiences and especially their speech and writing clarifying a relationship between homelessness and domestic unease, maternity, and disability in my own life. Although I do believe my pain is common, I do not pretend my experience is universal or that my thinking imparts wisdom for anyone else. I don't presume to make connections to readers whose experiences I can only imagine or to historical figures I see darkly through the glass of my own partiality. And, like most academics, I don't harbor illusions about the salvific potential of my teaching, and certainly not of my writing. If there were more relief to be found in writing about grief, there'd be less written about it. Attempts to make grief meaningful are often so misguided they're worth rejecting outright, as Aleksandar Hemon does when he writes about his young daughter's death from a brain tumor: "[Her] suffering and death did nothing for her, or us, or the world. We learned no lessons worth learning; we acquired no experience that could benefit anyone. . . . Her indelible absence is now an organ in our bodies, whose sole function is a continuous secretion of sorrow." But the labor Hemon expends to publish these emotions belies the sentiment he expresses. Can writing about the meaning-lessness of grief make it meaningful? Despite a popular view of Puritans as fixed and fortified in their stern convictions, the early New England writings I contemplated in this book do not show us people who found meaning in loss, just people trying to find it. Because there's no meaning in the loss. There's only meaning in the trying.[10]

Afterword

In March 2020, I was living in an apartment in downtown Salt Lake City and had buried myself in research for the first chapter of this book, "Homeless." Halfway through the month, most of the world's population was directed, and some compelled, to stay home. Home, we were assured, provided the surest safety from pestilence. That must have been true, but I obeyed even as I sensed with mounting dread that our cramped flat offered scant protection from other kinds of danger. It did no good to face that fact head-on because there was no defensible alternative for people like me who could, in theory, work and socialize on the computer. There was no place like home, so there was no place but home. I willed myself to find diversion in caring for a toddler, in monitoring a high-risk pregnancy with the help of an obstetrician I had never met in person, in cooking, and in writing. But one morning in July, the troubles inside our home burst the bands of my sundry diversions, and my daughter and I left the apartment with nothing but a canvas shopping bag hanging next to the front door that I hoped contained a diaper and my wallet.

Instinctively, I began driving toward my parents' home. They live seven miles from downtown, in a house I have known all my life and that beckoned me in my distress. But I pulled over on the side of the arid highway that cuts north from Salt Lake, between a sprawling gravel pit to the east and an oil refinery to the west, to collect my wits and rethink my course. We hadn't been to the house in months because it would have been cruel, or at least careless, to expose my aging parents to a disease claiming the lives of so many people like them. How could I do it now? For the first time since we had self-isolated, I let myself take stock of our options. There were women's and children's shelters, but the sudden and totalizing at-homeness of the pandemic spawned or discovered so much domestic despondency that these centers were flooded just as their staff buckled under their own economic, physical, and psychological crises. In further crowding a shelter, weren't we exposing other vulnerable people to additional risk? I was seven months into a complicated pregnancy. What would happen to the baby if I got sick, or went into labor?

But beneath these virtuous concerns was the unvarnished truth that I didn't want to go to a women's shelter; I wanted to go home. Not to the pen we had fled, miserable for all my efforts to renovate and redecorate, but to a real home. Desperation is rarely rational, and I could imagine no other place worthy of the name or equal to our need than a 1970s tract home, tended by my modest parents and dignified by their rectitude, and warmth, and suffering.

The mainspring of my mother's suffering was, as I described in the Preface, late-stage Alzheimer's disease, although over the years we salted her wounds accidentally, the way children do. When I was in my early twenties, I asked her to pick me up at the airport without realizing dementia was stripping her brain. But she knew, and figured the assaults of the disease into her preparations for the errand, which meant she drove to the airport at dawn and spent the day parked in front of the electronic sign that would display my afternoon arrival. She had written the letters "BOS" in blue pen on the palm of her hand. I caught on, as basically decent children stumbling out of adolescence finally will, to her deeply compromised quality of life and insisted on picking up my brother when he flew in from Boston to visit my parents a few years later. We got dinner and dawdled over dessert on the way home, not for a moment considering that a person of our mother's austere commitments and outrageous devotion would obviously wait up to greet her son. It was almost midnight when we walked into the family home to find her sitting in the half-dark on the stone hearth of a fireplace she could no longer light, pretending to warm her hands behind her back and assuming she had missed her children through some failure of her own.

In the early twentieth century, Georg Lukács and Walter Benjamin read loss and longing in novels as an expression of a modern condition they called "transcendental homelessness." It's a haunting term, by which they meant that epic heroes lost their place in the world but knew their relation to the gods that guided them home, whereas characters in novels had lost their place in the cosmos and so searched for homes they never had, and could never find. The term encompassed those who were unmetaphorically homeless only incidentally, a poetic overreach politicians and activists resisted by naming those whose homelessness posed practical as well as existential threats to social forms: bums, hobos, tramps, vagrants, transients, and so forth. Later these groups were folded into a softer term, "the homeless," but those concerned with their condition noticed that the old prejudices clung to the new name, which also dissolved the distinctions the slurs, in all their sharpness, captured. Tramping called on a skill set and a network the bum didn't have, just as a person now can be sheltered but still homeless. New words like "unhoused" and "unsheltered"—adopted by the Centers for Disease Control and Prevention in its guidance on how to aid people during the pandemic—try to shed affective baggage and preserve material nuance, and that's all to the good. But my glancing acquaintance with the panic of having a baby inside me and a baby at my back and not knowing where to turn my sweltering car brought Lukács's metaphor home. If I were not alone in the universe, would I be idling across from a strip club on a forsaken highway, ten minutes from an apartment I'd paid for and ten minutes from the home of my birth, with no idea where I'd sleep that night?[1]

Hospice nurses tell me about a strange phenomenon: not always but sometimes, they see patients slip life just after the loved ones who attend their deathbeds turn their backs or step out of the room. It happens enough that the nurses comment on it. The family is stunned, devastated. They've done nothing but keep vigil, and still somehow missed the moment. But if it's a tragedy, I'm not sure it's a mistake. Of course it could be a coincidence. But it may be that after lifetimes in which they control so little and suffer so much, some of the dying exercise the power at least to let go, to decide when things seem settled, when to say *it's time*. Some people will find this blasphemous or delusional; if so, it's a heresy or delusion that has become precious to me. Because I drove home. It was indefensible—morally, civically, rationally. But it occurred to me, finally, that my mother might be waiting for us.

The people I write about in this book left their homes at various turns, and many of them lost them through disasters of some kind, but their transcendental homelessness was not a presumptive condition of early modern existence; it was a choice, or the tolerable consequence of a choice. They knew their gods and had faith in homes on high that were subject to neither violence nor entropy. But they cared enough for people on this earth that they would not neglect them or leave them behind, not in their pilgrimages through life and not even when they died. They spent their lives building and buttressing homes for their families that turned to ash and dust. They also made considerable—and, in the case of Caleb Cheeshateaumuck, ultimate—sacrifices to immortalize emotional qualities of these precarious domestic lives in literary compositions, so, instead of fixing their focus on heavenly forms, they seem to have bent their affections backward toward the buffeted kinsfolk who would survive them. Or, rather, they did both, their textual traces preserving people spliced between this world and another one. Their writings, as one of Cheeshateaumuck's modern descendants attests, have given readers a sense of being "at home" in otherwise strange and foreboding worlds. But at such a cost. I have always thought of home makers as the most housed and sheltered of people—almost too sheltered. Only now do I realize their loyalty to something so provisional means they are never settled themselves.[2]

I don't know how much continuity we can assume between this life and the next, and as far as I'm concerned, the less the better. But faith in the cosmic persistence of home united many early Americans. "In my Father's house are many mansions," as the scripture says. Well, I do believe he's given beauty for ashes before, so why not again, and forever? But if I am to extrapolate from history to eternity, then I know this: the only houses worth inheriting will be made so by someone who sits at a cold hearth as time sheds meaning, watching for the latecomers.[3]

Notes

PREFACE

1. John Milton, *Paradise Lost* (1667), with twelve photogravures after designs by William Strang (London, 1905), 15.

INTRODUCTION

1. For the sources in which these incidents are related, see "The Parsons of Springfield: A Family at Odds (1651–1652)," in David D. Hall, *Witch-Hunting in Seventeenth-Century New England: A Documentary History, 1638–1693*, 2d ed. (Boston, 1999), 29–60. On the connection between the witch hunts and fear, one influential piece of scholarship is Mary Beth Norton's *In the Devil's Snare*, which acknowledges King William's War as a backdrop of the Salem witch hunts. Norton writes, "[Essex] county's residents were then near the front lines of an armed conflict that today is little known but which at the time commanded their lives and thoughts" (Norton, *In the Devil's Snare: The Salem Witchcraft Crisis of 1692* [New York, 2002], 4). On a possible connection between witchcraft and grief, see Hall, *Worlds of Wonder, Days of Judgment: Popular Religious Belief in Early New England* (Cambridge, Mass., 1989), 145. The relationship between fear and grief is, of course, noted beyond the academy; C. S. Lewis opens his memoir *A Grief Observed* (1961) with the line, "No one ever told me that grief felt so like fear" (Lewis, *A Grief Observed* [New York, 1996], 3).

2. Hall, *Witch-Hunting*, 43.

3. Jeff Tavss, "Michael Haight Was Investigated for Child Abuse; Not Charged, Records Show," *Fox13 Salt Lake City*, Jan. 18, 2023, https://www.fox13now.com/news/local-news/michael-haight-was-investigated-for-child-abuse-not-charged-records-show; Sam Metz, "Utah Man Who Killed Family Faced 2020 Abuse Investigation," *Associated Press*, Jan. 18, 2023, https://apnews.com/article/crime-utah-suicide-child-abuse-a89f3343e069c5214154ef24cca5b40f ("afraid," "inability").

4. Malcolm Gaskill, *The Ruin of All Witches: Life and Death in the New World* (New York, 2022), XX ("moody"). See Joseph H. Smith, ed., *Colonial Justice in Western Massachusetts, 1639–1702: The Pynchon Court Record, an Original Judges' Diary of the Administration of Justice in the Springfield Courts in the Massachusetts Bay Colony* (Cambridge, Mass., 1961), 21.

5. Although invisible evidence presents problems notoriously manifested in the witchcraft trials, in everyday New England it was of the upmost importance to Puritans and especially their religious leaders, who needed to discern the quality of individuals' spiritual lives. To that end, as Sarah Rivett argues, "from the evidence produced by the convert's experience, ministers developed a particular spiritual science for discerning,

authenticating, collecting, and recording invisible knowledge of God as it became manifest in the human soul" (Rivett, *The Science of the Soul in Colonial New England* [Williamsburg, Va., and Chapel Hill, N.C., 2011], 5). On the psychological dimensions of conversion and its significance in Puritan life, see Charles Lloyd Cohen, *God's Caress: The Psychology of Puritan Religious Experience* (New York, 1986). In their introduction to the essays collected in *Feeling Godly: Religious Affections and Christian Contact in Early North America* (Amherst, Mass., 2021), editors Caroline Wigginton and Abram Van Engen point out the centrality of "the place of religious affections in scenes of contact with and between Christians in early North America" (6).

6. I use the term "early American" to describe a period from 1620 to 1820, although I readily acknowledge that, during the seventeenth century, none of the people I study would have recognized themselves in this label. I do so for convenience—because the term means something to scholars—but also because throughout the book I discuss affects and emotions that affiliated people living in the lands and waters that would later become the United States. The term includes early New Englanders, but I also mean it to include other groups who came to shape and share early New England grief, particularly Native Americans and Native Hawaiians. In using this term, I do not mean to imply that these groups identified as American or to minimize crucial distinctions among their cultures, homelands, or belief systems. The label "Puritan," originally a term of derision, is also vexed, as many scholars acknowledge. I use the term fairly loosely in the book to refer to people who fell under the wide net of Puritan culture in New England, not necessarily people who professed certain doctrinal views. For a more nuanced discussion of the term, see Cohen, *God's Caress*, 3–5.

7. Alec Ryrie and Tom Schwanda, "Introduction," in Ryrie and Schwanda, eds., *Puritanism and Emotion in the Early Modern World* (New York, 2016), 1, 7. For the scholarship on emotion, see, for example, the introduction and essays in Ryrie and Schwanda, eds., *Puritanism and Emotion*; Wigginton and Van Engen, eds., *Feeling Godly*; and Gail Kern Paster, Katherine Rowe, and Mary Floyd-Wilson, eds., *Reading the Early Modern Passions: Essays in the Cultural History of Emotion* (Philadelphia, 2004). See also Nicole Eustace, *Passion Is the Gale: Emotion, Power, and the Coming of the American Revolution* (Williamsburg, Va., and Chapel Hill, N.C., 2008); John Corrigan, *Emptiness: Feeling Christian in America* (Chicago, 2015); Ana Schwartz, *Unmoored: The Search for Sincerity in Colonial America* (Williamsburg, Va., and Chapel Hill, N.C., 2023); and Abram C. Van Engen, *Sympathetic Puritans: Calvinist Fellow Feeling in Early New England* (New York, 2015).

8. Barbara H. Rosenwein's concept of "emotional communities," or "groups in which people adhere to the same norms of emotional expression and value—or devalue—the same or related emotions," has been foundational for many scholars of Puritan emotion. In this book, the idea of emotional communities helps explain both the relief New Englanders found as suffering drew them into relation and the distress they experienced when those within a social unit they took for granted—such as a marriage or a church—could not understand their grief, did not value it, or actively contributed to their pain (Rosenwein, *Emotional Communities in the Early Middle Ages* [Ithaca, N.Y., 2006], 2.)

9. Jonathan Edwards, *A Treatise concerning Religious Affections* . . . (1746) (Philadelphia, 1821), 19 ("affections"), 42 ("emotion of the mind"). See Barbara H. Rosenwein and Riccardo Cristiani, *What Is the History of Emotions?* (Cambridge, Mass., 2018), 11.

10. For a discussion of the limits of this terminology, see Paster, Rowe, and Floyd-Wilson, "Introduction: Reading the Early Modern Passions," in Paster, Rowe, and Floyd-Wilson, eds., *Reading the Early Modern Passions*, 1–20, esp. 2–3.

11. Affect theorists hold that affects are those "vital forces insisting beyond emotion" and argue that affects are pre-emotional and may even inhibit emotion and thinking; see Gregory J. Seigworth and Melissa Gregg, "An Inventory of Shimmers," in Gregg and Seigworth, eds., *The Affect Theory Reader* (Durham, N.C., 2010), 1 (quotation), 2.

12. Rosenwein and Cristiani, *What Is the History of Emotions?* 110; Tobin Siebers, *Disability Theory* (Ann Arbor, Mich., 2008), 96; Dobbs v. Jackson Women's Health Organization, 597 U.S. ___ (2022). See Matthew Hale, "Concerning Felonies by Act of Parliament, and First concerning Rape," in Hale, *Historia Placitorum Coronae: The History of the Pleas of the Crown . . .* , 2 vols. ([London], 1736), I, 626–636, esp. 629; and Gilbert Gies and Ivan Bunn, *A Trial of Witches: A Seventeenth-Century Witchcraft Prosecution* (London, 1997).

13. Nathaniel Hawthorne, *The Scarlet Letter*, with an introduction by George Parsons Lathrop, Salem ed. (Boston, 1893), 59; Haley Swenson, "How the Murder of a Utah Family Sparked Another Online Battle over Mormonism," *Slate*, Jan. 20, 2023, https://slate.com /human-interest/2023/01/michael-haight-murders-mormon-obituary-gofundme.html.

14. Texts in this vein include Mitchell Robert Breitwieser, *American Puritanism and the Defense of Mourning: Religion, Grief, and Ethnology in Mary White Rowlandson's Captivity Narrative* (Madison, Wis., 1990); Jeffrey A. Hammond, *The American Puritan Elegy: A Literary and Cultural Study* (Cambridge, 2000); Susan M. Stabile, "In Memoriam," in Stabile, *Memory's Daughters: The Material Culture of Remembrance in Eighteenth-Century America* (Ithaca, N.Y., 2004), 178–227; Max Cavitch, *American Elegy: The Poetry of Mourning from the Puritans to Whitman* (Minneapolis, Minn., 2007); Erik R. Seeman, *Death in the New World: Cross Cultural Encounters, 1492–1800* (Philadelphia, 2010); David J. Stewart, *The Sea Their Graves: An Archaeology of Death and Remembrance in Maritime Culture* (Gainesville, Fla., 2011); Martina Will de Chaparro and Miruna Achim, eds., *Death and Dying in Colonial Spanish America* (Tucson, Ariz., 2011); and Dana Luciano, *Arranging Grief: Sacred Time and the Body in Nineteenth-Century America* (New York, 2007).

15. This point was brought to my attention by the provocative volume edited by Michael Goode and John Smolenski, *The Specter of Peace: Rethinking Violence and Power in the Colonial Atlantic* (Leiden, Neth., 2018). The volume challenges historians to take peace as seriously as violence as we schematize early American history. As I considered this argument, it occurred to me that grief accompanied, and affectively connected, periods of peace and violence, although historians' overemphasis on periods of violence means most studies of grief are associated with these epochs and the literary forms they provoked rather than the stretches of relative uneventfulness between them.

16. See, for example, Neal Salisbury, ed., *The Sovereignty and Goodness of God, Together with the Faithfulness of His Promises Displayed: Being a Narrative of the Captivity and Restoration of Mrs. Mary Rowlandson and Related Documents* (Boston, 1997); John Williams, *The Redeemed Captive Returning to Zion; or, The Captivity and Deliverance of Rev. John Williams of Deerfield*, 6th ed. (1707; rpt. Springfield, Mass., 1908); Perry Miller, *The New England Mind: The Seventeenth Century* (New York, 1939); Sacvan Bercovitch, *The Puritan Origins of the American Self* (New Haven, Conn., 1975).

17. Conversion was often a painful process in early New England, one that begins, as Charles Lloyd Cohen argues in *God's Caress*, "with the soul's initial conviction of sin" (202).

Sometimes illness and other tragedies impressed this conviction upon Puritans, but not always, so the language and psychology of conversion are not always the language and psychology of grief. For a variety of cases that illustrate commonalities and some idiosyncrasies in relations of conversion, see chapter 7, "Tales of Grace," ibid., 201–241. I owe an obvious and profound debt to two works that extend classic scholarship on mourning in America along lines more directly engaged with affect than questions of form and genre: Kathleen Donegan's *Seasons of Misery: Catastrophe and Colonial Settlement in Early America* (Philadelphia, 2013), and Van Engen's *Sympathetic Puritans*. In the process of theorizing misery and sympathy, both works subtilize and complicate our conceptions of crisis, as well.

18. Helene P. Foley and Jean E. Howard, "Introduction: The Urgency of Tragedy Now," *PMLA*, CXXIX (2014), 617. As Elaine Forman Crane argues, "In the not so distant past, pain was persistent and pervasive enough to make it a normal (rather than aberrant) condition of life, and one that acted as a dynamic of human society"; see Crane, "'I Have Suffer'd Much Today': The Defining Force of Pain in Early America," in Ronald Hoffman, Mechal Sobel, and Fredrika J. Teute, eds., *Through a Glass Darkly: Reflections on Personal Identity in Early America* (Williamsburg, Va., and Chapel Hill, N.C., 1997), 370–403.

19. Throughout the book, I use the terms *mood, atmosphere, affect, sentiment,* and *feeling* to describe the emotional charge of grief. When distinctions between these terms are germane to the argument, I elaborate on their nuances. Otherwise, I use them interchangeably, although I acknowledge that affect theorists and historians of emotions use them in specialized ways. For a discussion of these approaches, see Rosenwein and Cristiani, *What Is the History of Emotions?* 10–11.

20. Donegan, *Seasons of Misery*, 4 ("material"), 5 ("sieges"), 8 ("'situation'"); Alain Badiou, "On the Truth-Process: Followed by Interventions of S. Žižek and G. Agamben," talk delivered at the European Graduate School, August 2002, accessed Dec. 21, 2021, https://www .lacan.com/badeurope.htm. As Badiou puts it: "For the process of truth to begin, something must happen. Knowledge as such only gives us repetition, it is concerned only with what already is. For truth to affirm its newness, there must be a supplement. This supplement is committed to chance—it is unpredictable, incalculable, it is beyond what it is. I call it an event. A truth appears in its newness because an eventful supplement interrupts repetition." I might have used stronger language for the tenor of the psalmist, as Collin Cornell does in *Divine Aggression in Psalms and Inscriptions: Vengeful Gods and Loyal Kings* (Cambridge, 2001). On providentialism in the early modern world, which in fact "was not a marginal feature of the religious culture of early modern England, but part of the mainstream, a cluster of presuppositions which enjoyed near universal acceptance," see Alexandra Walsham, *Providence in Early Modern England* (Oxford, 1999), 2.

21. Breitwieser, *American Puritanism*, 9; Luciano, *Arranging Grief*, 39; Van Engen, *Sympathetic Puritans*, 155. The project of mourning coincided with other projects carried out discursively in early America—the project of conversion, the project of war, and so forth. See also Cavitch's thorough analysis of the centrality of elegies in these productions in *American Elegy*.

22. "A Narrative of the Captivity and Restauration of Mrs. Mary Rowlandson," in Salisbury, ed., *Sovereignty and Goodness of God*, 71 ("gone"), 89. For studies on depopulation, see, for example, Alfred W. Crosby, *Ecological Imperialism: The Biological Expansion of Europe, 900–1900* (New York, 1986); Crosby, "Hawaiian Depopulation as a Model for the Amerindian Experience," in Terence Ranger and Paul Slack, eds., *Epidemics and Ideas: Essays on the Historical*

Perception of Pestilence (Cambridge, 1992), 175–202; and David Stannard, *Before the Horror: The Population of Hawai'i on the Eve of Western Contact* (Honolulu, 1989). Seth Archer offers a conspicuous exception. In his book *Sharks upon the Land: Colonialism, Indigenous Health, and Culture in Hawai'i, 1778–1855* (Cambridge, 2018), Archer foregrounds the crisis of ill health and its influence on Hawaiian politics, economy, and culture in the era immediately following James Cook's voyages to the Hawaiian Archipelago. Archer's argument is revolutionary precisely because most historians have passed over this crisis rather than dwelling on it. His book provided a model for my analysis in Chapter 4, "Disabled."

23. For the late eighteenth and early nineteenth century, this group of grieving women is addressed in Shannon Withycombe, *Lost: Miscarriage in Nineteenth-Century America* (New Brunswick, N.J., 2018). By the nineteenth century, there were discursive forms available to bereaved mothers that were not available earlier, an impediment to mourning I consider in Chapter 3, "Stillborn."

24. See "The Declaration and Confession of Esther Rodgers," in Daniel E. Williams, ed., *Pillars of Salt: An Anthology of Early American Criminal Narratives* (Madison, Wis., 1993), 95–110. See also, for example, "A Faithful Narrative of the Wicked Life and Remarkable Conversion of Patience Boston," ibid., 119–142.

25. Dora Zhang, "Notes on Atmosphere," *Qui Parle*, XXVII (2018), 121–155 (quotation on 125); Rita Felski and Susan Fraiman, "Introduction," *New Literary History*, XLIII (2012), v–xii, esp. v ("ambient"), vii ("in a mood"); Tho[mas] Dermer, "To His Worshipfull Friend M. Samuel Purchas, Preacher of the Word, at the Church a Little within Ludgate, London," in Samuel Purchas, *Hakluytus Posthumus; or, Purchas His Pilgrimes: Contayning a History of the World in Sea Voyages and Lande Travells by Englishmen and Others*, XIX (Glasgow, 1906), 129 ("sicknesse"); Paula Peters, "Of Patuxet," in William Bradford, *Of Plimoth Plantation*, ed. Kenneth P. Minkema, Francis J. Bremer, and Jeremy D. Bangs, 400th anniversary ed. (Boston, 2020), 25–47 ("the Great Dying," 30); William Bradford, *History of Plymouth Plantation, 1620–1647*, 2 vols. (Boston, 1912), I, 156 ("summer").

26. For a brilliant analysis of the crisis attending English settlement in Patuxet, see Donegan, *Seasons of Misery*, 117–154. At least one English explorer, Thomas Dermer, saw in the devastation of Patuxet the creation of "the ideal site" for a new English colony. See Neal Salisbury, "Treacherous Waters: Tisquantum, the Red Atlantic, and the Beginnings of Plymouth Colony," *Early American Literature*, LVI (2021), 62. Late in the American history of legal witch hunts, Cotton Mather famously (and, by that point, controversially) aired this view of diabolical forces at work in New England in *The Wonders of the Invisible World*. See Mather, "The Wonders of the Invisible World: Observations as Well Historical as Theological, upon the Nature, the Number, and the Operations of the Devils (1693)," ed. Reiner Smolinski, *Electronic Texts in American Studies*, Libraries at University of Nebraska—Lincoln, 1998, https://digitalcommons.unl.edu/etas/19.

27. Terry Eagleton summarizes this history in the classic essay "The Rise of English," in Eagleton, *Literary Theory: An Introduction*, anniversary ed. (Minneapolis, Minn., 2008), 15–46. See also W. K. Wimsatt, Jr., and M. C. Beardsley, "The Intentional Fallacy," *Sewanee Review*, LIV (1946), 468–488.

28. Rita Felski, "Latour and Literary Studies," *PMLA*, CXXX (2015), 737–742 (quotations on 741); Felski, *The Limits of Critique* (Chicago, 2015), 1–13.

29. Hayden White, "The Historical Text as Literary Artifact," *Clio*, III (1974), 84.

30. John M. Bullard, ed., *Captain Edmund Gardner of Nantucket and New Bedford: His Journal and Family* (New Bedford, Mass., 1958), 67 ("depressed"); Elaine Scarry, *The Body in Pain: The Making and Unmaking of the World* (New York, 1985); Cathy Caruth, *Unclaimed Experience: Trauma, Narrative, and History* (1996; rpt. Baltimore, 2016). For body and trauma theorists, see, for example, Ann Cvetkovich, *An Archive of Feelings: Trauma, Sexuality, and Lesbian Public Cultures* (Durham, N.C., 2003); Greg Forter, *Gender, Race, and Mourning in American Modernism* (Cambridge, 2011); and Naomi Mandel, *Against the Unspeakable: Complicity, the Holocaust, and Slavery in America* (Charlottesville, Va., 2006).

31. Jill Lepore, *The Name of War: King Philip's War and the Origins of American Identity* (New York, 1999), 148. For a thoughtful discussion of the impediments the early American history of colonialism presents to the usual methods of trauma studies, see Donegan, *Seasons of Mercy*, 215 n. 40. On this form of disability oppression, see Tobin Siebers, "In the Name of Pain," in Jonathan M. Metzl and Anna Kirkland, eds., *Against Health: How Health Became the New Morality* (New York, 2010), 183–194.

32. *The New-England Primer Improved for the More Easy Attaining the True Reading of English; to Which Is Added the Assembly of Divines, and Mr. Cotton's Catechism* (Boston, 1777) (the pages are not numbered, but the letter J appears on image 20 of the 1777 edition viewable at https://archive.org/details/newenglandprimeroowest/page/n19/mode/2up); William Perkins, "The Estate of a Christian Man in This Life . . . ," in *The Whole Works of That Famous and Worthy Minister of Christ in the University of Cambridge, M. William Perkins* . . . (London, 1631), 364; Cohen, *God's Caress*, 5 ("desperation"), 79 (on Perkins); Adrian Chastain Weimer, "Affliction and the Stony Heart in Early New England," in Ryrie and Schwanda, eds., *Puritanism and Emotion*, 121–143 (quotation on 133). Elaine Forman Crane considers both personal, subjective, experiences of pain in early New England and the public discourses surrounding it in "'I Have Suffer'd Much Today,'" in Hoffman, Sobel, and Teute, eds., *Through a Glass Darkly*, 370–403.

33. Daniel Sennert, *Nine Books of Physick and Chirurgery Written by That Great and Learned Physitian, Dr. Sennertus* . . . (London, 1658), 40; John Browne, *A Compleat Discourse of Wounds Both in General and Particular: Whereunto Are Added the Several Fractures of the Skull, with Their Variety of Figures* . . . (London, 1678), 11. My thanks to Brice Peterson for bringing these two medical books to my attention and for sharing his insights into early modern conceptions of trauma.

34. 2 Peter 3:5–12 (Authorized [King James] Version); Kristen Poole, "'My Hand Would Dissolve, Or Seem to Melt': Poetic Dissolution and Stoic Cosmology," in Mary Floyd-Wilson and Garrett A. Sullivan, Jr., eds., *Geographies of Embodiment in Early Modern England* (Oxford, 2020), 152–176 (quotation on 158); "Upon the Sweeping Flood Aug: 13.14. 1683," in Donald E. Stanford, ed., *The Poems of Edward Taylor* (1960; rpt. Chapel Hill, N.C., 2014), 347. On the cosmology of the Stoics, see Peter Barker and Bernard R. Goldstein, "Is Seventh Century Physics Indebted to the Stoics?" *Centaurus*, XXVII (1984), 148–164, esp. 149.

35. Lisa Brooks, *Our Beloved Kin: A New History of King Philip's War* (New Haven, Conn., 2018).

36. Perry Miller's *Errand into the Wilderness* (Cambridge, Mass., 1956), for example, proposes an influential model of the mutations that gradually transformed Puritan thought that finds fault lines between generations, not lateral fissures between married couples.

37. Emily Dickinson, "Pain—Has an Element of Blank," in R. W. Franklin, ed., *The Poems of Emily Dickinson: Reading Edition* (Cambridge, Mass., 2005), 339–340 (an image of the

original can be viewed at https://www.edickinson.org/3editions/1/image_sets/1217570); Tiffany Lethabo King, *The Black Shoals: Offshore Formations of Black and Native Studies* (Durham, N.C., 2019), 2–3.

38. Giovanni Levi, "On Microhistory," in Peter Burke, ed., *New Perspectives on Historical Writing* (University Park, Pa., 1992), 93–113 (quotation on 95).

39. Barbara H. Rosenwein, *Generations of Feeling: A History of Emotions, 600–1700* (New York, 2016), 9, 12 ("judgmental"); Elena Carrera, *Emotions and Health, 1200–1700* (Leiden, Neth., 2013), 9; Peter N. Stearns, *Shame: A Brief History* (Urbana, Ill., 2017), 12.

40. Job 1:21 ("gave"), 3:1–12, 6:2 ("grief") (AV).

41. Job 11:16 (AV).

CHAPTER 1

1. Anne Bradstreet, "Here Followes Some Verses upon the Burning of Our House, July 10th, 1666," in John Harvard Ellis, ed., *The Works of Anne Bradstreet in Prose and Verse* (Charlestown, Mass., 1867), 41, 42; [Mary Rowlandson], *The Sovereignty and Goodness of God, Together, with the Faithfulness of His Promises Displayed; Being a Narrative of the Captivity and Restauration of Mrs. Mary Rowlandson . . . Written by Her own Hand . . .*, 2d ed., corr. (Cambridge, Mass., 1682), 2. The Ellis edition of Bradstreet's work does not contain line numbers, so page numbers are cited instead. Any edition of Bradstreet's poetry has its limitations—organization, accessibility in print, presentation of revisions, etc.—but I use this one (unless otherwise noted) because it is widely available and mostly includes the revisions to the poems in *The Tenth Muse* (1650) that Bradstreet made in the 1660s, which I closely read later in the chapter.

2. Bradstreet, "Here Followes Some Verses," in Ellis, ed., *Works*, 40.

3. I paraphrase Sacvan Bercovitch's summary of Puritan typology in *The Puritan Origins of the American Self* (New Haven, Conn., 1975), 35–39. For another discussion of typology, see Ursula Brumm, *American Thought and Religious Typology* (New Brunswick, N.J., 1970), 23–33. "Pillar of fire" appears first in the Old Testament in Exodus 13:22, but I cite here Samuel Mather, *The Figures or Types of the Old Testament, by Which Christ and the Heavenly Things of the Gospel Were Preached and Shadowed to the People of God of Old: Explain'd and Improv'd in Sundry Sermons*, 2d ed. (London, 1705), 59. For "Fire and Brimstone," see ibid., 83 (Mather cites Rev. 21:8 [Authorized (King James) Version (AV)]); "not in the fire" is from 1 Kings 19:12 (AV). For Jonathan Edwards's sermon, see Edwards, *Sinners in the Hands of an Angry God: A Sermon Preached at Enfield, July 8th, 1741 . . .* (Boston, 1741), 15.

4. *Catalogue of the Relics and Curiosities in Memorial Hall, Deerfield, Mass., U.S.A.: Collected by the Pocomtuck Valley Memorial Association* (Deerfield, Mass., 1886), 26 ("conflagration"); Isaac Addington to Fitz-John Winthrop, Mar. 6, 1703/4, in *The Winthrop Papers*, Massachusetts Historical Society, Collections, 6th Ser., III (Boston, 1889), 180.

5. For discussions of "unsettlement" as I use it here, see Anna Brickhouse, *The Unsettlement of America: Translation, Interpretation, and the Story of Don Luis de Velasco, 1560–1945* (New York, 2015), 2; and Kathleen Donegan, *Seasons of Misery: Catastrophe and Colonial Settlement in Early America* (Philadelphia, 2014), 9.

6. William Cronon, *Changes in the Land: Indians, Colonists, and the Ecology of New England*, 2d ed. (New York, 2003), 50 ("sprout hardwoods"), 51 ("subtler"); John Smith, "A Description of New England (1616): An Online Electronic Text Edition," ed. Paul Royster, in *Electronic*

Texts in American Studies (Lincoln, Neb., n.d.), 47, https://digitalcommons.unl.edu/cgi /viewcontent.cgi?article=1003&context=etas; Timothy Dwight, Travels; in New-England and New-York, IV (New Haven, Conn., 1822), 61; Nathaniel B. Shurtleff, ed., Records of the Governor and Company of the Massachusetts Bay in New England . . . , III (Boston, 1854), 281 ("subdueing"). In the King James Bible, Genesis 1:28 reads, "And God blessed them, and God said unto them, Be fruitful, and multiply, and replenish the earth, and subdue it: and have dominion over the fish of the sea, and over the fowl of the air, and over every living thing that moveth upon the earth." See also Stephen J. Pyne, Fire in America: A Cultural History of Wildland and Rural Fire, 2d ed. (Seattle, 1997), 46. For a recent example of the edge effect, see "Microclimate Edge Effect in Small Fragments of Temperate Forests in the Context of Climate Change," Forest Ecology and Management, CDXLVIII (Sept. 15, 2019), 48–56, https://doi .org/10.1016/j.foreco.2019.05.069.

7. Thomas M. Wickman, Snowshoe Country: An Environmental and Cultural History of Winter in the Early American Northeast (Cambridge, 2018); Strother E. Roberts, Colonial Ecology, Atlantic Economy: Transforming Nature in Early New England (Philadelphia 2019), 102, 103 (quotations). For more on these patterns of deforestation, see Cronon, Changes in the Land, 118.

8. Roger Williams, A Key into the Language of America (1643) (Bedford, Mass., 1997), 59–60.

9. Cotton Mather, "Decennium Luctuosum; or, The Remarkables of a Long War with Indian-Salvages," article XXV, "A Notable Exploit, wherein, Dux Faemina Facti," in Mather, Magnalia Christi Americana; or, The Ecclesiastial History of New-England, from Its First Planting in the Year 1620 unto the Year of Our Lord, 1698 (London, 1702), bk. 7, 90; [Rowlandson], Sovereignty and Goodness of God, 1; Lisa Brooks, "Turning the Looking Glass on King Philip's War: Locating American Literature in Native Space," American Literary History, XXV (2013), 737, 738.

10. [Rowlandson], Sovereignty and Goodness of God, 7 ("vast"); Brooks, "Turning the Looking Glass on King Philip's War," American Literary History, XXV, 730 ("homeland"), 734 ("environment"); James Kendall Hosmer, ed., Winthrop's Journal: "History of New England," 1630–1649, Original Narratives of Early American History, I (New York, 1908), 68; Thomas Shepard, The Clear Sun-Shine of the Gospel Breaking Forth upon the Indians in New-England; or, An Historicall Narration of Gods Wonderfull Workings upon Sundry of the Indians . . . (London, 1648; rpt. [Cambridge, Mass., 1834]), 41.

11. John Williams, The Redeemed Captive Returning to Zion; or, The Captivity and Deliverance of Rev. John Williams of Deerfield (1707) (Boston, 1795; rpt. Springfield, Mass., 1908), 13; George Sheldon, A History of Deerfield, Massachusetts . . . , 2 vols. (Deerfield, Mass., 1895–1896), I, 546; William Bradford, History of Plymouth Plantation . . . (1651), ed. Charles Deane (Boston, 1856), 10. For a detailed description of the months leading up to the 1704 attack and the conditions under which these homes were abandoned, see Evan Haefeli and Kevin Sweeney, Captors and Captives: The 1704 French and Indian Raid on Deerfield (Amherst, Mass., 2003), 95–112.

12. [Lucy Terry Prince], "Bars Fight," in Josiah Gilbert Holland, History of Western Massachusetts . . . , II, pt. 3 (Springfield, Mass., 1855), 360; Sheldon, History of Deerfield, II, 899; Frances Smith Foster, Written by Herself: Literary Production by African American Women, 1746–1892 (Bloomington, Ind., 1993), 24–25 (quotation from Wagner on 24); Sharon M. Harris, Executing Race: Early American Women's Narratives of Race, Society, and the Law (Columbus, Ohio, 2005), 172–174. The central account of the ten fires that started, deliberately or accidentally, in New York City in 1741 is Daniel Horsmanden, Journal of the Proceedings in the Detection of the Conspiracy Formed by Some White People, in Conjunction with Negro and Other Slaves, for Burning the

City of New-York in America, and Murdering the Inhabitants (New York, 1744). Jill Lepore presents extensive additional evidence in New York Burning: Liberty, Slavery, and Conspiracy in Eighteenth-Century Manhattan (New York, 2005).

13. Gretchen Holbrook Gerzina, Mr. and Mrs. Prince: How an Extraordinary Eighteenth-Century Family Moved out of Slavery and into Legend (New York, 2008), 64–66; Susan McGowan and Amelia F. Miller, Family and Landscape: Deerfield Homelots from 1671 (Deerfield, Mass., 1996), xvii, 119. Sheldon's record is in History of Deerfield, I, 617.

14. This is particularly notable in Gerzina, since she records a tour through the present Wells-Thorn home and speculates at some length about Terry's history in that house. See Gerzina, Mr. and Mrs. Prince, 68–71. See also David R. Proper, "Lucy Terry Prince: 'Singer of History,'" Contributions in Black Studies, nos. 9–10 (1990–1992), 187–214, which does not mention the fire.

15. Bill Flynt, "Wells-Thorn House, c. 1747, Historic Deerfield, Deerfield, MA" (unpublished report, 2004). On the 1726 record of the grant, see Sheldon, History of Deerfield, I, 502. Greenfield was, in 1726, still part of Deerfield, not yet incorporated into a separate town.

16. [Prince], "Bars Fight," in Holland, History of Western Massachusetts, II, pt. 3, 360. In the nineteenth century, the poem also appeared, with minor variations in spacing and punctuation, in Sheldon, History of Deerfield, I, 548–549.

17. Sheldon offers these details about the conflict in History of Deerfield, I, 545–547.

18. Stephen W[est] Williams, Biographical Memoir of the Rev. John Williams, First Minister of Deerfield, Massachusetts . . . (Greenfield, Mass., 1837), 123. This history is recounted in Geneviève Treyvaud and Michel Plourde, The Abenakis of Odanak: An Archaeological Journey (Quebec, 2017).

19. John Demos, The Unredeemed Captive: A Family Story from Early America (New York, 1994), 193 ("blankets"); Williams, Biographical Memoir, 123 ("shabbily"); Haefeli and Sweeney, Captors and Captives, 131, 153–154.

20. Official History of Guilford, Vermont, 1678–1961: With Genealogies and Biographical Sketches, ed. Broad Brook Grange No. 151 (Guilford, Vt., 1961), 145–146. For more on this history, see Harris, Executing Race, 158.

21. Ruth Wallis Herndon, Unwelcome Americans: Living on the Margin in Early New England (Philadelphia, 2001), 2, 5.

22. For a brief discussion of the history of the poem across oral, manuscript, and print forms, see Proper, "Lucy Terry Prince," Contributions in Black Studies, nos. 9–10 (1990–1992), 193.

23. Harris, Executing Race, 179 ("damning"). In Deirdre Mullane, ed., Crossing the Danger Water: Three Hundred Years of African-American Writing (New York, 1993), Mullane argues that Terry's poem "recalls the popular captivity narrative genre of the colonial period, in which the writer recounts his or her experience in captivity among the Indians" (24). But April Langley points out that "Terry's poem is curiously—and I would add consciously—devoid of even circumstantial reference to a God to which the young poet 'was [purportedly] early on devoted'" (Langley, "Lucy Terry Prince: The Cultural and Literary Legacy of Africana Womanism," Western Journal of Black Studies, XXV, no. 3 [2001], 157). Langley's point here is that if Terry was adopting the American captivity narrative genre, she was also adapting it to a discourse on race largely absent from—and precluded by the values of—mid-eighteenth-century print culture.

24. Sheldon, *History of Deerfield*, II, 900.

25. This obituary, published in the *Franklin Herald* (Greenfield, Mass.), Aug. 21, 1821, [3], is reprinted in Proper, "Lucy Terry Prince," *Contributions in Black Studies*, nos. 9–10 (1990–1992), 188. Terry's later history is sketched in Gerzina, *Mr. and Mrs. Prince*, 186–188.

26. Sheldon, *History of Deerfield*, I, 547.

27. Harris, *Executing Race*, 178; Foster, *Written by Herself*, 25. On the constraints of readings guided by the author's supposed intentions, see W. K. Wimsatt, Jr., and M. C. Beardsley, "The Intentional Fallacy," *Sewanee Review*, LIV (1946), 468–488. On the "suspiciously chauvinistic approach" of some twentieth-century literary critics to the writings of early African Americans, see Foster, *Written by Herself*, 28.

28. Tiffany Lethabo King, *The Black Shoals: Offshore Formations of Black and Native Studies* (Durham, N.C., 2019), 2 ("school"), 3 ("ecological"), 8–9 ("captive," 9).

29. Michael LeVan, "The Digital Shoals: On Becoming and Sensation in Performance," *Text and Performance Quarterly*, XXXII (2012), 211.

30. Proper, "Lucy Terry Prince," *Contributions in Black Studies*, nos. 9–10 (1990–1992), 187 ("accurate"); Holland, *History of Western Massachusetts*, II, pt. 3, 359 ("wit").

31. Bradstreet, "In Memory of My Dear Grand-Child Anne Bradstreet . . . ," in Ellis, ed., *Works*, 406 ("look"); Bradstreet, "Here Follows Some Verses," ibid., 40 ("dwelling place"); Hokulani K. Aikau et al., "Indigenous Feminisms Roundtable," *Frontiers*, XXXVI, no. 3 (2015), 94; Tiya Miles and Sharon P. Holland, "Introduction: Crossing Waters, Crossing Worlds," in Miles and Holland, eds., *Crossing Waters, Crossing Worlds: The African Diaspora in Indian Country* (Durham, N.C., 2006), 2–3.

32. Ayesha Ramachandran, *The Worldmakers: Global Imagining in Early Modern Europe* (Chicago, 2015), 7 ("synthesize"); Roland Greene, *Five Words: Critical Semantics in the Age of Shakespeare and Cervantes* (Chicago, 2013), 150 ("ideal"); Samuel Fallon, "Lately Sprung up in America: Anne Bradstreet's Untimely Worldmaking," *Journal for Early Modern Cultural Studies*, XVIII (2018), 100–123, esp. 102–103 (quotation); Heb. 11:3 (AV).

33. Lisa Brooks, *Our Beloved Kin: A New History of King Philip's War* (New Haven, Conn., 2018), 76.

34. Ibid., 90–91 (quotations), 95. I am also indebted to Brooks for her careful research into Caleb Cheeshateaumuck's and Joel Iacoomes's biographies.

35. Brooks, *Our Beloved Kin*, 101, 102 ("malnutrition"), 103 ("shipwreck"); Lorie M. Graham and Peter R. Golia, "In Caleb's Footsteps: The Harvard University Native American Program," in Duane Champagne and Jay Stauss, eds., *Native American Studies in Higher Education: Models for Collaboration between Universities and Indigenous Nations* (New York, 2002), 126 ("honors").

36. Bradstreet, "To My Dear Children," in Ellis, ed., *Works*, 5 ("found"); Charlotte Gordon, *Mistress Bradstreet: The Untold Life of America's First Poet* (New York, 2005), 227 ("six pounds"); Bradstreet, "The Four Elements," in Ellis, ed., *Works*, 105 ("Cooks"); Bradstreet, "Here Followes Some Verses," ibid., 40 ("fire"); "Simon Bradstreet," in John Langdon Sibley, *Biographical Sketches of Graduates of Harvard University . . .* , II, 1659–1677 (Cambridge, Mass., 1881), 55 ("books"), 56 ("ministers").

37. See Abram Van Engen, "Advertising the Domestic: Anne Bradstreet's Sentimental Poetics," *Legacy*, XXVIII (2011), 47–68.

38. Bradstreet, "Here Followes Some Verses," in Ellis, ed., *Works*, 40 ("look"), 41 ("pleasant"), 40–41 ("Thou hast"); Bradstreet, "A Dialogue between Old England and New;

concerning Their Present Troubles, Anno, 1642," ibid., 336 ("exile"); Bradstreet, "In Memory of My Dear Grand-Child Anne Bradstreet," ibid., 405 ("joy").

39. Bradstreet, "Here Followes Some Verses," in Ellis, ed., *Works*, 41 ("Adeiu," "mouldring"); Bradstreet, "To My Dear Children," ibid., 3 ("Book"); Bradstreet, "Before the Birth of One of Her Children," ibid., 394 ("kiss"). In the King James Bible, Ecclesiastes 1:2 reads, "Vanity of vanities, saith the Preacher, vanity of vanities; all is vanity."

40. [John Woodbridge], "Address to the Reader," in Ellis, *Works*, 83–84; Bradstreet, "Here Followes Some Verses," ibid., 41 ("Table"). On the scarcity of paper during this period of New England settlement, see Lyman Horace Weeks, *A History of Paper-Manufacturing in the United States, 1690–1916* (New York, 1916), 2.

41. Van Engen, "Advertising the Domestic," *Legacy*, XXVIII (2011), 52–53; Margaret Olofson Thickstun, "Contextualizing Anne Bradstreet's Literary Remains: Why We Need a New Edition of the Poems," *Early American Literature*, LII (2017), 398; Editorial note in Ellis, *Works*, 391; Bradstreet, "The Author to Her Book," ibid., 389 ("less wise"); Bradstreet, "The Prologue," ibid., 101. On the ways "The Prologue" must be read in the context of Bradstreet's manuscript circulation, as well as the print culture in which it appeared, see Meredith Marie Neuman, "Manuscript Culture," in Kristina Bross and Abram Van Engen, eds., *A History of American Puritan Literature* (New York, 2020), 259–274.

42. Bradstreet, "To My Dear Children," in Ellis, ed., *Works*, 3; Thickstun, "Contextualizing Anne Bradstreet's Literary Remains," *Early American Literature*, LII (2017), 400 ("booklet"); Bradstreet, "Here Followes Some Verses," in Ellis, ed., *Works*, 40 ("loose Paper"); Bradstreet, "Before the Birth of One of Her Children," ibid., 394 ("kiss"); Neuman, "Manuscript Culture," in Bross and Van Engen, *History of American Puritan Literature*, 266 ("absolutely"). As Neuman points out, "If not for the celebrated contingencies of Bradstreet's seventeenth-century print publication, her literary output might better be known as a particularly good example of puritan manuscript culture" (259). For examples of other writers circulating their work to families and friends this way, see Margaret P. Hannay, "The Countess of Pembroke's Agency in Print and Scribal Culture," in George L. Justice and Nathan Tinker, eds., *Women's Writing and the Circulation of Ideas: Manuscript Publication in England, 1550–1800* (Cambridge, 2002), 17–49, esp. 31–32; and Margaret J. M. Ezell, *Social Authorship and the Advent of Print* (Baltimore, 1999), 27.

43. Rege Sincera, *Observations Both Historical and Moral upon the Burning of London, September 1666; with an Account of the Losses . . .* (London, 1667), 3, 4.

44. See, for example, Gillian Wright, *Producing Women's Poetry, 1600–1730: Text and Paratext, Manuscript and Print* (Cambridge, 2013), 92. See also Susan Wiseman, *Conspiracy and Virtue: Women, Writing, and Politics in Seventeenth-Century England* (New York, 2006), 193; Kate Chedgzoy, *Women's Writing in the British Atlantic World: Memory, Place, and History, 1550–1700* (Cambridge, 2007), 125–126; and Mihoko Suzuki, "What's Political in Seventeenth-Century Women's Political Writing?" *Literature Compass*, VI (2009), 927–941.

45. Jane D. Eberwein, "Civil War and Bradstreet's 'Monarchies,'" *Early American Literature*, XXVI (1991), 122, 140; Bradstreet, "The Four Monarchies," in Ellis, ed., *Works*, 328; Wright, *Producing Women's Poetry*, 95. For more on the political contributions of Dudley and Woodbridge during the crisis in London, see ibid., 94.

46. Bradstreet, "The Four Monarchies," in Ellis, ed., *Works*, 322, 329; [Woodbridge], "Address to the Reader," ibid., 84.

47. Paula Kopacz, "'To Finish What's Begun': Anne Bradstreet's Last Words," *Early American Literature*, XXIII (1988), 175–187, esp. 178 (quotation); Wright, *Producing Women's Poetry*, 88; Andrea Brady, *English Funerary Elegy in the Seventeenth Century: Laws in Mourning* (Houndmills, U.K., 2006), 2 ("sociable"); Jeffrey A. Hammond, *The American Puritan Elegy: A Literary and Cultural Study* (Cambridge, 2000), 16; Max Cavitch, *American Elegy: The Poetry of Mourning from the Puritans to Whitman* (Minneapolis, Minn., 2007), 1.

48. Elizabeth Wade White, *Anne Bradstreet: "The Tenth Muse"* (New York, 1971), 236; Eberwein, "Civil War and Bradstreet's 'Monarchies,'" *Early American Literature*, XXVI (1991), 120; Adrienne Rich, "Anne Bradstreet and Her Poetry," in Jeannine Hensley, ed., *The Works of Anne Bradstreet* (Cambridge, Mass., 1967), ix–xxii ("listless," xiv); Fallon, "Lately Sprung up in America," 101, 104; Facsimile title page of [Anne Bradstreet], *The Tenth Muse Lately Sprung up in America; or, Severall Poems, Compiled with Great Variety of Wit and Learning, Full of Delight . . . Also a Dialogue between Old England and New, concerning the Late Troubles . . . by a Gentlewoman in Those Parts* (London, 1650), reprinted in Ellis, ed., *Works*, [79]; Bradstreet, "An Elegy upon That Honorable and Renowned Knight Sir Philip Sidney . . . ," in Hensley, ed., *Works of Anne Bradstreet*, 190.

49. For "inappropriate grief," see Allison Giffen, "'Let No Man Know': Negotiating the Gendered Discourse of Affliction in Anne Bradstreet's 'Here Follows Some Verses upon the Burning of Our House, July 10th, 1666,'" *Legacy*, XXVII (2010), 4.

50. Thickstun, "Contextualizing Anne Bradstreet's Literary Remains," *Early American Literature*, LII (2017), 403. Thickstun is here referencing a history developed much more extensively by Catharine Gray in *Women Writers and Public Debate in 17th-Century Britain* (New York, 2007).

51. Bradstreet, "The Vanity of All Worldly Things," in Ellis, ed., *Works*, 387; Bradstreet, "Here Followes Some Verses," ibid., 40, 41; Bradstreet, "For Deliverance from a Feaver," ibid., 12. For a discussion of these sermons on the Great Fire, see Jacob F. Field, *London, Londoners, and the Great Fire of 1666: Disaster and Recovery* (New York, 2018).

52. Giffen, "'Let No Man Know,'" *Legacy*, XXVII (2010), 9; Bradstreet, "Here Followes Some Verses," in Ellis, ed., *Works*, 40; John Putnam Demos, *Entertaining Satan: Witchcraft and the Culture of Early New England* (New York, 1982), 375 ("hundreds").

53. Brian McGrory, "Centuries of Interruption and a History Rejoined: Wampanoag Grad to Be Harvard's First Since 1665," *Boston.com* (May 11, 2011), http://archive.boston.com /news/local/massachusetts/articles/2011/05/11/wampanoag_grad_to_be_harvards_firfi _since_1665/?page=2, accessed May 1, 2020.

54. Daniel J. Philippon, "Sustainability and the Humanities: An Extensive Pleasure," *American Literary History*, XXIV (2012), 167 ("development"); John Evelyn, *Silva; or, A Discourse of Forest-Trees, and the Propagation of Timber in His Majesty's Dominions . . .* (London, 1706), [5], [7]. For a discussion of the debate on sustainability, see Philippon, "Sustainability and the Humanities," *American Literary History*, XXIV (2012), 163–179. For more on the etymology of the term *sustainability* (and the attendant cultural values it indexes), see Jeremy L. Caradonna, *Sustainability: A History* (New York, 2014), 7.

55. Bradstreet, "To the Memory of My Dear and Ever Honoured Father Thomas Dudley Esq . . . ," 366 ("After-comers"). For this history of paper, see Weeks, *History of Paper-Manufacturing in the United States*, 3; and Jonathan Senchyne, *The Intimacy of Paper in Early and Nineteenth-Century American Literature* (Amherst, Mass., 2020).

1. Edmund S. Morgan discusses the legal dissolution of marriages in early New England in Morgan, *The Puritan Family: Religion and Domestic Relations in Seventeenth-Century New England*, rev. ed. (New York, 1966), 34–39. Martin Schultz treats particular cases in more detail in Schultz, "Divorce in Early America: Origins and Patterns in Three North Central States," *Sociological Quarterly*, XXV (1984), 511–525.

2. Benj[amin] Wadsworth, *The Well-Ordered Family* . . . (Boston, 1712), 25; John Cotton, *A Practical Commentary, or an Exposition with Observations, Reasons, and Uses upon the First Epistel Generall of John*, 2d ed. (London, 1658), 126 ("transported"); Cotton, *A Meet Help; or, A Wedding Sermon Preached at New-Castle in New-England, June 19th 1694, at the Marriage of Mr. John Clark, and Mrs. Elizabeth Woodbridge* (Boston, 1699), 9 ("Matches"). See William Gouge, *Of Domesticall Duties: Eight Treatises* (London, 1622), esp. the first treatise, 33–35, 94–95, 118–121. For a discussion of the comparison of the relationships of husband and wife to Christ and his church, see Laurel Thatcher Ulrich, *Good Wives: Image and Reality in the Lives of Women in Northern New England, 1650–1750* (New York, 1980), 108. For an example of an idealized portrait of Puritan conjugal experience, see Belden C. Lane, *Ravished by Beauty: The Surprising Legacy of Reformed Spirituality* (New York, 2011). I discuss several extreme, catastrophic marriages in this chapter, but more examples can be found in Elaine Forman Crane, *Witches, Wife Beaters, and Whores: Common Law and Common Folk in Early America* (Ithaca, N.Y., 2011), esp. chap. 3 (84–118).

3. For an elaboration on the Puritan spiritual ideal of marriage, see Michael P. Winship, "Behold the Bridegroom Cometh! Marital Imagery in Massachusetts Preaching, 1630–1730," *Early American Literature*, XXVII (1992), 175; and Amanda Porterfield, *Feminine Spirituality in America: From Sarah Edwards to Martha Graham* (Philadelphia, 1980), chap. 2 (19–50).

4. Anne Bradstreet, "Before the Birth of One of Her Children," in Jeannine Hensley, ed., *The Works of Anne Bradstreet* (Cambridge, Mass., 1967), 224; Bradstreet, "To My Dear and Loving Husband," ibid., 225 ("if ever").

5. John Winthrop to Margaret Tyndal, Apr. 4, 1618, Papers of the Winthrop Family, I, 226–229 (quotations on 228), Winthrop Papers Digital Edition, Massachusetts Historical Society, https://www.masshist.org/publications/winthrop/index.php/view/PWF01d133; Edward Taylor to Elizabeth Fitch, July 8, 1674, in Thomas M. Davis and Virginia L. Davis, eds., *The Unpublished Writings of Edward Taylor*, III, *Edward Taylor's Minor Poetry* (Boston, 1981), 37–41 (quotation on 37). For another reading of this letter, see Richard Godbeer, *Sexual Revolution in Early America* (Baltimore, 2002), 52.

6. *Boston News-Letter*, Apr. 11–18, 1715, [2]. My thanks to Zach Hutchins for bringing this case, which he uncovered in his own research, to my attention and for sharing his copies of this material with me.

7. Gouge, *Of Domesticall Duties*, 230.

8. Consider, for example, Thomas Hooker's accusing the powerful Springfield trader and magistrate William Pynchon of a kind of diplomatic unfaithfulness as recounted in Perry Miller, *Errand into the Wilderness* (1956; rpt. Cambridge, Mass, 1984), 39.

9. Ibid., 8–9; H. L. Mencken, ed., *A Mencken Chrestomathy* (New York, 1949), 624; Hayden White, "The Historical Text as Literary Artifact," *Clio*, III (1974), 84; Paul Ricoeur, *Freud and Philosophy: An Essay on Interpretation*, trans. Denis Savage (New Haven, Conn., 1970), 32; Rita Felski, *The Limits of Critique* (Chicago, 2015), 5.

10. Ricoeur, *Freud and Philosophy*, 28.

11. William Bradford, *History of Plymouth Plantation, 1620–1647*, 2 vols. (Boston, 1912), I, 155 ("wellcome"), 156 ("hideous"), 225 ("faithfull"). Leo Marx treats this same passage from Bradford's history in *Machine in the Garden: Technology and the Pastoral Ideal in America* (New York, 1964), 41–42; and Kathleen Donegan analyzes it in *Seasons of Misery: Catastrophe and Colonial Settlement in Early America* (Philadelphia, 2014), 124.

12. Bradford, *History of Plymouth Plantation*, I, 253.

13. Ibid., 252 ("regarde"); Tho[mas] Dermer, "To His Worshipfull Friend M. Samuel Purchas, Preacher of the Word, at the Church a Little within Ludgate, London," in Samuel Purchas, *Hakluytus Posthumus; or, Purchas His Pilgrimes: Contayning a History of the World in Sea Voyages and Lande Travells by Englishmen and Others*, XIX (Glasgow, 1906), 129–130 ("arrived"); Neal Salisbury, "Treacherous Waters: Tisquantum, the Red Atlantic, and the Beginnings of Plymouth Colony," *Early American Literature*, LVI (2021), 53–55, 58–62; Jace Weaver, *The Red Atlantic: American Indigenes and the Making of the Modern World, 1000–1927* (Chapel Hill, N.C., 2014). Paula Peters also discusses the scene when Tisquantum returns home in "Of Patuxet," in William Bradford, *Of Plimouth Plantation*, ed. Kenneth P. Minkema, Francis J. Bremer, and Jeremy D. Bangs, 400th anniversary ed. (Boston, 2020), 25–47. For an extended discussion of the ways these "diseases and consequent deaths altered political alliances and rivalries among New England Natives," see Kelly Wisecup, *Medical Encounters: Knowledge and Identity in Early American Literatures* (Amherst, Mass., 2013), 67.

14. Anna Brickhouse, *The Unsettlement of America: Translation, Interpretation, and the Story of Don Luis de Velasco, 1560–1945* (New York, 2015), 19–26 (quotation on 25); Bradford, *History of Plymouth Plantation*, I, 253–255.

15. See, for example, Salisbury, "Treacherous Waters," *Early American Literature*, LVI (2021), 65; and Betty Booth Donohue, *Bradford's Indian Book: Being the True Roote and Rise of American Letters as Revealed by the Native Text Embedded in "Of Plimoth Plantation"* (Gainesville, Fla., 2011), 110. According to Donohue, "It would have been difficult for an unmarried man with few if any relatives to make a successful power play in Native society because he would not have had the support of women" (110).

16. Bradford, *History of Plymouth Plantation*, I, 150 ("loath"), 254 ("begane"), II, 49. On the conflicts between settlers at Plymouth and Merrymount, see ibid., II, 46–58.

17. Ibid., I, 254 ("plague"); Dwight B. Heath, ed., *A Journal of the Pilgrims at Plymouth: Mourt's Relation: A Relation or Journal of the English Plantation Settled at Plymouth in New England, by Certain English Adventurers Both Merchants and Others* (New York, 1963), 70 ("weeping"); Donohue, *Bradford's Indian Book*, 109, 110 ("amassing"); Salisbury, "Treacherous Waters," *Early American Literature*, LVI (2021), 65; Peters, "Of Patuxet," in Bradford, *Of Plimouth Plantation*, ed. Minkema, Bremer, and Bangs, 30; Dermer, "To His Worshipfull Friend M. Samuel Purchas," in Purchas, *Hakluytus Posthumus*, 129 ("remnant[s]").

18. Bradford, *History of Plymouth Plantation*, I, 253 ("Gov[erno]r"); Lisa Brooks, *Our Beloved Kin: A New History of King Philip's War* (New Haven, Conn., 2018), 67 ("deed"); Sydney V. James, Jr., ed., with an introduction by Samuel Eliot Morison, *Three Visitors to Early Plymouth: Letters about the Pilgrim Settlement in New England during Its First Seven Years*, by John Pory, Emmanuel Altham, and Isaack de Rasieres ([Plymouth, Mass.], 1963), 29. Emmanuel Altham, an English visitor to Plymouth, wrote that Ousamequin had five wives and spoke of Hobbamock's plural "wives" (ibid.).

19. Edward Winslow, *Good Newes from New England: A True Relation of Things Very Remarkable at the Plantation of Plimoth in New England* (1624) (Bedford, Mass., [1996]), 13; Donohue, *Bradford's Indian Book*, 110. See also Brooks, *Our Beloved Kin*, 42–43.

20. Winslow, *Good Newes*, 33.

21. Siobhan Senier, ed., *Dawnland Voices: An Anthology of Indigenous Writing from New England* (Lincoln, Neb., 2014), 391.

22. Bradford, *History of Plymouth Plantation*, II, 404; Cotton Mather, "The Life of William Bradford, esq; Governour of Plymouth Colony," in Mather, *Magnalia Christi Americana; or, The Ecclesiastial History of New-England, from Its First Planting in the Year 1620 unto the Year of Our Lord, 1698* (London, 1702), bk. 2, 4; Jane G[oodwin] Austin, "William Bradford's Love Life," *Harper's New Monthly Magazine*, XXXIX (June 1869), 139 ("precious"); Austin, "Preface," in Austin, *David Alden's Daughter and Other Stories of Colonial Times* (Boston, 1892), v–viii; Samuel Eliot Morison, "Introduction," in William Bradford, *Of Plymouth Plantation, 1620–1647*, new ed. (1952; rpt. New York, 2016), xxiv; Francis Murphy, "Introduction," in William Bradford, *Of Plymouth Plantation, 1620–1647* (New York, 1981), xiii. For a strident rejection of Austin's claims to private historical knowledge and a repudiation of the theory Dorothy died by suicide, see George Ernest Bowman, "Governor William Bradford's First Wife, Dorothy (May) Bradford, Did Not Commit Suicide," *Mayflower Descendant*, XXIX, no. 3 (July 1931), 97–102. I am indebted to Stacey Dearing's sensitive analysis of Dorothy Bradford's death in "Remembering Dorothy May Bradford's Death and Reframing 'Depression' in Colonial New England," *Early American Literature*, LVI (2021), 75–104.

23. Bradford, *History of Plymouth Plantation*, I, 149. For a breakdown of the mortality rate as it relates to couples, men, children, and servants, see Donegan, *Seasons of Misery*, 135–136. For a thoroughly innovative treatment of the cataclysmic years 1620–1623, including Bradford's remarriage to Alice Carpenter, see ibid., 117–154.

24. Donegan, *Seasons of Misery*, 8. Alain Badiou writes that the event is a supplement to everyday experience that constitutes a subject in the act of rupturing this experience: "Whatever convokes someone to the composition of a subject is something extra, something that happens in situations as something that they and the usual way of behaving in them cannot account for"—it is a happening "that cannot be reduced to its ordinary inscription in 'what there is'" (Badiou, *Ethics: An Essay on the Understanding of Evil*, trans. Peter Hallward [New York, 2001], 41).

25. Felski, *Limits of Critique*, 20.

26. Bradford, *History of Plymouth Plantation*, I, 162 ("discovere"), 164 ("partly"), 198–203, 252 ("jealocie"); Winslow, *Good Newes*, 38 ("love").

27. This phrase—"the terrible thing"—was used so poignantly by the late poet Nina Riggs in her memoir *The Bright Hour* about her experience living with terminal breast cancer that, try however I might, I could think of no phrase more apt to describe the sense of confirmed dread that winds its way through so much of Bradford's history. I acknowledge my debt to her (Riggs, *The Bright Hour: A Memoir of Living and Dying* [New York, 2017]), 14).

28. Hayden White, *Metahistory: The Historical Imagination in Nineteenth-Century Europe* (Baltimore, 1985), 7–9, 11; Senier, ed., *Dawnland Voices*, 391 ("treacherous").

29. David D. Hall describes the historical context of the Antinomian Controversy in *The Antinomian Controversy, 1636–1638: A Documentary History* (Durham, N.C., 1990). On "familists" being used more commonly during the controversy than "antinomians," see Michael P.

Winship, review of *Martyrs' Mirror: Persecution and Holiness in Early New England*, by Adrian Chastain Weimer, *Journal of American History*, XCIX (2012), 574–575.

30. Overwhelmingly, articles and books about Anne Hutchinson focus on her thought, speech, and behavior leading up to, during, or in the wake of the Antinomian Controversy, although most mention her marriage. I summarize here by way of biographical context. A notable exception is Emery Battis, *Saints and Sectaries: Anne Hutchinson and the Antinomian Controversy in the Massachusetts Bay Colony* (Williamsburg, Va., and Chapel Hill, N.C., 1962), which I discuss later in the chapter. A more representative treatment of the Hutchinson marriage is in Kai T. Erikson, *Wayward Puritans: A Study in the Sociology of Deviance* (New York, 1966), which stages the Antinomian Controversy at "a private home in Boston where William Hutchinson lived with his wife Anne" (77). William is not mentioned after this, but the "home" is, suggesting that the Hutchinson household functions metonymically for Anne Hutchinson's theological views and activities.

31. Hall, *Antinomian Controversy*, 262, 390, 392.

32. James Kendall Hosmer, ed., *Winthrop's Journal: "History of New England," 1630–1649*, I (New York, 1908), 299 ("man"); Hall, *Antinomian Controversy*, 204 ("laboured"), 262 ("head"), 315 ("rule"), 316 ("clash," "seduce"), 382–383 ("stept"); Titus 2:3–5 (Geneva Bible); Mary Beth Norton, *Founding Mothers and Fathers: Gendered Power and the Forming of American Society* (New York, 1996), 394 ("monsters"). See also Everett Emerson, ed., *Letters from New England: The Massachusetts Bay Colony, 1629–1638* (Amherst, Mass., 1976), 229–230.

33. Michael P. Winship, *Making Heretics: Militant Protestantism and Free Grace in Massachusetts, 1636–1641* (Princeton, N.J., 2002), 53–55; Hall, *Antinomian Controversy*, 269 ("argument"); Battis, *Saints and Sectaries*, 51–52 (quotation on 51); Francis J. Bremer, ed., *Anne Hutchinson, Troubler of the Puritan Zion* (Huntington, N.Y., 1981), 12–13. Mary Beth Norton's brief reference to William Hutchinson's "wealth and standing" is characteristic of the way he is treated in more recent scholarship; see Norton, *Founding Mothers and Fathers*, 361. For a more sustained discussion of Hutchinson's economic and social status, see Michelle Burnham, "Anne Hutchinson and the Economics of Antinomian Selfhood in Colonial New England," *Criticism*, XXXIX (1997), 337–358.

34. Abram C. Van Engen, *Sympathetic Puritans: Calvinist Fellow Feeling in Early New England* (New York, 2015), 179; Gouge, *Of Domesticall Duties*, 20–21.

35. Neal Salisbury, "Introduction," in Salisbury, ed., *The Sovereignty and Goodness of God, Together with the Faithfulness of His Promises Displayed: Being a Narrative of the Captivity and Restoration of Mrs. Mary Rowlandson and Related Documents* (New York, 1997), 1–60 (quotation on 25).

36. Brooks, *Our Beloved Kin*, 67 (quotations), 237–245; Salisbury, "Introduction," in Salisbury, ed., *Sovereignty and Goodness of God*, 21–22. Brooks, in *Our Beloved Kin*, writes, "Yet Pocasset families found here a temporary refuge from their war-torn home, a harvest to replace their destroyed fields, and a coalition against 'a common threat'—all of which was expected from families bound by marriage" (237).

37. Salisbury, "Introduction," in Salisbury, ed., *Sovereignty and Goodness of God*, 15–18 (quotation on 16).

38. Ibid., 24–25, 32–33; Brooks, *Our Beloved Kin*, 304–317.

39. Salisbury, "Introduction," in Salisbury, ed., *Sovereignty and Goodness of God*, 33; "A Narrative of the Captivity and Restauration of Mrs. Mary Rowlandson," ibid., 71 ("gone"), 97 ("well"); Mitchell Robert Breitwieser, *American Puritanism and the Defense of Mourning: Religion,*

Grief, and Ethnology in Mary White Rowlandson's Captivity Narrative (Madison, Wis., 1990), 73 ("havoc"), 79 ("leap").

40. "Narrative," in Salisbury, ed., Sovereignty and Goodness of God, 66 ("coy"), 89 ("some"), 107 ("not one"); Breitwieser, American Puritanism, 144.

41. "Narrative," in Salisbury, ed., Sovereignty and Goodness of God, 97–98 ("Saggamores"); Salisbury, "Introduction," ibid., 35; Senier, Dawnland Voices, 375 ("Governor").

42. Salisbury, "Introduction," in Salisbury, ed., Sovereignty and Goodness of God, 35; Brooks, Our Beloved Kin, 323–326. See also Gina M. Martino-Trutor, "'As Potent a Prince as Any Round About Her': Rethinking Weetamoo of the Pocasset and Native Female Leadership in Early America," Journal of Women's History, XXVII, no. 3 (Fall 2015), 37.

43. Senier, Dawnland Voices, 470–471.

44. See Paul B. Moyer, Detestable and Wicked Arts: New England and Witchcraft in the Early Modern Atlantic World (Ithaca, N.Y., 2020), which mentions Hugh and Mary Parsons throughout; David D. Hall, ed., Witch-Hunting in Seventeenth-Century New England: A Documentary History, 1638–1693, 2d ed. (Boston, 1999), 29–60, which presents the primary documents associated with the Parsonses' cases; John Putnam Demos, Entertaining Satan: Witchcraft and the Culture of Early New England, updated ed. (Oxford, 2004), 74; Marion Gibson, Witchcraft Myths in American Culture (New York, 2007), 81–87; Stephen Innes, Labor in a New Land: Economy and Society in Seventeenth-Century Springfield (Princeton, N.J., 1983), 137–141; and Carol F. Karlsen, The Devil in the Shape of a Woman: Witchcraft in Colonial New England (New York, 1998), 22–23. For a discussion of the ways witchcraft and witch hunts might have provided a "release from grief," "a search for satisfaction," "a search for release from the message of the minsters," or release from other social pressures and pains, see David D. Hall, Worlds of Wonder, Days of Judgment: Popular Religious Belief in Early New England (Cambridge, Mass., 1989), 144–150 (quotations on 145).

45. Morgan, The Puritan Family, 40 ("admonish't"); Allyn Bailey Forbes, ed., Records of the Suffolk County Court, 1671–1680, Part 1, Publications of the Colonial Society of Massachusetts, Collections, XXIX (Boston, 1933), 524, https://www.colonialsociety.org/node/695.

46. Cruelty was often alleged in successful divorce suits in early New England and eventually became legal grounds for divorce in old England (See [D.] Kelly Weisberg, "'Under Greet Temptations Heer': Women and Divorce in Puritan Massachusetts," Feminist Studies, II, no. 2 [1975], 183–193, esp. 185). However, the uneven (or nonexistent) codification and application of divorce laws in seventeenth-century America and England complicate some historians' claim that cruelty was a legitimate reason for divorce in early New England (see, for example, Ulrich, Good Wives, 110). John Milton's five tracts on the potential benefits of divorce for both men and women, published between August 1643 and March 1645, make it apparent that most people wedded to cruel partners (or partners unsatisfactory in any other way) in England had little legal recourse and no hope of dissolving the marriage contract (see Sara J. van den Berg and W. Scott Howard, eds., The Divorce Tracts of John Milton: Texts and Contexts [Pittsburgh, 2010]). An examination of the cases cited in the scholarship about divorce in early New England reveals cruelty to be a compounding factor in divorces (usually granted for desertion or adultery) rather than the sole cause. For example, Weisberg finds, "in order for women to be successful in adultery petitions, the act had to be compounded by desertion, cruelty, or failure to provide" (Weisberg, "'Under Greet Temptations Heer,'" Feminist Studies, II, no. 2 [1975], 187). And Nancy F. Cott writes that between 1639 and 1692

the Massachusetts courts "annulled marriages on grounds of consanguinity, bigamy, and sexual incapacity, and dissolved them for long absence and for adultery alone or in combination with desertion, neglect, or cruelty" (Cott, "Divorce and the Changing Status of Women in Eighteenth-Century Massachusetts," *William and Mary Quarterly*, 3d Ser., XXXIII [1976], 589). M. Michelle Jarrett Morris also discusses cases of domestic cruelty in divorces granted on the technical grounds of desertion or adultery in *Under Household Government: Sex and Family in Puritan Massachusetts* (Cambridge, Mass., 2013), 69–71. Morris writes, "Although Massachusetts Bay never passed legislation specifying legitimate grounds for divorce, the superior courts granted divorces for desertion and non-support, marital infidelity, and . . . male sexual incapacity" (81).

47. Morgan, *The Puritan Family*, 36, 40; Joseph H. Smith, ed., *Colonial Justice in Western Massachusetts (1639–1702): The Pynchon Court Record; an Original Judges' Diary of the Administration of Justice in the Springfield Courts in the Massachusetts Bay Colony* (Cambridge, Mass., 1961), 21; John Allin, *A Defence of the Answer . . .* (London, 1648), 15. As William Gouge explains it in *Of Domesticall Duties*, "desertion" referred to people who left the faith—who "withdraw him or her selfe from all societie with the other, and live among Infidels, Idolaters, heretiques, or other such persecutors, as a faithfull Christian with safetie of life, or a good conscience, cannot abide among" (215).

48. Innes, *Labor*, 137; William Pynchon to John Winthrop, Sept. 15, 1645, in *Winthrop Papers*, V, 1645–1649 (Boston, 1947), 45–46 ("7 years," "league," 45); Smith, *Colonial Justice*, 20–21; Hall, ed., *Witch-Hunting*, 29–30, 45 ("midnight").

49. Hall, ed., *Witch-Hunting*, 41 ("occasion"), 45 ("know"). At least since the publication of Mary Beth Norton's *In the Devil's Snare: The Salem Witchcraft Crisis of 1692* (New York, 2002), scholars have been sensitive to the ways witch hunts might have reflected New Englanders' fears about the porous boundaries around settlements and the threats and realities of Native-Anglo military conflicts. Diabolism was commonly associated with foreign or racialized bodies. But Mary's complaint about Hugh—"When I say anything to anybody never so secretly to such friends as I am sure would not speak of it, yet he would come to know it"—alerts us to other, interpersonal, boundaries breached in New England colonies and settlements (Hall, ed., *Witch-Hunting*, 45). The analog in cases like the Parsonses' was not foreign invasion; it was treason.

50. Hall, ed., *Witch-Hunting*, 42 ("sorrow"), 43 ("blamed"), 44; Smith, *Colonial Justice*, 21.

51. Hall, ed., *Witch-Hunting*, 31–32 ("discontented"), 35 (Bedortha), 49, 53 (Lombard), 55 (Branch); Innes, *Labor*, 137. Innes arrives at this high proportion of accusers to Springfield residents by consulting the tax list of 1646.

52. Ulrich, *Good Wives*, 100 ("creatures"), 102 ("forty"); these cases are presented and analyzed on 99–103. Ulrich's interest is in the sexual nature of these cases and what they illustrate about New England's responses to female sexuality, rather than a consideration of these sexual crimes and threats as examples of emotional and psychological abuse.

53. Smith, *Colonial Justice*, 21, 22 ("sufficient"); Hall, ed., *Witch-Hunting*, 41 ("enemy"). Mary was found not guilty of witchcraft, and Hugh was found guilty.

54. According to Smith, the "Pynchon Court Record" refers "to two examinations, one on March 1, 1650/1 and one later, perhaps on March 18. However, the manuscript contains statements made under oath before Pynchon on thirteen different days, starting as early as February 25, 1650/1 and extending to April 7" (Smith, *Colonial Justice*, 21). Mary was present

on at least one of these days, since she testified against Hugh, and she was possibly present on more than one day, although she was taken into custody and transported to the Bay sometime before the Massachusetts General Court indicted her for witchcraft on May 13, 1651.

55. Hall, *Witch-Hunting*, 43 ("husband"), 51 ("dreamer").

56. Smith, *Colonial Justice*, 24. For example, in Utah, where I live, a victim of abuse can only get a restraining or protective order against their abuser based on a past incident or current threat of physical violence. See "Protection from Abuse," Utah State Courts, https://www.utcourts.gov/en/self-help/categories/protect-order.html.

57. As Smith points out in *Colonial Justice*, "Neither Mary nor Hugh was 'tried' at Springfield; the offenses charged were beyond Pynchon's jurisdiction to hear and determine" (22). Based on the examinations at Springfield, however, Pynchon bound Hugh Parsons over to the Court of Assistants to be formally tried for witchcraft, where the trial jury found him guilty.

58. On the court's decision to overturn the trial jury's verdict and acquit Hugh, see Smith, *Colonial Justice*, 23.

59. J[osiah] G[ilbert] Holland, *The Bay-Path; a Tale of New England Colonial Life* (New York, 1857), 21; Ebenezer W. Peirce [and Zerviah G. Mitchell], *Indian History, Biography, and Genealogy: Pertaining to the Good Sachem Massasoit of the Wampanoag Tribe, and His Descendants; with an Appendix* (North Abington, Mass., 1878), 45, 46–47.

60. Nathaniel Hawthorne, "Mrs. Hutchinson," in *Tales, Sketches, and Other Papers* . . . (Boston, 1886), 225; "The Duston Family," *American Magazine of Useful and Entertaining Knowledge*, II, no. 9 (May 1836), 395. In 1778, Jonathan Carver wrote of Duston's experience, "The woman, whose name, if I mistake not, was Rowe, formed a resolution worthy of the most intrepid hero"; see "Jonathan Carver from *Travels Through America* (1778)," in Wayne Franklin, ed., *American Voices, American Lives: A Documentary Reader* (New York, 1997), 118–119 (quotation on 119).

61. Lydia Maria Child, *Hobomok: A Tale of Early Times* (Boston, 1824), 174 ("far"), 182 ("laws"), 185 ("young").

62. Hall, ed., *Witch-Hunting*, 56 ("boy").

CHAPTER 3

1. The authoritative source here is Robert Woods, *Death before Birth: Fetal Health and Mortality in Historical Perspective* (New York, 2009), 100. Shannon Withycombe traces a history of childbearing disasters (primarily miscarriage, not stillbirth) in America through the nineteenth and early twentieth centuries in *Lost: Miscarriage in Nineteenth-Century America* (New Brunswick, N.J., 2019).

2. *Diary of Samuel Sewall, 1674–1729*, I, 1674–1700, May 18, 1696, in Massachusetts Historical Society, *Collections*, 5th Ser., V (Boston, 1878), 426; C. Alice Baker and Emma L. Coleman, *Epitaphs in the Old Burying-Ground at Deerfield, Massachusetts* (1924; rpt. Westminster, Md., 2007), 23; Robert Baker, *Before Bioethics: A History of American Medical Ethics from the Colonial Period to the Bioethics Revolution* (New York, 2013), 29.

3. "Complaint against John Evans by Sarah Smith," Aug. 4, 1694, [1], in L02.148, Memorial Hall Museum Online Collection, https://memorialhalldeerfield.catalogaccess

.com/library/21764; Cotton Mather, *Pillars of Salt: An History of Some Criminals Executed in This Land for Capital Crimes* . . . (Boston, 1699), 104 ("Dead"). For details of the allegation that Martin Smith committed sexual assault, see Richard I. Melvoin, *New England Outpost: War and Society in Colonial Deerfield* (New York, 1989), 81.

4. "A Faithful Narrative of the Wicked Life and Remarkable Conversion of Patience Boston," in Daniel E. Williams, ed., *Pillars of Salt: An Anthology of Early American Criminal Narratives* (Madison, Wis., 1993), 119–142 (quotations on 121, 122); "The Declaration and Confession of Esther Rodgers," ibid., 95–109; John J. Currier, *History of Newbury, Mass., 1635–1902* (Boston, 1902), 254 ("Barbadoes").

5. Puritans' heightened suspicion of women operating outside patriarchal control or protection is also evident in cases of early American witchcraft, many of which involved the same charges brought against Esther. As Carol F. Karlsen points out, in these witchcraft cases, "most of the accused were women who had no brothers or sons," and "many of these same women had committed or were thought to have committed fornication, infanticide, or other sexual or sexually related offenses." The women tended to be accused by their own neighbors rather than legal or religious authorities, which suggests that as early as the 1640s "signs of female independence had also become objectionable to the larger community" (Karlsen, *The Devil in the Shape of a Woman: Witchcraft in Colonial New England* [New York, 1998], 196, 197).

6. "Declaration and Confession," in Williams, ed., *Pillars of Salt*, 96 ("Mr. Cottons"), 108. More on the Woodbridge family can be found in John Langdon Sibley, *Biographical Sketches of Graduates of Harvard University* . . . , II, 1659–1677 (Cambridge, Mass., 1881), 57. Biblical scholar John Rogers was executed for heresy during the reign of Mary I of England in February 1555, or February 1554 according to the Julian calendar. For a discussion of Rogers's biography, especially his compilation of "Thomas Matthew's Bible," see David Daniell, *The Bible in English: Its History and Influence* (New Haven, Conn., 2003), 190–197. John Cotton's catechism *Spiritual Milk for Boston Babes* . . . (Cambridge, Mass., 1656) was first published as *Milk for Babes* . . . (London, 1646). Cotton's catechism and one of several images of John Rogers were published in *The New-England Primer Improved for the More Easy Attaining the True Reading of English; to Which Is Added the Assembly of Divines, and Mr. Cotton's Catechism* (Boston, 1777). The images of John Rogers and his "Advice to His Children" appear as images 38 and 39 at https://archive .org/details/newenglandprimer00west/page/n37/mode/2up. For a close reading of the primer as it was used in the education of Puritan girls like Esther Rodgers, see Elizabeth Reis, *Damned Women: Sinners and Witches in Puritan New England* (Ithaca, N.Y., 1997).

7. "Declaration and Confession," in Williams, ed., *Pillars of Salt*, 97.

8. I arrived at this statistic by consulting *Vital Records of Newbury Massachusetts to the End of the Year 1849*, I, Births (Salem, Mass., 1911). My point is not to argue for the significance or reliability of this figure but to insist on its inadequacy and the deficits of any statistics regarding early pregnancy loss in early New England, since so many cases of neonatal loss were kept private by mothers or were not recorded by the people (mostly women) privy to labor and childbirth. In *Good Wives*, Laurel Thatcher Ulrich examines a cluster of childbearing cases—mostly recorded in men's diaries and letters but a few in court cases—that attest to the ever-present danger of stillbirth and Puritans' determination to make meaning out of early stage reproductive disasters like Anne Hutchinson's and Mary Dyer's (Ulrich, *Good Wives: Image and Reality in the Lives of Women in Northern New England, 1650–1750* [1982; rpt. New York, 1983], 126–145.)

9. For a discussion of modern pregnancy loss, see Gabriela Weigel, Laurie Sobel, and Alina Salganicoff, "Understanding Pregnancy Loss in the Context of Abortion Restrictions and Fetal Harm Laws," Dec. 4, 2019, https://www.supremecourt.gov/opinions/URLs_Cited /OT2021/19-1392/19-1392-12.pdf. As a midwife in Maine in the late eighteenth century, Martha Ballard recorded instances of stillbirth, providing a valuable and detailed, if necessarily incomplete, record of this possible maternal outcome. See Laurel Thatcher Ulrich, *A Midwife's Tale: The Life of Martha Ballard, Based on Her Diary, 1785–1812* (New York, 1990), 174. For a discussion of the early New England birth rate, see Daniel Scott Smith, "The Demographic History of Colonial New England," *Journal of Economic History*, XXXII (1972), 165–183.

10. John Rogers, *Death the Certain Wages of Sin to the Impenitent: Life the Sure Reward of Grace to the Penitent: Together with the Only Way for Youth to Avoid the Former, and Attain the Latter . . .* (Boston, 1701), 153. For examples of the interest in Christian martyrologies among New England Puritans, see Donald E. Stanford's *A Transcript of Edward Taylor's Metrical History of Christianity* (Ann Arbor, Mich., 1962); and John Cotton's response to colleagues who challenged his interpretation of the covenant of works, among other doctrines ("Mr. Cottons Rejoynder," in David D. Hall, *The Antinomian Controversy, 1636–1638: A Documentary History*, 2d ed. [Durham, N.C., 1990], 78–151). For a discussion of the ways Catholics and Protestants negotiated competing interpretations of Christian doctrines and truth claims, "especially regarding who counted as heretics, martyrs, and saints," see Abram Van Engen, "Claiming the High Ground: Catholics, Protestants, and the City on a Hill," in Bryce Traister, ed., *American Literature and the New Puritan Studies* (Cambridge, 2017), 206–219 (quotation on 212).

11. Rogers, *Death the Certain Wages of Sin*, 122.

12. Mather, *Pillars of Salt*, 104; John Williams, *Warnings to the Unclean: In a Discourse from Rev. XXI. 8. Preacht at Springfield Lecture, August 25th. 1698. at the Execution of Sarah Smith* (Boston, 1699), 63.

13. John Hancock, Sermon Notes, Commonplace Book, 1687, MS Am 121.1, Houghton Library, Harvard University, Cambridge, Mass., cited in Sarah Rivett, *The Science of the Soul in Colonial New England* (Williamsburg, Va., and Chapel Hill, N.C., 2011), 174 ("How good"); Adrian Chastain Weimer, *Martyrs' Mirror: Persecution and Holiness in Early New England* (New York, 2011), 5 ("category"), 7 ("Christian"). Weimer discusses specific examples of Puritan deathbed confessions presenting their subjects as martyrs on 6–7.

14. Rivett, *Science of the Soul*, 176 ("social"), 177 ("exaggerated").

15. Judg. 11:30–40 (Authorized [King James] Version [AV]); Cotton Mather, *Biblia Americana: America's First Bible Commentary; a Synoptic Commentary on the Old and New Testaments*, III, *Joshua–2 Chronicles*, ed. Kenneth P. Minkema (Tübingen, Ger., 2013), 192 ("Real"), 199 ("fearful"); Abram Van Engen, "A Medieval Puritan Welcomes the Early American Enlightenment: What Bible Commentaries Can Offer Postsecular and Literary Studies," *Early American Literature*, LII (2017), 426 ("obscure"). On the phenomenon of real or imagined human sacrifices in Mesoamerica, see, for example, Álvar Núñez Cabeza de Vaca, *The Narrative of Cabeza de Vaca*, ed. and trans. Rolena Adorno and Patrick Charles Pautz (Lincoln, Neb., 1999), 87–88.

16. Anne Bradstreet, "Before the Birth of One of Her Children," in Jeannine Hensley, ed., *The Works of Anne Bradstreet* (Cambridge, Mass., 1967), 224 ("death's"), 239; Bradstreet, "To the Memory of My Dear Daughter-in-Law, Mrs. Mercy Bradstreet . . . ," ibid., 238 ("Him"); Helkiah Crooke, *Mikrokosmographia: A Description of the Body of Man, Together with the Controversies Thereto Belonging . . .* (London, 1615), 252 ("between"), 311; Hall, *Antinomian Controversy*, 214 ("deformed"). Bryce Traister affirms "the centrality of gender issues to this famous

chapter in American colonial history" even as he argues for a wider view of "the gender of antinomianism" that accounts for "the significance of male gender roles and sexuality to the texture of this early colonial struggle." See Traister, "Anne Hutchinson's 'Monstrous Birth' and the Feminization of Antinomianism," *Canadian Review of American Studies/Revue canadienne d'études américaines*, XXVII, no. 2 (1997), 133–158, esp. 136. On Eve's transgression, see Gen. 3:16 (AV).

17. Zach Hutchins, "Deborah's Ghost," *Women's Studies*, XLIII (2014), 332–345 ("free will offering," 341); Jean Marie Lutes, "Negotiating Theology and Gynecology: Anne Brad-street's Representations of the Female Body," *Signs*, XXII (1997), 309–340 ("visitations," 328); "Faithful Narrative," in Williams, ed., *Pillars of Salt*, 140 ("Saint").

18. Mather, *New-England Primer*, n.p. (image 35); "Declaration and Confession," in Wil-liams, ed., *Pillars of Salt*, 95; Rogers, *Death the Certain Wages of Sin*, [A4], 153. See also "A Com-fortable Letter of Pomponius Algerius, an Italian Martyr," in John Foxe, *The Unabridged Acts and Monuments Online* (TAMO) (1576 ed.) (The Digital Humanities Institute, Sheffield, U.K., 2011), bk. 7, 1110 [1110, original pagination], https://www.dhi.ac.uk/foxe/.

19. Mather, *Pillars of Salt*, 31; Daniel E. Williams, "Introduction," in Williams, ed., *Pillars of Salt*, 5. One could trace this discourse beyond the Puritan moment. As reform movements took shape in the late eighteenth century, Louis P. Masur finds, criminals were captive to the initiatives of "a middle-class culture that dreaded vice, craved order, advocated self-control, and valued social privacy," such as solitary confinement, which replaced the injuries of pub-lic punishment with new harms to prisoners (Masur, *Rites of Execution: Capital Punishment and the Transformation of American Culture, 1776–1865* [New York, 1989], 8). For more on these re-form movements, see Scott D. Seay, *Hanging between Heaven and Earth: Capital Crime, Execution Preaching, and Theology in Early New England* (DeKalb, Ill., 2009); Jen Manion, *Liberty's Prisoners: Carceral Culture in Early America* (Philadelphia, 2015); and Jodi Schorb, *Reading Prisoners: Liter-ature, Literacy, and the Transformation of American Punishment, 1700–1845* (New Brunswick, N.J., 2014).

20. Wendy Brown, *States of Injury: Power and Freedom in Late Modernity* (Princeton, N.J., 1995), 157. Elizabeth Maddock Dillon relates this passage to her larger argument about the role of women's presumed encumbrances in the fictions that imagined the American liberal political arena as a single-sex environment even as American liberalism relied for its very construction and conception on feminized identities and private spaces. See Dillon, *The Gender of Freedom: Fictions of Liberalism and the Literary Public Sphere* (Stanford, Calif., 2004), 15.

21. On the insights scholars have offered into the way Esther's criminal status operated in the public sphere generally or print culture specifically, see Daniel A. Cohen, *Pillars of Salt, Monuments of Grace: New England Crime Literature and the Origins of American Popular Culture, 1674–1860* (Amherst, Mass., 1993); Williams, ed., *Pillars of Salt*; Sharon M. Harris, *Executing Race: Early American Women's Narratives of Race, Society, and the Law* (Columbus, Ohio, 2005); Dillon, *Gender of Freedom*; Seay, *Hanging between Heaven and Earth*; and Schorb, *Reading Prisoners*.

22. Elizabeth Maddock Dillon, Laura Henigman, and Sharon M. Harris take Esther's guilt for granted. As Dillon argues, even if she is redeemed as "she confesses fully to her guilt and, more importantly, demonstrates a sense of her own 'conviction' of her sin," a concealed baby's body, itself evidence of extramarital interracial sexual congress, presents overwhelming problems to a case for Esther's legal innocence. See Dillon, *Gender of Freedom*, 212 (quotation); Laura Henigman, *Coming into Communion: Pastoral Dialogues in Colonial New*

England (Albany, N.Y., 1999), 48; Harris, *Executing Race*, 33. See also Schorb, *Reading Prisoners*, 31.

23. Edgar J. McManus, *Law and Liberty in Early New England: Criminal Justice and Due Process, 1620–1692* (Amherst, Mass., 1993), 5 ("resemblance"), 6 ("special"), 54 ("almost"). Two cases that demonstrate the elasticity of the judgments around infanticide and ambiguous childbearing disasters in Puritan New England are examined in M. Michelle Jarrett Morris, *Under Household Government: Sex and Family in Puritan Massachusetts* (Cambridge, Mass., 2013), 178–208. For a discussion of the principle of equity in administering New England's legal codes, see David D. Hall, *A Reforming People: Puritanism and the Transformation of Public Life in New England* (New York, 2011), 145. Justices of the peace (including John Winthrop) were given "much of the burden for bringing order and efficiency to the legal system" through their interpretation of laws in local circumstances, as David Konig discusses at length in *Law and Society in Puritan Massachusetts: Essex County, 1629–1692* (Chapel Hill, N.C., 1979), 16. On eighteenth-century juries' disinclination to convict women of infanticide, see, for example, the case of Patience Boston, who, on or just before 1734, told her husband—with whom she shared a volatile, even violent, relationship—she had murdered their newborn infant. She sought out and confessed to a justice three times before he agreed to send her to prison, but at trial she pleaded not guilty; she was acquitted and released from prison shortly after ("Faithful Narrative," in Williams, ed., *Pillars of Salt*, 119–141). See also Dillon, *Gender of Freedom*, 201.

24. Steven Wilf, *Law's Imagined Republic: Popular Politics and Criminal Justice in Revolutionary America* (Cambridge, 2010), 81 ("burden"); McManus, *Law and Liberty*, 54. See also Schorb, *Reading Prisoners*, 295. Infanticide was a "peculiar" crime in early America in this sense, as Steven Wilf notes. According to the Stuart Bastard Neonaticide Act of 1624, adopted in New England in the 1690s, "any woman concealing the death of an illegitimate child shall suffer death as in the case of murder" (Wilf, *Law's Imagined Republic*, 81).

25. Rogers, *Death the Certain Wages of Sin*, 122; *Vital Records of Newbury Massachusetts*, I; Currier, *History of Newbury*, 254 ("negro servants"). Wendy Warren details this network of relationships in *New England Bound: Slavery and Colonization in Early America* (New York, 2016), giving special attention to the circumstances of enslaved laborers in Puritan towns and villages "where laborers were differentiated by race, even while their labor was not" (118). Race becomes visible in the historical record of early New England only in particular contexts, such as, notably, when domestic servants and enslaved laborers had children (sometimes with each other, sometimes with their white employers and owners), as Warren discusses on 153–186.

26. Samuel Sewall, *The Selling of Joseph: A Memorial* (Boston, 1700), 2; "Declaration and Confession," in Williams, ed., *Pillars of Salt*, 97.

27. "Declaration and Confession," in Williams, ed., *Pillars of Salt*, 97.

28. Mather, *Pillars of Salt*, 72, 87; Rogers, *Death the Certain Wages of Sin*, 122. See also "Life, Last Words, and Dying Confession of Rachel Wall," in Williams, ed., *Pillars of Salt*, 283–287.

29. Rogers, *Death the Certain Wages of Sin*, 153. For a discussion of affective responses to martyrdom, see Caleb Smith, *The Oracle and the Curse: A Poetics of Justice from the Revolution to the Civil War* (Cambridge, Mass., 2013), 33.

30. Stephen Reed Cattley, ed., *The Actes and Monuments of John Foxe*, III (London, 1837), 720; *The Passion of Saints Perpetua and Felicity*, trans. W. H. Shewring (London, 1931), Internet

Medieval Sourcebook, Fordham University, n.p., sec. 18, http://sourcebooks.fordham.edu /Halsall/source/perpetua.asp; Charles A. Goodrich, Book of Martyrs; or, A History of the Lives, Sufferings, and Triumphant Deaths, of the Primitive as Well as Protestant Martyrs . . . (Hartford, Conn., 1830). For full, searchable texts of the 1563, 1570, 1576, and 1583 editions of Foxe's Actes and Monuments, see TAMO, http//www.dhi.ac.uk/foxe.

31. Rogers, Death the Certain Wages of Sin, 152 ("irresistible"); The Passion of Saints Perpetua and Felicity, trans. Shewring, prologue, n.p., sec. 21 ("God"), http://sourcebooks.fordham .edu/Halsall/source/perpetua.asp. See also Tamara Harvey, "'Taken from Her Mouth': Narrative Authority and the Conversion of Patience Boston," Narrative, VI (1998), 256–270.

32. For a discussion of the discrepancies in published versions of this incident, see Wayne Franklin, ed., American Voices, American Lives: A Documentary Reader (New York, 1997).

33. Cotton Mather, "Decennium Luctuosum; or, The Remarkables of a Long War with Indian-Salvages," article XXV, "A Notable Exploit, wherein, Dux Faemina Facti," in Mather, Magnalia Christi Americana; or, the Ecclesiastical History of New-England, from Its First Planting in the Year 1620 unto the Year of Our Lord, 1698 (London, 1702), bk. 7, 91.

34. "Declaration and Confession," in Williams, ed., Pillars of Salt, 108; "Quene Mary. M. Rogers. The History of Laurence Saunders, Martyr," in Foxe, TAMO (1570 ed.), bk. 11, 1703 [1664], http//www.dhi.ac.uk/foxe; "The Martyrdom of Polycarp," in The Apostolic Fathers; with an English Translation by Kirsopp Lake, 2 vols. (London, 1912–1913), II, 317; Mark 15:37 (AV); Luke 23:46 (AV); John 19:30 (AV). Daniel Boyarin discusses the "ritualized and performative speech act associated with a statement of pure essence" as "the central action of the martyrology" in Boyarin, Dying for God: Martyrdom and the Making of Christianity and Judaism (Stanford, Calif., 1999), 95.

35. Acts 7:59–60 (AV); "The Martyrdom of Polycarp," in Apostolic Fathers, II, 331, 335.

36. Nancy Ruttenburg theorizes the legal and literary significance of these speech acts and their relationship to early American political developments in Ruttenburg, Democratic Personality: Popular Voice and the Trial of American Authorship (Stanford, Calif., 1998). She proposes "that democracy be reconceived as a dynamic symbolic system or theater, historically realized in an untheorized and irrational practice of compulsive public utterance which gave rise, as popular voice, to a distinctive mode of political (and later, literary) subjectivity" (3).

37. "Faithful Narrative," in Williams, ed., Pillars of Salt, 119, 131, 139. Joseph Moody began wearing a white handkerchief over his face in 1738. Daniel E. Williams makes a suggestive connection between this action and the content of Boston's narrative. "It is interesting to note," he writes, "that 'Moody's mind cracked' at about the same time he and his father were ministering to Boston, as the preface they wrote for the narrative was dated 'April 24th. 1738'" (141).

38. Ibid., 124.

39. "Declaration and Confession," ibid., 98–99; Diary of Samuel Sewall, 1674–1729, II, 1699– 1700–1714, in MHS, Colls., 5th Ser., VI (Boston, 1879), 39.

40. "Faithful Narrative," in Williams, ed., Pillars of Salt, 130–131.

41. "Declaration and Confession," ibid., 107; "Faithful Narrative," ibid., 140.

42. Judg. 11:30–31, 35, 36–37.

43. Judg. 11:35.

44. The story is so problematic many early commentators favored a reading in which Jephthah's daughter was condemned to a life of virginity, rather than death. Cotton Mather

rejects this interpretation for a variety of reasons, including a lack of biblical precedent for this kind of punishment and, more critically, the impossibility of a man of God refusing (perhaps even being *able* to refuse) to fulfill his vow—which specifically promised death. See Mather's commentary in *Biblia Americana*, III, 188–201.

45. Mather, *Biblia Americana*, III, 200 ("Power"), 201. For more on John Winthrop's objections to the Bay Colony's first written body of laws, see McManus, *Law and Liberty*, 4–5.

46. "Declaration and Confession," in Williams, ed., *Pillars of Salt*, 105; Rogers, *Death the Certain Wages of Sin*, [A4].

47. This objection is surmountable; after all, Puritans' moral abhorrence of human sacrifice did not always prevent them from killing morally (if not legally) innocent people for symbolic reasons. For example, see John Putnam Demos's treatment of the functions of witch-hunting in *Entertaining Satan: Witchcraft and the Culture of Early New England* (1982; rpt. New York, 2004), 277–278, 299–300.

48. For commentary on the agency of Jephthah's daughter, see Cotton Mather's interpretations of the writings of Ludovicus de Dieu (192), John Owen (193), Clemens Alexandrinus (195), Albertus Crantzius (199), and Ludovicus Capellus (Louis Cappel) (199) in *Biblia Americana*, III.

CHAPTER 4

1. See George M. Bodge, *Soldiers in King Philip's War: Containing Lists of the Soldiers of Massachusetts Colony, Who Served in the Indian War of 1675–1677* (Boston, 1891), 116–117; Anne Bradstreet, "Before the Birth of One of Her Children," in Jeannine Hensley, ed., *The Works of Anne Bradstreet* (Cambridge, Mass., 1967), 224; John Wingate Thornton, *The Landing at Cape Ann* (Boston, 1854), 50 ("trials"); Clifford K. Shipton, *Roger Conant, a Founder of Massachusetts* (Cambridge, Mass., 1944), 55 ("good ground"); Frank A. Gardner, *Thomas Gardner Planter and Some of His Descendants* (Salem, Mass., 1907), 15 ("'present'"); Will Gardner, *The Triumphant Captain John and Gardners and Gardiners: Twelve Founders of Families* (Cambridge, Mass., 1958), 20, 48. For an elaborated discussion of the influence of this kind of pain in America through the long eighteenth century, see Elaine Forman Crane, "'I Have Suffer'd Much Today': The Defining Force of Pain in Early America," in Ronald Hoffman, Mechal Sobel, and Fredrika J. Teute, eds., *Through a Glass Darkly: Reflections on Personal Identity in Early America* (Williamsburg, Va., and Chapel Hill, N.C., 1997), 370–403.

2. Gardner, *Thomas Gardner Planter*, 6; Gardner, *Triumphant Captain John*, 36 ("father"); Anne Bradstreet, "To My Dear Children," in John Harvard Ellis, ed., *The Works of Anne Bradstreet in Prose and Verse* (Charlestown, Mass., 1867), 5 ("lingering"). I quote from Frank A. Gardner's collection of the Gardner family's documents in *Thomas Gardner Planter*.

3. Christian Wiman, "Mortify Our Wolves: The Struggle Back to Life and Faith in the Face of Pain and the Certainty of Death," *American Scholar*, LXXXI, no. 4 (Autumn 2012), 59–71 (quotations on 62); Bradstreet, "For Deliverance from a Feaver," in Ellis, ed., *Works of Anne Bradstreet*, 12.

4. John M. Bullard, ed., *Captain Edmund Gardner of Nantucket and New Bedford: His Journal and Family* (New Bedford, Mass., 1958), 5.

5. According to John M. Bullard: "Another item of interest in [Gardner's] adventurous, though comparatively short, career on the sea was his being one of the first two whaling

captains to bring his ship into what he called the Sandwich, and we now call the Hawaiian, Islands. The other captain, Folger, and he were keeping their ships the 'Balaena' and the 'Equator' hunting together when this event occurred." See ibid., 2.

6. Ibid., 35. At least one foreign visitor to Hawai'i wanted to imagine Ke'eaumoku as part of this 1779 event, although he was not born when Cook died. Gilbert Farquhar Mathison claimed Ke'eaumoku was "a mere boy" when the disaster occurred, "but the event . . . was too important not to be deeply impressed on his memory." See Mathison, *Narrative of a Visit to Brazil, Chile, Peru, and the Sandwich Islands, during the Years 1821 and 1822* . . . (London, 1825), 408.

7. Bullard, ed., *Captain Edmund Gardner*, 35 ("you lie," "often"); Samuel M[ānaiakalani] Kamakau, *Ruling Chiefs of Hawaii*, [ed. and trans. Mary Kawena Pukui et al.], rev. ed. (Honolulu, 1992), 389; Mathison, *Narrative of a Visit*, 393; William Ellis, quoted in C. S. Stewart, *A Residence in the Sandwich Islands*, including an introduction and notes by William Ellis, 5th ed., enl. (Boston, 1839), 210n. On Ellis's language abilities in Tahitian and Hawaiian, see Seth Archer, *Sharks upon the Land: Colonialism, Indigenous Health, and Culture in Hawai'i* (Cambridge, 2018), 154 n. 127; William Ellis to George Burden, July 9, 1922, Council for World Mission / London Missionary Society, box 3B, folder 10, University of London School of Oriental and Asian Studies Archives and Special Collections, cited ibid. ("'plain'"). On Ke'eaumoku's proficiency in English, see Kamakau, *Ruling Chiefs of Hawaii*, 389. Another missionary, Hiram Bingham, said Ke'eaumoku spoke "barbarous English, which [he] had acquired by intercourse with sea-faring men." See Bingham, *A Residence of Twenty-One Years in the Sandwich Islands* . . . , 2d ed. (Hartford, Conn., 1848), 103.

8. James Kenneth Munford, ed., *John Ledyard's Journal of Captain Cook's Last Voyage*, with an introduction by Sinclair H. Hitchings (Corvallis, Ore., 1963), 135–139. This quotation from one of Cook's men appears in a number of sources, including Anne Salmond, *The Trial of the Cannibal Dog: The Remarkable Story of Captain Cook's Encounters in the South Seas* (New Haven, Conn., 2003), 409; and Marshall Sahlins, *How "Natives" Think: About Captain Cook, for Example* (Chicago, 1995), 80–81.

9. J. Susan Corley and M. Puakea Nogelmeier, "Notes and Queries: Kalanimoku's Lost Letter," *Hawaiian Journal of History*, XLIV (2010), 91, 99 (quotations). For a history of Hawaiian exploration before and after Cook's voyages (in which Ke'eaumoku, as admiral of the king's fleet, played an important role), see David A. Chang, *The World and All Things upon It: Native Hawaiian Geographies of Exploration* (Minneapolis, Minn., 2016); and David Igler, *The Great Ocean: Pacific Worlds from Captain Cook to the Gold Rush* (Oxford, 2013), 20. On the commerce initiated by Cook's voyages, see Archer, *Sharks upon the Land*. For more commentary on Kalanimoku's letter, see ibid., 2.

10. Although neither Cook nor Ke'eaumoku were early Americans, and I do not read Hawaiian history teleologically as if the encounters I study prefigure the American occupation of Hawai'i, the spaces, interests, and concerns they shared with Gardner are evidence of the Pacific's global significance from the late 1700s onward and the elemental ways early American experience involved people and environments beyond the American continent. On the commonness of disability, the disability theorist Rosemarie Garland-Thomson writes, "Every life devolves into disability [as it also begins], making it perhaps the essential characteristic of being human" (Garland-Thomson, "Disability and Representation," *PMLA*, CXX [2005], 524). Some activists call those who consider themselves outside the

world of disability TABs, or the "temporarily able-bodied." See David T. Mitchell and Sharon L. Snyder, *Narrative Prosthesis: Disability and the Dependencies of Discourse* (Ann Arbor, Mich., 2000), 18; and Rachel Adams, Benjamin Reiss, and David Serlin, "Disability," in Adams, Reiss, and Serlin, eds., *Keywords for Disability Studies* (New York, 2015), 5–11 (quotation on 5). See also Lennard Davis's explanation of his use of the term "temporarily abled" in the introduction to *Enforcing Normalcy: Disability, Deafness, and the Body* (London, 1995), 172 n. 8. For an overview of the current state of the field of disability studies, which has evolved from an understanding of disability as a social construct to a fuller view of disability as a constitutive feature of complex embodiment, see Michael Davidson, review of *Disability Theory*, by Tobin Siebers, *Disability Studies Quarterly*, XXVIII, no. 4 (Fall 2008), https://dsq-sds .org/article/view/160/160. See also David T. Mitchell, Susan Antebi, and Sharon L. Snyder, "Introduction," 1–38, and Tobin Siebers, "Returning the Social to the Social Model," 39–47, both in Mitchell, Antebi, and Snyder, eds., *The Matter of Disability: Materiality, Biopolitics, Crip Affect* (Ann Arbor, Mich., 2019).

11. Although it is a late entry to the genre of medical guidebooks for mariners, the illustrations on pages 166–167 of Fred A. Barker's *The Mariner's Medical Guide* (Gloucester, Mass., 1921) give a vivid sense of what an operation at sea entailed. See also Joan Druett, *Rough Medicine: Surgeons at Sea in the Age of Sail* (New York, 2000), 10–25. A history of injury related to oceanic labor and warfare is chronicled throughout Kamakau's book *Ruling Chiefs of Hawaii*. Fairly detailed descriptions of illnesses and disabilities on the Hawaiian Islands can be found in Marion Kelly, ed., *Hawai'i in 1819: A Narrative Account by Louis Claude de Saulses de Freycinet*, trans. Ella L. Wiswell, Pacific Anthropological Records 26 (Honolulu, 1978) (hereafter cited as Freycinet, *Narrative Account*).

12. By "oceanic framework," I mean I let what Paul Lyons and Ty P. Kāwika Tengan call "Oceanic Reason," or "a different kind of 'common sense' that circulates among Islanders, one based in a fluidity of being in the world," guide my understanding of the disabilities of Native Hawaiians and of mariners, many of whom were Indigenous people and many of them islanders by birth (Lyons and Tengan, "Introduction: Pacific Currents," *American Quarterly*, LXVII [2015], 545–574). I realize I risk flattening material and cultural distinctions among ships, islands, and archipelagoes and am conscious that my focus on Hawai'i vastly underrepresents Oceania's diversity. Three works that discuss the significant participation of Indigenous mariners in the oceanic workforce are Matthew R. Bahar, *Storm of the Sea: Indians and Empires in the Atlantic's Age of Sail* (New York, 2019); John A. Strong, *America's Early Whalemen: Indian Shore Whalers on Long Island, 1650–1750* (Tucson, Ariz., 2018); and Jace Weaver, *The Red Atlantic: American Indigenes and the Making of the Modern World, 1000–1927* (Chapel Hill, N.C., 2014). Although the books would appear to focus on the Atlantic, they together make a compelling case for the essential interconnectedness of the globe's oceans, islands, archipelagoes, and continents.

13. For the "Cook books" and the writings of Protestant missionaries, see Daniel W. Clayton, *Islands of Truth: The Imperial Fashioning of Vancouver Island* (Vancouver, 2000), 50–62. For "passing" and "masquerade," see Tobin Siebers, *Disability Theory* (Ann Arbor, Mich., 2008), 96–119. For more on protheses, representation, and disability, see Mitchell and Snyder, *Narrative Prosthesis*.

14. Tobin Siebers, "In the Name of Pain," in Jonathan M. Metzl and Anna Kirkland, eds., *Against Health: How Health Became the New Morality* (New York, 2010), 183, 184. For a discussion

of the state of early American disability studies, see Sari Altschuler and Cristobal Silva, "Early American Disability Studies," *Early American Literature*, LII (2017), 1–27. On Indigenous disability, in particular, see Sarah Jaquette Ray and Jay Sibara, eds., *Disability Studies and the Environmental Humanities: Toward an Eco-Crip Theory* (Lincoln, Neb., 2017); Laurence J. Kirmayer et al., "Rethinking Resilience from Indigenous Perspectives," *Canadian Journal of Psychiatry*, LVI (2011), 84–91; Minerva Rivas Velarde, "Indigenous Perspectives of Disability," *Disability Studies Quarterly*, XXVIII, no. 4 (2018), https://dsq-sds.org/article/view/6114/5134.

15. Siebers, "In the Name of Pain," in Metzl and Kirkland, eds., *Against Health*, 187. For a collection of essays on the ways disability experience relates to the outcomes of geopolitical conflicts, health, humanitarian crises, and natural disasters, see David Mitchell and Valerie Karr, eds., *Crises, Conflict, and Disability: Ensuring Equality* (New York, 2014). The phrase "many people sick" appears throughout the journal of Don Francisco de Paula Marín, a Spaniard who treated Hawaiians, especially chiefs in and around Honolulu, in the nineteenth century. See *Don Francisco de Paula Marin: A Biography*, by Ross H. Gast; *The Letters and Journal of Francisco de Paula Marin*, ed. Agnes C. Conrad (Honolulu, 1973) (hereafter cited as Gast and Conrad, *Francisco de Paula Marin*).

16. Garland-Thomson, "Disability and Representation," *PMLA*, CXX (2005), 523.

17. J. C. Beaglehole, *The Life of Captain James Cook* (Stanford, Calif., 1974), 3, 80; Log of the *Grenville*, Aug. 19–20, 1764, Records of the Admiralty, Naval Forces, Royal Marines, Coastguard, and Related Bodies, Admiralty: Master's Logs, ADM 52/1263, The National Archives, Kew; Frank McLynn, *Captain Cook: Master of the Seas* (New Haven, Conn., 2011), 282, 283, 365; Christopher Lloyd and R. C. Anderson, eds., *A Memoir of James Trevenen* ([London], 1959), 20 ("relax"), 21 ("paroxysms").

18. Although Spanish helmets had been discovered on the Hawaiian archipelago, they were probably brought by Polynesian explorers. See McLynn, *Captain Cook*, 339.

19. Ibid., 369 ("cracked"), 383, 390 ("polar"); Christine Holmes, ed., *Captain Cook's Final Voyage: The Journal of Midshipman George Gilbert* (Honolulu, 1982), 104, quoted in Sahlins, *How "Natives" Think*, 81 ("Friendship"). For a discussion of the god Lono, see David Malo, *Hawaiian Antiquities (Moolelo Hawaii)*, trans. Nathaniel B. Emerson, 2d ed. (Honolulu, 1951), 141–159. Much controversy surrounds Cook's reception by the Hawaiians. For a treatment of two perspectives, see Gananath Obeyesekere's response to Marshall Sahlins in the 1997 edition of Obeyesekere, *The Apotheosis of Captain Cook: European Mythmaking in the Pacific*, with a new afterword by the author (Princeton, N.J., and Honolulu, 1997), 193–250.

20. James King, *A Voyage to the Pacific Ocean; Undertaken, by the Command of His Majesty, for Making Discoveries in the Northern Hemisphere . . .* , 2d ed., III (London, 1785), 80.

21. Bullard, ed., *Captain Edmund Gardner*, esp. 5 (quotations).

22. Ibid., 20, 21, 25, 27.

23. Ibid., 31, 32.

24. McLynn, *Captain Cook*, 284 ("hard"); Bullard, ed., *Captain Edmund Gardner*, esp. 46 (quotations).

25. Ellis, quoted in Stewart, *Residence in the Sandwich Islands*, 210n; Bingham, *Residence of Twenty-One Years*, 37, 80. For 1804 as the date of Keʻeaumoku Pāpaiaʻhiahi's death, see also Ralph Thomas Kam, *Death Rites and Hawaiian Royalty: Funerary Practices in the Kamehameha and Kalākaua Dynasties, 1819–1953* (Jefferson, N.C., 2017), 5.

26. Kamakau, *Ruling Chiefs of Hawaii*, 389; Frank J. A. Broeze, ed. and trans., *A Merchant's Perspective: Captain Jacobus Boelen's Narrative of His Visit to Hawai'i in 1828* (Honolulu, 1988), 17–18; Freycinet, *Narrative Account*, 8; Patrick Vinton Kirch and Marhsall Sahlins, *Anahulu: The Anthropology of History in the Kingdom of Hawaii*, vol. I, Sahlins, *Historical Ethnography* (Chicago, 1994), 84; [Sammy Amalu] Kapiikauinamoku, "Peleuli II Brought Up in Kamehameha's Court," in *The Story of Maui Royalty* (Honolulu, 1956?), [100], https://puke.ulukau.org /ulukau-books/?a=d&d=EBOOK-SOMR.2.1.1&e=-------en-20--1--txt-txPT.

27. Kirch and Sahlins, *Anahulu*, I, 84; Mathison, *Narrative of a Visit*, 393, 408–409 ("adduced").

28. Mathison, *Narrative of a Visit*, 393, 434; Ellis, quoted in Stewart, *Residence in the Sandwich Islands*, 211n; Freycinet, *Narrative Account*, 14; Bingham, *Residence of Twenty-One Years*, 156; Kamakau, *Ruling Chiefs of Hawaii*, 246–258.

29. Kamakau, *Ruling Chiefs of Hawaii*, 254; "Sandwich Island Mission Journal to ABCFM, Boston—1824," Mar. 24, 1824, no. 6, 10 (MS page 482), Sandwich Island Mission Journal, 1819–1825, typescript, 6 vols., *Hawaiian Mission Houses Digital Archive*, https://hmha .missionhouses.org/items/show/86. Kamakau's history reports that Ka'ahumanu was called home in February 1823, but other accounts of Ke'eaumoku's death suggest he did not become seriously ill until 1824 (see, for example, Gast and Conrad, *Francisco de Paula Marin*, 286). Ellis, though, refers to "frequent attacks of disease that he experienced during the last years of his life" (Ellis, quoted in Stewart, *Residence in the Sandwich Islands*, 210n).

30. I recognize that the field of disability studies has moved beyond a model of disability as wholly or even primarily shaped by social forces. In the next section of this chapter, I follow the field in considering these historical figures in terms of more complex conceptions of embodiment, but it is worth pausing on the undeniable fact that the social and spatial environments in which people with disabilities exist influence the ways they are perceived and represented. Field founders advanced this argument in sources such as Michael Davidson and Tobin Siebers, "Conference on Disability Studies and the University: Introduction," *PMLA*, CXX (2005), 498–501; and Davis, *Enforcing Normalcy*, 23–49.

31. Davis, *Enforcing Normalcy*, 2, and, for a discussion of the "norm" as it relates to bodies, 23–49; Siebers, *Disability Theory*, 8.

32. Stewart, *Residence in the Sandwich Islands*, 43–44. For more detailed descriptions of these injuries, see Druett, *Rough Medicine*.

33. Bullard, ed., *Captain Edmund Gardner*, 29 ("early"), 30 ("born"), 31 ("fighting"); Salmond, *Trial of the Cannibal Dog*, 434–437; McLynn, *Captain Cook*, 305; Peter Linebaugh and Marcus Rediker, *The Many-Headed Hydra: Sailors, Slaves, Commoners, and the Hidden History of the Revolutionary Atlantic* (Boston, 2000); Druett, *Rough Medicine*, 127.

34. Bullard, ed., *Captain Edmund Gardner*, 6 ("signs"), 26 ("Capitan"), 34 ("shut"), 35; Boelen, *A Merchant's Perspective*, 74–75 (quotation on 74); Herman Melville, *Billy Budd, Sailor* (1924), in *Billy Budd, Sailor and Other Stories*, with an introduction by Frederick Busch (New York, 1986), 287–385; Beaglehole, *Life of Captain James Cook*, 523–526; McLynn, *Captain Cook*, 293.

35. Melville, *Billy Budd, Sailor*, in *Billy Budd, Sailor and Other Stories*, 293 ("plump"), 299–300 ("showed"), 327 ("view").

36. Melville, 293, 319; Druett, *Rough Medicine*, 129 ("herringbone"). Lisa Herschbach points out that Confederate soldiers after the Civil War rejected Northern industrialists'

attempts to re-member disabled veterans with mass-produced prosthetics. They sought instead to remember the war. They held that "showing, not hiding, their disfigurement was part of a broadly perceived social imperative against historical amnesia." See Herschbach, "Prosthetic Reconstructions: Making the Industry, Re-Making the Body, Modeling the Nation," *History Workshop Journal*, XLIV, no. 1 (Autumn 1997), 22–57 (quotation on 50).

37. David Samwell, *A Narrative of the Death of Captain James Cook* . . . (London, 1786), 8.

38. Kamakau, *Ruling Chiefs of Hawaii*, 103–104. See John McAleer and Nigel Rigby, *Captain Cook and the Pacific: Art, Exploration, and Empire* (New Haven, Conn., 2017), esp. chap. 4.

39. Bullard, ed., *Captain Edmund Gardner*, 77; *Morning Mercury* (New Bedford, Mass.), Nov. 7, 1919, quoted ibid., 85.

40. Bullard, ed., *Captain Edmund Gardner*, 24, 26.

41. A[lexandre] O[livier] Exquemelin, *Bucaniers of America; or, A True Account of the Most Remarkable Assaults Committed of Late Years upon the Coasts of the West-Indies* . . . (London, 1684), Part III, 9, https://quod.lib.umich.edu/cgi/t/text/text-idx?c=eebo;idno=A39081.0001.001.

42. Patrick Vinton Kirch, *A Shark Going Inland Is My Chief: The Island Civilization of Ancient Hawai'i* (Los Angeles, 2012), 8. As Seth Archer writes, "Roving from district to district accompanied by their train of subchiefs, the ali'i 'ate' the land; hence the common title, ali'i 'ai moku (chief who eats the island/district)." See Archer, *Sharks upon the Land*, 26.

43. Kamakau, *Ruling Chiefs of Hawaii*, 198–199. According to Patrick Kirch and Marshall Sahlins, "Often it seems that the workers were not fed by the landholding ali'i, or only badly fed, and only exceptionally did any of the proceeds come into the people's possession" (Kirch and Sahlins, *Anahulu*, I, 83).

44. Freycinet, *Narrative Account*, 59; Noenoe K. Silva, *Aloha Betrayed: Native Hawaiian Resistance to American Colonialism* (Durham, N.C., 2004), 41; Kamakau, *Ruling Chiefs of Hawaii*, 91, 169–170. On the structure of Hawaiian chiefly authority, see Patrick Vinton Kirch, *Feathered Gods and Fishhooks: An Introduction to Hawaiian Archaeology and Prehistory* (Honolulu, 1985), 235–236.

45. Bullard, ed., *Captain Edmund Gardner*, 21 ("pronounced"), 52 ("mechanical genius," "one of the men"); Louis Coffin, ed., *The Coffin Family*, with an introduction by Will Gardner (Nantucket, Mass., [1962]), 77 ("my leg") (for a slightly different version of this legend, see Druett, *Rough Medicine*, 130); Robert Dampier, *To the Sandwich Islands on H.M.S. Blonde*, ed. Pauline King Joerger (Honolulu, 1971), 125 ("thereafter"); Kamakau, *Ruling Chiefs of Hawaii*, 390 ("patron"). On Hawaiian gender roles, see Archer, *Sharks upon the Land*, 31–33. Patrick Vinton Kirch makes the argument that "Hawaiian civilization at the time of Cook's arrival was based on principles of divine kingship"; see Kirch, *Shark Going Inland*, 4. Herman Melville's novel was first published in America as *Moby-Dick; or, The Whale* (New York, 1851).

46. Siebers, *Disability Theory*, 62–63.

47. Judith Butler, *Bodies That Matter: On the Discursive Limits of "Sex"* (New York, 1993), 3; McLynn, *Captain Cook*, 283 ("mania").

48. Elaine Scarry, *The Body in Pain: The Making and Unmaking of the World* (New York, 1985); Bullard, ed., *Captain Edmund Gardner*, 20 ("clothes"), 21 ("first"), 22 ("hand"), 60 ("extinct"), 64 ("cripple"). The history of whaling is summarized in an engaging way in "Whales and Hunting," New Bedford Whaling Museum, accessed Apr. 29, 2024, https://www.whalingmuseum.org/learn/research-topics/whaling-history/whales-and-hunting/.

49. For a discussion of "realism" as it relates to identities and bodies, see Siebers, *Disability Theory*, chaps. 3, 4, 6. Siebers clarifies: "By 'realism' I understand neither a positivistic claim about reality unmediated by social representations, nor a linguistic claim about reality unmediated by objects of representation, but a theory that describes reality as a mediation, no less real for being such, between representation and its social objects" (30).

50. Archer, *Sharks upon the Land*, 2, 3 ("disease"), 15 ("depopulation"), 59, 134; David Malo, "On the Decrease of Population on the Hawaiian Islands," trans. Lorrin Andrews, *Hawaiian Spectator*, II (1839), 121–131; Kirch and Sahlins, *Anahulu*, I, 57; David Stannard, *Before the Horror: The Population of Hawai'i on the Eve of Western Contact* (Honolulu, 1989), 57. For a discussion of the disastrous impacts—personal and cultural—of the international sandalwood trade from 1804 to 1843, see 'Iwalani R. N. Else, "The Breakdown of the *Kapu* System and Its Effect on Native Hawaiian Health and Diet," *Hūlili: Multidisciplinary Research on Hawaiian Well-Being*, I, no. 1 (2004), 249. On leprosy's impact on Hawai'i, see RDK Herman, "Out of Sight, Out of Mind, Out of Power: Leprosy, Race, and Colonization in Hawai'i," *Journal of Historical Geography*, XXVII, no. 3 (July 2001), 319–347; and Michelle T. Moran, *Colonizing Leprosy: Imperialism and the Politics of Public Health in the United States* (Chapel Hill, N.C., 2007).

51. Gast and Conrad, *Francisco de Paula Marin*, 286 ("much sickness"); Adam Smith, *The Theory of Moral Sentiments*, 2d ed. (London, 1761), 2 ("immediate"); Freycinet, *Narrative Account*, 58 ("personally"); Siebers, *Disability Theory*, 48. For an extended discussion of Indigenous disability, see Susan Antebi, *Carnal Inscriptions: Spanish / American Narratives of Corporeal Difference and Disability* (New York, 2009).

52. Freycinet, *Narrative Account*, 53 ("monstrous"), 57–58 ("eight-year-old").

53. Gast and Conrad, *Francisco de Paula Marin*, 286 ("many people sick"); Freycinet, *Narrative Account*, 58 ("mad dogs"); Siebers, *Disability Theory*, 62 ("enemy").

54. Gast and Conrad, *Francisco de Paula Marin*, 286–287; Else, "The Breakdown of the *Kapu* System," *Hūlili*, I, no. 1 (2004), 244. This history is evocatively documented and described in Lilikalā Kame'eleihiwa, *Native Land and Foreign Desires: Pehea lā e Pono ai?* (Honolulu, 1992).

55. Freycinet, *Narrative Account*, 19 ("complaining"); Bingham, *Residence of Twenty-One Years*, 79 ("defect"), 149 ("restored"); Peter Corney, *Voyages in the Northern Pacific: Narrative of Several Trading Voyages from 1813 to 1818, between the Northwest Coast of America, the Hawaiian Islands, and China, with a Description of the Russian Establishments on the Northwest Coast . . .*, ed. W. D. Alexander (Honolulu, 1896), 102; Ellis, quoted in Kirch and Sahlins, *Anahulu*, I, 85. The original quotation appears in "Sandwich Islands: Extracts of a Letter from Mr. William Ellis, Missionary, to Messrs. Tyerman and Bennet, (then at Sydney,) Dated 26th October, 1824 . . . ," *Missionary Chronicle for August 1825*, in *Evangelical Magazine and Missionary Chronicle*, III, new ser. (London, 1825), 349.

56. Ellis, quoted in Stewart, *Residence in the Sandwich Islands*, 210n.

57. Siebers, *Disability Theory*, 10 ("narcissists"); Bullard, ed., *Captain Edmund Gardner*, 73 ("few"); Else, "The Breakdown of the *Kapu* System," *Hūlili*, I, no. 1 (2004), 242.

58. Davis, *Enforcing Normalcy*, xix; Davidson and Siebers, "Conference on Disability Studies and the University: Introduction," *PMLA*, CXX (2005), 499 ("ability"); Altschuler and Silva, "Early American Disability Studies," *Early American Literature*, LII (2017), 1–27.

59. Else, "The Breakdown of the *Kapu* System," *Hūlili*, I, no. 1 (2004), 243. Although they inherit suffering from the past, Native Hawaiians inherit wisdom to cope, as well. Pomai

Weigert writes of "Sustainable Aloha," or "the spiritual aspect to our survival," which is the ability to face "death, natural disaster, terminal illness, depression, [or] failure" with "the ancient and unbreakable understanding that there is light at the end of every tunnel and gratitude in every struggle." See Weigert, "Sustainable Aloha," in Brother Noland, ed., *The Hawaiian Survival Handbook* (Honolulu, 2014), 153.

60. Corley and Nogelmeier, "Notes and Queries," *Hawaiian Journal of History*, XLIV (2010), 99. For important discussions of the study of Indigenous disability, see Antebi, *Carnal Inscriptions*; and Velarde, "Indigenous Perspectives of Disability," *Disability Studies Quarterly*, XXVIII, no. 4 (2018), https://dsq-sds.org/article/view/6114/5134.

61. I am indebted to Seth Archer for this translation (Archer, *Sharks upon the Land*, 1 n. 1).

62. Bullard, ed., *Captain Edmund Gardner*, 36 ("pumped"), 37 ("increase"), 38 ("dropsical"); Barbara Del Piano, "Kalanimoku: Iron Cable of the Hawaiian Kingdom, 1769–1827," *Hawaiian Journal of History*, XLIII (2009), 27, https://core.ac.uk/download/pdf/5026231.pdf; Gast and Conrad, *Francisco de Paula Marin*, 295. See Margrit Shildrick, *Leaky Bodies and Boundaries: Feminism, Postmodernism, and (Bio) Ethics* (New York, 1997).

63. On fraternity among whalemen, see for example, Edmund Gardner, who arrived in Hawai'i for the first time in company with Captain Elisha Folger of the ship *Equator*; the two captains joined Hawaiian hunters to chase a large sperm whale and "agreed" they "would divide what [they] obtained" (Bullard, ed., *Captain Edmund Gardner*, 34).

64. The classic study treating the way critical reception influenced both the status and the publication histories of sentimental American texts is Jane Tompkins, *Sensational Designs: The Cultural Work of American Fiction, 1790–1860* (New York, 1985). The circumstances of the recovery of Kalanimoku's letter are described in Corley and Nogelmeier, "Notes and Queries," *Hawaiian Journal of History*, XLIV (2010), 91–100.

65. Bullard, ed., *Captain Edmund Gardner*, 80, 82; Siebers, "In the Name of Pain," in Metzl and Kirkland, eds., *Against Health*, 190. For more on this view of God and disability, see Nancy L. Eiesland, *The Disabled God: Toward a Liberatory Theology of Disability* (Nashville, Tenn., 1994).

66. Bullard, ed., *Captain Edmund Gardner*, 5; "The Will of Anne Bradstreet, the Second Wife of Gov. Simon Bradstreet," in *Historical Collections of the Essex Institute*, IV (Salem, Mass., 1862), 186; Bradstreet, "Before the Birth of One of Her Children," in Hensley, ed., *Works of Anne Bradstreet*, 224. On the gendered rhetorical conventions of legal documents, see Vivian Bruce Conger, *The Widow's Might: Widowhood and Gender in Early British America* (New York, 2009), esp. 2 ("economic").

67. Photograph of Edmund Gardner, in Bullard, ed., *Captain Edmund Gardner*, between 84 and 85; Aleksandar Hemon, "The Aquarium: A Child's Isolating Illness," *New Yorker*, June 6, 2011, https://www.newyorker.com/magazine/2011/06/13/the-aquarium; Noland, ed., *The Hawaiian Survival Handbook*, 17.

CONCLUSION

1. Mary Eyring, Christopher Hodson, and Matthew Mason, "Introduction: The Global Turn and Early American Studies," *Early American Studies*, XVI (2018), 3–4 (quotation). In the wake of global turns in literary and historical scholarship, critics have cautioned about the potential pitfalls of these approaches to the past. For example,

historian Frederick Cooper criticizes the "totalizing pretensions" of globalists who, in his view, downplay the complexity of historical power relations and capital in an effort to describe and emphasize a "single system of connection"; see Cooper, *Colonialism in Question: Theory, Knowledge, History* (Berkeley, Calif., 2005), 91 ("single"), 94 ("totalizing"). For literary and anthropological critiques of global studies, see Sebastian Conrad, *What Is Global History?* (Princeton, N.J., 2016), 210–212; David A. Bell, "Questioning the Global Turn: The Case of the French Revolution," *French Historical Studies*, XXXVII (2014), 1–24; Lynn Hunt, *Writing History in the Global Era* (New York, 2014), 51. See also Jeremy Adelman, "What Is Global History Now?" *Aeon*, Mar. 2, 2017, https://aeon.co/essays/is-global-history-still-possible-or-has-it-had-its-moment.

2. Bryce Traister, *Female Piety and the Invention of American Puritanism* (Columbus, Ohio, 2016), 4; John 16:33 (Authorized [King James] Version). Joanna Bourke conceptualizes pain as "a way-of-being in the world," in Bourke, *The Story of Pain: From Prayer to Painkillers* (Oxford, 2014), 17.

3. Barbara H. Rosenwein and Riccardo Cristiani, *What Is the History of Emotions?* (Cambridge, Mass., 2018), 63 ("bounded"), 81–82.

4. Henri Lefebvre, *The Production of Space* (1974), trans. Donald Nicholson-Smith (1991; rpt. Oxford, 1994), 7; William Bradford, *History of Plymouth Plantation, 1620–1647*, 2 vols. (Boston, 1912), I, 155; John Putnam Demos, *Entertaining Satan: Witchcraft and the Culture of Early New England*, updated ed. (Oxford, 2004), 377.

5. William Rueckert, "Literature and Ecology: An Experiment in Ecocriticism," from "Into and Out of the Void: Two Essays," *Iowa Review*, IX, no. 1 (1978), 71–86 (quotations on 71, 74).

6. John M. Bullard, ed., *Captain Edmund Gardner of Nantucket and New Bedford: His Journal and Family* (New Bedford, Mass., 1958), 5, 82.

7. Anne Bradstreet, "Before the Birth of One of Her Children," in John Harvard Ellis, ed., *The Works of Anne Bradstreet in Prose and Verse* (Charlestown, Mass., 1867), 394; Bullard, ed., *Captain Edmund Gardner*, 3; Terry Eagleton, *Literary Theory: An Introduction*, anniversary ed. (Minneapolis, Minn., 2008), 7.

8. Gregory J. Seigworth and Melissa Gregg, "An Inventory of Shimmers," in Gregg and Seigworth, eds., *The Affect Theory Reader* (Durham, N.C., 2010), 4 ("theories"); Rosenwein and Cristiani, *What Is the History of Emotions?* 108; Rosenwein, *Generations of Feeling: A History of Emotions, 600–1700* (Cambridge, 2016), 9; Stephanie Trigg, "Introduction: Emotional Histories—Beyond the Personalization of the Past and the Abstraction of Affect Theory," *Exemplaria*, XXVI (2014), 3–15 (quotation on 9).

9. Vincent Gillespie, "Vernacular Theology," in Paul Strohm, ed., *Middle English*, Oxford Twenty-First Century Approaches to Literature (Oxford, 2007), 401–420, esp. 406 ("overstatement"); D. Vance Smith, "The Application of Thought to Medieval Studies: The Twenty-First Century," *Exemplaria*, XXII (2010), 85–94, esp. 85 ("creeping"), 87 ("redemptive"), 89 ("authenticity"); Sarah Tarlow, "Death and Commemoration," *Industrial Archaeology Review*, XXVII 1 (2005), 163–169 (quotation on 163); Carolyn Dinshaw, *Getting Medieval: Sexualities and Communities, Pre- and Postmodern* (Durham, N.C., 1999), 34; Trigg, "Introduction," *Exemplaria*, XXVI (2014), 11; Rita Felski, *The Limits of Critique* (Chicago, 2015), 4. Felski defends affinity and attachment as affective states that might produce rather than stymie generative engagements with works of art in *Hooked: Art and Attachment* (Chicago, 2020).

10. Aleksandar Hemon, "The Aquarium," *New Yorker*, June 6, 2011, https://www.newyorker.com/magazine/2011/06/13/the-aquarium.

AFTERWORD

1. Georg Lukács, *The Theory of the Novel: A Historico-philosophical Essay on the Forms of Great Epic Literature*, trans. Anna Bostock (1920) (Cambridge, Mass., 1971), 41, 61; Lukács, quoted in Walter Benjamin, "The Storyteller: Reflections on the Works of Nikolai Leskov," in Dorothy J. Hale, ed., *The Novel: An Anthology of Criticism and Theory, 1900–2000* (Malden, Mass., 2006), 371; Elizabeth Allen et al., *Communicating COVID-19 Risks and Prevention Measures among People Experiencing Homelessness: Communication Plan*, Centers for Disease Control and Prevention and Oak Ridge Associated Universities, Nov. 21, 2022, 8 ("unhoused"), 24 ("unsheltered"), https://www.cdc.gov/orr/homelessness/downloads/Communication-Plan-COVID-19-and-People-Experiencing-Homelessness.pdf. For a discussion of the history of these earlier terms for the homeless in political context, see Philip Webb, *Homeless Lives in American Cities: Interrogating Myth and Locating Community* (New York, 2014).

2. Brian McGrory, "Centuries of Interruption and a History Rejoined: Wampanoag Grad to Be Harvard's First Since 1665," *Boston.com*, May 11, 2011, accessed May 1, 2020, http://archive.boston.com/news/local/massachusetts/articles/2011/05/11/wampanoag_grad_to_be_harvards_firfi_since_1665/?page=2.

3. John 14:2 (Authorized [King James] Version).

Index

Page numbers in italics refer to illustrations.

Bradstreet, Simon, Jr., 54–55
Bradstreet, Simon, Sr., 49–51, 57, 67–68, 151, 200
Browne, John, 16
Burning homes: significance of, 24–25; ubiquity of fire and, 26; and captivity narratives, 29–31; Princes and, 38–39; Bradstreets and, 50–51, 54, 58–60, 63; as spiritual epiphany, 61–62; world crossing and, 64–65

Captivity narratives, 7, 29–30, 40, 139. See also "Bars Fight" (Terry); Duston, Hannah; Narrative of the Captivity of Mrs. Mary Rowlandson (Rowlandson)
Cheeshateaumuck, Caleb, 46–49, 47, 63–65
Child, Lydia Maria, 110
Class solidarity and disability, 173, 176, 185–187
Clerke, Charles, 163–164
Coffin, Seth, 186–187
Colonialism: English writing about, 8–9; promiscuity of pain and, 17–18; maritime industries and, 20; dislocation and, 23, 207–208; and disease, 158–159, 168–169, 190–194
Colton, George, 111
Comedy and disability, 186–187, 198
Conflagration of 1704. See Deerfield raid
Conversion, 15, 221–222n. 17. See also Criminal-martyrology
Cook, James: voyage to Hawai'i, 156–157, 163–164; oceanic disability and, 158–159, 244n. 10; background and disability of, 162–163; disability of, 163–164, 179–184, 181, 182; punishment and, 175–176; pain and, 188–190
Corbitant, 75, 79, 85
Cotton, John, 15, 67
Criminal-martyrology: reproductive tragedies and, 119, 121–122, 124–131; agency and, 126–128, 148–149; historical references and, 129;

murderers and, 135–136, 138, 141–144; sacrifice and, 144–150. See also Rodgers, Esther
Criminal narratives, 70, 114, 122, 131–135, 139, 148. See also Criminal-martyrology; Rodgers, Esther

Dance-Holland, Nathaniel, 180
Death, 6–7, 9, 66, 81–83, 188–192, 218
Deathbed confessions, 124–125
Death the Certain Wages of Sin (Rogers), 122–125, 123, 128–130, 135–136, 149. See also Rogers, John
Deerfield raid, 25, 32–37. See also "Bars Fight" (Terry)
Dermer, Thomas, 75
Dickinson, Emily, 19
Diplomatic crisis of 1622 (Wampanoag-Anglo): background of, 73–75; suspicion and, 75–76, 80, 84–85; marital relations and, 76–79
Disability: invisibility of, 10; pain and, 15; records of, 153–154, 160–161; connection and, 155–156; lying and, 156–157, 159–161, 180, 194–195, 203; maritime occupations and, 158–159, 174–179; injury and, 159–160, 174–177, 184; Indigenous people and, 160, 188, 191–194, 197; religious conviction and, 161; Cook and, 162–164, 179–183; Gardner and, 167, 183–184; Ke'eaumoku and, 168, 173; class solidarity and, 173, 176, 185–187; signification and, 173–174; illness and, 174, 190–192, 197, 208; punishment and, 175–176; Billy Budd and, 176–179; Native Hawaiians and, 179–180; comedy and, 186–187, 198; observation of pain and, 191–192, 194–195; inclusivity and, 196; theory of, 196, 247n. 30; recovery work and, 198–200, 203. See also Mental illness; Scars
Disability oppression, 186, 189–190, 197

and, 131–132; cheerfulness and, 136; criminal-martyrology and, 139, 141; vulnerability and, 150

Rodgers, Esther: reproductive tragedies of, 6, 10, 119–122; vulnerability and, 6, 117; agency and, 14, 130, 135, 139, 145, 149; legal judgment in case against, 115, 123–124, 131–135; isolation of, 118–119; criminal-martyrology and, 124–126, 128–131, 135–139, 142–144, 147–148, 207; salvation and, 143–144, 146; resignation and relief for, 145–148, 207

Rogers, John: criminal narrative of, 122–124, 123, 130–132; agency and, 125–126, 130, 135, 139, 142; martyrology and, 128–131, 135–137, 147

Rogers, John (martyr), 119–120, 120, 124, 128–129

Rowlandson, Joseph, 91, 93–95, 97

Rowlandson, Mary: familial separation and, 9–10, 17, 91–97; burning home and, 23–24, 65; Native spaces and, 30, 32. See also Narrative of the Captivity of Mrs. Mary Rowlandson (Rowlandson)

Sacrifice, 126–128, 144–148, 150

Saltwater, 17

Salvation, 61–62, 161, 199. See also Criminal-martyrology; Religious conviction; Rodgers, Esther

Scars, 162, 164, 175, 178–180, 182–183, 185

Sennert, Daniel, 16

Settlers, 9, 17–18, 27–30, 86, 205–208. See also Colonialism; Deerfield raid; Diplomatic crisis of 1622 (Wampanoag-Anglo); Hawaiian-Anglo relations; Plymouth Colony

Sewell, Samuel, 133, 142

Shephard, Thomas, 30

Ship captains, 168, 175, 184–188. See also Whaling

Shoals/sandbars, 19, 41–44

Silva (Evelyn), 64–65

Slavery, 34–35, 42–44, 75–76, 133, 205

Smalley, Tiffany, 63–64

Smith, Sarah, 114–117, 116–117, 124

"Some Verses upon the Burning of Our House" (Bradstreet), 58, 60–63

Southworth, Alice Carpenter, 81

Stephen (martyr), 140

Stewart, Charles Samuel, 174–175

Stillbirths. See Reproductive tragedies

Suffering, 15. See also Pain

Surgeons, 158, 162

Suspicion: Puritan faith and, 71–72; marital, 72, 81, 83, 87, 99; vulnerability and, 72; Wampanoag-Anglo relations and, 73–76, 84–85; unattached men and, 76–78; familial separation and, 94; as protective measure, 99; communal support and, 108, 112, 117–118; clues of emotional distress and, 111; transience and, 118–120; interracial sexual relations and, 133. See also Faith in faithlessness; Marital unease

Sustainability, 64–65

Sympathy, Puritan, 3, 6, 117–118, 191

Taylor, Edward, 16–17, 67, 69

Taylor, Elizabeth, 67

Tenth Muse, The (Bradstreet), 53–54, 56, 59, 63

Terry, Lucy, 34–41, 44, 65, 227n. 23. See also "Bars Fight" (Terry)

Tisquantum, 10–11, 73–78, 85

Tragedy, 7–8, 86–87

"Transcendental homelessness," 216–217

Transience and reproductive tragedies, 118–120, 130. See also Homelessness

Trauma, 13–17, 44, 199. See also Domestic abuse/violence; Reproductive tragedies

Ulysses, 65

Unattached men, 76–78, 81

"Upon the Sweeping Flood" (Taylor), 16–17

Vane, Henry, 88, 90–91
"Vanity of All Worldly Things, The" (Bradstreet), 61

Wampanoag-Anglo relations. *See* Diplomatic crisis of 1622 (Wampanoag-Anglo)
Wampanoags, 73–79, 84–85, 93, 96–98
"Warning out," 39
Water and grief, 16–17, 21–22
Webber, John, 180–182
Weetamoo: sorrow and, 17, 112; Rowlandson captivity and, 91; marriage and, 93, 95, 97–98, 109
Weld, Thomas, 127
Wells, Ebenezer, 35
Wells-Thorn House, 35–36, 36, 227n. 14
Whaling, 158–159, 174–178, 189. *See also* Maritime occupations and disability; Ship captains

"William Bradford's Love Life" (Austin), 81, 110, 110
Williams, John, 32, 65
Williams, Roger, 28–29
Winslow, Edward, 77, 79–80, 85
Winthrop, Fitz-John, 25
Winthrop, John, 30, 67–69, 89–90, 132
Winthrop, Margaret, 67–69
Witchcraft: Parsons case and, 1–2, 4, 99, 102–103, 105–107; fear and, 219n. 1; female agency and, 238n. 5
Wood, 27–29, 64. *See also* Fire
World crossing: home making and, 45; discourse of, 45–46; Cheeshateaumuck letter and, 46–49, 47; Native Americans and, 49; Bradstreet and, 49–50, 53–54, 58–62; fire and, 61; Reformed theology and, 61; global turn and, 62; paper and, 63–64; burning homes and, 64
Wowas (James Printer), 97

Index